To     Dean Rougeau

Jianfei Li

Beijing

3/4/2019

Introduction to Chinese Laws

中国法丛书 （英文版）

# LABOR LAW AND SOCIAL SECURITY LAW OF CHINA

## 中国劳动法与社会保障法

Jianfei Li　黎建飞 著

中国人民大学出版社

·北京·

# Introduction

This is a professional book systematically discussing about the labor law and the social security law in China. The author elaborates the basic theories of labor law, introduces the labor law system, expounds the legislative background and intent of labor law, and analyzes the problems of legislation and legal practice.

Among the systematic elaboration of the basic contents, relevant essential materials, cases and examples are involved in each chapter, for example, how to understand the employer's liability of preventing workplace sexual harassment after defining the legislative intent? The object of labor law is labor relations. However, the pioneering study is needed on theoretical divergences and disputes of interests about the issues such as the peasant-worker, the dispatched labor and the illegal employment. In the theoretical discussion and practical research, it's not only to analyze problems on the criminal responsibility of the social insurance funds embezzlement and the occupation introduction, but also to care about legal means of sanctions against the arrears of the peasant-workers' wage, and the basic and additional wages in developed countries.

With the concerns of issues like the insurance agent's legal status, the taxi drivers' labor relations, the entertainment contract's legal character, the abolishment and reform of the labor arbitration's pre-procedure, the corporate social responsibility and the labor rights and interests, the international standards of the special protection for women workers, this book makes readers realize the synchrony of the labor law and the society's reform and development, and furthermore, makes readers think about persons and events relevant to the labor and social security relations around them.

Besides, the book has the following features:

It defines and distinguishes, in theory, *the employment relations and the labor relations*, *the employer and the employing entity*, *the employee and the labor*, *the civil contract and the labor contract*, etc.

It analyzes, in practice, the recent typical cases of labor law and social security law in China, such as *equal pay for equal work for the temporary worker and the formal worker*, *the company compensation for its employee fired for pregnancy*, etc.

It pays much attention to the researches on the hot issues of labor law and social security law in daily life, such as *three issues about the age of retirement*, *the court shouldn't enforce the social insurance funds*, etc.

It discusses important issues in the theoretical work, such as the reasons of unemployment, the theoretical base of the work-related injury certification on one's way to and from work.

From this book, readers will know and understand the progress and development of labor law and social security law in China, and know the current situation and the future of the legal construction of labor law and social security law in China.

# Contents

中国劳动法与社会保障法

**Chapter Ⅰ    Basic Theory of Labor Law**                                    1

Section 1    Concept and Significance of Labor Law                            1

Section 2    The Functions and Significance of Labor Law                      11

Section 3    The Evolution of Labor Legislation and the Labor Law
             System in China                                                  16


**Chapter Ⅱ    Legislative Purposes of Labor Law**                            27

Section 1    The Significance of the Legislative Purposes of the
             Labor Law                                                        27

Section 2    Legislative Purposes in the Chinese Labor Law                    32


**Chapter Ⅲ    Subject Matter of the Labor Law**                              38

Section 1    Labor Relationships as a Subject Matter of the
             Labor Law                                                        38

Section 2    Personal Scope of Application of the Labor Law                   48


**Chapter Ⅳ    Employment Law**                                               52

Section 1    Introduction                                                     52

Section 2    Basic Principles of Employment                                   64

Section 3    Employment Security for Special Employment Groups                68

Section 4    Employment Security for College Graduates and Students
             Returned back to China after Finishing Overseas Study            78

Section 5    Prohibition of Child Labor                                       87


**Chapter Ⅴ    Labor Contract Law**                                           91

Section 1    Introduction to Labor Contracts                                  91

Section 2    Conclusion, Modification, Termination and Invalidity
             of Labor Contracts                                               103

Section 3   Contents, Formats and Terms of Labor Contracts         111
Section 4   Dissolution of Labor Contracts                         122
Section 5   Legal Liability for Breach of Labor Contracts          135
Section 6   Differences between Labor Contracts and Civil Contracts   139

Chapter VI   Labor Conditions Law                                  172
Section 1   Concepts and Legal Principles of Labor Remuneration    172
Section 2   Minimum Wage System                                    181
Section 3   Wage Payment Security                                  186
Section 4   The Right to Work and Right to Rest and the
            Significance                                           190
Section 5   Rest and Vacation                                      199
Section 6   Extension of Working Hours and Limitations             205

Chapter VII   Labor Protection Law                                 211
Section 1   Overview of Legislation on Work Safety and Health      211
Section 2   Content of Labor Safety and Health Law                 216
Section 3   Reporting and Legal Liability of Occupational Diseases   219
Section 4   Legislation and Significance of Special Protection for
            Female Employees                                       225
Section 5   Content of Special Protection for Female Employees     229
Section 6   Special Protection for Juvenile Employees              239

Chapter VIII   Social Security Law                                 243
Section 1   Concept of Social Security Law                         243
Section 2   Development and Reform of Chinese Social Security Law   249

Chapter IX   Social Insurance Law                                  255
Section 1   Concept of Social Insurance Law                        255
Section 2   Principles of Social Insurance Law                     259

Chapter X   Endowment Insurance Law                                263
Section 1   Concept and Functions of the Endowment Insurance       263
Section 2   Legislation and Reform of Endowment Insurance          265
Section 3   Raising of Pension Funds                               269
Section 4   Distribution of Pensions                               274
Section 5   Supplementary Endowment Insurance                      279

**Chapter XI  Unemployment Insurance Law**  282

  Section 1  Overview of Unemployment Insurance and Its Significance  282

  Section 2  China's Unemployment Insurance Legislation  286

  Section 3  Targets and Scope of Unemployment Insurance  288

  Section 4  Distribution of Unemployment Insurance Funds  291

**Chapter XII  Medical Insurance**  299

  Section 1  Concept and Significance of Medical Insurance  299

  Section 2  Contents of Chinese Medical Insurance  302

**Chapter XIII  Work-related Injury Insurance**  309

  Section 1  Concept and Principles of Work-related Injury
              Insurance  309

  Section 2  Scope of Work-related Injury Insurance  316

  Section 3  Identification of Work-related Injury and Prevention of
              Occupational Diseases  318

  Section 4  Liability Principles of Work-related Injury Insurance  325

  Section 5  Work-related Injury Insurance Benefits  328

**Chapter XIV  Maternity Insurance Law**  332

  Section 1  Concept and Significance of Maternity Insurance  332

  Section 2  Maternity Insurance Funds  337

  Section 3  Maternity Insurance Benefits  341

**Chapter XV  Other Legal Systems on Social Security**  345

  Section 1  Overview of Social Welfare System  345

  Section 2  Social Relief  350

  Section 3  Social Preferential Treatment  356

**Chapter XVI  Law on Labor Dispute Settlement**  365

  Section 1  Overview of Labor Dispute Settlement  365

  Section 2  Mediation for Labor Dispute  378

  Section 3  Arbitration for Labor Dispute  384

  Section 4  Labor Dispute Litigation  401

**Chapter XVII  Legal Liabilities**  407

● Chapter Ⅰ

# Basic Theory of Labor Law

Labor Law emerged in the 19th century against the special background of the western society. It started as a part of private law, but later acquired the characteristics of public law, which is a result of continuous evolution of the labor law and embodies the social nature of law.

This chapter introduces the concept, the subjects, the status and the role of labor law and explains the labor legislation system in China through a review of the process of adoption of the Chinese Labor Law.

## Section 1   Concept and Significance of Labor Law

### Ⅰ. The Concept of Labor Law

Labor law is a generic term referring to legal norms that regulate labor relations and other relations closely related to labor relations. In China, it is an important and independent branch of the socialist legal system. The purpose of labor law is to regulate through law labor relations and certain other relations closely related to labor relations, so as to protect lawful rights and interests of laborers, establish, sustain and develop stable and harmonious relationships between employing units and laborers, and promote economic development and social progress.

Since labor law came into being in the 19th century, it has played a special role in stabilizing labor relations and promoting social and economic development. The status and role of labor law have been universally recognized by countries around the world and, as a result, the law has gained rapid development throughout the world.

The Oxford Companion to Law defines labor law as the body of all legal principles and rules pertaining to hired labor. Roughly the same as industrial law, it governs legal issues relating to employment contracts and labor or industrial relations.① In his book *Theory of Labor Law*, Shi Shangkuan defines labor law as "the law on labor relationships. More specifically, it is the entire body of legal systems regulating labor relationships and all other subordinate relationships".② As far as its content is concerned, labor law covers employees and employers in labor relationship, labor contracts, collective contracts, labor organizations (trade unions), labor disputes, labor protection, labor adjustment, labor remedies, and labor insurance.

As regards foreign labor law and labor law scholarship, German scholars and experts hold that labor law is the entire body of labor-related legal norms and, therefore, not drawing upon a concept on physical activities, but upon an economic concept instead, covering both physical and mental work. For example, the work performed by a computer programmer, a photographer's model, and a doorman at a hospital is all labor under the labor law.③ In Japan, the labor law refers to the entire body of legal norms regulating employment relationships. Also called labor-capital relationship by Japanese economists, such employment relationships refer to the passive labor relationship whereby a laborer is hired by an employer and performs work under his order.④ The labor law in South Korea is the law that regulates the labor relationships between laborers and employees for the purpose of ensuring the subsistence of the former.⑤ The Singapore labor law regulates the labor relationships between employees and employers and applies to employees who work for their employers under labor contracts. It does not apply to any person occupying a managerial, an executive, or a confidential position to seamen, domestic workers, or any person employed by a Statutory Board or the Government.⑥ The Swedish labor law applies to all employees and employers.⑦ The Russian labor law regulates the relationships among all employees and employers. The labor contract under the Russian labor law is an agreement between the employee (worker) and the employer (enterprise, a government organ, or an organization) according to which the employee undertakes to perform certain professional, technical, or office work determined by such agreement and

---

① David M. Walker, *The Oxford Companion to Law*, Chinese edition, Beijing: Guangming Daily Press, 1988, p. 511.

② Shi Shangkuan, *Theory of Labor Law*, Shanghai: Zhengda Press, 1934, p. 1.

③ Wang Yiying (ed.), *Foreign Labor Law and Social Security Law*, Beijing: Renmin University of China Press, 2001, p. 71.

④ Wang Yiying (ed.), ibid., p. 408.

⑤ Ibid., p. 487.

⑥ Ibid., p. 578.

⑦ Ibid., p. 652.

comply with the internal work regulations of the employer while the employer undertakes to pay remuneration to the employee for the work he has done and to ensure the work conditions as stipulated by the labor law, collective contract, and relevant agreements between the two parties. ①

Professor Douglas L. Leslie of Virginia University discusses in his book Labor Law in a Nutshell the legal norms mediating labor-capital relationships, including judicial control of trade union activities before the promulgation of the Wagner Act, such as penalization of the workers' or trade unions' activities aimed at raising wages or improving work conditions; the selection of representatives for collective bargaining; the competence of and procedures before the National Labor Relations Board; the lawfulness of peaceful picketing during a dispute between the employer and employees; the lawfulness of direct and indirect measures taken by an employer against the collective mutual assistance and mutual protection actions taken by employees; the methods and procedures of collective bargaining, the implementation of collective contract, etc. Compared with the labor law in the traditional sense, the above provisions apparently have their unique characteristics. ②

The Labor Standards Act of the Taiwan province provides for the minimum standard of work conditions, requiring that the terms and conditions of any agreement between an employer and a worker shall not be lower than such minimum standards. The Act is applicable to the business (or industries) of mining and quarrying, manufacturing, construction, water, electricity and gas supply, transportation, warehousing and telecommunications, mass communication, and other businesses (or industries) designated by the relevant competent authority. As far as its content is concerned, the Act covers labor contract, wages, working hours, rest and vocation, child workers, female workers, retirement, compensation for industrial injuries, apprentice, work rules, supervision, inspection, and penal provisions.

Although the above definitions of labor law focus on different elements, their commonalities are obvious: firstly, as far as "act" (or "behavior") is concerned, all labor laws are legal norms that regulate "labor"; secondly, as far as "actor" is concerned, all labor laws are legal norms that regulate "workers" and "employing units" (or "employees" and "employers"); and finally, as far as "legal

---

① Ibid., p. 676.

② See Douglas L. Leslie, *Labor Law in a Nutshell*, Chinese edition (Zhang Qiang et al. transl.), Beijing: China Social Sciences Publishing House, 1997.

relationship" is concerned, all labor laws are legal norms that regulate "labor relationships".

## II. Act in Labor Law

### ( I ) The Meaning of "Labor"

Compared with the "labor" in its ordinary sense, the "labor" under the terms of labor law has some special connotations. Since the regulation by law of social relationships is embodied in legal rights and obligations, which in turn are linked to the legally prescribed conditions, it is the conditions of "labor" laid down by law that give special meanings to "labor" under labor law. First of all, the law requires that laborers must meet certain legal conditions regarding their qualifications; the remuneration for the labor must enable laborers to meet the basic living needs of himself and of his family; such labor must be done for someone other then the laborer himself or his family and therefore has an obvious social nature; such labor must also be based on a labor contract or employment relationship. The laborer must be subordinate to and accept the management by certain employing unit or employer. Therefore, the basic elements of "labor" include: legal obligation (as different from labor performed as voluntary help); labor contract relationship (as different from labor performed within spousal relationship or parent-child relationship); remuneration (as different from voluntary labor based on ethical considerations); and its occupational nature (namely, as a means of earning a living as different from internship and other non-occupational labor).

Shi Shangkuan also held that the "labor" under labor law should be different from the "labor" in general sense and must meet certain conditions: "The labor in general sense refers to the conscientious and purposeful physical and mental exertion by human beings whereas the labor under labor law must contain the following elements: (a) it is the fulfillment of legal obligations; (b) it is based a contract relationship (rather than based on spousal relationship or parent-child relationship under civil law); (c) it is paid; (d) it is occupational; (e) there is a relationship of subordination. From the above elements we can see that the labor under the labor law is a paid occupational labor based on contractual obligation and performed in a relationship of subordination. "[1]

### ( II ) "Labor" and "Employment"

According to the above-discussed understanding of labor, the "labor" that

---

[1]  Shi Shangkuan, *supra* note 2, p. 1.

contains the above-mentioned elements can be equaled with the "employment" under labor law. In fact, under labor law, "labor" is almost identical with "employment," because occupation and income are the basic elements of the realization of laborers' labor rights. "Individual laborers have already selected the locations of the social labor they engaged in when the entrepreneurs have purchased and allocated factors of production and recruited employees. Social production begins when employees arrive at their work posts and begin to work (namely when they are employed): they are transformed from merely ordinary consumers into social producers, employees and consumers."[1] However, "employment", as another important concept of labor law, is contrary to the concept of "unemployment".

Labor and social security authorities in China have given the following definitions to "employment" and "unemployment": "the unemployed" refers to persons who are of legal working age (namely 16 – 60 for men and 16 – 55 for women) and have the ability to work, but who are currently jobless and actively seeking for a job. Those who engage in certain social labor, but whose remuneration for labor is lower than the minimum living standard for local urban residents should be considered as unemployed persons. "Employed persons" refers to persons who are of the legal working ages (namely 16 – 60 for men and 16 – 55 for women), engage in certain social economic activities and receive lawful remuneration for their work or obtain income from operation of business. Among them, those whose remuneration for work reaches or exceeds the local minimum wage standard are fully employed; those whose working hours are less than those prescribed by law and whose remunerations for work are lower than the local minimum wage standard but higher than the minimum living standard for local urban residents, and who wish to engage in more work are underemployed.[2] Since this standard not only takes labor as a precondition for "employment", but also contains specific requirements on "remuneration for work", it makes a clearer distinction between "labor" and "employment" and therefore has a more practical significance.

---

[1]   Yao Yuqun, *Employment Theory and Employment Promotion*, Beijing: China Labor Publishing House, 1996, p. 4.

[2]   Bai Tianliang, "Redefining the Concepts of Employment and Unemployment and Setting the Target for the Control of Unemployment Rate at 4. 5%", http: //www. chinanews. com/, May 13, 2003.

### III. Actors in Labor Law: "Laborers" and "Employing Units"

( I ) Meanings and Scopes of "Laborers" and "Employing Units"

The term "actors" in labor law refers to the parties to a labor relationship, more specifically, laborers and employing units. Generally, the latter two terms appear easy to understand. However, they have special meanings under labor law and, therefore, need to be understood in a more specific way.

In China, "laborers" are natural persons who provide labor to employing units. They are referred to as "workers" or "employees". The term "laborers" in labor relationship refers to natural persons who engage in physical or mental work for and receive remuneration from an employing unit in accordance with the labor law and the labor contract. A laborer must meet the following legally prescribed conditions:

(1) Age. Chinese Labor Law provides that the minimum working age for Chinese citizens is 16. Persons under the age of 16 may not be employed by or establish any labor law relationship with an employing unit. Employing units may not recruit citizens under the age of 16, or will bear the corresponding legal responsibilities. Persons under the age of 18 are prohibited from engaging in occupations or work that may endanger the health, safety or moral of minors. For example, the Labor Law prohibits employing units from engaging workers under the age of 18 in heavy work, work exposed to toxic or hazardous substances or other work harmful to their physical or mental health, or other dangerous operations.

(2) Labor capacity. Since laborers must do the labor personally, they must have the capacity for labor. Moreover, for certain industries, labor capacity includes the capacity to meet special requirements of these industries. For example, people suffering from certain infectious diseases are not allowed to work in the catering industry. Broadly speaking, labor capacity should also include the laborer's freedom of action, which enables the laborer to participate in labor with his free action. Therefore, citizens who are deprived of personal freedom in accordance with law, such as those placed under re-education through labor or sentenced to fix-term imprisonment may not establish labor relationship with an employing unit.

Furthermore, Chinese law contains no restrictive rule on the nationality of laborers. Anyone, regardless of whether he or she is a Chinese citizen, a foreign citizen or stateless person, can become a laborer in China as long as he or she meets the relevant requirements set out in Chinese labor law.

"Employing units" is also called "business owners", "the capital", "employers," or the "hirers". In the Chinese law, they are uniformly called "employing units", which refers to entities that hire, manage, and bear corresponding responsibilities to laborers.

There are different types of employing units in China:

(1) Enterprises lawfully registered in China, including enterprises of various ownerships and organizational forms, such as state-owned enterprises, collectively-owned enterprises, private enterprises, foreign-invested enterprises, Hong Kong, Macao and Taiwanese enterprises, hybrid enterprises, joint-equity enterprises, joint ventures, and township enterprises.

(2) Lawfully registered individual economic organizations, namely individually-owned businesses having acquired business license in accordance with law. Individually owned enterprises have the right to hire helpers and apprentices.

(3) Institutions established in accordance with law, including cultural, educational, health, and scientific research institutions, for example, schools, hospitals, and publishing houses. These institutions have the right to employ laborers within the competence prescribed by law.

(4) State organs established in accordance with law. They have the right to employ laborers within their competence as prescribed by law.

(5) Mass organizations established in accordance with law, including trade unions, women's federations, research societies, and associations. They have the right to employ laborers within their competence as prescribed by law.

( II ) Specific Obligations of "Laborers" and "Employing Units"

With regard to the "actors" in labor law, the labor law provides for not only the minimum age for work but also the basic rights and obligations of laborers and employing units. More importantly, the basic rights and obligations refer to neither citizens' constitutional rights, nor laborers' rights and obligations in a general sense, but rights and obligations that are common in all labor relationships. There are correlations between such rights and obligations, namely the rights of one party usually constitute or correspond to the obligation of the other party.

Generally speaking, the laborers have the following five obligations:

1. A labor obligation, namely the obligation to deliver labor in accordance with a labor contract—This obligation has an exclusive nature, i. e., the labor obligation can be fulfilled only by the party to a labor contract. In some countries such as Germany, there are two exceptions to this rule of exclusiveness: first, the employer agrees or usually allows a third party to carry out the labor on behalf of

the employee; and second, it makes no difference whether the labor is carried out by the employee himself or by a third party on behalf of the employee. In view of the exclusive nature of the labor obligation, the employer's right to request labor is also exclusive. In principle, such right cannot be transferred to a third party without the consent of the laborer himself. However, such right can be transferred if the employer is lawfully changed without changing the content of the laborer's obligations. Under such circumstances, the employer's obligation will also be transferred along with the right. In addition, the laborers' labor obligation must not contradict relevant laws. A laborer has the right to reject his or her employer's order, which is malicious in nature, against public morals, or harmful to the health of the laborer. Moreover, a laborer has the right to reject labor obligations not provided for in the labor contract, unless there is an emergent situation or special occupational practice. The location of the fulfillment of labor obligation must also be agreed upon in the labor contract. If the employer wants the laborer to work in a location other than that specified in the labor contract, he must get the consent of the laborer and pay extra expenses. This is also true for the time of fulfillment of labor obligation. Unless there is an emergency or occupational practice, the laborer has the right to refuse to work outside the time prescribed in labor contract.

2. The obligation to obey the employer's orders, namely the laborer's obligation to accept the command and supervision by an employer during work—A laborer must not only comply with the relevant laws, the labor contract and any special agreement, but also follow the instructions of the employer with respect to the method, location, and time of work. Nonetheless, the laborer has the right to disobey an employer's order which is unlawful, immoral or harmful to the laborer's lawful rights and interests. As a rule, a laborer has no obligation to obey his employer's instructions outside the working hours, unless in case of emergency or household labor.

3. The obligation of confidentiality, namely the laborer's obligation not to disclose any confidential information relating to his employer's production or business—The laborer must keep confidential any commercial or technical information of his employer which the latter wishes to keep from any third party. The laborer is especially prohibited from providing such information to his employer's competitors, whether for a pay or not. In case of domestic work, a laborer may not disclose private information or violate the privacy of his employer. A laborer operating a business on behalf of his employer may not operate another business of the same kind for himself or for a third party, or become a shareholder

of a same kind of employing unit, without the consent of his employer. Otherwise, the employer has the right to claim any profit the laborer has thus made as compensation.

4. The obligation to improve the work efficiency of the employer—All laborers have the obligation to increase the work efficiency of their employers, namely they should fulfill their duties with due diligence and make to their employer any proposals that can improve the work efficiency of their employers. Moreover, they may not accept bribery or engage in any other activities harmful to the interest of their employers. Here arises the issue of "secondary labor" in labor law, or "second job" in popular terms. The labor laws in some countries provide that an employee may not conclude a new labor contract with a third party without the consent of his current employer, unless the new labor contract will not impede the implementation of the current labor contract. An additional condition is that "the secondary labor may not fall within the employer's scope of business". This prohibition draws upon two considerations: firstly, an employee who took on too much work will not be able to fulfill his labor obligation to his employer; secondly, an employee who engages in secondary labor falling within his employer's scope of business will inevitably compete with the employer and therefore harm the interest of his employer.

5. The obligation to pay compensation for damage—Also called collateral obligation by some scholars, this obligation means that the laborer should pay compensation for the damages caused by non-fulfillment or incomplete fulfillment of his labor obligation. Meanwhile, a laborer must also compensate for any damage to the employer's production materials, machines, or instruments caused by him either intentionally or unintentionally. Several different legislative regimes can be adopted for the establishment of this obligation. It can be provided for as part of the system of damage for breach of contract under the civil law, in an agreement between the two parties, or in the collective contract or industrial regulations.

Generally speaking, the employers have the following five obligations to their employees:

1. The obligation to pay labor remuneration—This obligation correlates with the laborer's labor obligation; or it can be said that it corresponds to the right to labor remuneration of a laborer who has fulfilled his labor obligation. Usually, labor remuneration is explicitly provided for in labor contracts or collective contracts and takes three forms: monetary payment, payment in kind, and a mixture of monetary payment and payment in kind. In the past, payment in kind was the main form of labor remuneration. Later, it was gradually replaced by

monetary payment. Monetary payment is not limited to payment in cash, but also includes payment in bonds or negotiable instruments. It is not limited to payment in domestic currency, but also includes payment in foreign currencies, depending on the law in each country. In China, although current law provides that labor remuneration can only be paid in Renminbi (RMB), employees in foreign invested enterprises are in fact not restricted by this rule. Nor is payment in kind limited to the payment in material goods. In some countries, housing, right to the use of land, and income opportunities are all listed as payment in kind. However, such payments in kind should not be confused with the welfare benefits to which a laborer is entitled. The difference between the two kinds of payments is that the employer provides the former on a non-regular basis. The mixed form of payment of labor remuneration normally applies in the field of domestic work.

2. The obligation to protect, namely the employer has the obligation to protect the laborer's life and health—In case of domestic work, this obligation also includes the provision of safe and healthy living conditions and food. Here, the obligation to protect is different from the protection of occupational health and safety provided for in state legislation since the latter is explicitly provided for by the state law and is imposed by the state on employers. Contrarily, the employer's obligation to protect here corresponds to the laborer's obligation of following the employer's order and is based on the personal-relationship nature of labor contract. Therefore, the content of the obligation to protect should not be expanded arbitrarily or without any restriction, but must be based on generally recognized criteria or rules.

3. The obligation to provide the work conditions necessary for the labor to be carried out—In labor legislation, work conditions in a broad sense include both human conditions and equipment conditions. As a rule, the employer has no labor obligation to the laborer. However, under certain special circumstances, the employer has such as obligation to create work conditions for employees. For example, under the condition of existence of a profit-sharing agreement between an actor and his employer, the actor has the right to demand that his employer carry out publicity and other activities so as to raise the actor's popularity, to ensure the expected effect of his performance, and to increase profit. Unless otherwise provided for by special agreements or industrial rules, an employer has the obligation to provide employees with places, tools and materials necessary for them to carry out the labor. An employee has the right to demand the employer who violates this obligation to fulfill the obligation or to pay compensation. [1]

---

[1]  See Shi Shangkuan, *supra* note 2, p. 46.

4. The obligation of reimbursement—The employer has the obligation to reimburse the laborer any expenses he has incurred in order to carry out the labor. Such a reimbursement is different from the payment of labor remuneration. For example, some laws provide that: "If, for a business-related reason, an employer finds it necessary for an employee to work in a place other than the one specified in the labor contract, it must, in addition to paying the remuneration for the work that employee has done in such another place, reimburse the travel expenses thus incurred by the employee."

5. The obligation to grant laborers leaves necessary for them to exercise their rights as citizens or fulfill their legal obligations, including their obligations as a witness, expert witness, deputies to a people's congress, etc. This kind of leave is different from paid leaves or vacations in that it is not common or regular. Nonetheless, this does not exempt the employer from the obligation.

## Section 2　The Functions and Significance of Labor Law

### I. The Functions

The functions of law testify to the impact of law on society. As a kind of social norm, law regulates people's behavior. Labor law, as a branch of law, regulates people's behavior in labor relationships. Generally, it has two functions: to establish norms of labor behavior and to provide legal basis for the resolution of labor disputes. In specific, it has the following four functions:

( I ) Establishing Norms of Labor Behavior and Protecting Lawful Rights and Interests of Both Parties to a Labor Relationship

As a kind of social norm, law determines people's code of conduct or mode of behavior, tells people what they can do, what they should do, and what they may not do; it also serves as a criterion for judging the lawfulness or unlawfulness of people's behavior. In short, the labor law exists first and foremost as a "criterion" or "basis" in labor administration, its main task being to establish the rules of labor conduct and to protect lawful rights and interests of the parties to labor relationships.

In law, rights and obligations are complimentary to each other. When a party enjoys certain rights, he or she must also fulfill certain obligations. There is no right without obligation, just as there is no obligation without right. For the parties to labor relationship, the rights of one party are the obligations of the other party and vice versa. It follows that labor law must embody the principle of fairness in protecting the rights and interests of parties to labor relationship and must protect the lawful rights and interests of the parties in a fair way. While emphasizing the rights and interests of laborers, the labor law must not ignore the lawful rights and interests of employers. Laborers have the right to labor remuneration as well as the obligation to perform labor. Correspondingly, employers have the right to use labor as well as the obligation to pay labor remuneration. This is true for all labor relationships under any type of market economy system. Therefore, generally speaking, the labor law protects the lawful rights and interests of both parties to a labor relationship, rather than catering only to the demands of laborers while ignoring the interests of the other party to labor relationship, namely the employers. Otherwise it will become difficult both to maintain labor relationships and for society to effectively regulate labor relationships.

Understandably, from a social point of view, laborers are in a disadvantaged position as compared to employers and therefore need greater protection by labor law, just as the British legal economist J. M. Oliver says, "The law has been concerned with unfortunate victims of the competitive system rather than those who have gained fortunate benefits. "[1] However, such protection must not deviate from the principle of fairness, let alone meet the interest needs of one party by depriving the lawful rights and interests of the other.

( II ) Reasonably Allocating Social Labor Resources and Organizing Social Labor

The organization of social labor affects directly the allocation and utilization of labor resources and equipment capacity, and the level of labor productivity. Before the "reform and opening up", a centralized labor allocation system was implemented in China, namely the labor force was monopolized and allocated by the state in a unified way. Such a system was not flexible enough to meet the actual needs of society. Furthermore, because of the underdeveloped productive force, unbalanced economic structure, and slow increase in the number of work posts, there were always a large number of people waiting for the assignment of

---

[1]  J. M. Oliver, *Law and Economics*, Chinese edition, Wuhan: Wuhan University Press, 1986, p. 32.

job by the state each year. However, on the other hand, once they got jobs, their "placement" in various employing units resulted in such problems as surplus manpower, overstaffing and decreasing productivity in these units. Under the socialist market economy, the state should give full play to the role of labor law in organizing social labor and managing the organization of social labor. For example, labor force transfer is one way to solve the problems caused by the imbalance between demand and supply of labor force, yet it needs to be legally regulated. Corresponding employment legal norms need to be adopted for both the export of labor force and the use of imported labor force. China is a country with very limited per capita arable land. The increase of labor productivity has resulted in large amount of surplus labor force in rural areas. The uncontrolled flow of surplus rural labor force into cities will result in many difficulties in city administration and traffic management. Therefore, legal countermeasures need to be adopted to regulate the flow of labor force and to reduce social losses resulting from such flow.

(Ⅲ) Adjusting the Payment of Labor Remuneration and Safeguarding the Basic Rights of Laborers

Labor remuneration is the compensation for the provision of labor by laborers. It is the only or main way by which laborers maintain and improve their livelihood as well as the main obligation of employers in the labor relationship. Under the product/planned economy, the form, level and standard of labor remuneration and the payment of allowances and bonuses were uniformly arranged by the relevant government departments and the promotion and adjustment of salaries of employees were also uniformly provided for by state regulations. Apparently, such a system was not compatible with the market economy. In Western countries under the market economy, labor remuneration is in principle negotiated between the two parties to labor relationship. The function of labor law is to establish the basic method and procedure for such negotiation so as to ensure that it can be carried out smoothly. The law also provides for the method of payment of labor remuneration, the time period of payment, emergency payment, allowances for work stoppage, paid leave, etc. Meanwhile, many countries have adopted laws on minimum wage and laws on the minimum standard of work conditions so as to safeguard the minimum income of laborers. In Germany, however, the minimum wage is regulated by collective contracts, which have higher legal effect than labor contracts.

Notoriously, the labor law under market economy should neither regulate all the details relating to labor remuneration, nor adopt a laisser-faire approach and let the parties to labor relationship to do whatever they like with regard to labor remuneration. The functions of the labor law with respect to labor remuneration are: firstly, to establish the basic principles of labor remuneration so as to ensure that labor remuneration can be enjoyed by laborers in a timely, direct and genuine way; and secondly, to establish standard of minimum wage so as to safeguard the laborers' right to basic income and, more importantly, to protect laborers' lawful income from the infringement by employers in situations in which there is an oversupply of labor force.

### ( Ⅳ ) Resolving Labor Disputes and Maintaining Stable Labor Order

The establishment of the labor relationship in accordance with law does not mean the realization of such relationship. Only if both parties to a labor relationship strictly fulfill their obligations can their rights and interests be realized. The non-fulfillment or incomplete fulfillment by either party to a labor relationship will harm not only the interest of the other party, but also, to varying degrees, the interest of society. In the process of realizing rights and fulfilling obligations by both parties to labor relationship, the implementation of labor contract is often affected by various subjective or objective factors resulting in labor disputes. In order to solve such disputes in a fair and reasonable way, it is necessary to take labor law as the criterion to determine the merits of each case, to identify responsibilities and to investigate and affix legal liabilities of the relevant parties.

The resolution of labor disputes by means of labor law usually takes mediation as its main form. This is due to the dual nature of labor relationship as both economic and social relationship. Apart from the complimentary right-obligation relationship, there is also a relationship of cooperation between the laborer and the employer. Maintaining a stable labor relationship not only is beneficial to both parties to the relationship, but also has a direct bearing on social stability. Therefore, the best solution to disputes between the two parties to labor relationship is not by litigation, but by a way that focuses on maintaining a harmonious and interdependent relationship between the two parties and is conducive to continuing cooperation between them after the resolution of the dispute.

Most enterprises in China have established labor dispute mediation committees, which, as a kind of grassroots organization, can prevent effectively labor disputes, thereby mitigating the conflicts between employees and employers and maintaining the stability of labor relationship. Furthermore, in any one of the following situation, labor disputes can be submitted to a local labor dispute arbitration committee for arbitration: (1) if the parties involved in the labor dispute are reluctant to apply for a mediation; (2) if the mediation fails; or (3) if the labor dispute is not suitable to be resolved through mediation by a labor mediation committee. The arbitration committee will first encourage parties to a dispute to reach a conciliation agreement. It will make a ruling only once the parties have failed to reach a conciliation agreement. A party disagreeing to an arbitral award may bring the dispute to a people's court. The people's court shall decide such cases in accordance with law.

## Ⅱ. The Significance of Labor Law

The significance of labor law can be analyzed from many different angles. Here, the author discusses the social significance of the promulgation of the Labor Law in China.

During the period of planned economy in China, the balance between the supply of and demand for labor force and the stabilization of labor relationship were mainly achieved through the exercise of administrative power. Nevertheless, the essential role and special functions of labor law at the historical stage of market economy had led to the emergence of a large number of separate labor law norms during that period. With the establishment and development of the socialist market economy, the existing system of labor law and regulations adopted in view of different industries, different ownership systems and different status of laborers, was no longer compatible with the market economy and therefore had to be coordinated and unified through the adoption of a basic labor law.

From the perspective of the actual reform needs, the Labor Law was a legal safeguard for the reform of the labor system as well as for the reform of the entire economic system. Since 1979, China has carried out a series of reforms with remarkable achievements on labor system, wage system and social insurance system with a view to transforming enterprise operating mechanism and invigorating enterprises. As regards the labor system, the state abolished the centralized labor force allocation system, implemented the labor contract system, and introduced the mechanism of two-way selection between employing units and laborers. In terms of wage distribution system, enterprises were given the autonomy in the distribution of wage. As regards social insurance, relevant reforms were carried out on the system of social pooling of employees' pension expenses, the unemployment insurance system and the system of insurance against work-related injuries. These reforms embody the transition of the nature of regulation of labor relationship from that by administrative authorities to that by law.

Given its pivotal role in adapting the Chinese socialist legal system, the labor law is a key branch of the law in China. It has the force of fundamental law, the legal effect of which is second only to the Constitution. The labor law regulates very common and important social relationships that have a direct bearing on the personal interests of broad masses of laborers, the development of the economy and the stability of society. The absence of such a basic law in the past led to the lack of legislative basis for the adoption of concrete laws and regulations or the adoption of repetitive, contradictory or uncoordinated laws and regulations, affecting negatively not only the construction and improvement of the legal system but also the regulation of labor relationship. In some areas, the cases of violation of laborers' lawful rights and interests and number of labor disputes were increasing. The lack of applicable law in some cases even led to prolonged petitions by some laborers and resulted in serious events. All these had demonstrated an urgent need for labor law in China.

From the perspective of international labor relationship, an imminent adoption of a labor law was necessary for the implementation of ILO conventions. China, as one of the founding members of the ILO, has ratified many ILO conventions. According to the ILO Constitution, each member state should enable laws to implement the conventions recognized by it. In international labor exchange and technical cooperation, the labor law is also indispensable for the protection of labor export and lawful rights and interests of exported laborers.

## Section 3　The Evolution of Labor Legislation and the Labor Law System in China

### I. Labor Legislation in China: 1949—1978

The Common Program of the Chinese People's Political Consultative Conference, adopted at the eve of the establishment of the People's Republic of China as a temporary constitution, provided for the basic principles regulating labor relationships, including those governing laborers' right of association, the democratic management of enterprises, working hours, minimum wage, labor insurance and the system of inspection of factories and mines.

The 1954 Constitution contained more standardized provisions on the protection of various rights of citizens, including the right to work, the right to rest, the right to material assistance and the right to education. Later on, a series of labor laws and regulations, including the Trade Union Law, the Regulations on Labor Insurance, and the Provisions on the Procedures for the Resolution of Labor Disputes, were promulgated one after another. In the field of labor safety and industrial hygiene, the Chinese government promulgated in 1956 three regulations and one decision-the Regulations on the Safety and Hygiene in Factories, the Regulations on the Safety Technologies for Construction and Installation Projects, the Regulations on Reporting Industrial Casualty Accidents, and the Decision on the Prevention of Harms Caused by Siliceous Dust in Factories and Mines-and began establishing a safety and health inspection system. In the field of labor insurance, the State Council promulgated in 1958 the Interim Provisions on the Retirement of Workers and Employees and other related instruments. In the field of occupational training, an apprentice training system and a technical training school system were established. In 1956, Mr. Dong Biwu stressed the need for the adoption of a labor law at the first session of the Eighth National Congress of the Communist Party of China. In 1957, the Ministry of Labor set up a Labor Law Drafting Group consisting of experts from the All-China Federation of Trade Unions and the relevant colleges and universities and started the drafting of the Labor Law of the People's Republic of China (Draft).

However, labor legislation was later seriously affected by wrong ideologies. Some regulations, such as regulations on the resolution of labor disputes and regulations on piecework wages and incentive system, were no longer implemented and the drafting of some laws, such as the Labor Law and the Regulations on the Protection of Female Workers, was aborted. During the ten-year "Cultural Revolution", legal nihilism prevailed, socialist democracy and legal construction were trampled upon, no progress was made in labor legislation, and many laws and regulations were abolished (for example, regulations on piecework wages and incentive system were once again abolished and the implementation of the system of social pooling of labor insurance expenses for enterprises employees was suspended). Because some management agencies in charge of implementing labor laws and regulations had stopped activity meanwhile, those labor laws and regulations which were not abolished or suspended were not implemented in practice.

Since the downfall of the "Gang of Four" in 1976, labor legislation was gradually put on the right track. The 1978 Constitution restored various labor rights and relevant labor regulations were also restored and further improved.

## II. Labor Laws and Regulations after 1979

The 1982 Constitution contains over 20 labor-related provisions providing for laborers' rights to work, to rest, to material assistance, and to education. Based on these constitutional provisions, China has adopted a large number of labor laws and regulations in the process of "Reform and Opening up".

### 1. Employment

In 1981, the State Council promulgated Several Decisions on Increasing Employment Opportunities, Reinvigorating the Economy, and Solving Employment Problems in Urban Areas, which established a "three combinations" employment policy. Then the Ministry of Labor adopted regulations that established a labor service company management system and unemployment registration system. In January 1990, the Ministry of Labor promulgated the Interim Provisions on Employment Service, requiring that employment agencies should be established under employment service departments of local governments at various levels, in order to provide employment services to job seekers. Moreover, the Ministry of Labor and Personnel and the Ministry of Public Security jointly promulgated in 1987 the Provisions on the Employment of Foreigners Who Have Not Acquired Residence Permit and Foreigners Who Come to China for the Purpose of Study, providing for such matters as the relevant approval systems, work permits and the conditions for their issuance, and employment contracts.

The State Council and the relevant government departments have promulgated a series of instruments on recruitment system, including the Interim Provisions on the Recruitment of Workers by State-Owned Enterprises and the Interim Provisions on the System of Evaluation and Selection on Merit in the Recruitment of Workers. These provisions enshrine the following principles: training before employment; public recruitment open to all members of society; comprehensive evaluation and selection on merit in the recruitment of employees; prohibition of any form of internal recruitment by enterprises and abolition of the practice of replacing retiring workers with their children; giving priority to women when recruiting workers for jobs suitable for women; prohibition of recruitment of minors under the age of 16; and giving priority to demobilized compulsory servicemen in the recruitment of workers in rural areas.

### 2. Labor Contract

Promulgated by the State Council in July 1986, the Interim Provisions on the Implementation of Labor Contract System in State-Owned Enterprises are the main legal basis for the current labor contract system in China. The Provisions provide that enterprises recruiting workers for regular jobs within the targets of the state labor and wage plans should practice the unified labor contract system, except otherwise stipulated by the state; the contract system is also applicable to casual and seasonal workers with terms of less than a year; when signing the labor contract, the enterprise and the workers should abide by principles of equality, voluntariness and reaching consensus through negotiation; once the contract is signed, it comes under the protection of the law, requiring strict observance by the parties involved. Moreover, labor contract system is provided for in regulations governing Chinese-foreign equity joint ventures and private enterprises.

### 3. Vocational Training

The 1982 Constitution stipulates that the state provides necessary vocational training for citizens before they are employed. For this purpose, the relevant government departments had revised or adopted a number of regulations concerning vocational training, such as the Working Regulation on Technical Schools, the Opinions on Strengthening and Improving Apprentice Training Work, and the Interim Measures on Several Issues relating to Vocational Training. Meanwhile, in order to improve in-service training, the government promulgated the Decision on Strengthening the Work for Education of Employees and the Trial Measures on the Establishment of Secondary Specialized Schools for Employees. In July 1990, with the approval by the State Council, the Ministry of Labor promulgated the Regulations on Assessment of Workers, introducing the system of Assessment of Workers. The Regulations provide that the State enforces the system of assessment of workers. The assessment of workers should be combined with their employment, and their remunerations and other benefits should be determined in accordance with relevant regulations of the State. The Regulations also contain detailed rules on the kinds, content, methods, organization and management of the assessment of workers.

### 4. Working Hours and Hours of Rest

The Constitution provides that laborers have the right to rest and that the state prescribes working hours and vacations for workers and staff. However, currently China has not yet adopted any special legal provision on working hours, rest and vacations, except for those on holidays and overtime work.

### 5. Wages

In order to reform the wage system, the State Council had adopted a series of policy documents, including the Notice on the Issue of Wage Reform in State-

Owned Enterprises and Trial Measures for Its Implementation, the Notice on the Issue of the Wage System Reform for Employees in State Organs and Public Institutions and related reform schemes. Besides, the relevant laws and regulations lay down provisions on such issues as the system of bonus and allowance, the management of wage fund, and the restriction on wage deduction.

### 6. Labor Safety and Industrial Hygiene

In February 1982, the State Council promulgated the Provisional Regulations on Supervision and Inspection of the Safety of Boilers and Pressurized Containers, the Regulations on the Safety of Mines, and the Regulations on the Supervision and Inspection of the Safety of Mines. The implementation of these Regulations had greatly strengthened the supervision and inspection of labor safety and gradually formed a system that combined inspection by the state with the management by the relevant industries and the supervision by the public. In July 1984, the State Council issued the Decision on Strengthening Prevention of Harms Caused by Dust and Poison, requiring that, all regions and departments, when implementing capital construction projects or plant-wide technological transformation, must ensure that design and approval of control and treatment of dust and poison and safety facilities must be made simultaneously with that of the principal part of the projects, their construction, completion acceptance, and being put into operation must also be made at the same time as those of the principal part of the projects. The Regulations on the Prevention and Treatment of Pneumoconiosis, promulgated by the State Council in December 1987, stipulated that, if the dust concentration in a workplace exceeds the national health standard and no active measure is taken to control its harmful effect, thereby seriously endangering the safety and health of employees, an employee has the right to refuse to work in such a workplace. It is worth mentioning that, in January the same year, relevant departments issued rules, which enlarged the scope of occupational diseases and specified treatment methods for occupational disease patients. Moreover, the Interim Provisions on the Procedures for the Investigation of Extraordinary Serious Accidents, promulgated by the State Council in March 1989, provided for methods for investigating extraordinarily serious accidents. And in 1992, the first specialized labor law, the Law on the Safety of Mines, was promulgated.

### 7. Labor Protection of Female Employees

The Provisions on Labor Protection of Female Employees, promulgated in July 1988, was the first specialized regulations that systematically provided for the labor protection of female employees. They contain comprehensive provisions on such issues as the recruitment of female employees, categories of work to be avoided by women, maternity leave and related benefits, and facilities of labor protection.

### 8. Labor Protection of Minors

Currently no specialized regulations on the labor protection of minors have been adopted in China. However, some administrative regulations contain provisions on this subject. For example, the Regulations on the Prevention and Treatment of Pneumoconiosis provide in Article 12 (3) that: "It is prohibited to engage minors under the age of 18 in any work that exposes them to harmful dust."

### 9. Awards and Penalties for Enterprise Employees

The Regulations on the Awards and Penalties for Enterprise Employees, promulgated by the State Council in April 1982, were the main regulations in this respect. They laid down the basic principles for the awards and penalties for enterprise employees, the categories of awards and penalties and conditions of their application, appeal procedures, etc. In July 1986, the State Council promulgated the Interim Provisions on the Laying-off Employees of State-Owned Enterprises for Violation of Disciplines. As a supplement to the Regulations on the Awards and Penalties for Enterprise Employees, the Provisions provided for the conditions for the laying-off employees who violated labor disciplines or made serious mistakes but whose violations or mistakes were not serious enough for the punishment of dismissal.

### 10. Social Insurance

Following the approval by the Standing Committee of the National People's Congress in May 1978, the State Council, issued in June the same year the Interim Measures for the Arrangements of Cadres Who Are Old, Weak, ill or Disabled and Interim Measures for Workers' Retirement and Leaving of Posts. The State Council further promulgated the Interim Provisions on the Implementation of the Labor Contract System in State-Owned Enterprises in July 1986, and the Provisions on the Unemployment Insurance of Enterprise Employees in 1993, thereby establishing a primary pension insurance system for contract workers and an unemployment insurance system for enterprise employees.

### 11. Trade Unions and Democratic Management of Enterprises

The Law on Industrial Enterprises Owned by the Whole People, adopted by the National People's Congress in April 1988, provides for that "Trade unions in enterprises shall represent and safeguard the interests of the staff and workers and conduct their work independently according to law. The trade union in an enterprise shall organize the staff and workers for participation in democratic management of the enterprise and democratic supervision of the management of the enterprise" and that "The employees' congress shall be the basic form for practicing democratic management in an enterprise. " The Law also contains specific provisions on the functions and powers of the employees' congress.

### 12. Settlement of Labor Disputes

The main regulations in this field include the Provisional Regulations on the Settlement of Labor Disputes in State-Owned Enterprises, promulgated by the State Council in July 1987, and the Regulations on the Settlement of Labor Disputes in Enterprises as results of several revisions of the 1987 Regulations before promulgated by the State Council in 1993. These regulations establish a system of organs and procedures for the settlement of labor disputes. They are applicable to disputes between enterprises and employees resulting from the implementation of labor contract or from the dismissal, discharge or lay-off of employees for violation of disciplines. The main methods of settlement of disputes include mediation, arbitration and adjudication by court. Mediation is an optional procedure; arbitration is compulsory and must be completed before a dispute can be brought to a court. The court's ruling is the final instance.

## III. The Legislative Process of the Chinese Labor Law

The drafting of the Chinese Labor Law can be divided into two stages.

In January 1979, the Labor Law Drafting Group was set up and scholars and experts from the relevant institutions, including All-China Federation of Trade Unions, the Ministry of Agriculture, Peking University, Beijing Institute of Economics, China University of Political Science and Law, and the Institute of Law of the Chinese Academy of Social Sciences, were invited to participate in the discussion and drafting process of the Law. The first draft of Labor Law was completed in July 1979; the 17th draft was completed in March 1983 and was deliberated and agreed upon in principle by the Standing Committee of the State Council on March 29, 1983. In July 1983, the revised 18th draft was submitted to the Standing Committee of the National People's Congress ( NPC ) for deliberation. In February 1984, this 18th draft law was revised in accordance with the opinions of some leading members of the Legislative Affairs Commission of the NPC Standing Committee. However, for various reasons, the Draft Labor Law was not adopted and the drafting work was suspended.

Nevertheless, the Labor Law was urgently needed to regulate various labor relationships in practice; the deepening of the reform made the adoption of the Law even more urgent. Meanwhile, many grassroots cadres and employees called through various channels for the adoption of the Labor Law as soon as possible; many deputies to the NPC and members of the Chinese People's Political Consultative Conference had submitted proposals for the adoption of the Labor Law as soon as possible.

In February 1989, the drafting of the Labor Law was resumed with the establishment of a Labor Law Research Group and a Labor Law Drafting Group. In 1990, a Leading Group on the Drafting of the Labor Law and a Labor Law Drafting Office were respectively established, each consisting of representatives from the Ministry of Labor, the Bureau of Legislative Affairs of the State Council, All-China Federation of Trade Unions, the State Development and Planning Commission, the Production Commission under the State Council, the State Commission for Restructuring the Economic System, the Ministry of Health, the Ministry of Personnel, the Ministry of Machinery and Electronic Industry, the Ministry of Energy, and the Ministry of Agriculture. They carried out research on and redefined the basic principles and main contents of the Labor Law, collected and sorted out Chinese and foreign materials amounting close to 300,000 words of, translated and published the labor laws of over 50 countries. On the basis of this comprehensive research, a new Draft Labor Law was formulated.

In December 1989, a series of seminars were organized in order to solicit systematically opinions on the draft Labor Law. More than 200 participants attended the seminars, representing labor administration departments, trade unions, as well as enterprises, employees, and experts in the four main regions of China, namely North China, Northeast China, Northwest China, and East China. The Draft Labor Law was also discussed at the national conference of the heads of labor departments of governments at various levels and at the national conference of the heads of departments of labor laws and policies of governments at various levels. In August and November of 1990, a series of discussions attended by over 100 participants and two expert demonstrations were held in the cities of Beijing, Chengdu, Chongqing and Wuhan. Meanwhile, the Drafting Group also solicited opinions on the Draft Law from over 150 entities, including various ministries, commissions and bureaus under the State Council, enterprises, mass organizations, and democratic parties. Under the guidance of the Leading Group and the Bureau of Legislative Affairs of the State Council, the Draft Law was revised eight more times and, in July 1991, the 27th draft of the Law was agreed upon by the Leading Group and submitted to the State Council.

The Draft Law was also sent by the Bureau of Legislative Affairs of the State

Council to various provinces and municipalities to solicit further opinions. These were sorted out and discussed within relevant departments. The dominant opinion was that the Draft Law was basically feasible and should be adopted and promulgated as soon as possible. The Draft Law was revised once again on the basis of further investigations and then submitted to the executive meeting of the State Council for deliberation.

On January 7, 1994, the State Council adopted the Draft Labor Law in its 14th executive meeting. It held that it was necessary and feasible for China to adopt the Labor Law and submitted the Draft Law to the Standing Committee of the NPC for deliberation. After careful deliberation, the Standing Committee of the NPC adopted the Labor Law on July 5, 1994, and the Law came into force on January 1, 1995.

## Ⅳ. The Labor Law System in China

With a view to content, the Chinese labor law system mainly consists of the laws regulating the behavior of subjects in labor force market, the laws protecting the rights and interests of laborers, the laws regulating labor administration behaviors and the laws on the settlement of labor disputes. As regards the level of legislation, it consists of basic laws, ordinary laws, administrative regulations and administrative rules.

( Ⅰ ) Basic Laws

The Labor Law further specifies the provisions on labor relationships in the Constitution and provides legal basis for the adoption of other labor laws. As far as its content is concerned, it consists of the basic rights and obligations of the parties to labor relationships and standards and basic norms established in order to regulate the main aspects of labor relationship.

( Ⅱ ) Laws

### 1. Laws Regulating the Behaviors of the Subjects in Labor Force Market

(1) The employment law provides for the conditions of employment, rules of recruitment, restriction on unfair recruitment practices and employment protection of special social groups; it also defines the qualifications of subjects in labor force market and the preconditions for their participation in labor market activities.

(2) The labor contract law provides for the mandatory principles when establishing labor contract, the form, content, time period, termination and dissolution of labor contract. It serves as a legal basis for the establishment of labor relationships by the subjects in labor force market.

(3) The collective contract law provides for the mandatory principles in establishing collective contract, the form and content of collective contract, and legal responsibilities for the violation of collective contract. It further confirms the rights and interests of laborers and safeguards these rights and interests through the competence of trade unions.

(4) The law on job referral provides for the qualifications, methods and standards of, as well as for the rights and obligations and corresponding legal liabilities relating to job referral. The purpose of the law is to promote the establishment of labor relationship through intermediary service.

(5) The wage law, provides for the principles and methods of determination of remuneration for labor, forms, time, and location of payment of wages, the payment of wages under special circumstances, the guarantee of real wage level, minimum wage guarantee, etc.

(6) The law on vocational training provides for the rights and obligations of the state and employing units as regards the vocational training for laborers so as to improve quality of the labor force and enhance the employment ability of laborers.

### 2. Laws on the Protection of Laborers' Rights and Interests

(1) The law on production safety provides for the obligations of employers towards laborers with respect to labor safety and industrial hygiene, so as to protect the health and safety of laborers.

(2) The law on unemployment relief provides for the rights enjoyed by laborers in time of unemployment, so as to guarantee their source of income in such time.

(3) The law on the welfare of employees provides for the welfare benefits and facilities that shall be provided by employing units to laborers, so as to guarantee the adequate working and living conditions of laborers.

(4) The law on social insurances provides for the benefits laborers should be able to enjoy in time of work-related injury, illness, old age, and childbirth, the sources and use of social insurance fund and the social insurance management system, so as to guarantee the basic living standard of laborers who are in the above-mentioned situations.

### 3. Laws Regulating Labor Administration Behaviors

(1) The law on labor inspection provides for the establishment and the functions of labor inspection organs, the methods, content, and procedures of labor inspection and the related legal responsibilities, so as to ensure that labor inspection is conducted in accordance with law and that those who violate labor

laws are investigated for corresponding legal responsibilities.

(2) The law on labor law enforcement is mainly applicable to labor administration organs and aimes at strengthening the enforcement of labor law through supervision at various levels, including the supervision over ordinary administrative acts and the supervision over labor inspection. This law regulates mainly the methods and content of inspection and the corresponding legal responsibilities.

### 4. Laws on the Settlement of Labor Disputes

(1) The laws on the settlement of labor disputes provides for the principles, organs and methods of settlement of labor disputes, including the procedures and legal effect of mediation and arbitration of labor disputes, etc.

(2) The laws on procedures for the trial of labor disputes by courts provides for the judicial bodies, methods and procedures for trial of labor-dispute cases, related legal responsibilities, as well as the legal effects of the judgments.

# Chapter II

# Legislative Purposes of Labor Law

The legislative purposes of Labor Law underlie entire system of labor laws and regulations. A careful study of the legislative purposes and spirit of the Labor Law is necessary to both understand the Law adequately and apply it properly. According to Article 1 of the Labor Law, the legislative purposes of the Law include: to protect the legitimate rights and interests of laborers; to establish, sustain and develop stable labor relationships; and to promote economic development and social progress.

## Section 1    The Significance of the Legislative Purposes of the Labor Law

### I. The Significance of the Legislative Purposes

Since law-making is a human activity, any law has its legislative purposes. It is on the basis of the purposiveness of human activities that Karl Marx distinguishes human self-consciousness from animal instincts: "A spider conducts operations that resemble those of a weaver, and a bee puts to shame many an architect in the construction of her cells. But what distinguishes the worst architect from the best of bees is this, that the architect raises his structure in imagination before he erects it in reality. At the end of every labor-process, we get a result that already existed in the imagination of the laborer at its commencement. He not only effects a change of form in the material on which he works, but he also realises a purpose of his own that gives the law to his modus operandi, and to which he must subordinate his will."[1] Human purposiveness is a

---

[1]  Karl Marx and Friedrich Engels, *The Complete Works of Marx and Engles*, Chinese Edition, Beijing: People's Publishing House, 1980, Vol. 46, p. 202.

motivating force that guides human activities and directly determines the directions, processes and results of such activities. As far as legislation is concerned, legislators must first and foremost have clear legislative purposes. In this way they can engage in concrete legislative activities, ensure that these activities are carried out around the legislative purposes, and control and adjust them in light of legislative purposes.

After the legislative purposes have been established, legislators carry out their work and formulate legal norms regulating specific social relationships, telling members of society what they can do, what they cannot do, and what they should or must do within a specific social relationship. American Jurist Roscoe Pound points out that: "A legal system attains the end of the legal order, or at any rate strives to do so, by recognizing certain of these interests, by defining the limits within which those interests shall be recognized and given effect through legal precepts developed and applied by the judicial (and today the administrative) process according to an authoritative technique, and by endeavoring to secure the interests so recognized within defined limits. "[1] The Guide on the Preparation of Law and Legislative Techniques, prepared by German Society for Technical Cooperation (Deutsche Gesellschaft für Technische Zusammenarbeit) for the Chinese Ministry of Labor and Social Security, also points out that the main task at the first stage of legislation, namely the "stage of preparation", is to analyse such issues as "What the law is trying to achieve?" "What are the purposes of the law?" and "What problems are to be solved through the adoption of the law?"[2]

Legislative purpose enables people to have an accurate understanding of legislators' subjective pursuits behind existing legal norms, analyse the value orientation of legal documents and determine the actual meanings of legal norms in the process of enforcement of such norms. Just as various U. S. courts have pointed out in interpreting the U. S. Constitution: "The primary rule of constitutional interpretation is to determine and respect the intents and purposes of the framers of the Constitution"[3] and that "the construction of every constitutional

---

① Roscoe Pound, *Social Control Through Law*, Chinese Edition (translated by Shen Zongling and Dong Shizhong), Beijing: Commercial Press, 1984, p. 35.

② See Lang Gena, "The Guide on the Preparation of Law and Legislative Techniques", in *Collected Papers on Chinese-German Labor and Social Law Cooperation* (1996—1999), German Society for Technical Cooperation (Deutsche Gesellschaft für Technische Zusammenarbeit) and Chinese Ministry of Labor and Social Security (eds. ), 1999, p. 22.

③ See Li Jianfei, *U. S. Constitutional Case Law and Its Interpretation*, Beijing: China University of Political Science and Law Press, 1999, p. 68.

provision must be the expression of the intent of the framers". ①

## II . The Significance of the Legislative Purposes of Labor Law

In the same vein, the legislative purposes of the Chinese Labor Law underpin the entire system of labor laws and regulations. All labor law systems and labor law norms must clearly serve the legislative purposes. Only by carefully studying and understanding the legislative purposes and spirit of the Labor Law can we adequately master and apply the Law in the process of its implementation.

The Chinese Labor Law stipulates in Article 1 that: "This Law is formulated in accordance with the Constitution in order to protect the legitimate rights and interests of laborers, adjust labor relationships, establish and sustain a labor system compatible with the socialist market economy, and promote economic development and social progress." According to this provision, the Chinese Labor Law entails the following three legislative purposes: to protect the legitimate rights and interests of laborers; to establish, sustain and develop stable and harmonious labor relationships; and to promote economic development and social progress.

The significance of the legislative purposes of the Chinese Labor Law is first and foremost manifested in their role as guidance in legislation. It took some time for the Chinese legislators to recognize "the protection of the legitimate rights and interests of laborers" as one of the main purposes of the Labor Law. The first several drafts of the Labor Law had used the expression: "to protect the legitimate rights and interests of laborers and employing units" —which was more in conformity with the general principles of law, because a law that regulates social relationship should be based on the principles of "impartiality" and "fairness". The most prominent manifestation of "impartiality" in the regulatory function of law is the equal protection of the lawful rights and interests and equal constraint on the behaviors of both parties to a legal relationship. On the face of it, the Chinese Labor Law, by taking the protection of the rights and interests of one party to a labor relationship as its primary objective, is unfair to the other party. But actually only in this way can the real equality between parties to labor relationships be truly realized. This is determined by the disadvantaged position of the laborers in labor relationship and the way the law upholds social equality and justice.

In modern society, it has become a general consensus as well as the basic

---

① Ibid. p. 68.

constitutional principle that laborers should have the same legal status and enjoy the same rights as their employers. However, the equality in legal status is not identical to the equality in concrete social relationships. For example, although husband and wife in a marital relationship are equal, in reality it is necessary to put emphasis on the protection of the rights and interests of the wife. This is especially true in labor relationships because in such relationships the laborers are in an obviously disadvantaged position.

The relationship between supply and demand in the labor force market and the significance of labor to laborers are the main causes putting laborers into a disadvantaged position in reality. The oversupply of labor force is a universal phenomenon of modern society. "Full employment" is no doubt an ideal expectation by all people, but it does not mean that every laborer will be able to find a job. The concept itself implies a certain level of unemployment rate. ① Even in a period of rapid economic growth and even if we exclude the unemployment caused by the absolute oversupply of labor force, there will still be frictional unemployment, structure unemployment, cyclical unemployment and seasonal unemployment caused by various other factors, including those related to laborers themselves.

In China, a country with a huge population, the phenomenon of oversupply of labor force is especially prominent. Primer Wen Jiabao, in a press conference held on March 18, 2003, pointed out frankly that: "China has a huge labor force of 740 million, while the combined labor force for developed countries in Europe and North America is just 430 million. Each year China sees the increase of some 10 million new urban laborers, and the country's laid-off and jobless people now total

---

①  The concept of "full employment", which was first used by British Economist John Maynard Keynes, refers to the economic condition in which "everyone who wishes to work at the going wage rate for their type of labor is employed", namely there is no involuntary unemployment. See John Maynard Keynes, *The General Theory of Employment, Interest, and Money*, Chinese edition, Beijing: Commercial Press, 1963, p. 19. In the theoretical circle, different definitions have been given to the concept of full employment. Roughly these definitions can be divided into two kinds: (1) "full employment" is a state in which the labor force and production facilities of a country are utilized to their maximum; (2) "full employment" means not zero unemployment rate, but that the total rate of unemployment equals the "natural rate of unemployment" (This concept was first put forward by Milton Friedman). Besides, some people use certain concrete employment indicators to describe full employment. With the passage of time, the level the natural rate of unemployment, which is used to describe full employment, has been gradually rising, for example, from the 3%—4% in the 1950s to the 6% in the 1980s. The International Labor Organization points out that full employment means that all men and women of working age who are willing and able to work can get paid, freely-chosen and productive employment, http://www. chinajob. gov. cn/, last visited May 28, 2002.

nearly 14 million. The size of rural migrant workers in cities is regularly kept at around 120 million, putting China under immense employment pressure. "① Huge labor force base means that even relatively low unemployment rate will lead to huge "reserve of the unemployed" in China. Whereas the unemployment puts the government and society under pressure, it puts much more than a pressure on unemployed laborers: it lowers the income and the living standard of the unemployed and their family; it leads to the degeneration and outdating of laborers' labor skill; it causes psychological harms to the unemployed and their family members, frustrating and reducing their self-confidence and sense of achievement, leading them to lose gradually the contact with society as a result of unemployment. Moreover, it challenges seriously the stability of their families, as evidenced by the high divorce rate among the unemployed or laid-off workers, especially among the unemployed and laid-off men. Apparently, the unemployment affects the survival of not only the unemployed, but also that of their family members and even their families as a whole.

The significance of the ratio between supply and demand in the labor force market to employing units or employers is very different from that to the laborers. The fact that it is difficult for laborers to find a job means that employers can easily find the laborers they need and that they can employ them at a very low price. Moreover, even if employers are unable to find laborers, the "pressure" they face cannot be compared with that faced by laborers who are unable to find a job, because an investment is made with the means of production rather than with the means of livelihood, and the majority of enterprises are entitled with "limited liability"; namely, even if they go bankrupt due to the lack of laborers, their investors' livelihood will not be affected. This again determines "disadvantaged position" of laborers.

Furthermore, even after a laborer has already found a job, he or she is still in a disadvantaged position in the labor relationship that has already been established. Notoriously, one of the characteristics of labor relationship is the dependence of employees on their employers; obeying the management and command of and the supervision by their employers is one of the basic labor obligations of laborers constituting the main content of the labor law, labor contract and internal rules of employing units. Laborers in their daily work must subject themselves to the management and command of and the supervision by

---

① See "Primer Wen Jiabao Meets the Press: a Full Text of Questions and Answers", available at www. npcnews. com. cn, last visited March 19, 2003.

their employing units. In case of a labor dispute between a laborer and his employer, it is often difficult for the laborer to collect evidence because of the internal rules or the management style of the employer or because of the unwillingness of other employees to give evidence, fearing retaliation by the employer. Even if he has collected enough evidence, he still faces many obstacles in bringing his employer to the court: he cannot afford to pay the litigation fee or is not capable to fight against the professional lawyers hired by his employer; or worries that it will be very difficult for him to find another job after bringing his employer to court, which means losing his current job, especially if the legal dispute is exposed by the media. None of these issues pose any problem for employers: they will be able to easily find a new laborer to replace him; the litigation fee and lawyer's fee are listed in their budget as the production cost and need not to be borne by any individual; their legal representative in court are either professional lawyers or head of human resource department who have rich experience in such kind of litigation and no worry about time and money spent on the litigation.

The way in which the law upholds social equality and justice has determined that the labor law must undertake the task of protecting the rights and interests of laborers who are in a disadvantaged position in labor relationships. The law achieves the social objective of helping the weak to achieve equality with the strong by restricting and punishing the violations by the latter of the rights of the former. The law of human society is essentially the law of the weak: "The law has been concerned with unfortunate victims of the competitive system rather than those who have gained fortunate benefits. "[1]

## Section 2　Legislative Purposes in the Chinese Labor Law

### I. To Protect Laborers' Lawful Rights and Interests

Laborers' lawful rights and interests are based on the various rights and interests enjoyed by laborers under state laws and administrative regulations. The

---

[1]　J. M. Oliver, *Law and Economics*, Chinese edition, Wuhan: Wuhan University Press, 1986, p. 32.

fact that the Chinese Labor Law takes the protection of laborers' lawful rights and interests as its primary purpose is determined by the nature of socialist law. In socialist countries, the law embodies the will of the people and takes the protection of the interests of the broad masses of people as its basic objective. Laborers are the creators of social wealth and the main subjects of social life. Therefore, the Labor Law must first and foremost embody and protect the various interests of laborers. Meanwhile, laborers' interest-based needs are their internal motive and driving force for engaging in productive labor. Laborers are most creative in their labor when their interest-based needs are satisfied and protected. The purpose of the Labor Law is precisely to satisfy, support, and protect by legal means laborers' material interest needs. In short, the Labor Law would be meaningless if it fails to take the protection of laborers' lawful rights and interests as its basic legislative purpose.

On the other hand, the protection of laborers' lawful rights and interests is also the precondition and safeguard for establishing a stable labor relationship, maintaining a normal labor order, and promoting economic development and social progress. Without effective protection of laborers' lawful rights and interests there will be no harmonious and stable labor relationship and normal labor order. Long-term negligence of and infringement upon laborers' lawful rights and interests will inevitably impede social and economic development. Hence is the level of protection of laborers' lawful rights and interests an important indicator of social progress in a country. Therefore, protecting laborers' lawful rights and interests is the foundational legislative purpose of the Chinese Labor Law.

In order to ensure the genuine realization of the legislative purpose of protecting the lawful rights and interests of laborers, the Chinese Labor Law, in accordance with the relevant provisions of the Constitution, establishes a comprehensive legal system of protection of laborers' lawful rights and interests. More specifically, this system includes: (1) the structured system of legal norms as embodied in Article 3 of the Labor Law and other provisions on the protection of laborers lawful rights and interests in various Chapters of the Law; (2) the system of legal norms materialising further laborers' rights and interests, embodied in the provisions on the protection of laborers' rights to employment, to democratic management, to rest, to remuneration for work, to safety and health, to the special protection of female and minor laborers, to vocational education and training, to labor insurance and welfare, and to legal remedies in case of infringement of labor rights; (3) the system of legal measures and methods for the protection of rights and interests, including the protection by administrative law, protection by civil law, protection by economic law, and the protection by criminal law.

## II. To Establish, Protect and Develop Stable and Harmonious Labor Relations

The Legislative purposes of Chinese Labor Law include not only protecting laborers' lawful rights and interests, but also establishing, protecting and developing stable and harmonious labor relationships between employing units and laborers.

Both the historical process of the emergence and development of human labor law and the reality of social production have shown that, as long as people get together to engage in social labor, certain labor rules must be established and followed in order to maintain a well functioning labor order, which can only be established on the basis of stable and harmonious labor relations. Without stable and harmonious labor relations, there will be no stable and well functioning production order or social order. Therefore, labor law has undertaken the mission of protecting a well functioning labor order ever since its emergence in human society.

The essence of the legislative purpose of establishing stable and harmonious labor relationships between employing units and laborers is to require that laborers and employing units, when establishing labor relationships, must base themselves on the principles of equality, voluntariness and unanimity through consultation, taking into full consideration the interest demands of both parties, so as to establish good and healthy labor relationships in accordance with law and to avoid various factors that may lead to conflicts between them. This legislative purpose is realized mainly through the legal systems provided for in Chapter II ( "Employment Promotion") and Chapter III ( "Labor Contract") of the Chinese Labor Law. According to the employment promotion law, an equal employment mechanism should be established to ensure that employing units, when establishing labor relationships, treat all laborers equally, regardless of their ethnic origin, gender, religion, etc. More importantly, a labor contract law system should be established to ensure that laborers and employers conclude labor contracts on the basis of the principle equality, voluntariness and unanimity through consultation, so as to reasonably realize the wills of both laborers and employers and to create a harmonious interpersonal environment for the formation of stable and harmonious labor relationships.

To provide legal guarantees sustaining a stable and harmonious labor relationship between laborers and employers means strengthening through various legal systems and measures the good labor relationships that have already been formed between laborers and employers. The establishment of stable and harmonious labor relationships is a regular and long-term requirement by the legislative purposes of Labor Law on the quality of labor relationships. The establishment of good and healthy labor relationships is only a good start in the formation of stable and harmonious labor relationships. It cannot alone guarantee the establishment of a well functioning labor order. Therefore, the Labor Law not only requires the establishment of stable and harmonious labor relationships, but, more importantly, also sustains and strengthens the stable and harmonious labor relationships that have already been established. The Labor Law materialises this legislative purpose in the following provisions: (1) on the prevention and punishment through labor disciplines and labor supervision of acts of sabotaging stable and harmonious labor relationships; (2) on the strengthening of labor relationships that have already been formed through the conclusion of collective contracts,; and (3) on the settlement and elimination through labor dispute settlement procedures conflicts and disputes between employing units and laborers.

Developing stable and harmonious labor relationships between employing units and laborers is one of the important legislative purposes of the Chinese labor Law, which requires to establish, sustain and develop stable and harmonious labor relations and to set up the labor system under the socialist market economy. This legislative purpose not only places stable and harmonious labor relationships in a condition of constant change, but also makes them more realistic and thus easier to realize. Meanwhile, it raises higher demands on stable and harmonious labor relationships, requiring them to fully develop laborers' labor initiative, creativity and enthusiasm, thereby continuously improving the quality of such relationships. This legislative purpose in the Labor Law has been mainly implemented in the following provisions: (1) on laborers' right to democratic management of enterprises, which cultivate and strengthen laborers' sense of ownership and responsibility and enable laborers and employing units to carry out coordinated labor on the basis of convergence of basic interest; (2) on the establishment of the labor competition system, the rationalization proposal system and the incentive system, which enhance laborers' labor creativity and enthusiasm, and enable laborers to participate in the labor process in a happy and cheerful mood; (3) on the establishment of the vocational training system, which promotes the further deepening of the labor relationships between employing units and laborers and provisions on plans for the training of employees within the term of labor relationship, which enable the employers and laborers to establish new labor relationships after the termination of their current labor contracts; (4) on the establishment of the labor safety and industrial hygiene system, the labor protection system, the social insurance and welfare system, and the labor disputes resolution system, which continuously improve the quality of and give new contents to the stable and harmonious relationships between employing units and laborers.

## Ⅲ. To Promote Economic Development and Social Progress

All laws relating to the market economy serve the purpose of promoting economic construction, either directly or indirectly. The Chinese Labor Law takes the promotion of economic development and social progress as one of its legislative purposes, thereby confirming through legislation the dialectic of the relationship between economic development and social progress and embodying the principle of "giving priority to efficiency with due consideration to fairness".

Labor is the basis of economic development and social progress, which in turn constitutes an important precondition for people to carry out productive labor activities and continuously satisfy their own material and cultural needs. The Labor Law promotes economic development and social progress by protecting laborers' lawful rights and interests, adjusting labor relationships, and enhancing laborers' enthusiasm for production.

In order to implement and fulfill the legislative purpose of promoting economic development, the Chinese Labor Law establishes the following legal systems: the allocation of labor resources under the market system based on the labor contract system and complemented by the system of legal conditions for the dissolution of labor contract and the social insurance system; the labor remuneration system based on the principle of "giving priority to efficiency with due consideration to fairness", which encourages laborers to raise their labor productivity for the sake of their own material interest, and for the ultimate goal for promoting the social economy; and the fair competition system according to which rapid economic development depends on intense competition, which in turn depends on a legal environment of fair competition.

Advancing social progress and promoting economic development are two of the main State tasks in a given historical period. The Chinese Labor Law also takes the advancement of social progress as one of its important purposes. This purpose requires that the Chinese Labor Law, while promoting economic development, must also take social progress into consideration and, while adopting concrete measures for the promotion of economic development and improvement of labor productivity, the Law must also guarantee that these measures will not affect negatively or endanger social progress. In cases where implementation of an economic promotion mechanism or system negatively affects social progress, corresponding remedial measures must be taken to eliminate such negative effects and improve the mechanism or system.

The above-discussed legislative purpose in the Chinese Labor Law has been materialised by establishing and guaranteeing the principle of equality for achieving the social progress, which is embedded in various specific provisions of the Labor Law, such as the provisions on safeguarding the right to equal employment, the right to equality in the selection of occupation, and the right to equality in labor remuneration, as well as the provisions on labor and production safety, industrial hygiene, labor protection, vocational training, social insurance, and settlement of labor disputes.

The Chinese Labor Law establishes a vocational training system in order to promote social progress. The Law not only provides for in the Chapter on General Provisions the laborers' basic obligations of improving their vocational skills and observing labor discipline and professional ethics and the state's duty of developing vocational education, but also devotes a special Chapter (Chapter VIII) on vocational training, regulating the status, roles and obligations of the state, the employing units and laborers in vocational training. The Chinese Labor Law also promotes social progress by gradually raising the levels of labor safety, industrial hygiene, labor protection, and insurance benefits. In this regard, the Law includes chapters that contain detailed and concrete provisions on such matters as labor safety and health, labor protection facilities and equipment, special labor protection of women and minor laborers, and multi-level and extensive social insurance system.

● Chapter Ⅲ

# Subject Matter of the Labor Law

Any independent branch of law must have its specific subject matter. The subject matter regulated by the Chinese Labor Law are labor relationships. An adequate understanding of the labor relationships governed by the Labor Law is necessary to understand the scope of application of the Law.

This Chapter discusses two issues: labor relationships as a subject matter of the Labor Law (I) and personal and spatial scope of application of the Labor Law (II).

## Section 1 Labor Relationships as a Subject Matter of the Labor Law

### Ⅰ. The Concept and Characteristics of Labor Relationship

(Ⅰ) The Concept of Labor Relationship

Labor relationship is a social relationship that a laborer establishes with his employing unit in the process of engaging his labor capacity in social labor. Labor promotes the development of human society: "In order to produce, they enter into definite connections and relations with one another and only within these social connections and relations does their action on nature, does production, take place." ① The status and significance of labor in society determines the status and importance of labor relationships. Therefore, labor relationships must be regulated by an autonomous branch of law, so as to ensure that social relations within labor are governed by an effective regulatory policy. This basic process constitutes the

---

① Karl Marx and Friedrich Engels, *The Complete Works of Marx and Engels*, Chinese Edition, Beijing: People's Publishing House, 1980, vol. 1, p. 362.

theoretical and social basis of the Chinese Labor Law as an independent branch of law.

### 1. Laborers

In China, "a laborer" as one party to labor relationship refers to a natural person who provides labor force to an employing unit. He or she is also referred to as "worker" or "employee". A laborer in labor relationship engages in physical or mental work in an employing unit and receives remuneration in accordance with labor law or labor contract.

A laborer must fulfil the following legal requirements:

(1) Age requirement: According to Chinese labor law, a minimum age for employment for Chinese citizens is 16 years old. Citizens under the age of 16 cannot be admitted to employment and may not enter into labor relationship with an employing unit. Employing units are prohibited to employ citizens under the age of 16, or will bear corresponding legal responsibilities. Citizens under the age of 18 are prohibited to engage in occupations or works that may endanger health, safety or moral of the minors. For example, the Labor Law prohibits employing units from assigning laborers under the age of 18 to any over-strenuous jobs, jobs exposed to toxic or hazardous substances, or other jobs that imperil their physical or mental health, or any dangerous operations.

Generally, the minimum age for employment is determined by laborers' physiological conditions and educational level, but non-physiological factors may also play an important role in this respect. For example, the minimum age for employment in China is higher than that in many other countries. This is not because the physiological conditions of Chinese laborers are poorer than those in other countries, but mainly because of the huge working population in China. Providing for relatively higher minimum age for employment can delay laborers' employment for a certain period of time, thereby alleviating the employment pressure on society.

Related to the minimum age for employment is the retirement age, an issue often ignored by many people. Law prescribes the retirement age. Just like a person who has not yet reached legally prescribed minimum age for work, a person who has reached legally prescribed retirement age can not engage in labor in the sense of the Labor Law, nor can he or she enjoy all the labor rights, especially laborer's right to social insurance, like a normal laborer. Otherwise it will lead to some unreasonable consequences. For example, China allows retired persons to be "re-employed by their former employing units after retirement" or find other jobs so as to enable them to "make some contributions in their remaining years". This practice, although indeed enables retired persons to play a positive role in social life, has also led to many problems: some employing units stop paying pension to retired persons who have found new jobs after retirement; some retired persons, after finding a new job in foreign-invested enterprises, do not know how to bring these enterprises to pay various social insurance fees for them. An even more difficult question is: can retirement persons enjoy the benefits of work-related injury insurance once they are killed or injured in an industrial accident on a job they found after their retirement? The solution to this problem involves a complicated system, because everyone knows about negative consequences of allowing persons to be re-employed after retirement. They receive pension from the social insurance fund every month and enjoy various other insurance benefits while at the same time occupying job posts without paying various social insurance fees, which otherwise would have been paid to social insurance management agencies by the occupiers of these posts or their employers.

Current retirement ages in China were established in the beginning of 1950s. At that time, people's retirement ages were almost the same as their life. Compared with the average length of life at that time, today Chinese people's life expectancy has increased almost by 30 years, and their health condition has also been greatly improved. In many other countries the retirement age is 65 or higher. In some countries it is as high as 69. In China, however, due to the employment pressure and many other considerations, the retirement ages have not been raised since early 1950s, which leads to many problems.

## A Typical Case

Mr. He Wen (fictitious name), a 62-year-old man, worked at a seafood restaurant in Baiyun District of Guangzhou City. One day, while working at the restaurant, he was beaten and wounded by a customer. He submitted an application to the local social security bureau (hereinafter referred to as the Social Security Bureau) for the determination of work-related injury. The Social Security Bureau rejected the application on grounds that Mr. He had passed the retirement age of 60 at the time when he was injured. Mr. He filed a lawsuit against the Social Security Bureau at a local court. The court ruled in favor of Mr. He.

Mr. He was born in 1936. After his retirement in 1998, he began to work as a security guard at a seafood restaurant in Baiyun District of Guangzhou City. In October 1998, he was beaten by a customer while working in the restaurant. He was wounded in the head and had to be hospitalized for a long period of time. In May 1999, he went to the Social Security Bureau of Baiyun District to apply for the confirmation of his injury as work-related injury. The Bureau found that Mr. He's descriptions of his work and the circumstance of his injury were truthful. With regard to Mr. He's request for the confirmation of work-related injury, the Bureau held that, since Mr. He was already 62 years old— far exceeding the legal retirement age of 60 years—when he began to work for the seafood restaurant, his injury did not fall within the scope of application of the relevant labor laws and regulations. Therefore the Bureau, based on the relevant provisions of the Interim Measures of the State Council Concerning the Retirement and Resignation of Workers, Article 10 of the Explanations on Several Articles of the Labor Law issued by the General Office of the former Ministry of Labor, and Article 7 of the Summary of the Opinions of the Intermediate People's Court of Guangzhou Municipality on Several Questions relating to the Trial of Cases of Labor Disputes, issued a decision that rejected Mr. He's request to confirm his injury as work-related injury.

Mr. He refused to accept the Decision and filed an administrative lawsuit against the Social Security Bureau at the Court of Baiyun District, requesting the Court to annual the Decision. The Court, after hearing the case, held that the Chinese Constitution protects citizens' right to work and that everyone with work capacity has the legally protected right to work. The purpose of the legal provisions on retirement age is not to prohibit persons who have reached retirement age from working, but to implement the social security system and ensure that laborers are provided for with adequate benefits after they become old. The Labor Law has only provided for the minimum, but not the maximum age for employment. The Social Security Bureau's Decision, which refused to recognize Mr. He's injury as work-related injury on ground that he had reached the retirement age and therefore his injury did not fall within the scope of application of relevant laws and regulations, was erroneous in the application of law. The Court ruled that the Decision made by the Social Security Bureau was null and void and that the court costs of the case should be borne by the defendant. ①

(2) Labor capacity requirement. Since laborers must perform labor by themselves, they must have labor capacity. Moreover, for some special

---

① See Luo Ying and He Qianli, 'No Work-related Injury for People Who Have Reached the Retirement Age?' in *Yangcheng Evening Paper*, January 10, 2003.

industries, labor capacity also means that laborers must meet some special requirements of the industry. For example, people suffering from infectious diseases may not work in the catering industry. Unlike civil law, allowing activities to be carried out by a third party in accordance with law, in specific labor relationships, labor must be carried out by the laborer himself, not by any third party on his behalf. In the 1980s, when China was still implementing the system of life-time employees and urban areas were facing with great employment pressure, state-owned enterprises adopted the policy of "internal recruitment", an employee's job being given to his son or daughter after his retirement. "This practice had led to the decline of the quality of employees and contributed to the 'dependence mentality' of unemployed young people whose parents were working in state-owned enterprises. "① In 1986, the State Council issued the Interim Provisions on the Recruitment of Workers by State-Owned Enterprises, which abolished the system of "internal recruitment" and replaced it with the system obliging state-owned enterprises to recruit laborers through public and fair competition, conduct comprehensive assessment of applications' morality, intelligence and physique, and choose the outstanding ones from among them. This system is compatible with the objective law of the establishment of labor relationships.

In practice, labor disputes resulting from the performance a labor's work duty by one of his family members on his behalf occur now and then, and are often very difficult to resolve. For example, there was a couple that worked in the same workshop of a factory. One day, the husband who was scheduled to work in the workshop on that day had to go home to deal with some urgent family affairs. Upon the consent of the workshop manager, the wife went to the workshop to do her husband's work on his behalf and was unfortunately injured during the work. The factory refused to recognize such injury as a work-related injury, because the woman was not on duty herself but was doing her husband's work when she was injured. Another example, a rural laborer from Hunan Province went to work in Zhuhai City of Guangdong Province and was killed in an industrial accident. He was entitled to benefits of work-related injury insurance because his employing units had paid the work-related injury insurance fees for him. However, the insurance management agency refused to pay insurance benefits, because it found out that the man who died in the industrial accident was not the real beneficiary of

① He Guang (ed.), *Management of Labor Force in Contemporary China*, Beijing: Social Sciences Publishing House, 1990, p. 26.

work-related injury insurance. At the time of the accident, he was working in Zhuhai City using the name of his brother, who was the real beneficiary of the work-related injury insurance. The main cause of such disputes is the separation of actual labor relationship from the nominal labor relationship, resulting in the laborer's failure to meet the legal requirement of specificity of the laborer in a labor relationship.

In a broader sense, a laborer's labor capacity should also include freedom of action, because only a citizen free to act can actively participate in labor. Citizens deprived of personal freedom, such as those being placed under re-education through labor or sentenced to imprison, cannot establish labor relationship with an employing unit. It is exactly for this reason that the loss of personal freedom is one of the legal conditions under which an employing unit can terminate its labor contract with a laborer.

Moreover, Chinese law does not contain any restrictive provision on the nationality of laborers. Any person, whether he is a Chinese citizen, a foreign citizen or a stateless person, can become a laborer in China as long as he meets the relevant requirements set forth by the Chinese law.

### 2. Employing Units

Employing units are also called " business owners ", " the capital ", "employers", or "hirers". In Chinese law, they are uniformly called "employing units", which refer to entities that hire, manage, and undertake corresponding responsibilities for laborers.

There are different types of employing unit in China:

First, the enterprises lawfully registered in China, including enterprises of various ownerships and organizational forms such as state-owned enterprises, collectively-owned enterprises, private enterprises, foreign-invested enterprises, Hong Kong, Macao and Taiwanese enterprises, hybrid enterprises, joint-equity enterprises, joint ventures, and township enterprises.

Second, lawfully registered individual economic organizations, namely individually-owned businesses having acquired business license in accordance with law. Individually-owned enterprises have the right to hire helpers and apprentices.

Third, public institutions established in accordance with law, including cultural, educational, health, and scientific research institutions; for example, schools, colleges, hospitals, and publishing houses. These institutions have the right to employ laborers within the competence prescribed by law.

Fourth, state organs established in accordance with law. They have the right to employ laborers within the competence prescribed by law.

Fifth, mass organizations established in accordance with law, including trade unions, women's federations, research societies, and associations. They have the right to employ laborers within the competence prescribed by law.

### 3. Labor Behaviour

Labor behaviour consists of the rights and obligations by contracting parties in a labor relationship. The primary obligation of a laborer is to carry out labor behaviours, complete his labor tasks, and do his job well while the primary task of an employing unit is to pay labor remuneration.

Since labor behaviour is the target of labor relationship, after the establishment of a labor relationship, a laborer must participate in the production or other work of the employing unit, become an employee of the employing unit, enjoy corresponding rights, and undertake corresponding obligations. Employing unit as organizer and manager of production and business activities, while demanding laborers to complete their tasks in production and other work, must provide laborers with labor conditions necessary for the laborer to complete labor activities agreed upon by both parties. Labor conditions include not only workplace and facilities and tools of production, but also facilities and appliances of labor protection, industrial hygiene and production safety.

Given the identification of laborer with labor at the level of rights, an employing unit should not merely pay its employees for their labor, but must also undertake comprehensive responsibility for their employees' labor safety and health, insurance, and welfare. For example, no private person should be allowed to operate employment agencies because labor is not a commodity and nobody is allowed to benefit from employment service. Laborers' overtime work is strictly limited. A laborer's working hour may not exceed a legally prescribed limit, even if the employer is willing to pay the double remuneration. This clearly shows that laborer's labor cannot be bought freely with money.

( Ⅱ ) Characteristics of Labor Relationships

Labor relationships governed by labor law have the following characteristics distinguishing them from relationships governed by other branches of law:

### 1. Labor Relationships Can be Established only in the Process of Labor

The labor process is the precondition and basis of the establishment of labor relationships. No labor relationship can be established without the labor process and any relationship not established in the labor process is not labor relationship. Because of this characteristic of labor relationship, the scope of application of the labor law is limited only to the labor process.

Strictly speaking, the Labor Law as a set of legal norms regulating labor relationships should not be applicable to the employment process before the establishment of a labor relationship. However, since China is a country with a huge labor force, employment is a social problem that will affect social and economic development and stability for a long period of time. Meanwhile, employment has especially close ties with labor relationship. In view of this situation, the Chinese Labor Law extends its scope of application to cover employment process and contains a special chapter (Chapter II) on this subject.

**2. Labor Relationships Can be Established only between a Laborer and an Employing Unit**

Both laborers and employing units may establish social relationships different in nature with different social subjects and in different social activities. However, only the relationship established between a laborer and an employing unit in the process of labor constitutes a labor relationship governed by labor law. Moreover, according to the Chinese Labor Law, the labor relationship between a laborer and an employing unit is exclusive: a laborer, as a natural person, can conclude a labor contract and establish labor relationship with only one employing unit at a time. No laborer can conclude labor contract and establish labor relationship with two or more employing units at the same time. Likewise, no two employing units may conclude separate labor contracts and establish separate labor relationships with the same laborer at the same time. Otherwise, they violate related provisions of the Labor Law and have to bear corresponding legal liabilities under Article 99 of the Labor Law.

**3. Labor Relationships Take Labor as a Purpose of Their Existence**

The purpose of establishing labor relationships between employing units and laborers is to realize the labor process and social production. Without this specific purpose, a labor relationship will lose the value and meaning of its existence. Because of this characteristic of labor relationship, an employing unit must have the right to engage/use laborers in accordance with law and a laborer must have certain legal capacity as well as the capacity for act. For example, an employing unit has the right to employ and manage laborers in accordance with laws and contracts. According to Chinese Labor Law, a labor contract between an employing unit and a laborer can be of fixed time limit, of flexible time limit or of time limits for the completion of certain amount of work. An employing unit can also exercise its right to use labor through carrying out internal labor rules, which are supplementary to and have the same legal effects as labor contracts.

It is exactly because of this characteristic of labor relationship that, after the establishment of labor relationship, a laborer must participate in the production and work of an employing unit, become an employee of the employing unit, enjoy the corresponding rights, and undertake the corresponding obligations. An employing unit, as an organizer and manager of production and business activities, while demanding laborers to complete their tasks in production and other work, must provide laborers with the labor conditions necessary for a laborer to complete of the labor activities agreed upon by both parties. These labor conditions include not only workplace, facilities and tools of production, but also facilities and appliances of labor protection, industrial hygiene and production safety.

Moreover, since the purpose of labor contract is to realize the labor process, rather than to deliver the result of labor, the result of a laborer's labor belongs to the employing unit. In other words, the laborer performs labor under the management of the employing unit for the realization of the interest of the employing unit. As a result, the relationship between a laborer and an employing unit has some special characteristics. An employing unit has certain legal responsibilities to a laborer who is injured or encounters difficulties in life, irrespective of its responsibility for the injury or difficulties. For example, an employing unit has the obligation to pay non-fault compensation to an employee who has suffered work-related injuries, maternity benefits to a child-bearing female employee, or the expenses for treatment and recovery of an employee who suffers from illness or is injured in a non work-related accident, even if it is not responsible for the difficulties encountered by the employees. Conversely, even if a laborer has caused damage to his employing unit due to his own fault, the employing unit cannot demand him to compensate the damage according to the civil law principle of compensating for the actual loss. Moreover, with respect to the method of payment of compensation, it is not bona fide to force a laborer to pay compensation with his personal or family property. Rather, the compensation can be deducted from the laborer monthly salary and the amount of deduction must be strictly limited by law, so as to guarantee the basic livelihood of the laborer and his family members. ①

**4. Labor Relationships Have a Dual Nature of Equality in Law between the Two Parties to a Relationship and Subordination of One Party to the Other in the Process of Realization of the Objectives of the Relationship**

Legally speaking, the two parties to a labor relationship enjoy equal rights:

---

① Li Jianfei, "Analysis of the Differences between Labor Disputes and Civil Disputes", in Shen Deyong (ed.), *Guidance to and References for Case Filling Work*, vol. 1, Beijing: People's Court Publishing House, 2002, p. 2002.

the laborer provides labor or service to the employing unit and the employing unit pays labor remuneration to the laborer. The rights and obligations of the two parties are agreed upon through the conclusion of labor contract on the basis of equality and voluntariness. More specifically, in the process of realization of the objectives of labor relationship the employing unit has the functions and powers of organizing, directing, coordinating and supervising the production, while the laborer has the duty of accepting the direction and abiding by the various labor rules made by the employing unit.

This characteristic of labor relationship not only leads to the laborer's obligation to obey the orders of the employing unit, but also constitutes the basis for the subordination of the laborer to the employing unit. Because of the relationship of subordination between laborers and their employing unit, laborers depend on their employing unit for the satisfaction of many of their normal needs. Establishing labor relationship with employing units and engaging in actual labor activities embody laborers' right to work as well as the guarantee of the livelihood of laborers and their family members. Under the socialist market economy, labor is still laborers' basic means of livelihood. By providing labor to and producing products for society they acquire labor remuneration necessary for meeting the basic living needs of themselves and their family members. Moreover, laborers must satisfy through labor not only the basic living needs of both themselves and their family members at the time when they are able to work, but also for the time when they are not able to work. Therefore, the content of labor relationships involves the process of reproduction of laborers themselves.

It is due to this reproductive characteristic of laborers that the labor relationships established between laborers and employing units must involve not only the rights and obligations of the two parties to the relationship, but also the right to material assistance of the immediate family members of laborers; it must take into consideration that not only the basic living needs, such as the needs for food and clothing of laborers, but also the housing need of laborers and their family members, the educational needs of the children of laborers, and other needs of laborers and their family members. In order to help overcome the difficulties encountered by laborers who have lost labor capacity temporarily or permanently. Therefore, labor remuneration because of old age, illness, work-related injuries, disability, or death, the employing units and society must not only provide laborers with various social insurance benefits, but also give certain material assistance to laborers' immediate family members who are dependent on the laborers.

## Section 2    Personal Scope of Application
## of the Labor Law

### Ⅰ. The Principle

Labor relationship is a kind of very extensive social relationship. According to different standards, they can be divided into many different categories, each with its own special characteristics. As far as subjects of relationship are concerned, labor relationships include labor relationships of enterprises, labor relationships of public institutions, labor relationships of state organs, labor relationships of social groups, labor relationships of individual economic organizations, etc. Labor relationships of enterprises can be further divided into those of state-owned enterprises, collective enterprises, private enterprises, Chinese-foreign joint ventures, Chinese-foreign cooperative enterprises, exclusively foreign-owned enterprises, and jointly operated enterprises.

During the period of planned economy in China, the government adopted regulatory policy introducing separate laws for each category of labor relationship in light of their special characteristics. For example, labor relationships in foreign-invested enterprises were mainly governed by the Regulations on Labor Management in Chinese-Foreign Joint Ventures and the measures for their implementation, and the Provisions on the Autonomous Right to Employ Workers of and the Wages and Salaries and the Expenses for Insurance and Welfare Benefits of Workers in Foreign Invested Enterprises; labor relationships in private enterprises were mainly regulated by the Interim Provisions on Labor Management in Private Enterprises. This system of regulating labor relationships according to the nature of employing units (for example, state-owned or collectively-owned) and the status of laborers (cadres, workers, temporary workers, peasant workers, etc.) was not only incompatible with the market economy, but also thwarted the implementation of law. Under the market economy, the fairness of competition is especially important for both laborers and employing units. It is incompatible with equal and fair market environment to divide laborers in the same enterprise into different hierarchies or to implement different legal systems in different employing units. Therefore, with respect to the scope of application, the Labor Law establishes the principle of equality and fairness, abolishes the outdated regulatory mode of giving different treatments to different employing units according to their ownership system or to laborers according to their status; the same legal regulation system applies to all employing units and laborers within the Chinese territory.

## Ⅱ. The Scope of Application

In view of the complexity and comprehensiveness of labor relationships, three different proposals for the personal scope of application of the Labor Law were put forward in the drafting process of the Law: according to the first draft, the Law would apply to all employing units and all laborers; the second draft differed by providing for the exception of civil servants who were already covered by the Regulations on Civil Servants; according to the third proposal, the Law applied only to enterprises and their employees. Among the three drafts, the first accommodated the demand of market economy, namely that a set of unified labor law norms should be applicable to all employing units and laborers having entered the labor market. However, personal scope of application of the Labor Law was too broad to reflect special characteristics of labor relationships. Moreover, "all laborers" included servicemen in the armed forces and farmers engaging in agricultural production either individually or as a member of a family. These two categories of laborers do not form labor relationship with any employing unit and therefore do not fall within the scope of application of the Labor Law. Under the third draft, personal scope of application of the Law was too narrow to meet the demand of the market economy for the establishment of a unified labor market and corresponding legal rules, or to be compatible with international practices. The second draft was adopted because it basically covered all labor relationships while at the same time taking special circumstances into consideration.

Article 2 of the Labor Law stipulates, "This Law applies to all enterprises and individual economic organizations within the territory of the People's Republic of China and laborers who form a labor relationship therewith. State organs, public institutions and social groups as well as laborers who form a labor contract relationship therewith shall follow this Law." Meanwhile, the Opinions on Several Issues relating to the Implementation of the Labor Law of the People's Republic of China provide that: "The Labor Law shall apply where a labor relationship is established between a laborer and an enterprise or an individual economic organization, namely as long as a laborer has in fact become a member of and provides paid labor to an enterprise or individual economic organization."

The above-cited provisions show that the Labor Law applies to all economic units engaging in production, circulation or service and carrying out independent accounting, including enterprises of various ownerships such as factories, farms, companies, and individual economic organizations.

1. "Enterprises" refer to all enterprises located within the Chinese territory, regardless the nationality of their investors or the nature of their ownership, including incorporated and unincorporated enterprise, state-owned enterprises and non-state-owned enterprise, domestic enterprise and foreign-related enterprises.

2. "Individual economic organizations" refer to privately or individually-owned businesses that hire seven or less employees, including private enterprises with legal personality and individual businesses without legal personality but having undergone registration formalities with the administrative department for industry and commerce. The former fall under "enterprises within the Chinese territory", the latter refer to individual businesses that hire employees.

3. State organs, public institutions and social groups: State organs refer to government organs at central or various local levels that engage in state administration or exercise state power and whose activities are independently financed by state budget, including organs of state power (the National People's Congress and people's congresses at various local levels and their standing committees), state administrative organs (the State Council, various ministries and commissions under the State Council, commissions, offices, and bureaus under local governments at various levels), state adjudicatory organs and legal supervision organs (people's courts and people's procuratorates at various levels), state military organs (the Central Military Commission and organs and units of the People's Liberation Army at various levels). Public institutions refer to social organizations engaging in various social undertakings and having independent fund or property, such as news agencies, publishing houses, movie studios, museums, theatrical troupes, schools, colleges, universities, research institutes, and medical and health institutions. Social groups are various social organizations formed by some individuals on a voluntary basis for the realization of a common objective. They include political parties (including democratic parties such as the Revolutionary Committee of the Chinese Kuomingtang, China Democratic League, Jiusan Society, China Democratic National Construction Association, and China Association Promoting Democracy), people's mass organizations (such as trade unions, communist youth leagues, women's federations, students' federations, youth federations, associations of industry and commerce, etc.), literary artistic, and sports organizations (such as federations of literary and art circles, soccer associations, and volleyball associations), academic organizations (such as philosophical societies, finance societies, and enterprise management societies),

social-economic organizations (such as various trade associations (for example, China Association of Privately-Owned Businesses), professional associations, and economic and technical consultancy agencies), religious organizations (such as Catholic Patriotic Association and Buddhist Society), amateur societies (such as philatelic societies and game fishing societies), and other mass organizations (such as societies of aged people).

The Labor Law applies to state organs and social groups only if they have established labor relationships with their staff members through the conclusion or implementation of labor contract. The Labor Law applies to public institutions that have implemented enterprise-style management system and to those that have or should have established labor relationships with their staff members through the conclusion of labor contract (employment contract).

● 
○ 
● 
○ 
● Chapter Ⅳ

# Employment Law

China is a country with huge labor resources and it has prominent employment problems.

This chapter discusses the concept of employment, explains in detail various forms of employment, and introduces some basic principles to be followed in employment, especially the principle of the state's obligation to promote employment, market principle and the principle of equality. It further explores the principle of gender equality in employment and the principle of employment protection of special groups of people. To highlight the protection of minors, this chapter contains a special section on the prohibition of child labor.

## Section 1 Introduction

### Ⅰ. Definition and Basic Elements of Employment

#### (Ⅰ) Definition

Employment is the act of a person with labor capacity enabling him an access to means of production so as to realize labor process and obtain labor remuneration or operating income. From the perspective of employment system, employment in essence is the combination of labor force with means of production for the purpose of realizing the labor process, producing for society, and promoting social progress and development. It is because of this important social function of employment that governments of countries worldwide are making great efforts in improving their employment polices and in establishing a scientific, reasonable and effective employment system. The Chinese Labor Law contains a special chapter on the promotion of employment aimed at establishing an employment system in which the market plays a basic role in the allocation of labor resources.

According to the definition given by relevant international organization, "a person in employment" refers to any person above a specified age who meets one of the following conditions: (1) "at work", namely, is engaging in a paid occupation during a specified period of time; (2) "with a job but not at work", namely has a formal attachment to a job but is temporarily not at work due to such reasons as illness, accident, labor dispute, vacation, temporary absence without leave, or bad weather, mechanical breakdown, etc. ; (3) is an employer, a self-employed, or a member of a family who is helping the family running an enterprise or farm without remuneration and whose working hour during a specified period of time is more than one third of the normal working hour. The scope of employment usually covers only the workforce in various sectors of national economy, not the servicemen in the armed forces or students in schools or colleges.

The labor rights enjoyed by laborers can be realized only through employment. Before employment, labor rights exist only in name. They can be realized only by combining laborers and the means of production through employment. Therefore, employment usually should contain the following elements:

### 1. Working Age

Working age is a basic indicator used for the confirmation by law of a citizen's capacity for the enjoyment of labor rights. According to the relevant Chinese regulations, the minimum and maximum working ages are 16 and 60 for men and 16 and 55 for women. However, this does not exclude the lowering of minimum working age or the raising of maximum working age under special circumstances. Unless otherwise provided for by law, nobody may conclude labor contract with a citizen under the age of 16. Meanwhile, only citizens who have reached the age of 18 have full labor capacity and can engage in any kind of labor not restricted by law. The maximum working age is the same as the retirement age, which does not mean that a citizen at this age has actually lost his labor capacity, but only that he has lost his labor capacity in the legal sense and that he should withdraw from the labor market. ①

### 2. Labor Capacity

Since employment objectives are the realization of labor process and manufacturing of products, it naturally requires a laborer to possess the actual capacity for labor, including the professional skills required by a specific

---

① "A population can be divided according to its natural features, such as age. Usually a population can be divided according to "working age". Those who are above the minimum working age and below the maximum working age are called "working-age population", which is roughly the same as "the labor force. " Yao Yuqun, *Employment Theory and Employment Promotion under the Market Economy*, Beijing: China Labor Publishing House, 1996, p. 33.

occupation or work post. For example, health condition can affect a laborer's labor capacity. Only laborers with a strong and healthy body can perform labor in a satisfactory manner. A laborer with poor health condition has limited scope of work. People with certain illnesses are not allowed to engage in certain occupations. For example, laborers with infectious diseases are prohibited from working in the catering industry. Likewise, a laborer's employment can also be affected by his levels of intelligence, education, technical proficiency, and personal freedom. Disabled persons who have lost all labor capacity cannot engage in any kind of labor whereas partially disabled persons can engage in work suitable for their health conditions. Those who have lost their labor capacity cannot therefore get employed but receive social assistance instead.

### 3. Willingness to Work

In essence, labor is a fundamental right of the laborer. The exercise of right should not be compulsory. It is for this reason that the Forced Labor Convention (No. 29) and the Abolition of Forced Labor Convention (No. 105) adopted by the International Labor Organization require state parties to abolish all forms of forced or compulsory labor within the shortest possible period of time. ILO Convention No. 29, when defining forced or compulsory labor, provides for five kinds of work or service that do not belong to forced or compulsory labor, namely, any work or service exacted in virtue of compulsory military service laws for work of a purely military character, any work or service which forms part of the normal civic obligations of the citizens of a fully self-governing country; any work or service exacted from any person as a consequence of a conviction in a court of law; any work or service exacted in cases of emergency, and minor communal services of a kind which are performed by the members of the community in the direct interest of the said community.

### 4. Participation in Social Labor

The basic role of employment is to realize the labor process by combining labor force with means of production. Therefore, it is necessary to participate in social labor as one of the basic elements of employment, so as to distinguish it from housework.

### 5. Corresponding Labor Remuneration or Operating Income

This basic element distinguishes the paid labor in employment from unpaid voluntary labor. Employment is the process in which laborers combine their own labor with means of social production and laborers obtain corresponding labor remuneration. No employment right is realized if a laborer engages in unpaid labor or if his income is not the remuneration for his labor. Therefore, participating in social labor and obtaining corresponding remuneration are the two indispensable aspects of employment.

## 6. Social Need for Labor

Although social need for labor may seem not to be an element of employment, it is indispensable for the realization of employment. According to economy theory: "employment is the effective combination of three basic elements of production—nature (land and material elements), labor and capital. Without such combination production would be impossible."[1] This shows that "employment" cannot be realized by laborers alone, but the existence of the need for labor is also necessary for its realization. When the supply of labor force is greater than that needed by society, unemployment is inevitable: a laborer can not find a job even if he meets all the above requirements and those who are already employed will lose their job. Therefore, when there is an overall surplus of labor force, it is inevitable that some laborers will not be able to get employed. The element of social need for labor constitutes the basis of the government's social responsibility to promote employment.

## Ⅱ. Forms of Employment

### ( Ⅰ ) Employment through Direct Negotiation between Laborers and Employing Units

This form of employment is in fact the employment through competition by laborers, notably a fair competition for jobs between laborers. The usual method of competition is to participate in recruitment examination or assessment, with those who have passed the examination or assessment getting the jobs and realizing employment. For example, large-scale talent fairs are held across the country before the graduation of college students each year. On this occasion, college students who are about to graduate can directly meet and negotiate with employing units, as well as to realize employment through two-way selection.

The usual procedures for competitive employment of laborers are: ( 1 ) issuance of job vacancy announcements by employing units in the labor market and submission of applications by job seekers. Laborers decide whether or not to apply for a job according to their own preferences and in light of their own

---

[1]   A population can be divided according to its natural features, such as age. Usually a population can be divided according to "working age". Those who are above the minimum working age and below the maximum working age are called "working-age population", which is roughly the same as "the labor force." Yao Yuqun, *Employment Theory and Employment Promotion under the Market Economy*, Beijing: China Labor Publishing House, 1996, p. 70.

qualifications. Those who decide to apply for a job should submit to the employing unit the relevant certificates and documents, such as diplomas and certificates of qualification as requested, and prepare for the written examinations in accordance with the general rules of recruitment made by the employing unit; (2) review of applicants' qualification, and educational backgrounds, etc. ; ( 3 ) written examination for applicants and physical examination for those who have passed written examination; (4) interview of applicants by the employing unit; (5) decision by the employing unit on whether or not to employ an applicant and notification of such decision to the applicant; (6) negotiation and signing of labor contract and going through the procedure for the establishment of labor relationship.

The form of employment through direct negotiation between laborers and employing units is directly related to the fair competition between laborers and the examination and assessment by employing units. Because of the prominent and long-standing problem of oversupply of labor force in the labor market, employment competition between laborers becomes increasingly intense and the requirement by employing units on the quality of the laborers becomes higher and higher. Under such circumstances, laborers should be aware of labor risk and employment competition and try their best to enhance their own labor ability and skills, so as to get more employment choices.

( Ⅱ ) Employment through the Services of Employment Agencies

The realization of employment can also take place through various services provided by employment agencies, such as introducing laborers to employing units and providing employment guidance to job-seekers. Employment agencies are specialized agencies established in accordance with law and engaged in providing professional intermediary services to the job seekers and employing entities. According to the relevant Chinese legal provisions, employment agencies should have a fixed business space, a particular number of full time employees and corresponding facilities. They promote the full utilization of labor resources by providing employment services to and facilitating the two-way selection between job seekers and employers.

Employment agencies in China can be divided into three categories: those run by labor departments of the government; those run by non-labor departments of the government, and those run by private citizens. Before 1984, employment agencies run by labor departments of the government were mainly specialized employment agencies namely, each of them targeted a particular group of people: urban youth waiting for job assignments, rural migrant workers in cities, or employed skilled workers in cities. After the promulgation by the State Council of regulations on the reform of the labor system in October 1986, specialized employment agencies established by labor departments began to merger with each other, founding comprehensive employment agencies mainly run by labor service companies. Since then, the scope of business of employment agencies has been expanding continuously, from state-owned enterprises to collectively-owned enterprises and foreign-funded enterprises, then to township enterprises and, finally, to private or individual enterprises.

Personnel departments of the government began to establish employment agencies and personnel exchange centres in early 1980s. Their scope of service has expanded from helping those who have resigned from their jobs or are on leave without pay to be re-employed, to providing employment services to new college graduates. The trade union system began to establish employment agencies specialized in providing services to laid-off employees of state-owned enterprises in 1988. Industries and enterprises have also set up employment agencies. The purpose of employment agencies set up by industries is to solve the problem of surplus labor force within each industry while the establishment of employment agencies by enterprises began with optimising the organization of labor. Furthermore, private citizens began setting up profit-making employment agencies in early 1980s, when the rural labor force began to flow into cities.

The Ministry of Labor promulgated the Interim Provisions on Employment Service in April 1990, the Circular on the Management of Private Employment Agencies in July 1993, and the Provisions on Employment Service in November 1995; the Ministry of Labor and the State Administration for Industry and Commerce jointly issued the Notice on Strengthening the Administration of Employment Agencies in July 1996; and the Ministry of Labor and Social Security promulgated the Provisions on the Administration of the Labor Force Market in December 2000.

On 9 October 2001, the Ministry of Labor and Social Security and the State Administration for Industry and Commerce jointly issued the Interim Provisions on the Administration of the Establishment of Sino-foreign Equity Joint and Sino-foreign Cooperative Employment Agencies; on 14 May 2002, the Ministry of Labor and Social Security, the Ministry of Public Security, and the State Administration for Industry and Commerce jointly promulgated the Provisions on the Administration of Services for Overseas Employment, which is applicable to the administration of the intermediary activities within China providing services for overseas employment; on 28 October 2005, the Ministry of Labor and Social

Security, the Ministry of Commerce, and the State Administration for Industry and Commerce jointly issued the Notice about Permitting Hong Kong/Macao Service Providers to Establish Solely-funded Employment Agencies in the Mainland, which allows employment service providers from Hong Kong and Macao to set up independent employment agencies in the Mainland. The procedure for setting up such employment agencies is the same as that provided for in the Interim Provisions on the Administration of the Establishment of Sino-foreign Equity Joint and Sino-foreign Cooperative Employment Agencies.

### ( III ) Employment through Self-organization

This form of employment takes place when refers to the employment realized by laborers themselves, with the support from the state, organise voluntarily to establish various forms of collective economic organizations in such fields as capital, taxation, and place of business. Employment through self-organisation first emerged in the end of 1970s. Its main purpose then was to encourage educated urban youth who had been sent to work in the countryside and mountainous areas during the Cultural Revolution and returned to cities after the end of the Cultural Revolution to organize themselves and establish various forms of cooperatives responsible for their own profits and losses. This form of employment played a positive role in the settlement of educated urban youth returned from countryside, in the alleviation of employment pressure, and in the maintenance of social stability.

In 1979, collective enterprises established by unemployed youth who organized themselves on a voluntary basis and raised funds emerged throughout the country. These were cooperative economic organizations created by the laboring people themselves. They played an important role in improving the ownership structure, invigorating economic life, expanding employment, and satisfying the different needs of the people. Cooperatives were suitable not only for commerce and the service industry, but also for manufacturing, construction and other industries. They were responsible for their own profits and losses and were allowed to have independent bank accounts. Their start-up fund, apart from those raised by themselves, included loans from urban and rural overall development fund and the fund for the settlement of educated urban youth having returned from countryside, as well as low-interest bank loans. The state implemented the same for wholesale, with retail price system and goods assignment system for cooperatives engaging in commerce and catering business as those provided for state-owned enterprises. Laborers' working years in cooperative economic organizations were counted as their length of service.

Employees in well-run cooperative economic organizations might have higher wages or other welfare benefits than those in state-owned enterprises on condition that such cooperatives paid sufficient attention to the proper accumulation of assets. The state protected the ownership and autonomy in management of cooperative economic organizations. No government department, organization or individual was allowed to violate such ownership or autonomy under any excuse.

Today, this form of employment embodies the state policy of encouraging unemployed persons or laid-off employees in urban areas to voluntarily organize themselves and set up collective enterprises. For this purpose, the government has adopted many preferential polices, such as allowing unemployed and laid-off persons to set up employment service enterprises, which are collectively-owned joint-stock cooperative economic organizations. The main purpose of such enterprises is to provide employment to unemployed persons in urban areas. The state and society provide support to such enterprises in such matters as the conditions for starting business, supply of material, fixed assets, circulating capital, and loans, and give them such other preferential treatments as tax exemption or reduction, and reduction or exemption of occupation fee of state-owned assets. Enterprises, public institutions, state organs or other entities that sponsor or support employment service enterprises should provide support and help to such enterprises in matters of raising start-up fund, conditions for production or operations, procedures of licensing and business registration, guidance in the establishment of enterprise management system, and protecting the operational and managerial autonomy of enterprises. For example, the state provides that unemployed persons in large-or medium-sized cities, especially skilled workers and those who have business ability, are allowed to set up collective economic organizations in small cities, townships, or rural areas while retaining their registered permanent residence in their home cities.

( Ⅳ ) Self Employment

Self-employment is one of the important forms of entry to employment for Chinese laborers. It refers to the employment by laborers themselves through engaging in industrial or commercial operation, setting up private enterprises, or entering into partnership with others. With the development of market economy, self-employment has attracted more and more attention and is playing an increasingly important role in the re-employment of laid-off employees.

The state has adopted the following policies to support and encourage unemployed or laid-off persons to realize re-employment through self-employment:

First, tax reduction or exemption: A commercial enterprise, service enterprise (with the exception of advertising business, housing brokerage, pawn, sauna, massage and oxygen bars), processing enterprise among employment service enterprises or a small processing enterprise (entity) of a sub-district or residential community is entitled to deduction, within the prescribed limits, of business tax, urban maintenance and construction tax, educational surtax and individual income tax on the basis of the number of actually hired persons, on condition that it concludes 1-year or longer employment contracts with newly hired persons who are holding a Preferential Certificate for Re-employment to fill the newly created job vacancies for the current year and pays the social insurance premiums for them according to law. A person with a Preferential Certificate for Reemployment engaging in self-employed business may, on the basis of each household, be entitled to a maximum 8,000 Yuan deduction per year from the actual payable amount of the business tax, city maintenance and construction tax, educational surtax and individual income tax for the current year. An economic entity established by a medium or large state-owned enterprise for resettlement of redundant workers resulting from separation of the major and sideline businesses and system reform of sideline business shall be exempted from the enterprise income tax for 3 years, on condition that it meets the relevant requirements.

Second, financial support: Laid-off or unemployed workers, urban demobilized servicemen, and other registered unemployed urban residents who organize themselves to engage in individual or partnership business operation but lack the necessary fund may apply for small-amount security loans to banks by virtue of their Preferential Certificates for Reemployment, certificate of demobilization of serviceman, or certification of unemployment registration that are verified by their neighborhood labor security agency (or the neighborhood committee entrusted by neighborhood labor security agency) and upon the commitment and security of local loan guarantee organizations. Those who apply for a small-sum secured loan to be engaged in a merger-profit project shall be given discount interest out of the government finance. Among them, the holders of Preferential Certificates for Re-employment and urban demobilized servicemen may be entitled to full-amount discount interest granted by Central finance; other registered unemployed urban residents are entitled to an interest discount of 50% by government finance (of which 25% is borne by the Central finance and 25% by local finance).

Third, reduction and exemption of administrative charges for industrial and commercial administration: Laid-off employees who apply for starting individual business or cottage craft or establishing private enterprise shall be granted reduction or exemption of administrative charges for industrial and commercial administration within one year of the start of their business; those engaging in services to community residents shall be granted exemption of administrative charges for industrial and commercial administration within three years of the start of business.

Fourth, vocational training subsidy: Holders of Preferential Certificates for Re-employment, other registered unemployed urban residents, and rural laborers working in urban areas who attend vocational training programs are entitled to one-time vocational training subsidy provided by the government. The subsidy usually takes the form of reimbursement of the training fees. The government may adopt special support measures by which training agencies may apply for training subsidies from the local labor security department so that they can provide free training to those who really have difficulties in making ends meet and are unable to pay the reimbursable training fees. Where conditions permit, local governments may also adopt other forms of subsidy, such as training vouchers.

Fifth, free services: Public employment service agencies should provide free policy information, consultation and employment services to holders of Preferential Certificates for Re-employment, other registered unemployed urban residents, and rural laborers looking for job in cities; in addition, they should provide free assistance and guidance to holders of Preferential Certificates for Re-employment in accordance with the relevant support policies, and free one-to-one occupational guidance and employment assistance to persons identified as having difficulty in seeking employment. Various job intermediary agencies that have provided free employment services in accordance with relevant provisions may apply for employment service subsidies from local labor security department on the strength of the evidential materials showing the number of successful job introductions.

(Ⅴ) Job Arrangement by Government

Currently, the state still has the obligation to ensure entry to the first-time employment of some laborers in accordance with the employment policies adopted on the grounds of state interests.

Persons entitled to employment through job arrangement by government include: (1) Demobilized conscripts who have registered permanent residence in urban areas; (2) Demobilized conscripts who have registered permanent residence in rural areas but have won a second or higher class merit, or who suffer from second or third grade disability as a result of war or performance of duty; (3)

volunteer servicemen who have retired from active service. Those who retired from active service ahead of schedule as a result of serious violation of discipline or at their own insistence without justifiable reason shall be dealt with as retired conscripts; (4) demobilized military officers; (5) children of martyrs (only one child for each martyr) who has rural registered permanent residence; (6) Returned overseas Chinese, the family members of overseas Chinese, compatriots from Hong Kong, Macao and Taiwan who have settled down in the Mainland and their family members in the Mainland; (7) people who had been wronged, misjudged or unjustly charged in criminal cases and been released after their judgment was reversed, or being declared innocent or not being investigated for criminal responsibility in accordance with relevant laws and policies. Generally, this applies only to those who had been in job or those who become homeless after their release; (8) with respect to former military officers who have been sentenced to imprisonment for a negligent crime, those who showed good behavior while serving their prison terms and therefore are suitable to become a cadre can be transferred to civilian work; others will be treated as being demobilized; (9) other laborers who, according to the relevant state provisions, are entitled to employment through job arrangement by the government.

### (Ⅵ) Employment Modalities for Specific Groups of People

China has also adopted special provisions on the employment of rural laborers in urban areas, the employment of Chinese citizens in foreign countries, the employment of foreigners in China and the employment of Taiwan, Hong Kong and Macao residents in the Mainland.

Chinese Government allows foreigners who have not been issued residence permit and those who are under study programs in China to be employed in China. Foreigners who have not been issued residence permit include those who hold visas of F, L, C and G categories and those whose residence certificate is withdrawn by public security organs due to the change of their status; foreigners who are under study programs in China include those who hold visa of X category and are in China for study, training or internship purposes or scholars who are in China for research purpose. The above-mentioned persons who seek employment in China must meet the following requirements: (1) 18 years of age or older and in good health; (2) with valid passport or other international travel document in lieu of the passport; (3) with professional skills and knowledge required for the work of intended employment; (4) with no criminal record; (5) allowed by state law to engage in the work of intended employment as a foreigner.

On 22 January 1996, the Ministry of Labor, the Ministry of Public Security, the Ministry of Foreign Affairs and the Ministry of Foreign Trade and Economic Cooperation jointly promulgated the Provisions on the Administration of Employment of Foreigners in China. According to these Provisions, the employment of a foreigner in China means the acts of engaging in social labor and thus obtaining remuneration in accordance with the law by a foreigner who has not obtained the right of permanent residence. ① In order to employ a foreigner, an employer shall apply for employment permission for the foreigner and may employ the foreigner after obtaining the License of the People's Republic of China for Employment of Foreigners upon approval. The post that an employer intends to assign to an employed foreigner must require special capacities for which a competent domestic candidate is temporarily not available and provided it does not violate relevant state regulations. A foreigner approved to seek employment in China shall apply for an occupational visa at a Chinese embassy or a consulate in foreign countries by virtue of the Employment License issued by the Ministry of Labor, the visa notification letter issued by an authorized organization and the valid passport of his/her country or a passport equivalent document. An employer shall conclude a labor contract with the foreigner it intends to employ in accordance with the law. The maximum duration of such a labor contract shall not exceed five years. With respect to a foreigner whose residence permit has been denied by a Chinese public security authority due to his/her violation of Chinese laws, the employer shall terminate the labor contract thereof and the labor department shall revoke his/her employment permit. A labor dispute arising between an employer and its foreign employees shall be processed in accordance with the Labor Law of the People's Republic of China and the Regulations of the People's Republic of China on Handling Enterprise Labor Disputes.

There are some special administrative regulations and rules that require foreigners seeking employment in China to have a certificate of professional competence. Competent authorities may impose administrative sanctions on employing units that illegally employ foreigners or foreigners who seek illegal employment in China. For example, on 1 February 1999, the Public Health Bureau of Chaoyang District of Beijing Municipality imposed the administrative sanction by revoking the Practising License for Medical Institutions of Beijing Longtou Real Estate Development Co., Ltd. for illegally employing three Japanese

---

① These Provisions are applicable to the foreigners who are employed and the employers that employ foreigners within the territory of China, but not to the personnel of foreign consulates or embassies in China, representative institutions of the United Nations in China and other international organizations who are entitled to diplomatic privileges and immunities.

medical doctors as their public health technicians. According to the Measures for the Implementation of the Regulations for the Administration of Medical Institutions, in order to be engaged in the medical and health technical work, a person must obtain the qualification for medical and health technical personnel in accordance with the relevant laws, administrative rules and regulations. Foreign medical personnel practicing medicine in the People's Republic of China for short periods of time must register in China and obtain the "permit for foreign doctors to practice medicine for short term". Since the three Japanese medical doctors mentioned above had not obtained the permit, they were not allowed to engage in medical and health technical work in China. [1]

Foreigners who meet any of the following conditions are not required to hold employment licenses and employment permits in order to work in China: (1) foreign specialized technical and management personnel directly employed and paid by the Chinese government; foreign specialized technical and management personnel employed and paid by state organs or public institutions and with senior technical titles or special skill certificates acknowledged by authoritative technical management departments or trade associations of their home countries or international organizations, and holding the Foreign Expert Certificates issued by the State Administration of Foreign Experts; (2) foreign contract workers who engage in offshore oil operations through a Permit for Foreigners to Engage in Offshore Oil Operations in the People's Republic of China and who have special skills and do not need to go ashore; and (3) foreigners conducting art performances of a commercial nature through a License for Temporary Commercial Performances upon the approval of the Ministry of Culture.

## Section 2　Basic Principles of Employment

### Ⅰ. Equal Employment

(Ⅰ) The Meaning and Significance of the Principle of Equal Employment

All Chinese citizens have the right to equal employment opportunity, regardless of their ethnic origin, race, gender, or religious belief. More specifically, the principle has two aspects: first, the equality in employment

---

[1] Hong Shiheng (ed.), *Handbook on the Labor Rights and Interests and Social Security of Employees*, Beijing: China University of Political Science and Law Press, 2000, p. 30.

qualification. All citizens of the People's Republic of China have the same chance for employment, regardless of their ethic origin, race, gender, religious belief or level of education. All persons with labor capacity and their wish to work, regardless of their ethic origin, race, gender, or religious belief, should be able to choose their occupation freely and on equal terms, in accordance with their own interest and skill and in light of social need. Equal treatment in view of the employability standards is the second aspect. In an employment environment in which there is a considerable oversupply of labor force and a relative shortage of employment opportunity, equality also means that citizens should enjoy the right to equal competition in the employment process; namely, the same standard on assessing labor capacity should be applied to all citizens so as to ensure that laborers are employed through fair competition.

Laborers' right to equal employment embodies laborers' human rights in the field of labor—The competition under the market economy should be fair. Since the allocation of labor resource is realized through the market mechanism, competition is inevitable in employment. All competitors in the labor market should be entitled to legal safeguards for equal competition.

The opposite to equal employment is employment discrimination. The International Labor Organization defines "discrimination" as any distinction, exclusion or preference made on the basis of race, colour, sex, religion, political opinion, national extraction or social origin, which has the effect of nullifying or impairing equality of opportunity or treatment in employment or occupation. Such discrimination can take the form of law, fact or practice. "Discrimination in employment" includes not only discrimination in the access to employment or certain occupations, but also discrimination in vocational training, as well as in the terms and conditions of employment. The Chinese Law specifically prohibits discrimination in employment.

( Ⅱ ) Legal Safeguards for Equal Employment

The Chinese Labor Law provides in Article 12 that: "Laborers shall not be discriminated against in employment on the basis of their nationality, race, sex, or religious belief." This article prohibits employing units to impose restrictions based on nationality, race, sex, or religious belief: ( 1 ) in the provision of employment opportunities or in the recruitment brochure; ( 2 ) on laborers' access to certain occupations, for example, restricting someone's opportunity to engage in judicial work on ground of his religious belief; ( 3 ) on laborers' scope of profession, including in processional training before employment or in access to secondary specialized school or higher education.

In practice, the principle of equal employment means that employing units may not impose any occupational restrictions on laborers other than those provided for by law. In reality, many employing units take advantage of the oversupply of labor force to impose on job-seekers the recruitment conditions close to absurd, such as height and appearance. The governments of some areas adopt the policy of "occupational monopoly" or "occupational retention" by which non-local laborers are prohibited from or restricted in engaging in certain occupations so that local laborers can monopolize or have priority in engaging in these occupations.

## II. The Principle of Gender Equality in Employment

### ( I ) The Significance

The Chinese Constitution provides in Article 48 that "Women in the People's Republic of China enjoy equal rights with men in all spheres of life, including political, economic, cultural and social, and family life. " This basic constitutional principle has also been reaffirmed by the Law on the Protection of Women's Rights and Interests and the Provisions on Labor Protection of Women. This principle is materialised in the Labor Law through the equality of men and women in the right to employment. Article 13 of the Law provides that: "Women shall enjoy equal rights as men in employment. Sex shall not be used as a pretext for excluding women from employment during recruitment of workers unless the types of work or posts for which workers are being recruited are not suitable for women according to State regulations. Nor shall the standards of recruitment be raised when it comes to women. "

Women are an important part of labor force that has created great wealth for society. In China, 38% of the GDP of the country is created by women. For example, of the 8,940. 4 billion Yuan total GDP in China in the year 2000, 3,397. 3 billion Yuan was created by women. However, because of their physiological, physical and mental qualities, women have often less employment opportunities and are under greater employment pressure than men. They are unsuitable for many kinds of work because of their special physiological and physical conditions; given the low level of socialization of the compensation for women's childbirth, enterprises have become reluctant to recruit female employees; the low level of socialization of housework has also weakened women's competitiveness in the labor market; and in the transitional economic system, women are always under a greater employment pressure than men. All these factors have increased the difficulties faced by women in employment. Therefore, it is necessary to provide women with special safeguards so as to create more employment opportunities for women and enable them enjoy the employment right on equal footing with men.

### ( II ) Legal Safeguards for Equal Employment Right for Men and Women

The principle of equal employment right for men and women requires employment units:

#### 1. To Provide Equal Employment Opportunity to Male and Female Laborers

An employing unit may not refuse to recruit women for any work post that is suitable for women. Women have the same right as men to participate in job application and placement tests and to get the job through open recruitment and competition. Article 8 of the Interim Provisions on the Recruitment of Workers by State-Owned Enterprises provides, that "Enterprises shall employ female workers for any work or post suitable for women. " The Provisions on Labor Protection of Female Employees provides in Article 3 that "Any organization shall not refuse recruiting female employees for a work or post appropriate for women to work. " And the Law on the Protection of Women's Rights and Interests provides in paragraph 1 of Article 22 that "With the exception of special types of work or post unsuitable to women, no unit may, in employing staff and workers, refuse to employ women by reason of sex or raise the employment standards for women. " The same law also provides that "Anyone who refuses to employ women or raising the employment standards for women where women shall be employed in accordance with the provisions of relevant laws or regulations shall be ordered to make corrections by his or her unit or by an organ at a higher level, and the person who is held directly responsible may, in light of the specific circumstances, be subjected to administrative sanctions. "

"Work or post unsuitable for women" must be determined in strict accordance with legal provisions, and not according to the understanding by employing units themselves. The Provisions on the Scope of Work Prohibited for Female Employees contain the following types of work unsuitable for women: (1) operation in mines and pits; (2) logging, decking up logs, and floating logs downstream in the forest industry; (3) operation with intensity of physical work reaching level 4 as specified in the Standard of Classification of Intensity of Physical Work; (4) the assembling and dissembling of scaffold in the construction industry and laying wires high above ground in electricity or telecommunication industries; and (5) operation that requires the carrying of heavy load that exceeds 20kg each time for at least six times every hour or operation that requires the carrying of heavy load that exceeds 25kg each time on a discontinuous basis.

To ensure the implementation of this principle and protect the lawful rights and interests of female laborers, labor administrative departments should strengthen the administration of and supervision over the recruitment policy of the employing units. Those that have work posts suitable for women but refuse to employ women should be ordered to make remedy within a prescribed time limit or be punished in accordance with law.

### 2. No Gender-Based Discrimination in the Employment Standards

Providing equal employment opportunities to male and female laborers alone cannot guarantee effective realization of the principle of equal employment right for men and women. In case different employment standards or conditions are adopted for men and women, women's right to work still cannot be guaranteed even if they are given equal employment opportunity with men. Therefore, the principle of equal employment right for men and women also requires employing units not to raise the employment standards for women. This principle is of great significance because it ensures the effective implementation of women's right to equal employment.

Although the Chinese Constitution has established the principle of equality of men and women, the constitutional provision on gender equality is only programmatic. As a result, female workers' right to equality is frequently violated by employing units that arbitrarily raise the employment standard for women in the recruitment of employees.

## Section 3    Employment Security for Special Employment Groups

### I. The Principle of Employment Security for Special Employment Groups

Special employment groups refer to the groups of people who, for some special reasons, are in a disadvantaged position in the employment competition, including women, people with disability, members of ethnic minorities, and soldiers discharged from active service. They are in a disadvantaged position in the labor market not because of "laziness", but because of their gender, age, lack of education, skill, or work experience, etc. They include new college graduates, middle or old-aged low-skill workers, job-seekers from economically backward areas, and members of ethnic minorities. Special employment groups can also result from the policies or institutional reforms implemented in a specific historical period, such as the "job-awaiting youth", especially the urban youth who were sent to and work in the countryside and mountainous areas during the Cultural Revolution and returned to cities after the end of the Cultural Revolution, in late 1970s and early 1980s and laid-off workers in middle and late 1990s. Women, people with disability, members of ethnic minorities and soldiers discharged from active service are the special employment groups that exist in most countries, societies, and historical periods and therefore are the key recipients of employment support programs in various countries.

Apart from establishing generally applicable principles and regulatory systems, the state should also adopt special provisions governing special problems that have emerged in a specific period of time. Therefore, the system of employment security for special employment groups is an indispensable part of the Labor Law. The Chinese Labor Law adopts the policy of employment security for special groups of laborers on the ground of equal employment right for everyone and provides policy protections for some employment groups on the basis of principles of the labor market.

## Ⅱ. The Employment Security for Special Employment Groups

### (Ⅰ) People with Disability

It is a common responsibility of all members of society to understand, respect, and help people with disability. According to Article 2 of the Law on the Protection of Disabled Persons: "A disabled person refers to a person who suffers from the loss or abnormity of a certain organ or function, psychologically, physiologically or in human structure, and has lost all or a part of the ability to normally carry out certain activities. Disabled persons include persons with visual, aural, speech and physical disabilities, mental retardation, mental disorder, multiple disabilities, etc. " This definition is in line with the definitions given by the UN, the WHO, and embraced by countries worldwide. Disabled persons are a special group of people with difficulties in employment. Special employment safeguards should be given to disable persons so as to realize equal protection of the right to subsistence.

China has adopted the following measures to safeguard the employment right of disabled persons:

(1) Centralized arrangement of employment refers the employment of disable persons in various welfare enterprises, medical institutions, medical massage centres, etc. Welfare enterprises are special production units that make concent-

rated employment arrangement for disabled persons. In order to protect the labor rights of disabled persons and the lawful rights and interests of welfare enterprises and institutions, the law prohibits discrimination against disable persons in matters of recruitment, employment, obtainment of permanent status, promotion, determination of technical and professional titles, labor remunerations, welfare, etc.; no enterprises or institutions may deny to disabled graduates so assigned by the state an access to institutions of higher learning, polytechnic schools or technical schools solely on the ground of their disabilities; in case of such denial, the disabled graduates may appeal to departments competent to accord special protection and the relevant departments shall instruct the enterprises or institutions concerned to accept the said graduates; enterprises and institutions where disabled persons work shall provide disabled workers with appropriate working conditions and labor protection, and they shall provide in-service technical training to disabled employees with a view to upgrading their skills and techniques.

(2) Decentralized job arrangement for disabled persons. The state shall adopt the pro-rata-employment arrangement system for disabled persons, which means that state organs, social organizations, enterprises, public institutions, and urban and rural collective economic organizations should arrange employment of disabled persons according to a prescribed proportion, and choose proper types of work and posts for them. The people's governments of provinces, autonomous regions and municipalities directly under the Central Government shall determine the proportion in light of their actual situations. Each city must adopt a system of proportional employment of disabled persons by the order of the municipal government, taking the city (municipality directly under the Central Government, provincial cities, or county-level cities) as the basic implementing unit. The implementation of the system shall abide by the Law on the Protection of Disabled Persons and the measures for the implementation of the Law adopted by provincial people's congress. State organs, social organizations, enterprises and public institutions, as well as urban and rural economic organizations should arrange employment for disabled persons according to specific proportion determined by the government of province (autonomous region or municipality directly under the Central Government). Those that have not yet reached the prescribed proportion shall pay disabled persons out of employment security funds and in accordance with the Interim Provisions on the Administration of Disabled Persons Employment Security Funds promulgated by the Ministry of Finance.

(3) Encouraging and helping disabled persons to organize themselves to find

job or to start their own business, namely to engage in independent production or business operation so as to obtain labor remuneration or operating income. Industrial and commercial administrative departments, tax departments and other relevant government departments shall, in accordance with the Law on the Protection of Disabled Persons and the relevant tax laws and regulations, adopt and improve preferential policies that encourage and help disabled persons to organize themselves to find job or to start their own business and give them priority and preference in such matters as the issuance of business license, going through the relevant procedures, exemption or reduction of taxes and fees, and securing place of business. Employment service agencies for disabled persons at various levels shall support them to start their own business or organize themselves to find employment; actively provide them services in such matters as the choice of projects and the application of business license; help them to solve various problems encountered in production or business operation; actively assist relevant authorities to gradually bring under the coverage of social insurance the disabled persons in urban areas who engage in individual business or organize themselves to find employment.

---

### A Case Study:
### Providing Timely Help to Disabled Persons

Knowledge can change one's destiny. For an abled person, it means to make things better and better, whereas for a disabled person, it means a basis to provide timely help. Education is crucial to ensuring the subsistence and sustaining the human dignity of disabled persons. Compared with other members of society, disabled persons are in a disadvantaged position in employment, marriage and family, and other aspects of life. Receiving higher and more specialized education is the best way for them to compensate their disadvantages. Therefore, special consideration should be given to disabled persons in the allocation of educational resources and in the provision of educational opportunities and special method of education and lower admission requirements should be adopted for disabled persons in light of the types of their disability and levels of receptivity, so as to provide overall convenience and effective safeguards for the realization of their right to education.

In this sense, it has become a social consensus that it is the responsibility of the relevant government departments to satisfy further educational need of a disabled girl Dong Lina who won second class awards in a national "Xia Qing Cup" contest for broadcasting and anchor and who obtained Putonghua (mandarin) level One A certificate for broadcasters, and to provide convenience and create conditions necessary for her to receive as much professional education as possible.

Another example of a young girl who suffers from high paraplegia, with the help of society and through her own efforts, has managed to graduate from the Law School of Remin University of China and entered Harvard Law School as a Ph. D. candidate, demonstrates the necessity and feasibility of providing higher education to disabled persons.

China has made some progress in this respect in recent years.

First, in the field of mental health: Strictly speaking, only people suffering from serious mental illness can be counted as mentally disabled persons. According to statistics published by the Mental Health Centre of Chinese Centre for Disease Control and Prevention, in the beginning of 2009, over 100 million people in China were suffering from various kinds of mental diseases. However, the rate of public awareness of mental diseases was less than 50%, and the consultation rate was even lower. Another study shows that the number of people suffering from serious mental diseases in China has exceeded 16 million. China began to draft the mental health law in 1985. On 10 June 2011, after 26 years and ten revisions, the draft of the Mental Health Law was finally published by the Legislative Affairs Office of the State Council for soliciting opinions from society. It is said to be the slowest law-making process in the legislative history of the People's Republic of China. However, compared with the mental health laws of other countries and regions, this draft law is rather advanced as far as its legislative technique and quality are concerned.

Second, the creation of a barrier-free environment: The Regulations on the Creation of a Barrier-free Environment are supporting administrative regulations aimed at implementing Chapter VII of the Law on the Protection of Disabled Persons. The Beijing Olympic Games, the Beijing Paralympics, and the Shanghai World Expo have greatly promoted the creation of barrier-free environment in Beijing, Shanghai and other large cities in China. In the past five years, the Chinese government has carried out systematic work for constructing barrier-free facilities in 100 cities in the country. In the next five years, it will carry out in an orderly way the work of constructing barrier-free facilities in medium and small cities and in rural areas. Nevertheless, many problems still exist in the construction of barrier-free environment in China, including the low overall level of construction of barrier-free facilities, the extremely uneven development of barrier-free environment in large cities, medium and small cities, and rural areas, and the low levels of management and utilization of barrier-free facilities. On 25 April 2011, the Legislative Affairs Office of the State Council published the Draft of Regulations on the Creation of a Barrier-free Environment to solicit public opinions. This exposure draft contains specific provisions on the construction and management of barrier-free facilities, barrier-free exchange of information, and barrier-free services, as well as corres-ponding legal responsibilities.

Third, the Regulations on the Prevention of Disability and Rehabilitation of Disabled Persons are designed to support administrative regulations aimed at implementing Chapter II of the Law on the Protection of Disabled Persons. Currently, the regulations, mainly aimed at the rehabilitation of disabled persons and the prevention of disability are still in the drafting process and no Draft has been published.

Fourth, the Regulations on the Education of Disabled Persons: Promu-lgated by the State Council on 23 August 1994, these are the first specialized administrative regulations on the education of disabled persons in China. Their main purpose is to provide legal protection to the right of disabled persons to education and to promote the education of disabled persons. Currently, China is in the process of revising the Regulations in light of current conditions of social development, especially the growing need of disabled persons for education, so as to create more opportunities and better conditions for disabled persons to receive education and to participate in social life on an equal basis with other members of society.

In 1981, a new provision was included in the Constitution providing that the state and society shall help make arrangements for the work, livelihood and education of the blind, deaf-mutes and other disabled citizens. This was the beginning of the legislation on the protection of disabled persons in China. On 28 December 1990, the Standing Committee of the National People's Congress adopted the Law on the Protection of Disabled Persons, which indicated that the undertaking of protection of the rights and interests of disabled persons has become inseparable from the rule of law.

On 24 April 2008, the Standing Committee of the National People's Congress adopted the revised Law on the Protection of Disabled Persons. The revised Law contains new provisions on such matters as barrier-free environment and social security, strengthens the protection of disabled persons, expands the coverage of special support programs for disabled persons, and further defines legal responsibilities for violations of the rights of disabled persons. The revision of the Law coincided with the adoption process by the UN of the Convention on the Rights of Persons with Disabilities and the revised law incorporates adequately the basic principles and spirit of the Convention.

However, some problems in the Law on the Protection of Disabled Persons have caused public concern in its implementation.

Firstly, the Law contains too many general and declarative provisions that use such terms as "the state shall encourage (…) gradually", etc. The Law lacks specified implementation standard and operational implementation measures, resulting in poor implementation results.

Secondly, the Law contains many "sleeping provisions". For example, Article 36 of the Law provides that "The people's governments at and above the county level and relevant departments shall determine the products or projects which are appropriate for disabled persons to produce or operate, give priority to arranging welfare entities for disabled persons to produce or operate the said products or projects, and in light of the production features of welfare entities for disabled persons, determine some products to be exclusively produced by welfare entities for disabled persons. In the case of government procurement, under equal terms and conditions, priority shall be given to the purchase of products or services of welfare entities for disabled persons." These provisions have never been implemented in practice and are therefore basically "sleeping provisions".

Thirdly, the Law fails to clearly define the subjects of responsibility. Although the Law contains many provisions using such terms as "It shall be prohibited…", "shall…", these provisions do not specify the government organs' responsibilities for their implementation and are therefore difficult to implement in practice. For example, the Law provides that "It shall be prohibited to discriminate against disabled persons", but it neither defines "discrimination on the grounds of disability" nor specifies the government organs' responsibilities for rectifying such discrimination. Another example, some articles in the Law contain such formulations as "The government and the society shall…" without specifying the specific government organs' responsibilities for the implementation of such provisions.

A typical example in this respect is the experience of a blind girl named Dong Lina. Ms. Dong has had a passion for linguistic art since childhood. She has won a second prize in a national competition for broadcasting and anchor and acquired Putonghua (mandarin) Level One A Certificate for Broadcasters. However, when she applied to take self-taught higher education examination, she was rejected because she was blind. Ms. Dong had the capability, the qualification, as well as the legal right to receive education. She was denied the opportunity to receive education only because there was no precedent of admitting blind student by the educational institution she applied for. However, it is not clear in this case who should be held responsible for the infringement on Ms. Dong right to education, what kind of responsibility is involved for such infringement, and what effective legal remedies are available to Ms. Dong.

Fourthly, the Law has been infrequently referred to in judicial practice. There is a lack of understanding of the Law on the Protection of Disabled Persons among judges, who rarely invoke the provisions of the Law as the legal basis for their judgments or rulings even in cases of violation of the rights of disabled persons. [1]

( Ⅱ ) Employment Security for Servicemen Discharged from Active Service

The special employment safeguard for servicemen discharged from active service is mainly manifested in the form of employment. Both the Military Service Law and the Regulations on the Placement of Demobilized Conscripts provide that local governments shall arrange a job for demobilized conscripts who meet the relevant requirements. Such a job arrangement should follow the rules of job providing by the people's governments of counties, autonomous counties, cities or municipal districts where the conscripts were enlisted. Those who were employees of state organs, social organizations, and enterprises before enlistment shall be allowed to restore their formal work and position; for those who were urban residents and had no work experience before enlistment, the state shall make unified job arrangement in accordance with the principle of assigning job-arrangement tasks to employing units in different systems, with each of the receiving unit making appropriate job arrangement for demobilized servicemen assigned to it.

To be compatible with the market economy, the government should support and encourage demobilized servicemen to participate voluntarily in the competition in the labor market or seek self-employment. Where conditions permit, the

---

[1]  See Li Jianfei, "Openning the Legal Umbrella to Protect the Rights and Interests of Disable Persons", (2011) 22, *Law and Life*.

government may adopt the method of arranging job-seeking demobilized servicemen to meet potential employers to enable them to make two-way choices, and arranging job for those who fail to find job by this way. In April and May each year, the Working Group of the State Council for the Placement of Demobilized Military Officers, the Organization Department of the Central Committee of the Communist Party of China, the Ministry of Personnel and the General Political Department of the People's Liberation Army jointly hold a national conference on the placement of demobilized military officers to make unified planning of and raise specific demand on the work of job-arrangement for demobilized military officers. The relevant government departments of provinces, autonomous regions and municipalities directly under the Central Government carry out the work of job-arrangement for demobilized military officers, in accordance with the spirit of the national conference and in light of their local situations.

The procedures for the placement of demobilized military officers by state organs of the Central Government or enterprises located in Beijing under the administration of the Central Government are as follows: (a) convening a conference on the placement of demobilized military officers. The main purposes of the conference, usually held in the first quarter of the year, are to summarize the work experience of the previous year, to arrange for the work of the current year, and to issue plans for the job-arrangement for demobilized military officers by various state organs and enterprises. The conference is attended by the heads of the personnel departments of various ministries and commissions under the State Council, the organs directly under the Central Government, social organizations, enterprises, research institutions, colleges and universities, and other public institutions; (b) convening selection and transfer meetings. About one month after the plan for the arrangement of jobs for demobilized military officers is issued, the Office for the Placement of Demobilized Military Officers of the State Council shall hold assignment and transfer meetings in which military officers who meet the requirements for working in Beijing and employing units with the task of employing demobilized military officers can meet each other and make two-way choices. The army units of the demobilized military officers can introduce the demobilized military officers to the employing units, provide them with relevant materials and recommend demobilized officers in light of their actual needs. After the meeting, the employing units and demobilized military officers can contact each other directly and continue the selection and transfer process. (c) signing acceptance card. After an employment agreement is reached through two-way selection, demobilized military officers and the units that accept them should jointly fill out the Card of Acceptance of Demobilized Military Officer by Central State Organ (Enterprise). Both the demobilized military officers and the units that accept them must sign the card, certified with the official seal of the accepting unit, and report to the Office for the Placement of Demobilized Military Officers of the State Council for the record. Each demobilized military officer can fill out only one card (he can have only one accepting unit). The card takes legal effect and may not be changed once it is signed by both parties and certified with the official seal of the accepting unit.

### Ⅲ. Employment Security for Members of Ethnic Minorities

China is a unitary multi-ethnic country jointly created by its people of all ethnic groups. So far, a total of 56 ethnic groups (or nationalities) in China has been identified and recognized by the Central Government. The policy of special protection of members of ethnic minorities (or minority nationalities) is an important component of China's ethnic policy as well as an important means of promotion of the economic and social development in ethnic minority areas. Both the Chinese Constitution and the Law on Regional National Autonomy contain special provisions in this respect.

With respect to the employment of members of ethnic minorities, the Chinese government has adopted the following special preferential policies: (1) priority in the recruitment of employees. When recruiting personnel, enterprises and institutions in national autonomous areas shall give priority to minority nationalities. Enterprises and institutions affiliated to state organs at higher levels but located in national autonomous areas shall also give priority to local minority nationalities when recruiting personnel in accordance with the regulations of the State. When recruiting employees to fill up vacancies resulting from natural reduction of staff members and increase in work posts, state organs in ethnic minority areas should give priority to members of ethnic minorities. In the annual plan for the "change of household registration from agricultural one to non-agricultural one" made by higher-level governments, a certain quota should be reserved for farmers and herdsmen of ethnic minorities so that they can be recruited as employees of state organs; (2) The training of talents among members of ethnic minorities. The organs of self-government of national autonomous areas shall take various measures to train large numbers of cadres at different levels and various kinds of specialized personnel, including scientists, technicians and managerial executives, as well as skilled workers from among members of local ethnic groups. The State set up universities or colleges of nationalities and, in other universities or colleges of higher education, nationality-oriented classes and preparatory classes that exclusively or mainly enrol the students from minority nationalities. Preferred enrolment and preferred assignment of jobs may also be introduced. In the enrolment procedures, universities or colleges and secondary technical schools shall appropriately set lower standards and requirements for the admission of students from minority nationalities, so as to raise the college admission rate of students from ethnic minorities.

## Section 4 Employment Security for College Graduates and Students Returned back to China after Finishing Overseas Study

### Ⅰ. Employment Security for College Graduates

( Ⅰ ) Encouraging Small and Medium-sized Enterprises to Employ College Graduates

(1) For small and medium-sized enterprises that employ a certain number of college graduates, local governments should give them priorities in getting subsidies from the Development Funds for Small and Medium-sized Enterprises or discount interest on loans for technological updating; (2) A small labor-intensive enterprise that employs registered unemployed college graduates in the current year in a number accounting for 30% (15%, if the enterprise has more than 100 employees) or more of the total number of its current employees, and enters into labor contracts with a term of at least one year with them may be granted a small-sum secured loan of no more than 2 million Yuan and enjoy 50% interest discount; (3) College graduates employed by small and medium-sized enterprises shall enjoy the same treatments as personnel belonging to the same category in state-owned enterprises and public institutions in matters of assessment and determination of professional titles, application of fund for scientific research project, declaration of research results or awarding of honorary titles. On 1 February 2012, the State Council decided at its executive meeting to grant training subsidies and social insurance subsidies to small and micro enterprises that employ college graduates.

( Ⅱ ) Length of Service, Registration of Permanent Residence and Custody of Personal Records

For college graduates who are employed first by enterprises or social organizations and then by state organs, the years in which they have paid premiums for the basic pension scheme in accordance with relevant regulations shall be calculated on an aggregate basis as a continuous length of service. Municipal governments of various cities shall abolish restrictions on the registration of permanent local residence by college graduates who are not registered permanent local residents but employed by local enterprises ( In municipalities directly under the Central Government, the matter shall be dealt with in accordance with their respective provisions ). For college graduates employed by state organs, public institutions and state-owned enterprises that have the competence to manage personal records, their personal records shall be directly taken over and managed by their employing units; for those employed by entities that have no competence to manage personal records ( such as private enterprise or foreign enterprises), employment service centres may provide them with the personal records management and other personnel services. For college graduates who are not employed when leaving their colleges, colleges should transfer their personal records to the public employment service agencies of the localities where they have their registered permanent residence for custody. Individuals are not allowed to keep their personal records.

( Ⅲ ) Financial Support to Service Outsourcing Enterprises for the Employment of College Graduates

Service outsourcing enterprises that meet certain requirements and recruit more than one college graduates on a labor contract of over one year will be subsidized up to RMB 4,500 for the training of each of the college graduate employed; qualified training bodies, after training service outsourcing talents who have a university degree or above and who have passed the examinations of service outsourcing professional knowledge and skills, will be subsidized up to RMB 500 for the training of each college graduate, if that college graduate signs a labor contract for at least one year with a service outsourcing enterprise. Service outsourcing enterprises that arrange internship for employment for college graduates shall enjoy relevant financial subsidy. Service outsourcing enterprises employing college graduates with difficulties in employment shall enjoy social insurance subsidies and other preferential policies. College graduates with difficulties in employment who participate in the training in service outsourcing shall enjoy vocational training subsidy and subsidy for vocational skill assessment.

## (Ⅳ) Encouraging College Graduates to Work in Specific Areas

Grassroots work posts in the field of social administration or public service include: village officials; teachers, technicians, medical doctors and other professionals from urban areas assigned to rural areas for the purpose of improving the qualities of teaching, agricultural techniques and medical services, or to carry out poverty alleviation work in rural areas; and other work posts in the fields of legal aid, employment assistance, social security administration assistance, cultural, scientific and technological services, community service for the elderly, residential service for the disabled, and supporting services for low-rent housing in urban communities. College graduates who meet the requirements for public interest posts and engage in public interest work in the fields of social administration or public service in rural grassroots units and or urban communities shall be granted social insurance subsidy and public interest work post subsidy in accordance with the relevant state provisions on employment promotion. Those who work in other social administration and public service posts in rural grassroots units or urban communities shall be given salary subsidies or living allowances and covered by social insurance schemes in accordance with relevant state regulations; college graduates who work in grassroots units below the county level in central and western regions of the country or in remote areas with harsh living conditions or those drafted into the armed forces as compulsory servicemen shall have their tuition compensated or have their student loan paid by the state. Beginning from 2012, with the exception of certain special work posts, all civil servants in state organs at or above the provincial level should be recruited from those who have had more than 2 years of working experience at a grass-roots unit. State organs at or below the municipal (prefecture) level, especially those at county or township levels, should take effective measures to attract actively outstanding college graduates to take the civil service exam. The recruitment plan should be mainly used to recruit college graduates. In the enrolment of graduate students or recruitment of employees of public institutions, priority should be given to college graduates with grassroots work experience.

The policy of "free to come and free to go" should be adopted for college graduates who go to work in grassroots units in central and western regions of the country or in remote areas with harsh living conditions. They could keep their original registered permanent residence or they can change their permanent registered residence to the place of work according to their own wish. Their personal records should in principle be transferred to the human resource and social security department of the county-level government of their place of work and the public employment service agencies should provide them with free personnel agency services. Their political affiliation should be transferred to their employing units. For those who request to join the Communist Party of China while working at grassroots units, the matter should be dealt with by Party organizations at the township level in accordance prescribed procedures.

(Ⅴ) Employing College Graduates to Participate in Major National and Local Research Projects

Colleges and universities, research institutions, and enterprises engaged in Major National Special Projects of Science and Technology, 973 programs, 863 programs, National Key Technology R&D Programs, National Natural Science Foundation programs and other major or key research projects may employ outstanding college graduates as research assistants or supporting staff on these projects, including those graduated with doctoral, master's or bachelor's degrees from colleges, universities or research institutions that have the corresponding degree awarding authority. Such college graduates are not permanent employees of the institution in charge of the project. They must sign service agreement with the latter to clearly define the rights, responsibilities and obligations of both parties. Such a service agreement may not contain stipulations requiring college graduates to pay penalties for the breach of agreement. During the implementation of the service agreement, college graduates have the right to cancel the agreement. In case a project organisation wishes to cancel its service agreement with a college graduate, it must notify the college graduate in writing 30 days in advance. A research assistant whose service agreement is cancelled or has expired, may enjoy unemployment insurance benefits in accordance with relevant state provisions. A college graduate may seek another job if the project institution/organisation does not intend to continue employing him after the expiration of the service agreement. The state encourages the institution in charge of the project to give priority to college graduates who have worked as research assistant under the project when employing or recruiting permanent employees. After a research assistant is employed as permanent staff member, he can go through the formalities for the registration of permanent residence by strength of the letter of appointment issued by the employing unit, his labor contract, and his diploma. In this case, his length of service shall include the working time as research assistant under the research project plus his working time as a permanent employee of the employing unit. The same method shall be used for calculating the number of years when paying his social insurance premium.

(Ⅵ) Supporting College Graduates to Start Their Own Business or Make Flexible Employment Arrangement

Preferential polices for college graduates who start their own business include: (1) preferential tax policies: the holders of an Employment and Unemployment Registration Certificate (which indicates "Tax Policies on Self-employment" or is accompanied by a Self-employment Certificate for University and College Graduates) who engage in individual business operations within the year of graduation (the calendar year of graduation, namely, from January 1 to December 31) may enjoy the deduction of, in turn, the actually payable business tax, urban maintenance and construction tax, educational surtax and individual income tax for the current year in the amount of RMB 8,000 Yuan for each business owner per year within a period of three years. Small meagre-profit enterprises established by college graduates shall enjoy preferential tax policies in accordance with the relevant state provisions; (2) small-sum guarantee loans and interest discount loans: self-employed college graduates that meet certain requirements may apply for small-sum guarantee loans in the place where they start their own business in accordance with the relevant local regulations; those engaged in a meagre-profit project may enjoy interest discount for up to 100,000 Yuan loans. For those starting a partnership business or organizing themselves to get employed, the scale of loan may be increased to a proper extent in light of their actual need; (3) exemption of relevant administrative charges: college graduates within two years of graduation who are engaged in running self-employed businesses (with the exception of businesses restricted by the state) will be, within three years of their date of registration with the industrial and commercial authority, exempted from such requested kinds of administrative charges as for administration, registration and certificate/license issuing and other such purposes; (4) training subsidies. College graduates who have attended the business-starting training within the year of graduation and obtained the certificate of successful completion of the training program shall be granted training subsidies in light of their employment or business-starting situation and in accordance with the relevant state provisions; (5) free services relating to starting of a new business. College graduates intending to start their own business shall be entitled to free business-starting guidance provided by public employment service agencies; (6) abolition of restriction on the registration of permanent residence by college graduates in cities where they start their own business (In municipalities directly under the Central Government, the matter shall dealt with in accordance with the relevant state provisions).

(Ⅶ) Providing Internship Opportunities and Skill Trainings to College Graduates

Internship refers to the employment promotion measure whereby human resource and social security departments at various levels organize college graduates to work as interns with a view to accumulating work experience and improving their employability. Unemployed college graduates wishing to participate in internship programs may consult local human resource and social security department or local organizations of the Communist Youth League; they are responsible units for the arrangement of internship for college graduates. The term of internship is usually 3 – 12 months, after which the units of internship shall make an assessment of the performance of the interns and issue them a certificate of internship, to be used as one of the bases of selection and employment of college graduates by employing units. For college graduates who are formally employed by their unit of internship, their period of internship shall be calculated as a part of their full-time employment. Units of internship shall buy personal accident injury insurance for their interns during the period of internship.

Unemployed college graduates shall benefit from the following policies and services during internship: (1) basic living allowance (the expenses shall be shared by the unit of internship and the local government and the standard of allowance shall be determined and adjusted in a reasonable and timely manner by local government in light of local level of economic development and local price level); (2) free personnel agency services; (3) personal accident injury insurance; iv. continued employment guidance and services for interns who have not been employed after the expiration of the term of internship. Enterprises (or units) that accept unemployed college graduates to work as interns shall pay in advance the basic living allowance for the interns during the period of internship and later apply for reimbursement for internship subsidies from local human resource and social security department, as regulated by relevant provisions.

College graduates who participate in skill training or business-starting training within the year of graduation may apply for vocational training subsidies at local human resource and social security departments. College graduates who have gone through unemployment registration procedures after graduation may also apply for vocational training subsidies at local human resource and social security departments when participating in skill training or business-starting training. After the completion of training, those who have passed the appraisal of vocational skills and obtained a primary or higher vocational qualification certificate (or a certificate of specialized professional competence or certificate of successful completion of business-starting training in industries in which no national vocational skill standards has been adopted) and who have realized employment within six months of the training, shall be given 100% of the standard vocational training subsidy; those who have obtained a primary or higher vocational qualification certificate but have not been able to realize employment within six months shall be given 80% of the standard vocational training subsidy; and those who have obtained a certificate of specialized professional competence or a certificate of successful completion of business-starting training but have not been able to realize employment within six months shall be given 60% of the standard vocational training subsidy.

(Ⅷ) Supporting Policies for College Graduates from Families with Difficulties

College graduates from families with difficulties refer to those from families receiving minimum living allowance in cities and towns, families with a living standard close to the poverty line, poverty-stricken families in rural areas, and families with a disabled member. When recruiting employees, state organs and public institutions at various levels shall exempt registration fee and physical examination fee for college graduates from families with difficulties. To help them to look for employment, universities and colleges should provide them with job-seeking subsidies or to reward those who have found a job.

(Ⅸ) Registration and Providing Services to Unemployed College Graduates

Public employment service agencies at various levels should make a registration of unemployed college graduates, incorporate them into the scope of unified administration of unemployed persons at the place of their registered permanent residence, and provide them with the relevant supporting policies. Unemployed college graduates who register at the public employment service agencies at the place of their registered permanent residence shall enjoy free public employment services provided by local human resource and social security department. Registered unemployed college graduates are entitled to free policy consultation, vocational guidance, employment service, and custody of personal records and other services. Those who wish to participate in internship programs shall be provided with basic living allowance and one personal accident injury insurance; those who take part in vocational training and appraisal of vocational skills may apply for training subsidy and subsidy for the appraisal of vocational skills. Those who wish to start their own business shall enjoy preferential policies, such as tax reduction or exemption, small-sum secured loans and interest discount, reduction or exemption of administrative fees, and business-starting services.

## Ⅱ. Measures and Content of Services to Returned Overseas Chinese Students

### (Ⅰ) Main Measures

1. Further promotion policies on providing services to returned overseas Chinese students. Special efforts should be made to further improve preferential policies on such matters as entry and exit, residence, administration of registered permanent residence, social insurance, family planning, employment of spouse, schooling of children, professional qualification, project application, financial support, distribution of income, taxation, honours and rewards, protection of intellectual property, starting of business, and investment and financing, and the three-in-one policy system (overseas Chinese students return to China for work, for starting business, and for servicing the country) of providing services to overseas Chinese students who have returned to China "to work, to start business and to service the country".

2. Promoting the construction of the network of services to returned overseas Chinese students. This refers to the establishment of a service alliance that includes service centres, work stations, and business-establishing parks for returned overseas Chinese students, association of returned overseas Chinese students, and other social intermediary service institutions and organizations providing various services to returned overseas Chinese students. Its aim is to give full play to the role of relevant overseas organizations.

3. Strengthening the construction of a service information platform for returned overseas Chinese students that provides services to society and returned overseas Chinese students and promotes the exchange and sharing of information about talents, projects, policies, and funding relating to returned overseas Chinese students.

4. Establishing and improving the service system for returned overseas Chinese students, encouraging and supporting high-level talent markets and talent intermediary agencies to participate in the development of the market of high-level talents with overseas education background, strengthening the mechanism of cooperation between service agencies for returned overseas Chinese students, and further improving the coordination between government departments providing services to returned overseas Chinese students.

( Ⅱ ) The Types of Services

1. Implementing preferential policies for returned overseas Chinese students: to provide special services to high-level or top-ranking talents among returned overseas Chinese students in accordance with the principle of "handling special cases with special methods"; carrying out state policies on such matters as settlement, financial aid, facilities in entry, exit and residence, inspection and declaration of luggage at the customs, employment of spouse, schooling of children, calculation of length of service, evaluation of technical or professional titles, household registration, protection of intellectual property right, social insurance, and family planning, so as to facilitate and support oversees Chinese students to return to China to work, start business and serve the country.

2. Providing employment guidance: providing employment intermediary services to returned overseas Chinese students so as to give full play to market forces in the allocation of human resources; organizing in a systematic and focused manner various kinds of scientific and technological demonstrations and exchanges for returned overseas Chinese students by building exchange platforms, organizing special activities and making recommendations to employing units, so as to open up the channel of communication between returned overseas Chinese students and employing units.

3. Supporting returned overseas Chinese students to start their own business. More specifically: taking active measures to attract returned overseas Chinese students to enter into pioneer parks to engage in the development of new technologies and products and in the application of scientific and technological research results; encouraging returned overseas Chinese students to apply for various government funded scientific research projects and programs in an open, equal and fair manner; exploring the establishment of various investment and financing mechanisms, including financial support by the government, bank loans, venture capital investment, and technological property right transaction so as to help returned overseas Chinese students to overcome financial difficulties, and to promote the industrialization and commercialization of their research results.

4. Attracting overseas Chinese students to serve the country: supporting and encouraging overseas Chinese students or organizations of overseas Chinese students to participate in the construction of the motherland on a broader scope, at higher-level, and in more diversified forms, such as part-time work, cooperative research, lectures, academic and technological exchanges, field visits and

consultation, intermediary services, etc. ①

## Section 5 **Prohibition of Child Labor**

Child labor refers to a juvenile or child under the age 16 years who establishes labor relationship with a unit or an individual and engages in labor for economic income, or who engages in labor under sole proprietorship. Minors under the age of 16 are at a stage of adolescence and growth. Heavy manual labor is harmful to their health. They are also psychologically immature and at the stage of acquiring knowledge and cultivating sentiments and basic qualities, and therefore still do not meet the qualifications of laborers. The use of child labor not only deprives minors of their right to physical and mental development and their right to education, but also can negatively affect the future supply of labor force in a country. Therefore, the prohibition of child labor is an important element of the labor law in various countries. In China, the minimum age of employment is 16 years old and it is prohibited for any employing unit to employ minors under the age of 16.

In China, legal provisions on the protection of minors are included in the Constitution, the Labor Law, and the Law on the Protection of Minors. The State Council promulgated the Provisions on Prohibition of Child Labor in April 1991 and revised the Provisions on December 1, 2002. The above-mentioned laws and regulations form the legal system protecting minors in China. According to these laws and regulations, no state organ, social organization, enterprise, institution, private non-enterprise unit, or individual industrial and commercial businesses may recruit or hire minors under the age of 16 (namely child labor); all units and individuals are prohibited from providing job placement service to minors under the age of 16; and minors under the age of 16 are prohibited from starting business and engaging in individual business operations. In the case of use of child labor by an employing unit, the labor and social security administrative department shall be punished by the standard of fining 5,000—10,000 Yuan for each of the children employed per month.

More specific provisions in Chinese law on the prohibition of child labor include: no state organ, social organization, enterprise, public institution,

---

① Source: Ministry of Human Resource and Social Security, "Opinions on Strengthening the Construction of a Service System for Returned Overseas Chinese Students", Document No. 46 [2011] of the Ministry of Human Resources and Social Security, April 19, 2011.

individually-owned business, farmer or urban resident may use child labor; no employment agency, other unit or individual may provide job placement service to minors under the age of 16; industrial and commercial administrative departments at various levels are prohibited to issue license for individual business to minors under the age of 16; and no parent or other guardian may allow children under the age of 16 to work as child labor.

Illegal acts such as employing minors under the age of 14, employing minors under the age of 16 to engage in dangerous operations or operations under poisonous or harmful conditions that are prohibited for workers under the age of 18, or employing minors and resulting in death or severe injury to the minors pose great danger to physical and mental health of minors and therefore shall be punished by the Criminal Law.

Under the following three circumstances, the use of child labor constitutes a crime and should be investigated for criminal responsibilities:

1. Abducting children for use as laborer, which mainly constitutes the crime of abducting and trafficking in children and the crime of buying abducted children. With regard to the crime of abducting and trafficking in children, Article 240 of the Criminal Law provides that "Whoever abducts and traffics in a woman or child shall be sentenced to fixed-term imprisonment of not less than five years but not more than 10 years and shall also be fined; if he falls under any of the following categories, he shall be sentenced to fixed-term imprisonment of not less than 10 years or life imprisonment and shall also be fined or sentenced to confiscation of property; if the circumstances are especially serious, he shall be sentenced to death and also to confiscation of property: (1) being a ringleader of a gang engaged in abducting and trafficking in women and children; (2) abducting and trafficking in three or more women and/or children;... (7) causing serious injury or death to the woman or child who is abducted and trafficked in or to her or his relatives or any other serious consequences; or (8) selling a woman or a child out of the territory of China. " In the case of abducting children for use as laborer, the victims of the crime are child labor, namely minors under the age of 16. With regard to the crime of buying abducted children, Article 241 of the Criminal Law provides that "Whoever buys an abducted woman or child shall be sentenced to fixed-term imprisonment of not more than three years, criminal detention or public surveillance. " In the case of illegal use of child labor, the purpose of buying abducted children is to use them as child labor.

2. Forcing children to work, which mainly constitutes the crime of forced labor. Article 244 of the Criminal Law provides that "Where an employer, in

violation of the laws and regulations on labor administration, compels its employees to work by restricting their personal freedom, if the circumstances are serious, the persons who are directly responsible for the offence shall be sentenced to fixed-term imprisonment of not more than three years or criminal detention and shall also, or shall only, be fined. " Compelling minors to work by restricting their personal freedom seriously violates personal freedom and the labor rights and also severely harms physical and mental health of minors under the age of 16, and therefore shall be severely punished by the Criminal Law.

3. The most appropriate criminal charge against the acts of illegal use of child labor should be the crime of using child labor. [1] Illegal use of child labor mainly takes three forms: employing a child to be engaged in work high above the ground or down in the pit, work involving radioactive, highly poisonous, inflammable or explosive substances or work of the fourth degree labor intensity; employing a child under the age of 14; and causing death or severe injury to a child employed.

Under the following circumstances, the participation in labor by juveniles or children under 16 years old shall not fall within the category of child labor:

(1) Juveniles or children under 16 years old who participate in family chores, labor courses organized by their schools, or auxiliary labor activities that do not harm their physical and psychological health, correspond to their physical capacity and are permitted by the people's government of the province, autonomous region or municipality. However, it is prohibited to use child labor in the name of part-time study and part-time work programs.

(2) Arts, sports and units of special profession that genuinely need to recruit artistic workers, athletes and apprentices under the age of 16 shall obtain the consent of the parents or other legal guardians of the minors and apply to the labor

---

[1]  "In order to increase the efforts on cracking down the use of child labor, relevant government departments suggest that a new crime of 'using child labor' and the corresponding punishments be added to the Criminal Law. Currently the Legislative Affairs Commission of the Standing Committee of the National People's Congress is conducting studies on the suggestion with a view to drafting an amendment to the Criminal Law. Therefore, the Chinese Criminal Law would contain a new crime of 'using child labor' if the amendment was passed by the Standing Committee of the National People's Congress. In view of the fact that the revised Provisions on the Use of Child Labor will be promulgated before the promulgation of the amendment to the Criminal Law, it is not advisable for the term 'the crime of using child labor' to appear in the Draft Revision of the Regulations on Prohibition of Child Labor. Rather, the term 'other crimes' should be used to cover the crime. " Labor and Social Security Department of Legislative Affairs Office of the State Council and Legislative Affairs Department of the Ministry of Labor and Social Security (eds. ), *Explanations on the Provisions on Prohibition of Child Labor*, Beijing: China Legal System Publishing House, 2002, p. 31.

administration department at or above the county level for approval. Athletes refer to persons specializing in the training and competition in a particular sport; apprentices refer to persons who learn an artistic skill from a master in the fields of acrobatics, traditional (Chinese) opera, industrial art, etc.; and artistic workers refer to persons specialized in performance art. For artistic workers, athletes and apprentices under the age of 16 recruited pursuant to the relevant provisions, the recruiting units shall fully and effectively protect their physical and psychological health, so as to help them grow healthily in terms of morality, intelligence and physical fitness, and shall be responsible for creating conditions to ensure that the recruited receive compulsory education for the number of years prescribed pursuant to the law.

Chapter V

# Labor Contract Law

The labor contract law system is the most crucial system in labor law. Since 1986, China has implemented the labor contract law system, and labor contracts have become an essential legal mechanism for adjusting labor relations. Labor contracts are also the most important basis on which employers and laborers make their claims when labor disputes arise.

The contents, formats and terms of labor contracts are different. This chapter introduces the conclusion, modification, termination and invalidity of labor contracts, the contents, formats and terms of labor contracts, the dissolution of labor contracts as well as the legal liability for breach of labor contracts.

## Section 1  Introduction to Labor Contracts

### I. Legal Definition and Legal Characteristics of Labor Contracts

#### ( I ) Definition of Labor Contracts

Paragraph One of Article 16 of China's Labor Law provides that "Labor contracts are agreements reached between laborers and employing units to establish labor relations and define both parties' rights and obligations". Paragraph Two states that "Labor contracts shall be concluded when the labor relation is established". It means that labor contracts are the legal basis on which labor relations are formed. Employers and laborers that establish labor relations must conclude labor contracts. Labor contracts, once concluded, will become the legal basis for regulating the labor rights and obligations of both parties.

Whether a labor contract is concluded between both parties in labor relations, the labor contract may be classified as an oral labor contract and a written labor contract in terms of format and as a de facto labor relation and a statutory labor relation in terms of contents. The former refers to the de facto labor services arising from both parties in labor relations by means of oral agreement, which is applicable to short-term labor services on the basis of mutual trust. In a de facto labor relation, cases where both parties have concluded a labor contract but the labor contract is nullified due to statutory or other reasons must be included. Since it is difficult to define the rights and obligations of both parties in de facto labor relations, and the termination or dissolution of labor relations is relatively arbitrary, de facto labor relations are therefore not recommended in the modern society.

Another de facto labor relation is rather controversial with high frequency in real life, which is, a de facto labor relation is formed with a laborer and an employing unit when both parties have not terminated the labor contract upon expiry and the laborer continues to provide labor services. Article 14 of the Circular on Several Issues Concerning the Implementation of the Labor Contract System promulgated by the Ministry of Labor and Social Security in 1996 provides that: "Where a fixed term labor contract has expired and there is no termination or renewal due to the reasons of the employing unit and a labor relation is so formed, it shall be deemed as renewal of the labor contract. The employing unit shall timely negotiate the contract period with the laborer and handle the renewal formalities. Where a loss is so caused to the laborer, the employing unit shall assume compensation liability according to law. " A clear principle is formed on the responsibilities of both parties in labor relations after a de facto labor relation. In the same year, the Ministry of Labor further specified the requirements in the Official Reply on the Economic Compensation Requested by Employees Where No Labor Contracts are Concluded With Employing Units: Where an employing unit and a laborer have formed a labor relation, the employing unit intentionally delays the conclusion of the labor contract and dissolves the labor relation with the laborer, a labor dispute arises when the laborer requests compensation from the employing unit, if the laborer applies for arbitration with the labor dispute arbitration committee, the labor dispute arbitration committee shall accept the application and handle the case according to Article 98 of the Labor Law, the Measures for the Economic Compensation for the Violation and Dissolution of Labor Contracts and the Measures for the Compensation for the Violation of the Labor Contract Provisions in the Labor Law. If the laborer makes a report to the labor supervisory authority, the labor supervisory authority shall conduct investigation according to the Labor Law, the Measures for the Administrative Punishment in Violation of the Labor Law of the People's Republic of China and other provisions.

The diversified modes of employment of laborers can be classified into various forms of labor contracts, which form the basis for deciding the specific contents of labor contracts in other forms. For a long time, people only get used to the so-called regular employment, labor contracts are therefore associated with working in regular employing units with a regular mode of work. Following the improvement of market economy, other modes of employment on top of regular mode of employment have gained importance. These modes of employment are flexible and diversified modes of employment in terms of working hours, remunerations, working places, insurance welfare and labor relations, other than the traditional full-time mode of employment in the mainstream based on industrialization and modern factory system.

In the Opinions on Several Issues Concerning Non Full-time Labor Use promulgated by the Ministry of Labor and Social Security in 2003, these labor contracts are different from standard labor contracts because: (1) a laborer not engaging in full-time work may establish labor relations with one or more employing units. The employing units that establish labor relations with non full-time laborers shall conclude labor contracts. Labor contracts are generally in written form. Where the period of a labor contract is less than one month, a labor contract in oral form may be concluded with the consent of both parties after consultation. However, if the laborer requests for a written labor contract, the written form shall be adopted; (2) Where a laborer provides non full-time labor services to other units, families or individuals through a labor dispatch institution lawfully established, the labor dispatch institution shall conclude a labor contract with the non full-time laborer; (3) The contents of non full-time labor contracts are determined by both parties after negotiation, which shall include five essential provisions on working hours and period, job duties, labor remunerations, labor protection and labor conditions, but no probation period shall be agreed; (4) The conditions under which non full-time labor contracts are terminated shall be followed according to the agreement of both parties. Where a labor contract does not provide for the notice period for termination of the labor contract as agreed by both parties, either party may notify the other party of the termination any time. Where both parties have agreed on the liability for breach, compensation liability shall be assumed according to the agreements. From the perspectives of minimum wage standard, monthly wage payment, standard working hours, working on festive holidays or Sunday not equal to overtime work, employing units "must enter into written labor contracts" in the employment of personnel, there are special requirements for the sharing and contribution to various social insurance premiums, different from the provisions of prevailing labor legislation.

To understand what labor contracts are, distinction should be made between labor contracts and collective contracts, as well as labor contracts and civil contracts.

Collective contracts are written agreements concluded between labor unions (or employee's representatives) on behalf of employees and enterprises for labor remunerations or working conditions after consultation and negotiation. In collective contracts, labor standards are the core content of collective contracts, which impose constraints on individual labor contracts, covering labor remunerations, working hours, rest and leave, insurance, welfare benefits, job training, labor discipline, labor protection, etc. Collective contracts are formed and developed on the basis of labor contracts, but there are distinctive differences between the two: collective contracts are entered into between employers or employing organizations and trade union representatives on behalf of all employees. Labor contracts are entered into between employers and individual employees, that is, employing units and individual laborers. Collective contracts not only prescribe the general labor and living conditions of enterprises or industries, but also involve various aspects of labor relations. Labor contracts provide for the rights and obligations of individual laborers and employing units. Collective contracts have a greater impact than labor contracts as collective contracts apply to all employees of enterprises and labor contracts only impose constraints on individual laborers, and the relevant provisions of collective contracts must not be violated. When a collective contract states the minimum labor standards of an enterprise, all labor standards prescribed in the labor contract must not be less favorable than the provisions of the collective contract. Where the employing unit of a collective contract violates the provisions of the collective contract and infringes the lawful rights and interests of the trade union and all employees and causes losses, the employing unit shall assume the liability for compensation in kind. When a trade union fails to fulfill the provisions of the collective contract, no liability for compensation in kind will be assumed in general. Any party to the labor contract that violates the provisions may give rise to the dissolution of the labor contract, either party that causes economic loss to another party may make compensation subject to the consequences and losses.

Civil contracts are agreements to establish the civil rights and obligations of the parties. The parties that engage in contracting and processing may enter into civil contracts, which are relevant to labor services to a certain extent, but there are substantial differences. For example, the parties to a labor contract are specific. One party to a labor contract is the laborer and the other party is the employing unit. At least one of the parties is a natural person, and both parties are both in equal and subordinate labor relations. The parties to a civil contract are natural persons, legal persons or other organizations on an equal status with civil rights and obligations. In a labor relation, a laborer must join the employing unit to become an employee and comply with the internal labor rules of the unit. In a civil relation, the parties do not need to join the employing unit and are not subject to the internal labor rules of the employing unit. The employing unit, as a party in a labor relation, arranges labor services and enjoys labor control rights, it therefore has the obligation to undertake the liability of labor risks, while the labor service provider, as a party in a labor relation, arranges labor services on its own and undertakes the liability of labor risks by itself. Accordingly, the employing unit in a labor relation enjoys labor control rights, it therefore has the obligation to undertake the liability of labor risks. In a civil relation, one party arranges labor services on its own and undertakes the liability of labor risks on its own. The aim of a labor contract is to establish a labor legal relation. The aim of a civil contract is to establish, change or terminate a civil relation between natural persons, legal persons and other organizations. The contents of a labor contract consist of labor rights and obligations, to be revised by the Labor Law. The contents of a civil contract consist of civil rights and obligations, to be revised by the Civil Law.

( Ⅱ ) Legislation on Labor Contracts

The Labor Law of the Soviet Republic of China enacted in the land reform era in China gave a definition of labor contracts: "A labor contract is an agreement between a laborer or several laborers and the employer. Where the agreements of the labor contract or the conditions of the labor contract are less favorable than the Labor Law, prevailing labor orders and the requirements of collective contracts, no such contract shall be valid". The Labor Law, revised in October 1933, specified in detail the meaning, period, modification and dissolution of labor contracts by individual chapters. The Labor Protection Regulations of the Shan-Gan-Ning Border Region (Draft) enacted in the anti-Japanese war period made provisions on labor contracts. The resolution adopted at the 6th session of China's Labor Congress held in the liberation war period also required that "there must be an agreement on labor services".

After the liberation period to 1986, China did not make any legislation on labor contracts, private enterprises and other enterprises were only required to conclude labor contracts for the use of temporary employees, seasonal employees and rotation employees in the early days of the liberation period. The fixed term worker system was implemented for the majority of other workers, no provision on concluding labor contracts was stipulated in law. The Interim Measures of the All China Federation of Trade Unions on Employer-Employee Relations issued in November 1949 provide that "Where the relations between a private enterprise and the workers, employees, apprentices and office personnel employed do not fail within the provisions of these Measures, the employer and the employees shall enter into a collective or labor contract with the agreement of the employer and the employees." The Interim Provisions on the Recruitment of Workers by Various Regions issued by the Ministry of Labor in May 1951 state that "At the time of recruitment of workers, both the employer and the employee shall directly enter into a labor contract to provide for the wages, benefits, working hours, probation period and travelling fees and settling-in allowances for the recruitment of faraway employee, and a record shall be filed with the local labor administrative authority". The Measures for the Conclusion of Labor Contracts by Construction Project Enterprises that Go Aboard for the Employment and Use of Construction Workers promulgated by the Ministry of Labor in May 1954 provide that "Where a construction project unit goes abroad for the employment and use of temporary workers, the employing unit (hereinafter referred to as 'Party A') shall, regardless of the period of employment, enter into a labor contract with the worker or worker representative (hereinafter referred to as 'Party B') according to the labor use provisions of the labor administrative department at the place the project is located and strictly comply with such provisions". In early 1956, the Ministry of Labor and the All China Federation of Trade Unions prepared the Labor Contract Law of the People's Republic of China, which was renamed as the Interim Provisions on the Conclusion of Labor Contracts for Recruitment of Personnel by Enterprises, Institutions and Authorities (Draft) in 1957, provide that "An enterprise, institution or authority that employs new workers, new employees, new apprentices, seasonal workers, temporary workers and workers transferred or seconded to other units must enter into a labor contract. " In addition, the contents of labor contract, the procedures for conclusion and reasons for contract dissolution are also provided. This draft was sent to various regions for discussion without formal promulgation. The Interim Provisions on the Use of Temporary Workers by State-owned Enterprises promulgated by the State Council in October 1962 and the Interim Provisions on Improving the Use and Administration of Temporary Workers enacted in March 1965 provide that employing units must enter into labor contracts for the employment of temporary workers. Other provisions also stipulate that labor contracts must be signed for the use of industrial and peasant rotation workers by mining, transport, railway enterprises, and the use of seasonal workers by the relevant enterprises.

Since 1980, some regions have started implementing the labor contract system. The Circular on Active Trial Implementation of the Labor Contract System issued by the Ministry of Labor and Personnel in February 1983 requests employing units and employees to enter into labor contracts with legal validity to stipulate the rights and obligations of both parties when whole people-owned units or collectively-owned units above the county and district levels employ general or technical workers. The Interim Provisions on the Implementation of the Labor Contract System by State-owned Enterprises issued by the State Council on July 12, 1986 provide that upon the effectiveness of the Provisions on October 1, 1986, enterprises that employ workers for regular posts within the standard of the state labor wage plan must centrally implement the labor contract system unless there are special provisions otherwise provided by the State. The workers employed for regular posts by State authorities, institutions and social organizations shall refer to the Provisions. The employment of workers under the labor contract system, on-the-job, employment-seeking and retirement benefits and the legal system for the conclusion, modification, termination and dissolution of labor contracts are also included in the Provisions.

Following the development of the labor use system in China, the time is ripe for formulating designated labor contract law. In November 2005, the Standing Committee of the State Council deliberated the Labor Contract Law of the People's Republic of China (Draft) and submitted to the Standing Committee of the National People's Congress for deliberation. On December 24, 2005, the 19th Session of the Standing Committee of the 10th National People's Congress made a preliminary deliberation of the draft of the Labor Contract Law. On March 20, 2006, the full text of the draft was issued to the public to solicit opinions. A total of 191849 pieces of opinions were received within one month. On December 24, 2006, the new draft of the Labor Contract Law was submitted to the 25th Session of the Standing Committee of the State Council for deliberation. The legal committee of the National People's Congress made comprehensive response to the deliberation opinions of the Standing Committee of the National People's Congress and the opinions of the community to make revisions to the probation period, economic redundancy, conclusion and dissolution of non-fixed term labor contracts.

On June 29, 2007, the 28th Session of the Standing Committee of the 10th National People's Congress deliberated the Labor Contract Law which takes effect as of January 1, 2008. On July 6, 2012, the 27th Session of the Standing Committee of the 11th National People's Congress deliberated the Revision to the Labor Contract Law (Draft) regarding the issues in the implementation of the Labor Contract Law and published on the website of the National People's Congress to solicit opinions from the public. As of the deadline of August 5, 2013, a total of 557243 pieces of opinions were received, which hit a record high.

## II. Legal Characteristics of Labor Contracts

Labor contracts are a special type of contracts with legal characteristics in addition to the characteristics of general contracts:

### 1. Parties to a Labor Contract must be Designated Employing Units and Laborers

For the parties to a labor contract, one party must be an enterprise, institution, authority, social organization or an employer from the private sector, and the other party is the laborer. Agreements on the import and export of labor services between two parties are not labor contracts.

Labor contracts are contracts entered into for the use of labor power, therefore one party to a labor contract must be a person with labor power, meaning that the person must have manpower. The other party to a labor contract must then be a laborer in the capacity of a natural person. The laborer with labor power is the pre-condition for the establishment of labor relations, conclusion and performance of labor contracts. Similarly, it is essential that the employing unit with the demand for labor power should be the relative party, because the use of labor power means the use of labor power by other parties, or the laborer works for other parties. The labor services provided to the laborer on his own do not refer to the labor services in terms of labor contracts. A laborer will not provide labor services to another laborer unless the other laborer is in the capacity of an employer, by then he is no longer a laborer.

### 2. The Subject of a Labor Contract is the Labor Activity of a Laborer

After the conclusion of a labor contract, the laborer must join the employing unit for production and work, and become a member of the employing unit to enjoy the rights of an employee offered by the employing unit and undertake the obligations of an employee, which means that the laborer has the rights to obtain remunerations, social insurance and living benefits, and has the corresponding obligations to complete his labor activities. The employing unit has the right to arrange and manage laborers according to the provisions of labor contracts for laborers to complete the agreed labor activities, and certainly the employing unit has the obligations to pay remunerations to laborers, enroll employees in social insurance and provide living benefits.

With labor activities as the subject of a labor contract, it requires laborers to provide labor services according to the instructions of the employing unit. The provision of labor services by the laborer itself is the objective of the labor contract. Accordingly, a labor contract must be a contract performed by a designated laborer and the provision of labor services to an employing unit by a laborer must be continuous. The continuity of labor activities has determined the significance of the period of labor contract and the impacts on the rights and obligations of both parties in view of the duration of continuity. The more rights a laborer enjoys, the more obligations of an employing unit has to a laborer.

### 3. Inclusion of the Probation Period in a Labor Contract in General

Article 21 of China's Labor Law provides that "A probation period may be agreed upon in a labor contract. The period shall not exceed six months." The labor process is the integration process of two essential elements of labor power and production information, which is the process of demonstrating intelligence and physical power by laborers. The probation period in a labor contract is the period of examination of the integration of a laborer and production information to realize the best integration of the two essential elements to achieve optimal result of labor services.

The probation period in a labor contract is also called "labor relation on probation", and defined as "a complete and real labor relation, and both parties agree to the probation, therefore it is easier to dissolve the relation."[1] There is then a special phenomenon of the labor contract. The labor contract becomes valid and the contract is performed but both parties can be free to dissolve the labor contract to terminate the labor relation within a specified period. In this period, both parties are relieved from certain obligations for the dissolution or termination of labor relations within the validity period of the labor contract.

### 4. Inclusion of the Process of Completing Re-production in a Labor Contract

There is a natural aging process of labor power, which carries the characteristic of re-production. In concluding a labor contract, the rights and obligations of the employing unit and the laborer must be set out, and the right of

---

[1]  Huang Yueqin, *New Discussions on Labor Law*, Beijing, China University of Political Science and Law Press, 2003, p. 88

assistance in kind to the direct relatives of the laborer under certain circumstances must also be included. If an employee has lost his working ability on a temporary or permanent basis due to aging, illness, work-related injury, disability or death, and the suspension of labor services may not be entitled to labor remunerations, the employing unit must undertake the social insurance benefits of the employee himself and provide certain assistance in kind to the direct relatives dependent on the employee.

In this regard, the due significance of a labor contract is the provision of a wide range of living needs to a laborer by an employing unit, including collective benefits and facilities to provide living convenience to the laborer, such as employee housing, collective accommodation, canteen, nursery, bathroom, hair salon, internal shop, etc., to provide cultural and sports venues to enrich and light up the cultural entertainment life of employees such as library, sports center, club house, etc., and to establish various subsidies and grants to solve the living difficulties of the employee and his family, such as home visit leave, transport subsidy, personal living difficulty grant, rental subsidy, cleaning subsidy, etc. In this aspect, more benefits will be provided in economically developed countries.

**5. The Objective of a Labor Contract is the Realization of Labor Process, not the Grant of Labor Achievements**

The labor process is a complicated process of demonstrating physical power and intelligence, some labor services directly create value and some others indirectly realize value. Some labor achievements can be measured instantly and some other labor achievements can only be seen after a period of time. Accordingly, the objective of a labor contract is to establish a labor relation for the realization of labor process.

Given this objective of a labor contract, the remunerations given to the laborer by the employing unit must be money but not goods. A laborer engages in labor services to complete the production process rather than obtaining the products produced after labor services. Accordingly, the laborer obtains wages in monetary terms by completing the labor process to satisfy his living needs and those of his family, instead of bringing products home for self use. The replacement of wages with products violates the objective of labor contract and harms the lawful rights and interests of the laborer, because products that cannot be sold on the market by the employing unit can hardly be realized in money by the laborer.

---

**Typical Case**

Mr Zhao was employed by a company in Zhao Yuan City to work in a unit in another province in November to December 1996. During these periods, the company failed to give wages to Mr Zhao. Mr Zhao requested for his wages on many occasions, but the company only agreed to pay wages in physical goods or no payment will be made. Mr Zhao did not agree to offset wages by physical goods and the outstanding wages have not been recovered in July 2001. The labor arbitration commission opened a case and held that the Labor Law sets out that wages shall be paid to the laborer on a monthly basis in monetary terms, and the outstanding wages for November to December 1996 have not been paid in July 2001, which has violated the Labor Law. Article 5 of the Interim Provisions on Wage Payment provides that wages shall be paid in statutory currency and shall not be paid in kind or negotiable securities in lieu of such currency. The refusal of Mr Zhao to accept wages in physical goods was made on proper grounds, and the payment of wages in physical goods or no payment will be made by the company has violated the Interim Provisions on Wage Payment and shall not be supported[1].

---

### 6. The Subordinate and Non-compulsory Nature of Performance of a Labor Contract

The subordinate nature is firstly demonstrated in the situation that a laborer that engages in labor activities must give up his freedom in managing his own rest and leisure time, and follow the time arrangement of the employing unit. In terms of work, the laborer cannot decide the methods and contents of work on his own, and must follow the requirements of the employing unit to complete his labor process. In the labor process, the laborer must follow the instructions of the employing unit and the scope of instructions of the employing unit accepted by the laborer is much wider and specific than processing contracting and project contracting. The subordinate nature of instructions has expanded to the compliance with the punishment right of the employing unit. When the employing unit makes a punishment decision on the laborer and the decision is not negated in law at last, the laborer must accept and follow. The subordinate nature of the performance of a labor contract is also demonstrated in economic sense, that

---

[1]   Wang Qimei, *Salary can't be in Kind*, *an Authorization is required for Collecting Salary by Others*, China Labor Security News, July 29, 2003.

means the labor achievements created by the laborer do not belong to him, but are owned by the employing unit.

Despite the strong subordinate nature of the performance of a labor contract, the point that it is not compulsory for a laborer to perform the labor contract must be emphasized. Even though the laborer does not perform the labor contract intentionally, the employing unit cannot compel the laborer to perform the labor contract. The mandatory provision of labor services to the employing unit, regardless of whether the mandatory nature comes from lawsuits or means other than lawsuits, it is not compulsory for the laborer to perform the labor contract. The employing unit may engage in acts permitted by law and contract for the absence of a laborer or termination or dissolution of labor contract without prior notice, but it has no right to compel the laborer to work.

### 7. The Continuity of the Rights and Obligations of a Labor Contract

The continuity of the rights and obligations of a labor contract is originated from the natural nature of the re-production of labor power. This continuity is demonstrated in two aspects. One aspect is that a laborer still has the right to request for labor remunerations under certain conditions within the validity period of the labor contract even though no labor services have been provided to the employing unit by the laborer, and the employing unit still has the obligation to pay labor remunerations. For example, regular leave, leave, special leave and the participation in other statutory activities by the laborer within the validity period of the labor contract. Although no labor services are provided to the employing unit, the employing unit is still required to pay labor remunerations. The Interim Provisions on Wage Payment also provide that "Where the suspension of work or production is caused by reasons other than the laborer within a wage payment cycle, the employing unit shall make wage payment to the laborer according to the standards stipulated in the labor contract." The other aspect is that after the termination or dissolution of a labor contract, the employing unit still assumes corresponding liabilities to the laborer. In addition, the liabilities are wide-ranging. Where economic compensation is paid at the time of contract dissolution, the employing unit shall assume the liability for compensation when the potential work-related injury or occupational disease arises. More obviously, various social insurance premiums paid by the employing unit for the laborer during the labor service period are the benefits to be enjoyed by the laborer after the cease of labor contract relation or even after the complete discharge of labor obligations by the laborer.

### 8. The Legal Nature of the Contents of a Labor Contract

The basic essence of a contract lies in the meeting of the minds of both parties, which is the same for a labor contract. The difference lies in the inclusion of more statutory contents in a labor contract. On the one hand, this statutory nature is demonstrated in the direct regulation of labor contracts by law and both parties do not have the modification right, such as the employment and retirement ages of laborers, labor conditions for safety and health, undertaking and sharing ratio of social insurance premiums, etc. On the other hand, it is demonstrated in the choices of contents of labor contracts within legal standards, both parties cannot exceed the statutory standards, such as the maximum working hours, the maximum overtime work and minimum wage, etc.

The other side of the statutory nature of a labor contract is the statutory nature of legal liability. Since the employing unit takes a leading role in the labor activities of the laborer, labor risks must be borne by the employing unit. When the laborer suffers from injury caused by tools, raw materials or production facilities, compensation for occupational injury arises and the employing unit shall assume the no-fault liability provided by law. On the contrary, if the laborer has caused loss to the employing unit at work, his compensation liability is limited to willful acts in the subjective sense, in the case of faulty acts, liability shall be relieved or exempted according to the degree of fault and the outcome of harm. Furthermore, even if the laborer is required to assume compensation liability, his liability is limited to his actual ability in assuming the liability, such as wage deduction of the laborer, and the monthly deduction must not exceed 20% of the wage of the laborer of the current month. If the wage after deduction is less than the local minimum wage standard, the minimum wage standard must be followed, so as to protect the basic living of the laborer and his family.

## Section 2 Conclusion, Modification, Termination and Invalidity of Labor Contracts

### Ⅰ. Conclusion of Labor Contracts

( Ⅰ ) Conditions for Conclusion of Labor Contracts

The conditions for conclusion of labor contracts refer to the qualifications of performing the obligations and exercising the rights of an employing unit and a laborer after the establishment of a labor relation that is bound by rights and obligations.

### 1. Conditions for Conclusion of Labor Contracts by Employing Units

Article 2 of China's Labor Contract Law provides that this Law is applicable where organizations such as enterprises, individually-owned economic organizations and private non-enterprise units within the territory of the People's Republic of China (hereinafter referred to as employing units) establish labor relations with workers through concluding, performing, modifying, dissolving or terminating labor contracts with them. State organs, institutions and public organizations and the workers with whom they are to establish labor relations shall conclude, perform, modify, dissolve or terminate labor contracts in accordance with this Law. Article 96 also sets out that where there are stipulations made in other laws or administrative regulations or by the State Council to govern the conclusion, performance, modification, dissolution or termination of labor contracts between institutions and the persons employed by them under the employment system, such provisions shall prevail; otherwise, the relevant provisions in this Law shall apply.

From the above provisions, the party who is an employing unit is a legal person most of the time. The General Principles of the Civil Law of China expressly provide for legal person status. With these conditions, an employing unit can then exercise its right and perform its equivalent obligations. At the same time, some employing units may be a party to a labor contract despite the lack of legal person status, in particular in cases where an individually-owned economic organization is a party to a labor contract. For the conclusion of a labor contract between an individually-owned economic organization and a laborer, whether the employing unit is of credit ability at a certain level, whether it can make labor remunerations in full to the laborer on time have first to be taken into account regarding the principal status of the employing unit. For the conclusion of a labor contract by the laborer without legal person status, he shall consider the property and civil liability of the employing unit. By then, the labor contract concluded will be valid and the labor remunerations and other rights of the laborer can then be realized.

### 2. Conditions for Conclusion of Labor Contracts by Laborers

The conditions for conclusion of labor contracts by laborers refer to the principal status a laborer, as a party to a labor contract, must have. The conclusion of labor contracts is a channel through which citizens realize their labor rights and perform their labor obligations. As a party to a labor contract, there are certain restrictions on a laborer.

(1) Age. It means a laborer that concludes a labor contract must reach the statutory age for labor services. Paragraph Two of Article 58 of China's Labor Law provides that "underage workers refer to laborers aged over 16 but less than 18." This indicates that laborers that reach the age of 18 fulfill the conditions for conclusion of labor contracts. For laborers aged over 16 but less than 18, they must follow the relevant provisions of the Labor Law and the agreements of labor contracts and conclude labor contracts under the condition that the rights and obligations agreed in labor contracts do not violate laws and regulations.

(2) Working ability. It refers to the ability of a laborer to complete a certain task with his own intelligence or physical power. The working ability of different laborers may vary greatly. There are differences in the working abilities of intellectual laborers and physical laborers, adult and underage workers, as well as female laborers. At the time of concluding a labor contract, reference should be made to the contents of the labor contract to conclude the labor contract with a laborer with the corresponding working ability. The labor contract can be accurately performed accordingly.

According to China's Labor Law, employing units should enter into labor contracts with laborers, individually-owned industrial and commercial businesses should also conclude labor contracts with employees. State organs, institutions and public organizations that implement the labor contract system, logistics personnel under the contract law system according to provisions, personnel of institutions that implement enterprise management, and laborers that can only establish labor relations with state organs, institutions and public organizations through labor contracts must conclude labor contracts or employment contracts with employing units.

( II ) Principles for Conclusion of Labor Contracts

Paragraph One of Article 17 of China's Labor Law sets out that "the conclusion and modification of labor contracts shall follow the principles of equality, voluntariness and consensus through consultation, and shall not violate the provisions of laws and administrative regulations." From here, we can see the basic principles of China's Labor Law.

### 1. Principles of Equality and Voluntariness

Equality refers to equality in legal status when employing units and laborers conclude contracts. In the process of concluding labor contracts, both parties are the principals of labor relations on an equal status. Both parties must reach an agreement on the basis of consensus through consultation according to law, employing units must not take advantage of the higher labor supply than demand to include additional conditions which are unfair to laborers at the time of concluding labor contracts.

Voluntariness refers to the truthful will of both parties at the time of concluding labor contracts. Through meeting of the minds, they fully reflect their intention of entering into labor contracts and reach an agreement after equal consultation. Voluntariness mainly means that the parties independently express their wills to conclude labor contracts without the coercion of other parties.

### 2. Principle of Consensus through Consultation

Consensus through consultation means that the contents and clauses of labor contracts are determined by both parties after discussion and consultation within the scope permitted by laws with full consensus. After both parties have reached a consensus on the major clauses of contracts, the contracts can then become effective. In reality, it is common for employing units to prepare labor contracts and laborers will decide whether they will sign the contracts. According to the relevant provisions of the Contract Law, where a contract is concluded in standard clauses, the party that provides standard clauses shall comply with the principle of equality to determine the rights and obligations of the parties, and adopt reasonable methods to remind the other party of the clauses that exempt or restrict his liability, and give explanations to such clauses at the request of the other party.

### 3. Principle of Compliance with Laws and Regulations

To conclude a labor contract, compliance with legal requirements is a prerequisite for the validity of the labor contract under legal protection. Otherwise, the parties to a labor contract will not be protected and the corresponding legal liability will also be assumed.

To conclude a labor contract, the first issue is the legality of the labor contract. The objectives of concluding a labor contract cannot violate the provisions of laws and regulations, or go against basic morals and good customs of the society. Both parties must not cover up illegal intention in the disguise of concluding a labor contract in legal form. The rights and obligations agreed in the labor contract cannot breach the provisions of laws and regulations.

This principle requires that the contents of a labor contract must not be illegal or cause harm to social and public interests. For example, a laborer and an employing unit cannot conclude a contract for stealing the technological secrets of another enterprise, and a labor contract must follow the format required by law. The parties must comply with the conditions of legal provisions. When an employing unit openly recruits employees, it must comply with the principles of open recruitment, voluntary application, all-round evaluation of characters, intelligence and health, and selection of good candidates.

### (Ⅲ) Validity of Conclusion of Labor Contracts

Paragraph Two of Article 17 of China's Labor Law states that "Labor contracts shall be legally binding upon the conclusion thereof according to law. Parties concerned shall perform the obligations specified in labor contracts." This means that labor contracts are valid immediately at the time of conclusion, and both parties must perform the contracts, otherwise they will undertake the corresponding legal liability. In fact, this is only a situation after the conclusion of labor contracts, or to put it in another way, this is the most common phenomenon.

In the Official Reply of the Ministry of Labor to Zhejiang Labor Department on the Terms of Labor Contracts, it specifically provides that labor contracts that are concluded according to law are legally binding. The validity period of a labor contract is generally calculated from the time of concluding a labor contract and both parties have signed on the text of the labor contract. The date the contract is signed and the date agreed on the contract should be the same. If both parties have specified in the contract the validity date of the contract at the time of concluding a labor contract, the validity date is from the date of the effectiveness of the contract. The two circumstances of contract validity are illustrated, including the date of signing and the validity date specifically agreed in the contract.

There are some other unusual circumstances, such as engaging laborers before concluding labor contracts, or continuing to engage laborers without concluding labor contracts anymore. In this regard, Article 7 of the Labor Contract Law sets out that a labor relation is established by an employing unit with a laborer as of the date the former employs the latter. Article 10 provides that in the event that no written labor contract is concluded at the time when a labor relation is established, such a contract shall be concluded within one month as of the date when the employing unit employs a laborer. Where an employing unit and a laborer conclude a labor contract before the latter starts to work, the labor relation shall be established as of the date when the latter starts to work.

## Ⅱ. Modification of Labor Contracts

The modification of labor contracts refers to the revisions or supplements to the clauses of labor contracts that have become valid due to changes in statutory reasons or agreed conditions in the process of performing labor contracts.

### (Ⅰ) Conditions for Modification of Labor Contracts

The conditions for modification of labor contracts refer to the essential elements that give rise to modification of labor contracts. In the process of execution of labor contracts, there have been significant changes to objective circumstances, some clauses of the original labor contracts may not continue to fit new circumstances if there is no revision or supplementation. At the request of both parties or either party, parties to labor contracts may modify labor contracts after consultation according to laws and regulations.

(1) Both parties have reached a consensus after consultation.

(2) The laws or regulations on which labor contracts are based at the time of conclusion have been revised or repealed.

(3) There are significant changes to the objective circumstances in which labor contracts are based at the time of conclusion, leading to the non-performance of labor contracts.

The Labor Contract Law also provides that: 1) Where an employing unit alters its name, replaces its legal representative, the principal leading person or investor (s), etc., performance of the labor contract shall not be affected. 2) Where an employing unit is merged, divided, etc., the existing labor contract shall remain valid and continue to be performed by the employing unit which succeeds to its rights and obligations.

### (Ⅱ) Impacts on Modification of Labor Contracts

Attention should be drawn to the following for modification of labor contracts: (1) Article 17 of the Labor Law provides that the modification of labor contracts shall follow the principles of equality, voluntariness, consensus through consultation and legality, modification can only be made after full consultation and reaching a consensus within the scope permitted by laws and regulations of the State; (2) The modification of labor contracts must be made within the validity period of the original labor contracts, which means either party or both parties make a request for modification before the expiry of labor contracts. The expiry of labor contracts equals to termination of labor contracts, which is not related to modification; (3) The modification of labor contracts must be made in writing. The employing unit and the laborer shall each keep a copy of the modified text of labor contracts; (4) When labor contracts are modified and no consensus can be reached in the process of consultation, giving rise to a dispute, either party can apply for arbitration with the local labor dispute arbitration committee.

## III. Termination of Labor Contracts

The termination of labor contracts refers to the cease of legal force of labor contracts naturally or after ruling or judgment. The termination of labor contracts means the end of the labor relation established by both parties. The termination of labor contracts must comply with statutory conditions.

Apart from the termination of labor contracts upon expiry, labor contracts should also be terminated in the following circumstances:

(1) Where both parties to a labor contract have a labor dispute, the labor arbitration authority ruled or the people's court held that the labor contract must be terminated.

(2) Where the laborer reaches the retirement age, dies, is totally incapacitated for work, either party to the labor contract no longer exists or is incapacitated, the labor relation will be terminated naturally. Where the laborer reaches the retirement age, it means that the laborer is vacated from office naturally. Even if the labor contract has not expired, the formalities for retirement and termination of the labor contract should be undergone immediately when the laborer reaches the retirement age.

(3) The employing unit, a party in the original labor relation, no longer exists due to bankruptcy, or dissolution, cancellation or other statutory reasons, the labor contract shall also be terminated.

(4) Where the labor contract is held to be invalid by the labor arbitration authority or the people's court, it shall be terminated immediately.

(5) Other circumstances prescribed by laws and administrative regulations.

It must be noted that, labor contracts of female employees during pregnancy, maternity or breastfeeding cannot be terminated upon expiry. The labor contracts must be extended to the end of the pregnancy, maternity or breastfeeding before the labor contracts can be terminated. In addition, labor contracts should be extended until the following circumstances cease to exist: laborers engaging in operations in contact with occupational hazards without occupational health examination before vacation of office, or suspected occupational disease patients are in the diagnosis period or medical examination period; the laborers are sick or injured not related to work and within the prescribed medical period; the laborers have served in the company for 15 consecutive years and will reach statutory retirement age in less than 5 years. When the labor contracts of laborers who suffer from occupational diseases or work-related injuries and determined to be totally or partially incapacitated, the relevant provisions on work-related injury insurance of the State must also be observed.

## Ⅳ. Invalidity of Labor Contracts

Invalid labor contracts refer to the contracts without legal force because of the breach of laws and regulations or application of improper procedures for contract conclusion. A labor contract that violates the provisions of laws and regulations goes against the will of the State and the intention of laborers, therefore it is invalid. If one party to a labor contract concludes the contract by fraud or threat, intentionally concealing the truth and making falsehood to deceive another party or causes the other party to conclude the contract against his true intention, which violates the principle of conclusion of labor contracts and infringes the rights and interests of the other party, the contract must be invalid.

( Ⅰ ) Labor Contracts in Violation of the Mandatory Provisions of Laws and Regulations

Labor contracts in violation of laws and regulations mean that the contents of labor contracts violate the mandatory provisions of laws and administrative regulations. Mandatory legal provisions are mandatory legal guidelines that the parties must comply with the conclusion of labor contracts, or they breach the law. These mandatory guidelines mainly include labor protection provisions, provisions on working hours, provisions on basic rights of laborers, special protection provisions on women and underage. Some employing units may restrict female employment, or include provisions on no marriage or child birth as conditions of labor contracts, or longer working hours are prescribed in labor contracts.

( Ⅱ ) Labor Contracts Concluded by Fraud, Threat or Taking Advantage of Others

Fraud means a party intentionally fabricates falsehood, or distorts or conceals the truth, causing the other party to have a wrong understanding and a labor contract is then concluded, such as good benefits, high wages, favorable working conditions, etc. Threat means the use of real or potential hazards to induce another party to feel threatened and a labor contract is then concluded, such as threatening to harm the person-in-charge of an employing unit to force him to conclude a labor contract. Taking advantage of others means forcing the other party to accept obviously unfavorable conditions against his will by taking advantage of his urgent needs or his emergency to convey untruthful meaning.

In addition, a labor contract that exempts the statutory liability of an employing unit or excludes the rights of a laborer shall also be invalid.

An invalid labor contract is not legally binding since the time of conclusion. When a labor contract is determined to be partially invalid and the validity of the remaining part is not affected, the remaining part is still valid. According to this provision, a labor contract that is determined to be invalid is not legally binding since the time of conclusion. When a labor contract is determined to be partially invalid and the remaining part is still valid, such as the invalidity of the clause of keeping commercial secrets in a labor contract will not affect the validity of other clauses.

Although the validity of an invalid labor contract has not been recognized from the start, not everyone has the right to declare the invalidity of a labor contract. The authorities with the right to determine the invalidity of labor contracts in China are the labor dispute arbitration commission and people's courts.

The conclusion and performance of an invalid labor contract will cause losses to the parties. After a labor contract is determined to be invalid and a party to the contract suffers losses due to the invalid contract, the party at fault shall be responsible for compensation. If an employing unit using child labor has led to the disability of the child labor, the employing unit must undertake the corresponding compensation liability for such losses.

When a labor contract is determined to be invalid, and a laborer has provided labor services, the employing unit shall pay remunerations to the laborer. Reference shall be made to the remunerations of laborers taking up the same or similar positions to determine the amount of remunerations.

## Section 3   Contents, Formats and Terms of Labor Contracts

### Ⅰ. Contents of Labor Contracts

The contents of labor contracts refer to the specific provisions that set out the labor rights and obligations between a laborer and an employing unit. The contents of labor contracts directly affect the individual interests of laborers and employing units, and are also related to the implementation of labor laws, regulations and policies of the state, which are an important topic in the legal system of the labor contract.

The contents of labor contracts can be divided into essential clauses and supplementary clauses depending on the necessity of the clauses in labor contracts. Essential clauses are the essential contents of labor contracts, without such clauses labor contracts cannot be formed. Some essential clauses are prescribed by law and are the statutory contents that must be prescribed by the parties to labor contracts, and some others are the contents negotiated by the parties to labor contracts upon agreement. Supplementary clauses are not the essential conditions for forming labor contracts, without supplementary clauses labor contracts can also be formed. Supplementary clauses are the contents agreed by the parties.

## ( I ) Essential Clauses of Labor Contracts

From Article 19 of the Labor Law and Article 17 of the Labor Contract Law, the essential clauses of labor contracts include the name, domicile and legal representative or major responsible person of an employing unit, the name, domicile and number of the identity card or other valid identity document of a laborer. In addition to such information, three other aspects are particularly important.

### 1. Terms of Contracts

It means the validity period of a contract, commencing from the validity of the contract, and ending at the termination or dissolution of the contract. A labor contract may be fixed-term or non-fixed term, or a period for completing a certain assignment. A clause on the term must be specified in a labor contract, if there is no such provision and it is impossible to specify a necessary term by other means, the contract cannot be formed. For specific labor contracts, on the condition that the parties do not violate the prohibitive legal provisions, the term of the contract may be negotiated on their own.

### 2. Job Duties

Job duties refer to the labor services provided to an employing unit by a laborer, which are the major obligations that should be performed by the laborer. When a laborer is admitted to an employing unit, what type of work or duties he should do, what the desired job requirements are, and so on, should be specified in the labor contract. Both parties can specify the types of work the laborer should do and the targeted indicators of quantity and quality on the basis of consensus after consultation. Reference can also be made to the general situation of the same industry. Regarding laboring or working hours, places, methods and scopes, where unified legal provisions are available, such provisions shall prevail, otherwise, both parties can make their own provisions after consultation, but the basic legal provisions must not be violated.

### 3. Labor Remunerations

Employing units should pay labor remunerations to laborers. This is the major responsibility of employing units and the right of laborers to obtain the corresponding labor remunerations. Labor remunerations refer to various types of labor income obtained by laborers in labor relations as adjusted in the Labor Law. The major form of payment is wage payment, together with allowance and bonus. The amount of wages, payment method, amount of allowance and bonus and the conditions for eligibility should be specified in labor contracts. When there are express provisions in law, such provisions shall prevail, otherwise the parties can discuss with each other. In addition, insurance and benefits should also be specified.

Furthermore, labor contracts must agree on the working hours and rest days of laborers, set out the social insurance rights and items enjoyed by laborers, and include labor protection, working conditions and occupational hazard protection facilities provided to laborers. When a labor contract does not include specific labor remunerations and working conditions that give rise to a dispute, the employing unit and the laborer may negotiate afresh. If negotiation fails, the provisions of the collective contract shall apply. When there is no collective contract or no provision on labor remunerations is included in the collective contract, equal pay should be made to laborers of equal positions. When there is no collective contract or no provision on the standards of working conditions, the relevant State provisions shall apply.

### ( Ⅱ ) Supplementary Contents of Labor Contracts

Apart from the above essential contents, the parties to labor contracts can also agree on other contents on the basis of consensus after full consultation. Supplementary contents are not required in every labor contract, without these contents, the contract can still be formed, but it does not mean that supplementary contents are optional in a labor contract. Supplementary contents specify the rights, obligations and responsibilities of the parties, which are as important as essential contents. Similarly, supplementary contents cannot violate the relevant legal provisions.

Supplementary provisions may be set out by the parties with specific reference to the problems that may arise in specific legal relations, commonly including the agreement on probation period, clauses on maintaining commercial secrets, clauses to supplement insurance and benefits and clauses on damages and compensation for breach of contract.

## 1. Probation Period

A probation period refers to the period of probation for employees newly recruited. The objective is to examine whether the employee meets the conditions for employment, whether the working conditions introduced by the employing unit meet the actual circumstances, etc. In the probation period, the employee and the employing unit have a further understanding of each other, and make a decision on performing or dissolving the labor contract subject to specific circumstances. The employing unit may examine the basic quality and conduct of the employee to see if such quality and conduct can fit the job duties. If the employee is found to be incompetent or found not to meet the employment conditions, the employing unit may dissolve the labor contract any time. The laborer can further understand the situation of the employing unit during the probation period to see if the working conditions and benefits are identical to what was told during recruitment, whether he is suitable for the post, whether he is interested in the post and willing to work on a long-term basis. If he finds that he is not suitable for the post or the situation of the employing unit does not fit his expectations, the laborer may dissolve the labor contract any time.

Article 21 of China's Labor Law provides that a probation period may be agreed upon in a labor contract. The period shall not exceed six months. According to the prevailing provisions, a laborer that starts working for the first time or changes to a different post or type of work when he works again, a probation period may be agreed upon in a labor contract. The same employing unit shall only set out one probation period once for a laborer that does not change his post or type of work. Article 19 of the Labor Contract Law sets out that "if the term of a labor contract is more than three months but less than one year, the probation period may not exceed one month; if the term is more than one year but less than three years, the probation period may not exceed two months; and if the term is fixed for three or more years or is open-ended, the probation period may not exceed six months. No probation period may be stipulated in a labor contract that expires upon completion of a given job or in a labor contract for a term of less than three months. The probation period shall be included in the term of a labor contract. If a labor contract only provides for a probation period, that period shall not stand and the term provided for shall be the term of the labor contract."

When university graduates look for employment, they come across the problems of "internship period" and probation period. The internship system is a system for business familiarity and evaluation of fresh graduates in China applicable to the employment of fresh graduates by employing units. If they are found qualified after the internship period, employing units will handle the procedures for changing them to regular posts and give them post titles. If they cannot reach the internship requirements after the expiry of the internship period, the internship period may be extended for 6 months to one year, or the wage standard will be lowered. For graduates with exceptionally bad performance, employing units may consider dismissal. The probation period is a period for examination agreed by an employing unit and a laborer for mutual understanding and choice after a labor relation is established. It applies to laborers who enter the job market for the first time or change job position or type of work for employment. During the probation period, the laborer may inform the employing unit of dissolving the labor contract any time. According to the provisions of the Ministry of Labor in 1996, when high school or middle school graduates or technical school graduates are assigned to work in employing units, the one-year internship system shall also be followed according to the original provisions, and a probation period of not more than 6 months may be agreed within the internship period.

The "apprenticeship period" is also relevant. The apprenticeship period is a form of training to new recruits in certain positions for them to get familiar with business operations and enhance working skills. After the implementation of the labor contract system, this form of training continues to be adopted according to the periods of technical grading standards. In this regard, the differences of the three types of periods above lie in: (1) different terms. An apprenticeship period is determined according to the period required for technical grading standards. An internship period lasts for one year, and a probation period will not exceed 6 months; (2) different effectiveness. An apprenticeship period and an internship period originate from the existing policies and rules, and a probation period is agreed by both parties and they can determine the period on their own after consultation within a period of 6 months; (3) different applicability. An apprenticeship period mainly applies to new recruits of specific positions. An internship period applies to newly admitted high school or middle school graduates or technical school graduates. A probation period applies to laborers including the above personnel.

### 2. Confidentiality Clause

The clause on confidentiality of commercial secrets is also a common supplementary clause. The objective of this clause is to protect the economic benefits of employing units to prevent laborers who have knowledge of the commercial secrets of employing units from disclosing the commercial secrets of the employing units intentionally or without authorization, causing economic losses to employing units. Commercial secrets refer to technical information and business information that are practical, without the knowledge of the public, bringing about economic benefits to the information holders and on which confidentiality measures are adopted by the information holders, including management methods, production and sale strategies, client lists, information on sources of goods and other business information, as well as production formulas, technical workflow, technical skills, design drawings and other technical information. The characteristics of commercial secrets are non-open, without the knowledge of the public, bringing about benefits to operators, obtaining competitive edge, or containing potential commercial benefits.

The Civil Law, the Anti-unfair Competition Law and the relevant technology administration regulations of China provide that the theft, bribery or unauthorized acquisition of the commercial secrets of other parties constitutes infringement. The Anti-unfair Competition Law prohibits the infringement of commercial secrets of others as an anti-unfair competition act. The Criminal Law provides for the crime of infringement of commercial secrets. In stipulating this clause in a labor contract, the issues to be determined include the scope of commercial secrets to be maintained by laborers, the means of maintaining commercial secrets, the period for undertaking this obligation by laborers. The period for continuing to maintain the commercial secrets of laborers is generally one year after the termination of labor relations, but certain economic compensation must be given to laborers at the same time. Both parties may also agree on the liability for breach of contract and liability for compensation.

### 3. Liquidated Damages and Compensation Clause

The liquidated damages and compensation clause is used to agree on the liquidated damages and compensation payable for non-performance of labor contracts. It is the clause of economic liability to be borne by the party in default as agreed by both parties when a party to a labor contract breaches the contract by not performing the contract.

At present, the provisions on compensation by employing units in China include: (1) where an employing unit deducts or owes the wages of laborers without proper reasons, or refuses to pay wages and remunerations to laborers for extended working hours, the employing unit must make full payment to laborers within the specified time period and pay an additional 25% of wages and remunerations as economic compensation, and the labor and social security administrative department can order the employing unit to pay 1 - 5 times of the unpaid wages and remunerations as compensation; (2) where the wages paid to laborers by an employing unit are less than the local minimum wage standard, the employing unit must supplement the proportion lower than the standard, and pay 25% of the proportion lower than the standard as economic compensation, and the labor and social security administrative department can order the employing unit to pay 1 - 5 times of the unpaid minimum wages as compensation; (3) where an employing unit harms the physical health of laborers, causing occupational diseases or injuries or disabilities of laborers, the employing unit should give medical treatment according to the conditions prescribed by the State and guarantee that laborers are entitled to other insurance benefits. Where the employing unit dissolves the labor contract and does not pay economic compensation to laborers according to statutory standards, the employing unit must make economic compensation to laborers and the economic compensation must be paid in full to laborers as requested by laborers or ordered by the labor and social security administrative department, and pay 1 - 5 times of the unpaid economic compensation as compensation; (4) where an employing unit recruits a laborer who has not yet dissolved a labor contract, causing economic losses to the original employing unit, the laborer must assume direct compensation liability and the employing unit must assume joint and several compensation liability. The joint and several liability must not be less than 70% of the total economic losses caused to the original employing unit. Compensation must be made to the original employing unit for the following losses: (1) direct economic losses caused to production, operation and work; (2) economic losses caused to the original employing unit by obtaining commercial secrets. The compensation for the losses in item (2) must follow Article 20 of the Anti-unfair Competition Law. In this case, the laborer undertakes the liability for statutory compensation, and the maximum compensation in joint and several liability must not be lower than 30%. If the amount undertaken by the employing unit exceeds the statutory amount, it shall have the right to make claims from the laborer.

Where economic losses are caused to the employing unit by reasons of the laborer himself, the employing unit can request the laborer to make compensation of economic losses according to the contract. "Reasons of the laborer himself" mainly means that the laborer violates the labor discipline and rules and systems of the employing unit. If both parties have specific agreements in the labor contract, the laborer must assume the compensation liability, otherwise no such liability is assumed. There is also a restrictive provision on the amount of wage deduction of the laborer. Article 16 of the Interim Provisions on Wage Payment provides that

"Such compensation may be deducted from the laborer's wage, provided, however, that the monthly deduction shall not exceed 20% of the laborer's wage of the month. Where the wage remained after the deduction is lower than the local minimum wage standard, the wage shall be paid in accordance with minimum wage standard."

Where a laborer breaches the confidentiality clause as agreed and brings about economic losses to the employing unit, compensation must be made according to Article 20 of the Anti-unfair Competition Law. The scope of compensation includes: where losses are caused to the employing unit, the liability for damages must be assumed. Where it is difficult to ascertain the losses of the operator, the compensation amount will be the profits arising from infringement obtained by the infringing party in the period of infringement, as well as the reasonable expenses paid by the operator for investigating the anti-unfair competition acts that infringe his lawful rights and interests. Regarding this type of compensation liability, the laborer and the employing unit must provide for a confidentiality clause in the labor contract.

The Measures for Compensation in Violation of the Relevant Provisions on Labor Contracts in the Labor Law provide for the scope of compensation caused to employing units by laborers in violation of provisions of labor laws or agreements of labor contracts. Where a laborer dissolves the labor contract in violation of law or regulations or the agreements of the labor contract and causes losses to the employing unit, the laborer should compensate the employing unit for the following losses: (1) the expenses incurred by the employing unit for his recruitment; (2) the training fees paid by the employing unit on behalf of the laborer. If both parties have made separate agreements, such agreements shall prevail. Regarding the specific compensation standard for training fees, the Ministry of Labor has made a provision in the Official Reply on the Rationales for Handling the Dissolution of Labor Contracts During Probation Periods: "Where an employing unit contributes capital (which refers to the situation with proof of monetary payment) for the technical training of an employee, and the employee wishes to dissolve the labor contract with the employing unit during a probation period, the employing unit cannot request the laborer to pay such training fees. If the probation period is completed and the dissolution of labor contract is made during the contract period, the employing unit can request the laborer to pay such training fees. The specific payment method is: where the service period is agreed, the capital contribution shall be equally shared according to the service period, and the employee makes payment according to the remaining service period after deducting the service period in which he has worked. If no service period is agreed, the capital contribution shall be equally shared according to the labor contract period, and the employee makes payment after deducting the contract period he has performed. If no contract period is agreed, the capital contribution shall be equally shared according to a 5-year service period and the employee makes payment after deducting the contract period he has performed. Where both parties have agreed on the deduction calculation method, such agreement shall prevail. If the contract period expires, and the employee requests for contract termination, the employing unit cannot request the laborer to pay such training fees. If the employing unit recruits the employee with money contribution, and the employee dissolves the labor contract with the employing unit within the contract period (including the probation period), the employing unit may make a claim for compensation against the laborer according to Item 1 of Article 4 of the Measures for Compensation in Violation of the Relevant Provisions on Labor Contracts in the Labor Law. " (3) direct economic losses caused by production, operation and work; (4) other compensation agreed in the labor contract.

In addition, the employing unit and the laborer may also agree on the training, supplementary insurance and other welfare benefits. However, there is also express prohibition of certain issues by law. For example, when an employing unit concludes a labor contract with a laborer, no deposit, security money (goods) or collateral money (goods) in any form can be collected from the laborer. In the recruitment and admission of personnel, no money collection fee, training fee or medical check-up fee can be collected in disguise.

## Ⅰ. Terms of Labor Contracts

The terms of labor contracts refer to the validity of labor contracts in which the parties with labor relations exercise their rights and perform their obligations. After the conclusion of labor contracts, both parties have established labor relations with the constraints on rights and obligations, each party must exercise his rights and perform his obligations with his own acts. This binding relation with rights and obligations lasts for a certain term, be it long or short. Paragraph One of Article 20 of the Labor Law provides that "Terms of labor contracts include fixed term, non-fixed term and term for completing a specific assignment. "

### ( Ⅰ ) Fixed-term Labor Contracts

A fixed-term labor contract refers to the labor contract concluded by both parties to a labor contract that specifies the commencement and termination dates.

On the expiry of the term of a labor contract, the labor relation will also be terminated immediately. The contract may be renewed with the consent of both parties after consultation, but the term of the renewal of the labor contract is also specific. The specific term for a regular labor contract may be determined by both parties according to needs and actual circumstances. The application of a regular labor contract is wide with great adaptability, which can maintain the relative stability of a labor relation and facilitate the reasonable flow of manpower, while reducing unnecessary labor disputes.

( Ⅱ ) Non-fixed Term Labor Contracts

A non-fixed term labor contract, also called irregular labor contract, refers to a labor contract concluded by both parties to a labor contract without specific time limit. For concluding a non-fixed term labor contract, both parties should agree on the conditions for modification and dissolution of labor contract apart from laws and regulations.

A non-fixed term labor contract is not targeted at short-term labor activities, on the contrary, when a laborer works in an employing unit for a long period of time, the laborer will possess strong technical skills and have consecutive work experience in a position, which can be applied to industries with high technology involving advanced scientific technology and the need for confidentiality. In general circumstances when the conditions for the modification and dissolution of labor contracts as agreed in labor contracts do not exist, employing units cannot modify or dissolve labor contracts. Labor relations can only be terminated under the statutory or agreed conditions for dissolution of labor contracts. When compared with fixed-term labor contracts, non-fixed term labor contracts are more favorable to laborers. On the expiry of fixed-term labor contracts, employing units can refuse to conclude another labor contract with laborers. There is no expiry of non-fixed term labor contracts and dissolution of labor contracts is only possible due to statutory reasons or meeting of the minds of both parties.

There is a certain degree of flexibility in non-fixed term labor contracts. Paragraph Two of Article 20 of the Labor Law sets out that "where a laborer has been working for the same employing unit for over ten consecutive years and both parties agree on renewing the labor contract, if the laborer makes a request for concluding a labor contract with non-fixed term, such contract with non-fixed term shall be concluded. " The term "working for the same employing unit for over ten consecutive years" means that the term of a labor contract concluded between a laborer and an employing unit lasts for ten consecutive years, on the expiry of the labor contract and both parties agree to renew the labor contract, when the laborer requests for concluding a non-fixed term labor contract, the employing unit shall conclude a non-fixed term labor contract with the laborer.

Regarding the difficulty in concluding a non-fixed term labor contract in practice, Article 14 of the Labor Contract Law revises the relevant conditions as: (1) The laborer has been working for the employing unit for a consecutive period of 10 or more years; (2) The laborer has been working for the employing unit for a consecutive period of 10 or more years but less than 10 years away from the statutory retirement age when the employing unit introduces the labor contract system or when the State-owned enterprise has to conclude a new labor contract with him as a result of restructuring; or (3) The laborer intends to renew the labor contract after he has consecutively concluded a fixed-term labor contract with the employing unit twice. A provision is added to provide that where an employing unit does not conclude a labor contract with a laborer after labor use of one year or more, it shall be deemed that a non-fixed term labor contract is concluded between the employing unit and the laborer.

( Ⅲ ) Labor Contracts for Completion of a Certain Assignment

A labor contract for the completion of a certain task means that both parties have determined the commencement and termination dates of the contract with the completion of a certain task or project. The commencement date of a certain task or project shall be the commencement date of the contract, when the task or project is completed, the contract will expire immediately.

This type of labor contract is in fact a regular labor contract of a special nature in a different format. A general fixed-term labor contract is determined by the duration, while a labor contract for completion of a certain task is determined by the commencement and completion of a task or project. Since there is a time limit but unspecified, the period for completion of the task set out in the contract is the contract expiry period.

## Ⅲ. Formats of Labor Contracts

The formats of labor contracts refer to the manner in which the parties to a labor contract establish, modify or terminate the relation of labor rights and obligations. The conclusion, performance, modification and dissolution of labor contracts are realized through reflecting the minds of both parties. The reflection of the minds must be presented in a certain format, and labor contracts must be in a certain format. Article 19 of the Labor Law provides that labor contracts must be concluded in writing, therefore, labor contracts must be in written form.

Labor contracts in writing means the direct use of written languages to express the consensus of both parties that is reached after consultation to determine the rights and obligations. Labor contracts in writing are solemn and serious, the contents of contracts are written in black and white, which are accurate and reliable, and the basis can be substantiated. These contracts are conducive to the exercise of rights and performance of obligations by both parties, and facilitate the supervision and examination by the competent department and the labor contract administrative authority. When a dispute arises, accurate evidence can be obtained to investigate the facts and distinguish the right and wrong, so as to apply laws and regulations accurately to handle the dispute. In the relevant laws of China, labor contracts are required to be concluded in writing all along. For example, Article 7 of the Interim Provisions on the Implementation of the Labor Contract System by State-owned Enterprises promulgated by the State Council in 1986 sets out that "Where an enterprise and a worker recruited conclude a labor contract... the responsibilities, obligations and rights of both parties shall be specified in writing. " In addition, Article 8 of the Provisions on the Labor Administration of Foreign Investment Enterprises provides that "Labor contracts shall be concluded by individual employees and enterprises in writing. "

## Section 4    Dissolution of Labor Contracts

The dissolution of a labor contract refers to the legal act of terminating the effectiveness of a contract in advance by both parties due to a certain factor after they have concluded a labor contract without completion. In general, dissolution includes statutory dissolution and dissolution after consultation. Statutory dissolution means that the circumstances in which a labor contract may be dissolved are provided by state laws, regulations or contract provisions, without the mutual consent of both parties, the effectiveness of the contract can be terminated in advance naturally or unilaterally. Dissolution after consultation means that the effectiveness of a labor contract is terminated in advance by both parties for a certain reason out of their own will on the basis of consensus by both parties after consultation.

The dissolution of a labor contract is an interim stage that is foreseeable from the conclusion to performance of a labor contract. It is an unavoidable reality. The lawful dissolution of a labor contract is an important guarantee to protect the proper rights and interests of both parties to a labor contract. Since the dissolution of a labor contract will take place when the parties have not fully performed the legal acts prescribed in the contract. If the objectives of concluding a labor contract by both parties are not realized or fully realized, either party or both parties must be affected. In this regard, the dissolution of a labor contract involves the personal interests of both parties to the contract, therefore dissolution must be made according to law.

## Ⅰ. Dissolution of Labor Contracts by Employing Units and Restrictions

### ( Ⅰ ) Rights of Dissolution of Labor Contracts and Evolution

A labor contract that is dissolved by an employer or employing unit is also called "dismissal". In theory, the right of dismissal of employers has changed in the course of historical development. In the early times, the general view was that employers have the freedom to dismiss employees. They must take operating costs into consideration in view of operations and investment, the employment or dismissal of laborers is the basic freedom of operations of employers, which should not be interfered. On this basis, the claims on restricting the dismissal right are proposed subsequently, which means that on the condition that the freedom of dismissal of employers is affirmed, there must be proper reasons or no dismissal can be made. Since labor rights are the basic rights of laborers and relevant to the survival of laborers, there must be express legal provisions for employers to exercise the dismissal right, otherwise dismissal is not valid. Accordingly, designated provisions on the conditions of dissolving labor contracts by employers or employing units are made in labor legislation in various countries. Some countries have enacted the Dismissal Protection Law to restrict dismissal by employers and protect the labor rights of laborers.

### ( Ⅱ ) Provisions of Labor Legislation and Restrictions

Articles 25, 26, 27 and 28 of China's Labor Law and Articles 39 to 41 of the Labor Contract Law provide for the circumstances in which employing units can dissolve labor contracts and the restrictions. The dissolution of labor contracts by employing units can be divided into three circumstances:

**1. Employing Units Have Decided to Dissolve Labor Contracts based on the Subjective Working Performance of Laborers.**

Article 25 of China's Labor Law provides that "Under any of the following circumstances of a laborer, the employing unit may dissolve the labor contract: (1) The laborer has been proved not to meet the recruitment requirements during the probation period; (2) The laborer has seriously violated labor discipline or the employing unit's rules and systems; (3) The laborer has caused great harm and losses to the employing unit due to gross neglect of duty or malpractice; or (4) The laborer's criminal liability has been pursued in accordance with the law."

The above provision of the Labor Law is based on the work performance of the laborer in the employing unit as the legal basis provided by the employing unit for advance dissolution of labor contracts:

(1) The laborer has been proved not to meet the recruitment requirements during the probation period. The conclusion and performance of a labor contract is likely to rely on the value of manpower use. The Labor Law provides for the probation period in the labor contract is to give practical examination of the use value of the laborer. During the probation period, the employing unit will further conduct a comprehensive and stringent evaluation of different aspects of the laborer. If it is found that the clauses of the contract or the relevant provisions are not conformed, such as physical conditions, age, cultural level, individual profession, work ethics, individual cultural values, moral values and so on do not conform to the agreed recruitment requirements, or the laborer is still not competent for the requirements of the job after training in the probation period, the employing unit has the right to dissolve the labor contract.

(2) The laborer has seriously violated labor discipline or the employing unit's rules and systems. Labor discipline is the basis for organizing social labor, which is an essential condition for engaging in social labor. The rules and systems of the employing unit are based on the rules and systems of enterprises and institutions formulated according to state laws and regulations, which specifically provide for the requirements of labor discipline and become the criteria for labor activities conducted by all personnel of the employing unit in a coordinated and standardized manner. Accordingly, the laborer must comply with labor discipline and the rules and systems of the employing unit. Where the laborer seriously violates labor discipline, affects production, working discipline, seriously violates operating guidelines, damages facilities, tools, wastes raw materials, energy, causes economic losses to the employing unit, or demonstrates bad working attitude or service attitude and quarrels frequently with customers, harms the interests of consumers, disobeys regular job rotation, steals, gambles, sacrifices public interests for personal benefits, fights, or commits other serious mistakes, the employing unit has the right to dissolve his labor contract.

(3) The laborer has caused great harm and losses to the employing unit due to gross neglect of duty or malpractice. The essence of the labor contract is that the laborer remains in the job position and works whole-heartedly to complete the

tasks agreed in the labor contract. If the laborer is absent from duty without authorization, derelict of duty or sacrifices public interests for personal benefits, and causes huge economic losses to the employing unit, the employing unit has the right to dissolve the labor contract.

(4) The laborer's criminal liability has been pursued in accordance with the law. When the laborer is required to receive labor education or imposed punishment, and violates the relevant provisions of laws or security administration punishment laws, they will harm the society. When the laborer is required to receive labor education or imposed punishment which affects the accurate and timely performance of the labor contract, he has not only caused delay to the period for performing the labor contract due to the loss of personal freedom, but also violated labor discipline and the rules and systems of the employing unit due to illegal acts or criminal acts, and the production and working discipline of the employing unit cannot be ongoing as usual. The performance of the labor contract will then become unnecessary, the employing unit has the right to dissolve the labor contract.

(5) When the laborer establishes a labor relation with another employing unit concurrently, which seriously affects the completion of the tasks of the employing unit, or the laborer refuses to rectify at the request of the employing unit. This is the fourth item newly added to Article 39 of the Labor Contract Law, which prohibits part-time work of the laborer. Other countries usually do not make provisions on this issue, in particular no prohibitive provisions are made in labor legislation. This provision in the labor legislation of China should meet the needs of the employing unit, which is a related element of a labor relation. Since labor legislation has provided for various statutory obligations of the employing unit to the laborer, and required the laborer to perform the corresponding obligations and responsibilities, a necessary obligation is to be loyal to the employer.

In the Opinions of the Ministry of Labor on Several Issues Concerning the Thorough Implementation of the Labor Law of the People's Republic of China, Article 39 sets out that an employing unit that dissolves a labor contract according to Article 25 of the Labor Law can refuse to pay economic compensation to the laborer.

**2. Employing Units can Dissolve Labor Contracts According to the Changes of Objective Conditions during the Performance of Labor Contracts.**

Article 26 of the Labor Law provides that "Under any of the following circumstances, the employing unit may dissolve the labor contract but shall inform the laborer in written form 30 days in advance: (1) The laborer is unable to engage in his or her original work or any new work arranged separately by the employing unit after the expiration of the period of medical treatment for sickness or non-work related injury; (2) The laborer is incompetent for his or her work and still incompetent after training or change of posts; and (3) The objective conditions based on which the labor contract was concluded have changed significantly, which results in the failure to perform the original labor contract, and no agreement on contract change has been reached through consultation between the parties concerned. "

When the laborer is sick or suffers from non-work related injury, a medical treatment period will be given according to the length of service in the employing unit. According to the provisions of the Ministry of Labor on medical treatment period, such period will last for 3 to 24 months. For employees suffering from special illnesses (such as cancer, mental illness and paralysis) who cannot be recovered within 24 months, with the approval of the enterprise and the local labor department, the medical treatment period may be properly extended. The specific standards are as follows: (1) where the actual length of service is less than 10 years, and the length of service in the employing unit is less than 5 years, the medical treatment period will be 3 months; if it is more than 5 years, the medical treatment period will be 6 months; (2) where the actual length of service is more than 10 years, and the length of service in the employing unit is less than 5 years, the medical treatment period will be 6 months; if it is more than 5 years but less than 10 years, the medical treatment period will be 9 months; if it is more than 10 years but less than 15 years, the medical treatment period will be 12 months; if it is more than 15 years but less than 20 years, the medical treatment period will be 18 months; if it is more than 20 years, the medical treatment period will be 24 months. The medical treatment period is calculated from the date of sick leave, a medical treatment period of 3 months will be calculated according to accumulated sick leave period of 6 months. For a medical treatment period of 6 months, it will be calculated according to accumulated sick leave period within 12 months. For a medical treatment period of 9 months, it will be calculated according to accumulated sick leave period of 15 months. For a medical treatment period of 12 months, it will be calculated according to accumulated sick leave period of 18 months. For a medical treatment period of 18 months, it will be calculated according to accumulated sick leave period of 24 months. For a medical treatment period of 24 months, it will be calculated according to accumulated sick leave period of 30 months. After the medical treatment period, where the laborer cannot engage in the original work or he is still incompetent for the job after the employing unit has changed the job position, the employing unit must inform the laborer of the dissolution of the labor contract with one month's notice.

If the laborer is incompetent for the job after training or change of job position, the employing unit has changed the job position and the laborer is still incompetent for the new job after training, the employing unit has the right to dissolve the labor contract.

When the objective conditions based on which the labor contract was concluded have changed significantly, such as the repeal or revision of the laws and regulations the labor contract is based, which results in the failure to perform the original labor contract, and no agreement on contract change has been reached through consultation between the parties concerned, the employing unit may dissolve the labor contract. When the performance of the labor contract is rendered unnecessary due to force majeure, or the laborer is incompetent for the job after the change of the labor contract, and both parties fail to reach an agreement on modifying the labor contract, the employing unit may dissolve the labor contract.

In this regard, objective conditions include those of the employing unit and the laborer himself. The former may be caused by operational hardship, suspension of business or change of business, deficit or business contraction; or a decrease in the number of laborers because of changes of working conditions due to market conditions, international competition and technical reform. The latter may be caused by the implementation of automation or new production technology by the employing unit when the laborer was competent for the job at the beginning.

The dissolution of a labor contract due to changes of objective conditions is different from the dissolution of a labor contract due to the objective mistakes of the laborer, and the difference lies in "prior notice" or "advance notice". "Advance notice" aims at protecting the laborer. When the laborer receives an advance notice of dismissal, he may apply for leave during the working period to look for a new job.

Article 40 of the Labor Contract Law includes a new statutory condition of "or additional payment of one month of wages to the laborer", which allows the employing unit to pay one month of wages in lieu of "30 days of advance notice in writing". Since the implementation of the Labor Law, after the employing unit makes payment of one month of wages for dissolution of the labor contract, the laborer will apply for sick leave or leave for work-related injury, thereby the labor contract cannot be terminated as scheduled, and further giving rise to the consequences of labor arbitration and litigation. This condition is set out to dispel the worry of the employing unit.

### 3. Employing Units can Dissolve Labor Contracts due to Economic Dismissal.

Paragraph One of Article 27 of China's Labor Law provides that "during the statutory rectification of an employing unit when it is on the verge of bankruptcy or when an employing unit has a serious difficulty in production and business operation, where it is necessary to lay off workers, the employing unit shall explain the situation to the labor union or all its workers 30 days in advance, solicit their opinions and report to the labor administration department before laying off workers." Article 41 of the Labor Contract Law also includes the relevant contents: where there is change of production, significant technological reform or adjustment of the mode of operation of an enterprise, the enterprise still needs to lay off workers after the modification of labor contracts. Another reason includes the objective conditions based on which the labor contract was concluded have changed significantly, which results in the failure to perform the labor contract.

Enterprise bankruptcy means that an enterprise is in a serious deficit due to poor operations and management and fails to repay the debts due. It is a system in which the creditor or debtor makes an application according to law, and the people's court declares the bankruptcy of the enterprise according to law and repays the debts owed to the creditor in the statutory order. According to China's Enterprise Bankruptcy Law (Trial Implementation) and the Civil Procedure Law, the period in which an enterprise is on the verge of bankruptcy and undergoes statutory rectification means the creditor has applied for the bankruptcy of the enterprise, and the competent department at the higher level of the enterprise subject to the application for bankruptcy rectifies such enterprise. When there is serious difficulty in the production and operations of the employing unit, Article 2 of the Provisions on the Economic Dismissal of Staff by Enterprises states that the employing unit may lay off workers when it experiences serious difficulty in production and operations, and reaches the standard for enterprises in serious difficulty prescribed by the local government which genuinely requires the dismissal of workers.

The survival of the fittest is a natural principle in a market economy. From the angle of the whole society, it is certain that some enterprises may undergo rectification according to laws and regulations due to operational hardship or insolvency caused by objective reasons. During the rectification period, the employing unit may conduct economic dismissal of employees with the consent of the trade union or after consultation with all the employees of the employing unit, which is the dissolution of labor contracts with employees. When the employing unit is in serious difficulty in production and operations and input and output are seriously disproportional, the employing unit has the right to dissolve labor contracts with laborers with the consent of the trade union or after consultation with all the employees in order to reduce production cost and maintain normal production.

Regarding economic dismissal, the employing unit must follow statutory procedures to dissolve labor contracts with the staff dismissed: (1) the employing unit should explain the situation to the trade union or all the employees 30 days in advance and provide the relevant information on production and operations; (2) prepare a dismissal plan, including a list of dismissal, period of dismissal, steps for implementation, basis of laws and regulations, economic compensation measures; (3) solicit the opinions of the trade union and all the employees on the dismissal plan and revise the plan; (4) report the dismissal plan and opinions of the trade union and all the employees to the local labor security administrative department and listen to the opinions of the labor security administrative department; (5) announce the dismissal plan and dissolve labor contracts with the employees dismissed, pay economic compensation and issue dismissal certificate. For staff dismissal, the following personnel should be retained on priority: (1) employees that conclude a long period of fixed-term labor contracts with the employing unit; (2) employees that conclude non-fixed term labor contracts with the employing unit; (3) employees that are the only person in employment of the family with dependent elderly or underage. When the employing unit conducts a new round of recruitment within 6 months, the employing unit should inform the persons dismissed and recruit such persons on priority on equal terms.

( Ⅲ ) Payment of Economic Compensation by Employing Units for Dissolution of Labor Contracts

Article 28 of the Labor Law states that "where an employing unit dissolves a labor contract in accordance with the provisions of Articles 24, 26 and 27 of this Law, it shall make economic compensation in accordance with the relevant provisions of the State." The economic compensation from an employing unit for dissolution of labor contracts refer to the economic subsidy from the employing unit to the laborer after dissolution of the labor contract, which generally includes: living subsidy and medical subsidy. The subsidy offers the necessary protection to the laborer with basic living expenses and medical fees before the laborer can find a new job following the dissolution of the labor contract.

Economic compensation is made to the laborer according to his length of service in the employing unit, the payment should be made to the laborer according to the standard of one month of wages upon one full year of service. When the period is more than 6 months but less than 1 year, it should be counted as 1 year. When the period is less than 6 months, economic compensation of half a month should be made to the laborer. When the monthly wages of the laborer is 3 times higher than the average monthly wages of staff of the previous year of the region announced by the people's government at the level of municipality with districts, economic compensation of 3 times of the average monthly wages of staff should be made to the laborer, the maximum period of payment of economic compensation should not exceed 12 years. Monthly wages refer to the average wages of the laborer of 12 months before the dissolution or termination of the labor contract. The economic compensation to the laborer will be made at one time by the employing unit. Economic compensation is listed as expenses in the costs of the enterprise, and should not account for the welfare fees that should be withdrawn according to the required ratio of the enterprise. If the employing unit fails to make economic compensation according to provisions after dissolution of the labor contract, it should make economic compensation in full together with additional economic compensation at 50% of the amount of economic compensation.

On February 15, 1996, the General Office of the Ministry of Labor gave an official reply to the Request for Instructions on the Issues Relevant to the Computation and Payment of Economic Compensation for Termination or Dissolution of Labor Contracts, which states: after the full implementation of the labor contract system, where an employee is deployed or transferred to another working unit, he shall terminate the labor relation with the original employing unit and establish a labor relation with the new employing unit. Where the employee requests for deployment or transfer to a working unit, he shall dissolve the labor contract with the original employing unit to conclude a labor contract with the new employing unit. When the employing unit makes a request for dissolving the labor contract according to Article 24 of the Labor Law after the consultation of both parties, the employing unit should make economic compensation to the laborer. When the laborer proposes the dissolution of the labor contract, the employing unit does not need to make economic compensation. When the working unit is changed due to the merger, consolidation, joint venture, change of the nature of the unit or change of the name of the legal person, the working period before the change may be counted as the working period in the employing unit.

(Ⅳ) Restrictions on Dissolution of Labor Contracts by Employing Units

Article 29 of the Labor Law provides that under any of the following circumstances of a laborer, the employing unit shall not dissolve the labor contract in accordance with the provisions of Articles 26 and 27 of this Law: (1) The laborer suffers from occupational diseases or work-related injuries and determined to be totally or partially incapacitated; (2) The laborer receives medical treatment for a disease or an injury within the prescribed period of medical treatment; (3) The female laborer is during the period of pregnancy, the perinatal period or the period of lactation; (4) Other circumstances prescribed by laws and administrative regulations.

**1. The Laborer Suffers from Occupational Diseases or Work-related Injuries and Determined to be Totally or Partially Incapacitated.**

In the laboring process, a laborer may be exposed to the harm caused by poisonous or harmful gas, dust, dangerous goods, industrial noise, strong light, high temperature or low temperature. When a laborer is confirmed to suffer from occupational disease, his employing unit should arrange medical treatment or medical care to the laborer on the advice of the occupational disease diagnosis institution. After medical treatment or medical care, when the laborer is confirmed to be totally or partially incapacitated, the employing unit cannot dissolve the labor contract. If the laborer is partially incapacitated, the job position can be changed to arrange the laborer to engage in work he is competent. If the laborer is totally incapacitated, his living should be arranged according to the relevant state provisions on social insurance. Work-related injury refers to the injury suffered by the laborer in a work-related incident or the harm caused to the laborer for working reasons within the working area or other reasons within the scope of the Labor Law. When the laborer is totally incapacitated due to work-related injury, the work and living of the laborer should be arranged according to the relevant State insurance benefits for work-related injury. The employing unit cannot dissolve the labor contract.

**2. The Laborer Receives Medical Treatment for a Disease or an Injury within the Prescribed Period of Medical Treatment.**

Where a laborer is sick or suffers from work-related injury and suspends working for medical treatment and care, the employing unit must not dissolve the labor contract within the period of medical treatment according to Articles 26 and 27 of the Labor Law.

**3. The Female Laborer is during the Period of Pregnancy, the Perinatal Period or the Period of Lactation.**

In the process of production and working, female laborers are offered special labor protection during the menstruation period, the perinatal period and the period of lactation. The employing unit cannot dissolve the labor contract of a female laborer during the maternity period, the period of lactation and the menstruation period according to Articles 26 and 27 of the Labor Law, which shows the special protection offered to female laborers during the perinatal period, the period of lactation and the period of pregnancy.

The Labor Contract Law also adds the relevant contents: where a laborer in contact with hazardous operations of occupational diseases has not yet undergone health examination before vacation of office, or a suspected occupational disease sufferer is in the period of diagnosis or medical observation and has been working in the unit for 15 full years, and there is less than 5 years before his statutory retirement age, or in other circumstances prescribed by laws and administrative regulations, enhanced protection of dismissal is offered to a designated labor group.

Special attention should be drawn to the punitive provisions on illegal dissolution of labor contracts by employing units. Article 48 sets out that where an employing unit dissolves or terminates a labor contract in violation of provisions, the laborer requests for the continuous performance of the labor contract, the employing unit shall continue the performance. Where the laborer does not request for continuous performance of the labor contract or the labor contract cannot be performed, the employing unit should pay double amount of compensation.

## II. Dissolution of Labor Contracts by Laborers and Points to Note

Articles 31 and 32 of the Labor Law and Articles 37 and 38 of the Labor Contract Law provide that laborers that dissolve labor contracts can be divided into the following two circumstances:

### ( I ) Dissolution of Labor Contracts Requires Advance Notice to Employing Units

Article 31 of the Labor Law sets out that "A laborer who intends to dissolve a labor contract shall inform the employing unit in written form 30 days in advance. " The Labor Contract Law includes the phrase "inform the employing unit 3 days in advance within the probation period", which is the general situation for dissolution of labor contracts by the laborer.

Since a labor contract is concluded out of the will of the laborer, he should also have the right to dissolve it out of his will, as long as the dissolution conforms to laws and regulations. In particular, in a market economy where the reasonable flow of manpower is encouraged, the laborer should be allowed to select his occupation according to actual circumstances to give full play to his talents. Accordingly, the Labor Law provides for the dissolution of labor contracts by laborers to offer a legal basis to laborers for exercising the said right.

Nevertheless, laborers must note that 30 days of advance notice in writing to the employing unit is required in exercising the said right, so as to avoid causing unnecessary losses to the employing unit. Article 31 of the Explanations of Several Provisions of the Labor Law states that: "This provision provides for the right of resignation of laborers, in addition to the procedures set out in this provision, there is no other condition for laborers to exercise the right of resignation. However, laborers in breach of labor contracts shall assume the liability according to law. "

When a laborer unilaterally dissolves a labor contract, it is also called "resignation". Regarding this unilateral legal act of employees, the legislation of various countries only provides that advance notice is given without the acceptance of the other party to give legal force to resignation. An employee may end the subordinate labor relation with an enterprise any time. This act does not require excessive reasons because the request for the dissolution of the labor contract itself is already a sufficient reason. In other words, an employee that dissolves a labor contract is only required to comply with the provision on advance notice period. If a laborer resigns without giving advance notice, he shall make compensation to the enterprise for its losses and the amount usually equals to the wages obtained by the employee in the advance notice period.

( Ⅱ ) Dissolution of Labor Contracts not Requiring Advance Notice to Employing Units

Article 32 of the Labor Law states that: "Under any of the following circumstances, a laborer may inform the employing unit to dissolve the labor contract at any time: (1) within the probation period; (2) the employing unit forces the laborer to work by violence, intimidation or illegal restriction of personal freedom; or (3) the employing unit fails to pay labor remunerations or provide working conditions under the labor contract. " Article 38 is revised to: " (1) failing to provide labor protection or working conditions as agreed in the labor contract; (2) failing to pay labor remunerations on time and in full; (3) failing to pay social insurance premiums for the laborer in accordance with the law; (4) having rules and systems in violation of laws or regulations, thereby impairing the rights and interests of the laborer; (5) invalidating the labor contract as a result of one of the circumstances specified in paragraph one of Article 26 of this Law; (6) other circumstances in which a laborer may dissolve the labor contract as prescribed by laws and administrative regulations. " As emphasized in paragraph two: "if an employing unit forces a person to work by violence, intimidation or illegal restriction of personal freedom, or if it gives instructions in violation of rules and regulations or gives peremptory orders to the laborer to perform hazardous operations, which endanger his personal safety, the latter may dissolve the labor contract forthwith without notifying the employing unit of the matter in advance. "

## 1. Within the Probation Period.

A probation period is a period of examination for the employing unit to assess whether a laborer meets the conditions for recruitment, which is also a period for the selection of the employing unit by the laborer. Accordingly, when the laborer thinks that it is unnecessary to continue to perform the contract within the probation period, he may inform the employing unit at any time to dissolve the labor contract. After the implementation of this provision in the Labor Law for several years, in response to the opinions of employing units, "3 days of notice in advance within the probation period" is set out in the Labor Contract Law. This may only be a slight change, but gives rise to much trouble in practice: when a laborer informs the employing unit within the probation period for dissolution of the labor contract without giving 3 days of notice in advance, how should the act of the laborer in dissolving the labor contract and the time be determined?

## 2. The Employing Unit Forces the Laborer to Work by Violence, Intimidation or Illegal Restriction of Personal Freedom.

The conclusion of labor contracts should follow the principles of equality, voluntariness and consensus after consultation. Labor contracts concluded by means of fraud and threat are not valid. When the employing unit forces the laborer to work by violence, threat or illegal restriction of personal freedom, it is an act that seriously infringes the personal freedom of the laborer. If the circumstances are serious, a crime will be constituted, and criminal liability of the directly responsible person shall be pursued according to law. From the perspective of a labor contract, it is an illegal act that goes against the principle of conclusion of the labor contract, and the laborer has the right to inform the employing unit at any time to dissolve the labor contract that has been concluded.

"An employing unit gives instructions in violation of rules and regulations or gives peremptory orders to the laborer to perform hazardous operations, which endanger his personal safety" is an act prohibited by law, it is therefore necessary and reasonable to provide immediate dissolution right to the laborer.

**3. The Employing Unit Fails to Pay Labor Remunerations or Provide Working Conditions under the Labor Contract.**

The failure to pay labor remunerations under the labor contract includes deferred payment, short payment or non-payment of labor remunerations. The failure to provide working conditions under the labor contract mainly refers to poor working environment, lack of the necessary labor protection measures, or even the existence of factors endangering the life and health of employees. Both infringe the proper and lawful labor rights and interests of laborers, which are acts in obvious breach of the labor contract. Laborers certainly have the right to inform the employing unit to dissolve the labor contract any time. If the matter is not handled in a timely manner, it will give rise to grave consequences.

Also relevant is "failure to pay social insurance premiums for the laborer in accordance with the law", which is prohibited by law. The laborer may immediately dissolve the labor contract.

New provisions in the Labor Contract Law are "having rules and systems in violation of laws or regulations, thereby impairing the rights and interests of the laborer", as well as "invalidating the labor contract as a result of one of the circumstances specified in Paragraph One of Article 26", both will cause serious harm to the lawful rights and interests of the laborer. As a result, the laborer has the right to dissolve the labor contract on the same date.

## Section 5    Legal Liability for Breach of Labor Contracts

A labor contract, once effective, is legally binding. Both parties should consciously perform the contract. If a party fails to perform or improperly performs the contract, certain losses will be caused to the other party. Accordingly, to ensure the accurate performance of the labor contract, the law provides that anyone in breach of labor contracts must assume the corresponding legal liability. The legal liability for breach of labor contracts means that a party or both parties to the contract fail to perform or improperly perform the labor contract and undertake the legal obligation of compensation due to the economic losses caused to the other party.

## Ⅰ. Legal Liability Undertaken by Employing Units

If an invalid contract is concluded due to the reasons of the employing unit, which causes harm to the laborer, the employing unit must assume the liability for compensation. Article 97 of the Labor Law sets out that where an invalid contract is concluded due to the reasons of the employing unit and causes harm to the laborer, the employing unit must assume the liability for compensation. An invalid contract concluded due to the reasons of the employing unit refers to an invalid labor contract concluded with a laborer by an employing unit intentionally or by mistake which causes harm to the laborer, the employing unit must assume the liability for compensation. Pursuant to the Measures for Compensation in Violation of Labor Contract Provisions of the Labor Law, where an invalid labor contract is concluded due to the reasons of the employing unit, or a partially invalid labor contract is concluded, which causes loss of wage income of the laborer, the wage income to which the laborer is entitled together with compensation at 25% of such wage income should be paid to the laborer.

If the employing unit dissolves a labor contract in violation of the requirements of the Labor Law or willfully delays the conclusion of a labor contract, it must assume legal liability. The employing unit will assume civil liability for illegal dissolution of labor contracts. Article 98 of the Labor Law provides that where an employing unit, in violation of the conditions specified in this Law, terminates labor contracts or deliberately delays the conclusion of labor contracts, the labor administrative department shall order the employing unit to make corrections; where harm has been caused to laborers, the employing unit shall bear the liability for compensation. When a laborer violates the confidential matters agreed in a labor contract, the following prerequisites must be fulfilled for the laborer to undertake legal liability: firstly, both parties have agreed on the confidential matters under the labor contract; secondly, the laborer has performed acts in breach of the confidential matters agreed under the labor contract; thirdly, the facts of damages are available. The three elements must be present. It must be explained that there is a correlation between the acts of the laborer in breach of the confidential matters agreed under the labor contract and the losses caused to the employing unit. The violating acts are the reasons and the losses are the result. Article 5 of the Measures for Compensation in Violation of Labor Contract Provisions of the Labor Law sets out that where a laborer has violated the confidential matters agreed under a labor contract and caused losses to the employing unit, the matter shall be dealt with according to Article 20 of the Anti-unfair Competition Law, which states that if the losses of the infringed business operator are difficult to estimate, the damages shall be the profits derived from the infringement by the infringer during the period of infringement. The infringer shall also bear the reasonable expenses paid by the infringed business operator for investigating the infringer's unfair competition acts violating his lawful rights and interests.

Where an employing unit commits one of the following acts, the labor administrative department shall order it to pay the labor remuneration, give overtime payment or make other financial compensation within a time limit; if the labor remuneration is lower than the local minimum wage rate, it shall pay the difference. If it fails to make such payment at the expiration of the time limit, it shall be ordered to pay an additional compensation to the worker at a rate of not less than 50% but not more than 100% of the amount payable: (1) failing to pay a laborer his labor remuneration on time and in full as stipulated in the labor contract or as prescribed by the State; (2) paying labor remuneration at a rate below the local minimum wage rate; (3) arranging overtime work but giving no overtime payment; or (4) failing to pay the laborer financial compensation pursuant to Article 85 of the Labor Contract Law when dissolving or terminating a labor contract.

Where an employing unit forces a laborer to work by means of violence, threat or illegal restriction of personal freedom, gives instructions in violation of rules and regulations or gives peremptory orders to the laborer to perform hazardous operations, which endanger his personal safety, insults, inflicts corporal punishment, assaults, illegally searches or detains the laborer, working conditions are poor and environmental pollution is serious, which causes serious harm to the physical and mental health of the laborer, administrative punishment must be imposed according to Article 88 of the Labor Contract Law. Where a crime is constituted, criminal liability shall be pursued. Where damages are caused to the laborer, the liability for compensation shall be pursued.

In relation to the illegal criminal acts of an employing unit without the lawful operation qualifications, legal liability shall be pursued according to law. Where the laborer has provided labor services, the employing unit or its capital contribution party shall pay labor remunerations, economic compensation or compensation to the laborer according to the relevant provisions of this Law. Where damages are caused to the laborer, the liability for compensation shall be undertaken. Where an individual contracting business recruits a laborer in violation of the provisions of this Law, and causes damages to the laborer, the contracting party and the individual contracting business operator should undertake joint and several liability.

Where a labor deployment unit violates the provisions of this Law, the labor administrative department and other relevant competent departments shall order rectification. Where the circumstances are serious, punishment of over RMB 1000 but less than RMB 5000 per person shall be imposed, and the industry and commerce administrative department shall revoke the business license. Where damages are caused to the laborer deployed, the labor deployment unit and the employing unit shall undertake joint and several liability.

## II. Legal Liability Undertaken by Laborers

Where a laborer dissolves a labor contract in violation of the Labor Law or the Labor Contract Law and causes economic losses to the employing unit, he shall undertake the liability for compensation according to law. For example, the Labor Contract Regulations of Shandong Province set out that where an employing unit recruits a laborer that has not yet been dissolved a labor contract and causes economic losses to the original employing unit, the laborer shall undertake the liability for compensation and the new employing unit shall undertake joint and several liability. In relation to the compensation for damages by employees, it is different from private law in Germany, its characteristics lie in whether the employer should make compensation for the losses caused by the employee and the extent of compensation. "The prerequisite for the obligation of compensation for losses by employees is firstly the violation of the obligation of the labor contract by the employee which causes losses to the employer. It corresponds to general law on compensation for losses. However, in the Labor Law, there are other conditions on the liability of the employee. It also depends on the extent of losses caused by the employee. The employee will not be responsible for simple (minor) mistakes, the employer will undertake (enterprise) risks on its own. The losses caused by average mistakes are shared by the employee and the employer. The reasons for losses and the overall general consequences of losses must be considered and assessed from the perspectives of equality, reasonableness and the bearing ability. The employee is wholly responsible for serious mistakes in general, if there is no joint liability of the employer (caused by loopholes of organizational management, for example). "①

---

① Clemens Appeal: Federal Germany Labor Contract Law—Legal Foundation, Issues and Experience, German Technical Cooperation and Ministry of Labor and Social Security of China, Joint Collection of Sino-German Labor and Social Law (1996—1999), p. 69.

If a laborer violates the confidentiality obligation as agreed in a labor contract and causes economic losses to the employing unit, he shall undertake the liability for compensation according to law. Article 102 of the Labor Law provides that "where a laborer, in violation of the conditions specified in this Law, terminates the labor contract or violates the confidentiality clauses agreed upon in the labor contract thus causing economic losses to the employing unit, the laborer shall bear the liability for compensation in accordance with the law." Economic losses will generally be interpreted as direct economic losses. Pursuant to the Labor Law, a laborer that illegal dissolves a labor contract carries dual meaning: firstly, the laborer dissolves the labor contract illegally in terms of formalities; secondly, the laborer dissolves the labor contract illegally in terms of substance.

## Section 6　Differences between Labor Contracts and Civil Contracts

### Ⅰ. Contract Dissolution and Dismissal

Article 31 of the Labor Law is a legal provision on dissolution of labor contracts by laborers, which provides that laborers may dissolve labor contracts by informing employing units in writing 30 days in advance. This provision is also Article 37 of the Labor Contract Law, but the condition of 3 days of notice in advance is required for laborers dissolving labor contracts within the probation period. Other conditions remain the same. It is therefore easier for laborers to dissolve labor contracts than employing units. As usual, the Labor Law imposes considerable and stringent restrictions on the dissolution of labor contracts by employing units. Following the principles and provisions of civil law, both parties to a contract have equal rights to dissolve the contract, regardless of prerequisites for applicability or restrictive conditions, there will not be any differences in contract dissolution by the parties in a labor relation.

In relation to the rights of laborers to dissolve labor contracts, since the promulgation of the Labor Law effective as of January 1, 1995 to the present, there are great challenges in practice with undesirable implementation. The relevant departments and professional personnel inadvertently interpret the dissolution right as: laborers may request for the dissolution of labor contracts but employing units may not approve the request. In view of this interpretation, the degrees of difficulty in dissolving labor contracts and civil contracts are equal. To put it another way, two legal departments have adopted the same practice of contract dissolution. ①

In the 90s, the application of Article 31 of the Labor Law gives rise to the case of resignation of Beijing Liulihe Cement Factory head Lu Liang. ② In this case, Lu Liang has informed the employing unit in writing 30 days in advance, but the final judgment is that he cannot dissolve the labor contract. A civil court judge has discussed these cases in detail and thinks that Article 31 is extremely unfair. ③ Its unfairness is shown by imposing more restrictions on employers or employing units for dissolution of labor contracts. Articles 25 to 27, Article 29, Article 32 of the Labor Law all place restrictions on employing units, but it is not necessary for laborers to give any reasons for contract dissolution. However, it is a general labor rule that no reason is required for laborers to tender resignation. There are at least 3 supporting reasons: the first reason is personal freedom. The labor activities of the doer and the personal freedom of the doer are closely related, restriction on labor activities is equal to personal restriction. The second reason is

---

① Unilateral dissolution of labor contracts: commentary on Article 31 of the Labor Law: Article 31 of the Labor Law provides that a laborer who intends to dissolve a labor contract shall inform the employing unit in written form 30 days in advance. In terms of contract law jurisprudence, this provision actually grants the unilateral right of dissolution of labor contracts to laborers. This provision is made in the Labor Law to uphold the right of labor autonomy because most scholars in China believe that laborers take up a weak position in labor relations. However, from civil law theory and judicial practice, this provision is against jurisprudence. (Ma Qiang, *Study on Several Issues on Labor Contracts*, http://www.xianwang.net/mb/ht/10677 _ 4. html, date of access: 2011 - 06 - 26)

② Lu Liang, head of Beijing Liulihe Cement Factory, tendered resignation on November 13, 1995 and tendered another resignation on December 14, the 30-day advance notice as stipulated in Article 31 of the Labor Law, and took up the post of factory head in Beijing Chinefarge Cement Co. Ltd in the afternoon on the same day. Beijing Liulihe Cement Factory applied for arbitration. Beijing Fangshan District Labor Dispute Arbitration Commission held that Lu Liang and Beijing Chinefarge Cement Co. jointly made a compensation of RMB 1. 62 million to Beijing Liulihe Cement Factory. After the mediation of Beijing First Intermediate People's Court, a compensation of RMB 800,000 is required (RMB 760,000 from Beijing Chinefarge Cement Co. and Lu Liang must return to work in Beijing Liulihe Cement Factory together with compensation of RMB 40,000. ) (Xinhua Digest, Issue 1, 1998, p. 193)

③ "The Labor Law unconditionally grants the unilateral contract dissolution right to laborers which undoubtedly recognizes the legality of unilateral contract dissolution by laborers during the subsisting period of labor contracts (notification to employing units 30 days in advance), thereby creating contradiction between legal provisions and contractual agreements. " (Ma Qiang, *Study on Several Issues on Labor Contracts*, http://www.xianwang.net/mb/ht/10677 _ 4. html, date of access: 2011 - 06 - 26) In a strict sense, this provision has created contradiction in civil contracts, with the exception of labor contracts.

that labor activities are a free and basic right and forceful labor activities will only be liable to criminal liability. The third reason is that if the reasons for dissolution of labor contracts by laborers are stipulated by law or laborers are required to provide reasons by law, and the reasons of laborers cannot be substantiated, they will lose the case. However, such a judgment cannot be executed on a mandatory basis because no mandatory measures can be available along with the labor services of laborers. However, from the perspective of civil law, this is genuinely unfair. From the perspective of interpretation theory, Articles 93 and 94 of the Contract Law provide for the circumstances for dissolution of civil contracts by agreement and statutory dissolution of civil contracts. The key issue is that these circumstances apply to both parties without difference. Civil parties are on an equal footing in contract dissolution. Nevertheless, the basic principle of the Labor Law is "employment is easier than dismissal", this is the principle of labor law and the criterion of labor law. The Labor Law aims at protecting the interests of laborers, the only thing it can do is to create a barrier for dismissal, as long as employers cannot locate express legal provisions or express provisions in labor contracts, they cannot dismiss employees. The law prohibits employers from ordering employees to come and go at will, but the law does not impose such a restriction on employees. The supply in excess of demand in the labor market means that it is difficult for laborers to seek and keep a job, but to employing units, the situation is exactly opposite.

The differences in contract dissolution between parties in civil relations and parties in labor relations lie in: firstly, the Labor Law targets at general laborers, it does not focus on white collars such as senior personnel. The Labor Law is originated from the Factory Law, in the early 19th century, industry workers were not white collars. Accordingly, general workers such as assembly line workers, construction workers, mining or shaft workers or textile workers, it is not likely for them to terminate employment. In civil law, the contracting parties are on an equal status, a party will not be restricted by the other party due to hardship, there will not be any pressure due to contract dissolution. However, general workers rely heavily on work to earn a living for the whole family, and they will not dissolve the contract easily. Secondly, in the early implementation of the Labor Law in China, courts and arbitration institutions did request laborers to continue with their performance with labor contracts. Such a ruling will not be made in developed countries because it cannot be executed. Fuller has cited the words of Chief Justice Vaughan in his works, which read "A law which a man cannot obey, nor act according to it, is void and no law; and it is impossible to...

act according to them. "① Certainly, laborers can choose not to work, but it will mean that laborers cannot survive. Accordingly, no law in the world will provide that employers can force laborers to work.

No labor law in the world provides for the reasons for contract dissolution by laborers, thereby providing unequal protection for contract dissolution, which is a sharp contrast to the protection for contract dissolution in civil law. If Article 31 of the Labor Law is interpreted according to civil law, it is unfair. The Labor Law imposes a lot of restrictions on employers and employing units, this difference is obvious. It is obvious because it is labor law, not civil law, and it is not equal value exchange. The value does not correspond in full, and the rights and obligations of both parties are not fully corresponding, "it is precisely because the force of circumstances tends continually to destroy equality that the force of legislation should always tend to its maintenance. "② Contract dissolution in the civil law requires the adherence to the equality principle. In terms of labor law, termination by both parties is not proportional, thereby giving rise to Article 31 of the Labor Law, which is Article 37 of the Labor Contract Law. In theory, we always say laborers are the weak, between the weak and the strong, there is inequality. In terms of inequality, equality protection can only maintain the inequality of the equation. To turn inequality into equality, and to seek justice and fairness, there can only be tilt protection. Karl Larenz has said "if there is no such equality, the legal system must adopt measures to protect the interests of the typically weaker parties by creating a certain balance. "③ Due to equality in their acts, both parties with something added or reduced equivalently still means there is inequality, therefore the weak must be given something extra to make it an equation.

## Ⅱ. Agreement and Prohibition of Liquidated Damages

In the civil law, liquidated damages will be supported by courts in general as long as there is no violation of law or ethics of socialism. However, in the Labor Law, in particular the Labor Contract Law expressly provides that no agreement

---

① [US] Lon Fuller, *The Morality of Law*, translated into Chinese by Zheng Ge, the Commercial Press, 2005 edition, p. 40.

② [France] Jean-Jacques Rousseau, *The Social Contract*, translated into Chinese by He Zhaowu, the Commercial Press, 3rd edition in 2003, p. 67.

③ [Germany] Karl Larenz, *Allgemeiner Teil des Deutschen Bürgerlichen Rechts* Ⅰ, translated into Chinese by Wang Xiaoye, Shao Jiangdong, Cheng Jiangying, Xu Guojian and Xie Huaichi, the Law Press, 2003 edition, p. 70.

should be made on payment of liquidated damages by laborers except in the circumstances of Articles 22 and 23 of the Labor Contract Law. As pointed out by Professor Liang Huixing, "party autonomy does not mean it is not subject to restriction, out of the needs for protecting the interests of laborers, it is necessary for the state to enact special laws to properly restrict party autonomy."[1] Specifically speaking, in addition to the two circumstances set out in the Labor Contract Law, there are no other circumstances in which laborers are in breach of contract. These two circumstances are respectively: firstly, special training clause. Fee payment must also be made for special training, that means a third party invoice must be produced in judicial practice in order to give rise to the issue of liquidated damages specified in Article 22, and the amount is restricted to the training fee actually paid in training. Secondly, non-compete clause. Laborers may only be required to bear the unfavorable consequences of liquidated damages in these two circumstances. In terms of civil law, liquidated damages may apply to various circumstances.

The legislative intent of the Labor Contract Law on the prohibitive clause on liquidated damages is targeted at the excessive and abusive imposition of liquidated damages since the implementation of the Labor Law. In a district in Hebei, laborers are liable to liquidated damages of RMB 1.2 million. Liquidated damages of RMB 2 million are required in some districts, some require RMB 20,000 or RMB 100,000. If liquidated damages are used for performance of labor contracts, or for direct relief of the liability of labor contracts, together with Article 31 of the Labor Law, laborers will not have any problems with contract violation because laborers do not need any reasons for dissolution of labor contracts. Laborers are only required to inform employers in writing 30 days in advance. The legislative intent of the relevant provisions of the Labor Contract Law is to impose restrictions on employers so that laborers will not be liable to liquidated damages, in civil relations, liquidated damages are a form of liability for contract violation. Furthermore, if the law encourages employers to obtain liquidated damages from laborers, the liquidated damages from laborers can only come from the wages of laborers, which are income from the provision of labor services. On top of the income from labor services, laborers do not have other income. Laborers are not employers and they do not obtain profits. In this sense, requiring laborers to pay liquidated damages is the same as reducing or deducting the wages of laborers. Accordingly, in the domain of labor law, labor legislation all over the world

---

① Refer to Liang Huixing, *Civil Law Around You*, the Law Press, 2007 edition, p. 63.

generally negate the practice of liquidated damages to be borne by laborers. "The law forbids us to practise any vice. "①

China's Labor Contract Law provides for two circumstances in which laborers are liable to liquidated damages. One is training fee. From the point of view of Marxism, "In order to modify the human organism, so that it may acquire skill and handiness in a given branch of industry, and become labor-power of a special kind, a special education or training is requisite. "② Regarding social needs and social advancement, attributing training problems to laborers is not fair, there is a well-known saying in the United States: "no education is useless", the ultimate beneficiary of education is the whole society, the society should therefore undertake the responsibility of education and training. In overseas countries, such training will be undertaken by the government through tax reduction and exemption of employers as prescribed by law. Training fees are imposed on employing units according to Chinese laws, but employing units will request laborers to provide services after training is provided, which is a relief to the government by leaving laborers and employing units to deal with training fees and service periods. Anti-unfair competition is even so. In formulating the Labor Contract Law, an international seminar was held in Kunming, Yunnan to discuss the relevant clauses of the draft of the Labor Contract Law. Two renowned labor law experts from the United States and the United Kingdom said in the seminar that it was wrong to prohibit anti-unfair competition in China's Labor Law. Although anti-unfair competition provisions are allowed in overseas legislation, no such provisions can be made in the Labor Law, because the Labor Law aims at protecting the rights and interests of laborers, and anti-unfair competition provisions restrict the rights and interests of laborers. Accordingly, in terms of the legal system, no anti-unfair competition provisions should be made in the Labor Law, in particular the Labor Contract Law. In addition to these two provisions, Article 25 of the Labor Contract Law expressly provides that laborers should not be liable to liquidated damages. Here, it is different from civil law given the differences in standing points and perspectives.

## III. Freedom and Prohibition of Security

Article 9 of the Labor Contract Law on prohibition of security almost did not

---

① Refer to [Ancient Greece] Aristotle, *Nicomachean Ethics*, translated into Chinese by Liao Shenbai, the Commercial Press, 2003 edition, p. 133.

② [Germany] Karl Marx, *Capital* (*Volume 1*), translated into Chinese by the Central Compilation and Translation Bureau, People's Publishing House, 2nd edition in 2004, p. 200.

arouse controversy in the legislative process. However, in practice, especially in courts, there is a great variation in the knowledge of this type of issue. In labor relations, it is a common rule all over the world that provision of security by laborers is prohibited, because labor services and persons are inter-related, with security, detention or collateral, laborers no longer have freedom and employers may therefore restrict the personal rights of laborers. John Locke said, "all mankind...that being all equal and independent, no one ought to harm another in...liberty..."[1] No prohibitive clauses on provision of security are included in the Security Law and the Property Law, as provision of security reflects party autonomy of both parties. The provision of security will not restrict the personal freedom of security providers. In fact, the key lies in the absence of security in personam in civil law.

From the period of June 29, 2007 in which the Labor Contract Law is promulgated to January 1, 2008 in which the Labor Contract Law is enacted, a court in Shanghai made a judgment in August regarding a career change of an air hostess. On November 3, 2003, Yuan Shen, as guarantor of his daughter Lily, confirmed that her daughter had concluded an aviation industry training agreement with China Eastern Airline. Under the agreement, Lily must serve in China Eastern Airline for 8 years, if Lily dissolves the labor contract for personal reasons, she must pay liquidated damages at the standard rate of RMB 20,000 per annum. Lily stopped going to work after August 1, 2006 and both parties dissolved the labor contract on September 25. On September 30, China Eastern Airline applied to Changning District Labor Dispute Arbitration Commission for arbitration and the arbitration ruling required Lily to pay liquidated damages of RMB 130,000 to China Eastern Airline. However, without applying for execution of the arbitration ruling at court, China Eastern Airline sued Yuan Shen, father and guarantor of Lily, at Jingan court on June 14 this year after failing to look for Lily, and requested Yuan to pay RMB 130,300 (including arbitration fee of RMB 300) on behalf of Lily. After two times of court hearings, both parties are willing to settle the case and both parties have agreed on a mediation proposal in a mediation session chaired by the judge. [2] This case, included in the main page of www. chinacourt. org, is in no way problematic in terms of security from the

---

[1]   Refer to John Locke, translated into Chinese by Ye Qifan, Qu Junong, *Second Treatise of Government*, the Commercial Press, 1964 edition, p. 4.

[2]   "China Eastern Airline's air hostess quits job without resignation, father pays $70,000 compensation", http: //finance. ce. cn/law/home/sh/200708/28/t20070828 _ 12535883. shtml, date of access: 2011 − 06 − 26.

perspectives of the Security Law and the Property Law. There is no problem in this case when analyzing it according to contract principles. Both parties have expressed their intentions clearly without the use of force. Nevertheless, from the perspective of the Labor Law, this act is seriously in breach of law. Article 9 of the Labor Contract Law expressly prohibits the provision of security to laborers, and this piece of legislation was promulgated on June 29. Although it has not yet been formally implemented, courts should know very well about the basic principles of this Law, and thoroughly adhere to the prohibitive clause in labor relations. It should be stressed that security in personam is different from security in rem, the security included in the Security Law and the Property Law cannot be applied to security in personam. In the air hostess' case, her father's property is executed, which is not proper. A retiree needs to spend his own savings to make a settlement of her daughter's job with pension funds or wages will not be supported in labor laws of any communities.

In addition, it is not a normal social phenomenon to set up a security company for establishment of labor relations, because security in personam turns humans into a commodity of the security company, the profits of the security company come from the operation of humans, and humans become the business targets of the security company. It is a common sense in the modern society that humans cannot be a business. Prohibition of security in personam is thoroughly pursued in human rights law and basic law, the underlying rationale is that "laborers are not a commodity." Accordingly, security in personam is the provision of security to persons, which is not necessary both in terms of legal theory and legal practice. The approval of the establishment of security companies by industry and commerce registration authorities is an illegal act in itself.

Similarly, no legal theory can clearly justify the propriety of provision of collateral and security by laborers. Two problems will arise when laborers are required to provide collateral and security. Firstly, laborers must borrow money for their labor services (to obtain working opportunities). Laborers must look for money before getting a job. If the money comes from parents, it means the source of money comes from the wages of parents, a deduction of the wages of parents in disguise. The wages of parents eventually go to the hands of employers or employing units. Secondly, if the money comes from security companies, laborers are required to pay money to security companies. The wage income of laborers, income from provision of labor services, will be lost. As a result, the provision of security and collateral will bring losses to the wage income of parents, or laborers are indebted before starting a job, or future income of laborers from labor services will suffer.

These theories have demonstrated the differences in the security theory in civil law. The Security Law and the Property Law involve security in rem, rather than in personam, which does not apply to persons, in particular not apply to laborers who need to establish labor relations. The right of labor services is a natural right or obligation without additional support from other parties, or others' money as a prerequisite for obtaining a job. The Labor Law has never set such a prerequisite, the establishment of labor relations does not allow the addition of such a prerequisite. This is the reason why Article 9 of the Labor Contract Law emphasizes on the prohibition of security and collateral, and also the reason why this clause does not arouse any controversy. However, in the application process at courts, civil courts insist that contracts are above all trial rationales, upholding contracts is the legal point of view of judgment to maintain the legal force of the relevant contract clauses. It is indisputable in general civil cases, but not accepted in labor law domain.

## Ⅳ. Different Consequences of Contract Invalidity

Article 28 of the Labor Contract Law provides that if a labor contract is determined to be invalid but the laborer has performed it, the employing unit shall pay the laborer labor remunerations. It is different from civil law. In civil law, when a contract is determined to be invalid, it will go back to the original state as if nothing has taken place. It is different in labor law because no one can take the output of labor services at no cost regardless of how labor services are performed. The labor relations will be invalid when there is serious violation of law or use of underage workers, however, labor services provided by laborers must be remunerated and employers must make payment. In this regard, valid labor remunerations and rights are generated from invalid labor relations, and employing units must undertake the obligations and responsibilities of wage payment. Even if underage workers are used, the Labor Law still requires employers to pay remunerations to underage workers for the labor services provided, and the labor protection administrative department will order employing units to send underage workers back to their parents or guardians at their original places of residence, the required transportation and accommodation expenses must be borne by employing units in full.

Regarding the relation between an invalid labor contract and wage payment, the Labor Law implements the liability exemption system, in which there is no distinction of the liability of both parties in a labor relation for an invalid contract.

The distinction of liability is not allowed to reduce or harm the liability for payment of labor remunerations by employing units to laborers. There is a marked difference from civil law. In labor law, all labor services are remunerated. The Labor Law never recognizes non-remunerated labor services, because it implies that employers have taken the output of labor services at no cost. This is not allowed in modern society, no employers will be allowed to take the output of labor services of laborers gratuitously in modern society. [1] In civil law, there are many circumstances of non-remuneration, such as helpers, donation, and on loan, or even custody and commissioning.

In terms of the gratuitousness of labor services in the Labor Law, the Labor Law (Draft) of 1983 is worth mentioning. When opinions were solicited, some suggested that voluntary labor work advocated by the government in the Constitution Law should be included. Some feedbacks, however, are useful: if voluntary labor work is included in the Labor Law, there will be a direct conflict with the labor period provision, overtime work restriction and additional payment of overtime wages in the Labor Law. If these feedbacks are rather awkward at the time when state-owned enterprises assume a leading role, they are correct and appropriate under social and economic diversification in China.

The invalidity of labor contracts will not affect the rights and interests of laborers, it will otherwise be vividly reflected in work-related injury compensation. It is not only related to the no-fault principle in work-related injury insurance, but also obviously reflected in the labor law principle that employers should undertake labor risks in any circumstances rather than laborers. These basic principles of the Labor Law are not well-known in theory, but are replaced by the principle of fault liability in practice. For example, Xiao He worked in a manufacturing enterprise and his thumb was injured by a machine tool after he has worked for less than half a month. However, when determining work-related injury, the labor administration discovered that Xiao He did not resemble the photo on his identity document. He is actually Xiao Wang, but he is under 16 years of age and borrowed the identity document of Xiao He for work. The labor administration therefore refused to determine work-related injury, because the main entity of insurance enrolled by the employing unit does not match and no compensation can be made. The labor dispute arbitration commission held that the

---

[1] Rousseau has made a statement: "To say that a man gives himself gratuitously, is to say what is absurd and inconceivable", [France] Jean-Jacques Rousseau, *The Social Contract*, translated into Chinese by He Zhaowu, the Commercial Press, 3rd edition in 2003, p. 11.

employing unit should make compensation to Xiao Wang at half of the standard of work-related injury compensation. Xiao Wang opposed to the decision and initiated legal proceedings and made appeals, both parties eventually reached a mediation agreement in the appeal court that compensation will be made in half as soon as possible. ①

In the process of dealing with this case, the employing unit, the labor and social security bureau, the labor dispute arbitration commission, the court of second instance for first trial or second trial, and even Xiao Wang himself unanimously recognized that Xiao Wang was at fault, and Xiao Wang must undertake the corresponding liability for this fault. In work-related injury insurance where no-fault liability is strictly implemented, Xiao Wang cannot be exempted from liability, and compensation for his thumb lost at work should be made in half. The reasons are still that the labor contract between Xiao Wang and the employing unit is invalid, the social insurance relation between the employing unit and the social insurance institution is invalid, the insurance premiums paid by the employing unit to the social insurance institution for Xiao Wang also disappear. The headline of this typical work-related injury case used by the writer of the article and the feelings expressed by the writer have clearly illustrated this point: "the employing unit has made a big mistake simply because of doubt in the mismatch of employee and photo in labor employment, and made a compensation of more than RMB 100,000. How can we take it lightly and not learn from experience?" In fact, if Xiao He suffered from work-related injury, the employing unit should assume liability and compensation should be made from work-related injury insurance. If the injured party is not Xiao He, the employing unit must still undertake liability for his work-related injury, no matter whether this employee is Xiao He or Xiao Wang, the work-related injury insurance institution cannot be exempted from liability or refuse to make compensation. This is because we cannot find out the reasons for refusal of compensation from work-related injury insurance, nor find out to whom the liability for work-related injury insurance can be transferred after the refusal of compensation. Who has the rights and interests on work-related injury insurance premiums contributed by the employing unit? Even the work-related injury insurance institution cannot find the reasons and basis of improper benefits in law, not to mention that the rights and benefits should belong to the laborer who has lost an organ.

① Zhang Peng, "A big mistake caused by negligence", Xinmin Evening News (Shanghai), 2011 - 06 - 19.

## Ⅴ. Different Intents in the Same Jurisdiction

The legislative intent of civil law is to offer equal protection of the personal and property rights of both parties in a labor relation. There is no favoritism to either party or tilt protection towards the rights and interests of a certain party. Article 1 of the Labor Law provides that "this Law is formulated... in order to protect the lawful rights and interests of laborers. " The statement made in the first three drafts of the Labor Contract Law is basically consistent with the Labor Law, but employers later do not think that this statement merely represents "protect the lawful rights and interests of laborers. " Employers think that "the Labor Law and the Labor Contract Law protect the interests of laborers, who will protect my interests?" The civil law emphasizes on basic principles such as equality of main entities and equal value exchange. From the perspective of the civil law, equal treatment and protection should be given to the interests of both parties instead of the lawful rights and interests of one party. It can be achieved in civil relations, but it is different in labor relations. Hegel has once said, "By alienating the whole of my time, as crystallised in my work, and everything I produced, I would be making into another's property the substance of my being, my universal activity and actuality, my personality... The Athenian slave perhaps had an easier occupation and more intellectual work than is usually the case with our servants, but he was still a slave, because he had alienated to his master the whole range of his activity. "①

The relations between humans are different from the relations between humans and objects, the owners and users in labor relations are not on equal status. In front of employers, laborers are the weak. This is even the consensus of civil law and labor law scholars. ② The Labor Law is separated from the civil law, and the reason for separation is the difference in power, which is attributed to the characteristics of labor power.

The Labor Law is the product of industrial revolution. When land is used to construct factories, peasants will lose their land for cultivation and leasing, only

---

① Refer to [Germany] Georg Wilhelm Friedrich Hegel, *Elements of the Philosophy of Right*, translated into Chinese by Fan Yang and Zhang Qitai, the Commercial Press, 1961, p. 75.

② Professor Wang Liming has applied historical interpretation to illustrate the "legislative intent", Article 1 of the Labor Contract Law. The conclusion is that laborers are the weak and it is necessary to offer tilt protection to laborers. For specific illustration, please refer to Wang Liming, *Introduction to Legal Interpretation-From Perspective of Civil Law*, the Law Press, 2009 edition, pp. 357 – 358.

labor power is left, and they can only earn their living by selling labor power. It is exactly the case that capitalists also require peasants to sell their labor power for building factories. In this regard, Marx illustrated the ensuing process in the *Capital*: before the selling of labor power, both parties are equal. However, this equality also depends on whether you sell your labor power or not and to whom you sell the labor power (in these aspects laborers are free)[1]. However, when both parties meet their minds and labor relations are established, the situation will go worse immediately: "He, who before was the money-owner, now strides in front as capitalist; the possessor of labor-power follows as his laborer. The one with an air of importance, smirking, intent on business; the other, timid and holding back, like one who is bringing his own hide to market and has nothing to expect but—a hiding."[2] The imbalance in labor relations is called politely as "subordinate relation" between laborers and employing units in modern theory. This subordinate relation is presented as constraint or management by employing units on laborers in terms of format and substance, meaning that laborers must be subject to the supervision, guidance, management and deployment of employing units. This theory objectively and truthfully depicts the characteristics of labor relations, which expressly reflect the strong and the weak of the parties in labor relations.

What is worse is the scarcity of job positions since the industrial revolution. It is a common social phenomenon that supply of manpower is in excess of demand. No government can guarantee the full employment of its citizens. Unemployment has long existed and moved along with time. In a modern society, there is a weird situation that the growth in gross domestic product will lead to fewer job positions, because high technology means that fewer laborers are required for original positions or such positions can be phased out altogether. On surface, employment means possession of positions; in substance, employment means possession of social wealth, which is initial distribution of social wealth. Every position requires the back-up of social wealth, because any labor services refer to the combination of livelihood and labor power. They are indispensable, and the former is the prerequisite of the latter. For example, if you want to be a taxi driver, there is at least a taxi. If you want to be a teacher, there should be

---

① Refer to [Germany] Karl Marx, *Capital* (*Volume 1*), translated into Chinese by the Central Compilation and Translation Bureau, People's Publishing House, 2nd edition in 2004, p. 197, p. 204, pp. 821-822.

② Refer to [Germany] Karl Marx, *Capital* (*Volume 1*), translated into Chinese by the Central Compilation and Translation Bureau, People's Publishing House, 2nd edition in 2004, p. 205.

schools, classrooms and students. In a certain period of time, social resources are always limited, which will not be increased following an increase of laborers. Given the scarcity of positions, laborers who cannot get a job will become redundant in society; they will be degenerated from social men to organism. What is more problematic is that labor power cannot be stored, laborers who do not work today cannot work two times tomorrow, the idleness and loss of labor power become an irreversible loss.

When the law adjusts social relations, for the weak party, the legal balance must be appropriately tilted. If both parties have equal power, they will not need the law. If the strong and the weak can be easily distinguished, the strong will not need the law. In society, those who cannot do justice with their own powers, and the weak on whom justice cannot be done will be in genuine need of the law, those who must obtain legal assistance. This is what Hegel described: Injustice is a negation of justice, justice is a negation of injustice, through the negation of a negation, to affirmation. [1] The law represents the law of the weak, reflected in the Labor Law as protection of weak laborers. Certainly, it does not mean that the rights of employing units are not protected. In the whole legal system, the rights of employing units can be protected through the Company Law and the Property Law. From the start, the Labor Law aims at protecting the rights and interests of laborers, and the rights of employers are protected by many other laws.

In the labor domain, it is not necessary to place the rights and interests of employers as well as laborers on the same position, nor implement the so-called "dual protection". There is no need to deal with whether the interests of both parties should be equally protected or whether the rights and interest of laborers should be protected. [2] Otherwise, in the Law of the Protection of Rights and Interests of Women, every right of women means that men should also have the same right. The Law of the Protection of Wild Animals may also provide that animals should have the corresponding rights as humans. By then, legislation will become meaningless. Having said that, from the draft Labor Contract Law to its adoption, the legislative intent of the first draft being "protect the lawful rights and interest of laborers and promote the harmony and stability of labor relations" to the provision adopted being "specify the rights and obligations of both parties to

---

[1] Refer to [Germany] Georg Wilhelm Friedrich Hegel, *Elements of the Philosophy of Right*, translated into Chinese by Fan Yang and Zhang Qitai, the Commercial Press, 1961, pp. 91 – 109.

[2] Refer to Wang Jiaoping, "Underlying the Making of Labor Contract Law", *Workers Daily*, 17 – 11 – 2009.

labor contracts, construct and develop harmonious and stable labor relations and protect the lawful rights and interests of laborers" proves that the other party makes a compromise in the drafting of the Labor Contract Law when the initial legislative intent is to tilt towards laborers. The holding back in the legislative intent is practically manifested in legal provisions. For example, laborers should give 3 days of advance notice for contract dissolution during probation period, the rules and systems of employing units directly relevant to the personal interests of laborers are determined through the equal consultation of the trade union or the employees' representative instead of adopting through discussion by the trade union, the employees' assembly or the employees' representative, even though the authority emphasized that "there is a limited degree of compromise" in the Labor Contract Law. Nevertheless, the initial legislative intent that "as a piece of social law, an objective of the Labor Contract Law is to rectify this problem (author's note: infringement of the rights and interests of laborers)"[1] is not strictly adhered to.

## Ⅵ. Different Rights for the Same Age

The relation between age and rights is reflected in civil law as doers, either at different ages or different age ranges, are entitled to civil rights or enjoy various civil rights. In Labor Law, there is another state for the relation between the employment age of doers and labor rights. In September 2010, Vice Minister of the Ministry of Human Resources and Social Security Wang Xiaochu said in a press briefing that the extension of retirement age is still under study, but later the official said retirement age will not be extended for the time being.[2] Afterwards, Shanghai started the implementation of the flexible retirement age system on October 1, 2010, the retirement ages of men will generally be extended to 65 and women to 60.[3]

In legal practice, there is another view that labor is the right conferred to

---

① Quoted from Wang Jiaoping, "Underlying the Making of Labor Contract Law", *Workers Daily*, 17 - 11 - 2009.

② Zhao Peng, et al. , "MORHSS Vice Minister: extension of retirement age under study", Beijing Times, 11 - 09 - 2010. Bai Tianliang, "MORHSS: no adjustment of retirement age for the time being, only some suggestions on 'extension of retirement age' currently under study, no immediate change of existing policy", Southern Metropolis Daily, 17 - 09 - 2010.

③ "Shanghai soft policy of extension of retirement ages: men 65, women 60", Beijing News, 28 - 09 - 2010.

laborers by the Constitution, therefore laborers have the right to work any time. ①
In theory, this view is problematic because employment age is statutory and legal
in nature, it is not self-determined and of a natural nature. The statutory nature
of employment age covers both the upper and lower limits of employment age.
When the upper and lower limits of employment age are specified in law, it means
that the party beyond the age boundary does not have labor power according to law
(although the party may possess considerable labor power). The lower limit of
the employment age of laborers in China is set out in Article 15 of the Labor Law,
i. e. 16 years old. In reality, not merely citizens reaching the age of 16 have labor
power. In international labor treaty, the minimum employment age of developing
countries is recognized to be 14 years old. We do not lower the employment age
because of the immense employment pressure in China on the one hand, and
linking up the employment age and 9-year free education on the other hand. China
has set the highest employment age at 16 all over the world, which gives rise to
the use of underage workers. As the law sets out the age of 16 as the minimum
employment age, we must understand and follow, regardless of how abundant
labor power doers have before the age of 16.

The same goes for the upper limit of employment age. The legal history of
the upper limit of employment age can only be traced back to the Labor Insurance
Regulations in 1951 in which the retirement ages of men and female are 60 and 55
respectively. Although I, similar to many other people, oppose to this age
requirement, there is such a provision in law and we must understand and follow,
no matter how much labor power doers have after this age. In practice, the direct
consequence of not understanding or following the upper limit of employment age
is the legal ambiguity created by retirees that re-establish labor relations with
employing units. For instance, laborers must be covered by work-related injury

---

① Xia Jixiang, aged 63, was laid off by employing unit and requested for overtime wages and
economic compensation. The labor arbitration department has made a decision of non-acceptance
because Xia Jixiang is beyond the statutory retirement age of 60. Xia Jixiang, feeling helpless, resorts
to lawsuits. Xinjin County People's Court made the first instance judgment that Xia Jixiang and the
logistics company have established a labor relation and held that the logistics company should pay
wages of RMB 2000 for statutory rest days and economic compensation of RMB 2100. Head of
Administrative Tribunal of Xinjin County People's Court Cai Qingli said, according to the relevant
provisions of the existing Labor Contract Law, citizens at the age of 16 or above with labor power have
the right to labor, employing units are not prohibited from employing personnel reaching the statutory
retirement age nor personnel beyond the statutory retirement age are prohibited from labor power.
(Cai Xiaoli, "Economic compensation for dismissal of vehicle guard aged 63", Chengdu Economic
Daily, 21 - 06 - 2008)

insurance at work but retirees cannot enroll in any social insurance policy. Another example is that laborers injured at work should be covered by work-related injury insurance, but retirees cannot enroll in work-related injury, who will undertake the liability for injury? In legal aspect, personnel beyond the upper limit of employment age are people outside the labor force, who are no longer laborers, and employing units cannot employ them any longer. The reasons are: firstly, a normal job position should satisfy the need for employment of a laborer within the statutory employment age. Secondly, the job position and the laborer should make normal contribution to social insurance. That means premiums must be contributed to various social insurance policies and integrated into social insurance funds. By then, the usual cycle of labor relations and social insurance system can be maintained. If a retiree is allowed to take up the job, the job position and the personnel will not make contributions to social insurance premiums but receive social insurance from social insurance funds and enjoy preferential policies of social insurance. In a long term, no source of funding can be contributed to social insurance funds and the social insurance system will be empty. As such, all members of society will suffer. ①

---

### Typical Case
### Legal Force of Labor Contract Concluded with False Certificate

Facts:

In September 2007, Company R decided to employ a business officer for the Communications Section of the Software Business Department due to operational needs. The job requires academic qualification of bachelor's degree or above. Z provided Company R with a bachelor's degree certificate in computer engineering (including graduation certificate and degree certificate which are essential documents to prove his academic qualification), and include the full school name in the "highest qualification" column in the "job application form" of Company R, the specific date of graduation from that school in

---

① In May 1990, I observed a court hearing at Nurnberg Social Court in Germany. The party with suspension of unemployment subsidy sued the Labor Bureau for payment of unemployment subsidy. The Labor Bureau defended with the reason that the person has another job during the unemployment period, but finally lost the case due to insufficient evidence. After the court hearing, I consulted the presiding judge and asked what the outcome would be if the person was proved to have another job during unemployment period. The presiding judge gave a simple answer: the liability for breach of law or even criminal liability of the person would be pursued.

"graduation date", computer in "major" column, and "bachelor" in the "academic qualification" column. Company R decided to employ Z as business officer for the Communications Section of the Software Business Department in view of his academic qualification and work experience. Both parties established labor relations and entered into a labor contract in September 2007. The contract period lasts from September 3, 2007 to September 2, 2010. The contract provides that Company R may dissolve the labor contract if the documents provided by Z are forged or false. In September 2008, Company R performed the formalities for dissolution of labor contract and discovered that there is falsehood in academic qualification. It then verified with the technical university and there is no academic record of Z in the school file. Company R considers that Z has used false academic qualification and resume by fraud, the labor contract of both parties should be invalid, and the fraudulent act of Z has caused loss to Company R and Z should undertake compensation liability.

In August 2008, Company R applied for arbitration to a municipal labor dispute arbitration commission to request for confirmation of the invalidity of the labor contract and order Z to compensate Company R for the loss. The municipal labor dispute arbitration commission did not make a decision within the time limit. Company R then filed a lawsuit with the municipal people's court to request for confirmation of the invalidity of the labor contract and order Z to compensate company R for the loss. The court confirmed that both parties had established a labor relation and entered into a labor contract in November 2006. According to Article 8 of the labor contract, Company R may dissolve the labor contract if the documents provided by Z are forged or false. Z opposed to the judgment of the district people's court and made an appeal to an intermediate people's court. The second instance court also confirmed the facts and considered that according to Article 8 of the Labor Contract Law, Z included false academic qualification in the job application form, his act obviously goes against moral ethics such as faith and creditworthiness, the court made serious criticism against it. Company R said that the enterprise has stated the requirements on academic qualification and relevant work experience when Z applied for the job, but Z failed to provide supporting evidence, therefore Company R should not believe in the claim. Company R interviewed Z and was entitled to verify the truthfulness of personal information of the applicant, but Company R did not exercise this right in a timely manner, accordingly it has to undertake the corresponding consequences. Company R entered into a labor contract with Z after interview, despite the falsehood of academic qualification, his act does not constitute fraud or coercion in a legal sense, therefore the request of Company R for confirmation of the invalidity of the labor contract concluded with Z will not be supported. The first instance court held that the labor contract between Z and Company R is invalid, which is not proper, the second instance court should make another judgment.

Company R opposed to the judgment of the second instance court and applied for re-trial. After examination, the re-trial court held that the appellant entered into a labor contract with the respondent after interview. Although the respondent provided false academic qualification, both parties are deemed to have entered into a labor contract on the basis of voluntariness under the situation that the appellant fails to prove that academic qualification is a decisive factor of employing the respondent. The judgment of the second instance court is not improper and the application of Company R for re-trial should be rejected.

Question:

When a laborer uses false certificate to conclude a labor contract with an employing unit, does the labor contract carry legal force?

Analysis:

(Ⅰ) Truth of "Falsehood"

Entering the labor market on the strength of certificates starts from the reform of the labor use system in China. With the advancement of the labor market following the implementation of the Labor Law, it becomes more common for laborers to enter into labor contracts with employing units by deception. In practice, "false certificates" and "false resumes" become more prevalent. In December 2001, a reporter of Life Times interviewed a foreign-funded company. Liu Ming, Japanese translator, told the reporter that 1/3 of staff in his company hold false certificates. The manager of the company said, having worked as personnel manager for 7 years, 40% of more than 200 persons the company has recruited hold false certificates. [①] In March 2006, Legal Daily published the result of a professional psychological survey conducted by Faculty of Education of Nanjing Normal University on postgraduates of Nanjing higher institutions, which reveals that at least 1/4 of postgraduates do

---

① Chen Tan, "Criticism of the Personnel File System in China", http: //www. chinavalue. net/Article/Archive/2005/5/15/4649. html.

not change their resumes, make falsehood or tend to forge documents.[①] In 2009, Dongguan Academic Assessment Center found over a thousand false documents, including graduation certificates, degree certificates, self-study certificates, adult higher education certificates, involving several hundreds of universities throughout nearly 20 provinces and municipalities in China.[②] The falsehood made by quite a number of laborers not only affects the performance of labor contracts, but also gives rise to arbitrariness of employing units in dealing with false certificates of laborers, thereby leading to variation of labor arbitration and trial institutions in dealing with false certificates of laborers.

A "university student" is employed as the production supervisor of a company in Shenzhen on the strength of false certificates. The company dismissed the employee by the reason of "poor communication skills and incompetent for the job" after discovering the falsehood. However, the "university student" sued to the labor department with the dismissal letter and requested close to RMB 10,000 economic compensation from the company. What is more controversial is, the labor arbitration commission ruled that the dismissed supervisor had won the case, and compensation of RMB 1,665 should be made to the false university student. The director of the company is aggrieved: why compensation is required for dismissal of false university student? The person responsible for arbitration said it is not reasonable but

---

① Zhang Yirong, et al., "Job alert: labor contract rendered invalid with use of false resumes in job seeking", the Legal News, 20 – 03 – 2006. It must be explained that the sub-headlines of the news report are: "refund of remunerations and compensation for loss of employing unit", and in the body of the news, it reads that: "Li Jianfei, deputy director at Labor Law Research Institute of Renmin University of China, said that labor contracts concluded with false resume holders are of course invalid. This will not do any good to the forger, the labor contract that has not yet performed will not be performed, and the labor contract being performed will be terminated immediately. The wages, insurance benefits and common reserve obtained by the forger from the employing unit should be refunded to the employing unit, the household account and file will be returned to the original household and compensation for the loss so arises must be made to the employing unit." However, this is far from what I said in the interview. In particular, "the wages, insurance benefits and common reserve obtained by the forger from the employing unit should be refunded to the employing unit, the household account and file will be returned to the original household and compensation for the loss so arises must be made to the employing unit" is not based on law or contrary to legal provisions and the legislative intent, no matter now or back then.

② "These false certificates are well made with serial numbers and seals, it is difficult to distinguish whether they are real by perception and experience, and those available here are merely inspected by the assessment center recently." Yu Xiaoling: "Thousands of false certificates confiscated in Dongguan", Yangcheng Evening News, 03 – 03 – 2010.

lawful for the false certificate holder to win the case. "This person wins the case by taking advantage of legal loophole". ①

Xia Zhongjun, aged 36, comes from Lanzhou, Gansu. He graduated from Gansu Jiangong middle school. In April 2000, he worked in a pharmaceutical factory in Taizhou, Zhejiang, and was dismissed due to the lack of academic qualification. When he looked for a job in Hangzhou labor market, he experienced repeated failure due to the lack of academic certificates. He saw an advertisement about production of false certificates on an electric pole along West Lake, Hangzhou and spent RMB 400 with two color photos given. On the same day the forger gave him a blank "master's degree certificate" and a blank "postgraduate degree certificate" with photos affixed and printed words inside. The "master's degree certificate" is affixed with the seal of Shenyang Medical University and the "postgraduate degree certificate" is affixed with the seal of Shenyang Pharmaceutical University. As Xia knows there is no Shenyang Medical University, Xia requested the forger to make a change but his request was rejected and Xia can only leave it. With his "master's degree" and "experience" as the head and senior engineer of pharmaceutical quality department of a well-known pharmaceutical group in Northwest for a long time, a high school in Ningbo was interested in him and arranged an interview and trial lecture, and eventually employed him. In late March 2001, Xia Zhongjun reported duty at school. The school offered him the benefits for import of skilled personnel and arranged a flat with two rooms and one dining room to him. He was later appointed as the head of education and research section of the school to teach business management and industrial management courses. The school has repeatedly requested him to transfer his personal file to the school, but Xia made excuses by claiming that the original employing unit did not release the file or further work is required, and he requested for setting up a new personal file. Since he claimed he is a "senior pharmaceutical engineer" in resume, he has to forge another document of employment qualification and spent RMB 200 to make a forged seal of Gansu Department of Personnel in red. Xia passed this document and two false certificates to the school to set up personal file, but the school was in doubt and made a report to the police. Xia was detained by the police for criminal offence because of his suspected forgery of national authority documents, certificates and seals. ②

---

① Chen Wending, et al. , "University student with false certificate dismissed, request for economic compensation of almost ten thousand and win", Southern Metropolis Daily, 08 - 07 - 2002.

② Dong Bishui, "University teaching post obtained with false certificates, false master holder teaches at high school for more than a year", China Youth Daily, 20 - 06 - 2002.

In late November 2004, in the national job fair for senior skilled personnel held in Beijing, Liu Zhigang, a self-study candidate of Peking University, claimed to be a doctoral student of School of Economics, Peking University, and worked as "Assistant Researcher at China Securities Regulatory Commission" and "Telecommunications Planning Consultant at the Ministry of Industry and Information Technology". He was introduced to Zhengzhou Institute of Aeronautical Industry Management as senior skilled personnel, and was given RMB 40,000 for relocation fees, wages and allowances of almost RMB 6,000 and a flat of 120 square meters. Two months later, the Institute found that most information provided by Liu Zhigang is false and immediately reported to the police. Liu admitted that he had produced a false resume, but he insisted that his knowledge had reached the doctoral level of Peking University despite the absence of a school place. In May 2005, the court sentenced the "false doctor" to 3 years and 6 months of imprisonment on the charge of fraud. [1]

Singapore, one of the "four Asian tigers", attaches great importance to higher education qualifications of employees. Those who are graduated from famous universities can get better and senior jobs easily, and the certificates of these schools are frequently forged. In May 2002, Tianjin University received an official letter from the Consulate-General of the Republic of Singapore, stating that there are several cases of false Tianjin University certificates presented for employment in Singapore. After prosecution, the majority of false certificate holders candidly confessed the crime. They were sentenced to 3 months of imprisonment in Singapore and were repatriated to their countries of origin. However, one person refused to admit forgery of certificates and

---

[1] Han Junjie, et al., "Self-study candidate pretending as Peking University doctor with false resume is suspected of fraud", China Youth Daily, 07 - 05 - 2005. "Anyone who produces false certificates will be subject to moral condemnation and undertake liability under the Labor Law, or even subject to criminal sanction. Liu Zhigang was prosecuted because of production of false certificates. It serves as a warning to the abundance of false certificates and resumes." (Zhang Yirong, et al., "Job alert: labor contract rendered invalid with use of false resumes in job seeking", the Legal News, 20 - 03 - 2006) "On this point, extraterritorial experience may worth our attention. The Election Law of Korea expressly provides that: any political party that produces false or fabricates academic qualifications will have his election qualification revoked and be sentenced to less than 5 years of imprisonment. In Germany, false certificate holders will be dealt with as deception with penalty of over EUR1000. In Canada, there is zero tolerance to false certificates, false certificate producers will be subject to legal sanction and the liability of purchasers will also be pursued." ( "Risky to use false certificates", Beijing Daily, 15 - 07 - 2010)

claimed to be a graduate of Tianjin University. In this regard, the Consulate-General hoped that the university can provide evidence and send representatives to Singapore to coordinate with Singaporean court to close this case. Upon receipt of the letter, the Principal of Tianjin University Shan Pingdang signed a written proof and authorization letter and appointed designated personnel to fly to Singapore to assist the court in hearing the case. With the concerted efforts of the court and the school, Z can only accept punishment when faced with strong evidence. ①

In July 2008, Yang made an application to a company and claimed that he graduated from a famous university in Beijing and provided proof of academic qualification, the company employed Yang as head of corporate planning. One year later, Yang was found to have provided false academic qualification and he only graduated from a vocational college. In August of the same year, the company dissolved the labor contract with Yang. Afterwards, Yang applied for arbitration with the labor dispute arbitration commission to request the company to pay economic compensation of RMB 28,000, but the request was rejected by the labor dispute arbitration commission. Yang filed a lawsuit to court but lost the case. ②

In mid-January 2003, Wuhan Jiangxia District Civil Affairs Bureau held an open recruitment of 5 personnel with academic requirement of higher college or above. Among some 120 applicants, the results of written examination and interview of Mei Jing far exceed other candidates and Mei Jing ranks first. However, the examination department of the Civil Affairs Bureau received a letter to report that the higher college certificate used by Mei Jing for this examination is false. Upon receiving the report, Jiangxia District Discipline Inspection Commission and the Personnel Bureau paid a special visit to Wuhan Radio and TV University for certificate verification, which proves that Mei Jing presented a false "Wuhan Radio and TV University Finance and Accounting College" graduation certificate, but the Wuhan Radio and TV University degree graduation certificate provided by Mei Jing is verified to be authentic. Surprisingly, the college diploma provided by Mei Jing for application for admission to the degree program is false. According to provisions, the state will

---

① "False certificate holders sentenced to prison in Singapore", Xinhuanet, 07 – 06 – 2002.

② Qiao Xuehui (Beijing Fengtai district court), "risks unavoidable with false academic qualifications", Beijing Daily, 15 – 07 – 2010.

not recognize the degree certificate so obtained. After this incident, Wuhan Jiangxia District Civil Affairs Bureau was in a great dilemma: should Mei Jing be employed? Will the false certificate incident affect the reputation of the Civil Affairs Bureau? The employment list was scheduled for announcement one week after the completion of examination, but the announcement was further delayed due to "Mei Jing incident". An officer surnamed Liu said no conclusion on "Mei Jing incident" can be made. It is hard to tell whether Mei Jing should be employed. ①

Zhao Peng was assigned to work in a big hotel in Kunming after university graduation in 1997. He was promoted to the head of the Personnel Department one year after. In 1999, he was tasked to recruit a departmental manager. Li Lanfang, a fresh graduate of Renmin University of China, was employed as manager of Entertainment Club after several rounds of shortlisting. Half a year later, they went on a date. In late 2000, they decided to get married in Beijing. After arrival, Zhao found that Li was unfamiliar with Beijing and became skeptical. He asked Li whether she knew Renmin University at the school gate. Li cannot but confess that she had purchased a false certificate in Kunming. Being furious, Zhao Peng did not get married in the millennium and flied back to Kunming on the same day. He told his parents about the false certificate incident, and his father was outrageous because he included in his family tree "first son Zhao Peng married his wife Li Lanfang, graduate of Renmin University of China" and burnt the family tree in front of ancestors. He felt exceptionally disgraceful about the false certificate incident and advised his son to get a "divorce". Zhao also considered that he was involved in the false certificate incident and both of them may be laid off. He felt that even he cannot help himself. ②

(Ⅱ) Six Legal Provisions

A directly relevant provision is first seen in Article 18 (2) of the Labor Law: "labor contracts concluded by means of fraud and threat" are "invalid contracts". This provision was made to combat against the conclusion of labor contracts by employing units with laborers "by means of fraud and threat". For example, in a recruitment advertisement, higher wages and better benefits are

① "Perplexity of false certificate of top candidate", Jianghuai Morning Post, 18 - 01 - 2004.
② "False Renmin University graduate, husband wants a divorce", New Express Daily, 05 -01 - 2001.

claimed to be provided, but when a laborer starts working in an employing unit, it is not the case. At that time, it was extremely rare for laborers to conclude labor contracts with employing units "by means of fraud and threat", therefore laborers are not the target for legislation.

When the Labor Contract Law was drafted, it is common for laborers to use false certificates in the process of job application. The harm caused to labor relations becomes more obvious, which is an issue to be addressed and solved. The Labor Contract Law addresses the problems in practice and adds four legal provisions in limited legal provisions, namely Articles 8, 26, 39 and 86, so as to make specific regulation.

Article 8 of the Labor Contract Law provides that "the employing unit has the right to acquire the basic information of the laborer which is directly related to the labor contract, and the laborer shall truthfully provide the same". The legal intent is that where a laborer truthfully provides personal information, which is the basic ethics every laborer must have and the bottom line in law every laborer must comply for engaging in civil activities. It is also a statutory obligation laborers must perform at the time of job application. Since the law confers legal obligations on laborers, if laborers cannot truthfully provide individual information, causing employing units to convey a wrong meaning, laborers should undertake unfavorable legal consequences, rather than employing units. For employing units, the Labor Contract Law sets out that employing units have the right to acquire the basic information of laborers. Employing units are business entities, rather than government organizations specializing in investigating and confirming the authenticity of the academic qualifications and work experience of laborers. As such, the law only stipulates that employing units have the right to acquire the basic information of laborers, without imposing the obligation of confirming the authenticity of academic qualifications and work experience of laborers on employing units.

From the history of legislation, the obligation of truthful provision of laborers comes from the Insurance Law. The Insurance Law provides for this principle because of people. In insurance, in particular personal insurance, the dominant principle of truthfulness and creditworthiness in civil law has modified the utmost good faith principle. Considering that the insured has the best knowledge of his health conditions, the insurer requests the insured to follow the utmost good faith principle at the time of taking out insurance policy, that is, faithfully state his health conditions to the insurer or the insured will undertake the legal consequences of invalidity or dissolution of insurance contracts. This history also reflects the necessity and certainty of undertaking the relevant obligation by laborers.

On the basis of Article 18 (2) of the Labor Law, Article 26 (1) of the Labor Contract Law adds the condition of "conclusion or modification of the labor contract against the truthful meaning of the other party". Where a laborer provides false certificates to an employing unit to make falsehood, or distort or cover up the truth, thereby the employing unit concludes a labor contract with the laborer due to erroneous knowledge, the contract should not carry any effect.

Article 39 of the Labor Contract Law corresponds to Article 25 of the Labor Law, that means the dissolution of labor contract by the employing unit due to the mistake of the laborer is the most stringent situation regarding dissolution of labor contract, which is a punitive clause on the impropriety of laborers. In Article 39, " (5) invalidating the labor contract as a result of the circumstances specified in the first paragraph of Article 26 of this Law" is an added clause in the Labor Contract Law corresponding to the Labor Law to confer the right to employing units to dissolve labor contracts. This is not only a dual negation of such act by laborers in legislation, but also clearly state that employing units can deal with such act at various times. Since the law confers legal rights to employing units ( rather than obligations that must be performed), there is no limit on the time of exercising such right, employing units can decide on whether to exercise and when to exercise such rights, and not assume the unfavorable legal consequences arising from the illegal acts of non-performance of legal obligations. In this regard, the court's requirement that " the company is entitled to verify the truthfulness of the personal information of job applicants, failure to do so in a timely manner will lead to unfavorable consequences" is obviously added legal language, in which the legal "right" of the employing unit becomes a legal "obligation", attributing the legal liability arising from the illegal act of the laborer due to non-performance of legal obligation to the employing unit erroneously, thereby the employing unit assumes legal liability without legal basis.

Article 86 of the Labor Contract Law sets out the legal liability for Article 26 of the same law, which specifies that after confirmation of the invalidity of the labor contract, "harm is caused to the other party, the erroneous party shall undertake the liability for compensation". The two legislative intents should be reflected in judicial trials, the first legislative intent is that the legal consequence of such act is the "invalidity" of the labor contract, rather than "the court makes strong criticism against it". It is because China's law does not require laborers to be liable for the legal consequences of providing false academic qualifications and other information means that "the court makes strong criticism against it". Such judgment is identical to turning an illegal act prescribed by law into a general ethical problem not legally liable. The second legislative intent is that laborers providing false certificates to employing units may undertake the liability for compensation. It is also rare in labor legislation that laborers undertake legal liability, in particular in the circumstances of the liability for compensation, which is an added legal liability in the Labor Contract Law. The added provision of the Labor Contract Law has changed the unilateral liability of Article 97 of the Labor Law, which states that "where invalid contracts are concluded due to the reasons of the employing unit that cause harm to the laborer, the employing unit shall undertake the liability for compensation" into mutual liability. Before that, no matter whether the Labor Law or the Measures for the Compensation for Violation of the Relevant Provisions of Labor Contracts in the Labor Law promulgated by the former Ministry of Labor only provide that the employing unit should undertake the liability for compensation where an invalid labor contract is concluded due to the reasons of the employing unit which causes harm to the laborer, together with different compensation standards. Paragraph Two of Article 14 of the Interpretation of the Supreme People's Court on Certain Issues Concerning the Application of Law in Trying Cases Involving Labor Disputes is ancillary to this: "In accordance with the provisions of Article 97 of the Labor Law, where an invalid contract is concluded due to reasons attributable to the employer, causing harm to the laborer, the employer shall compensate the laborer for his/her economic loss caused by contract invalidity by reference to the payment standard for the economic compensation for dissolution of a labor contract".

The Implementing Regulations for the Labor Contract Law, which are subsequently promulgated and implemented, also specify in Article 19 a situation for dissolution of the labor contract with the laborer by the employing unit that "(6) The employee forces the employer to conclude or modify the labor contract against the employer's true will by means of deception, coercion or taking advantage of the employer's difficulties", thereby further specifying and detailing the relevant clauses and contents of "fraud" in the Labor Contract

Law.

### (Ⅲ) "Fraud" in Labor Relations

Article 68 of the Draft Opinion on Several Issues Concerning the Thorough Implementation of the General Principles of the Civil Law of the People's Republic of China of the Supreme People's Court provides that: "where a party willfully inform the other party of falsehood, or willfully conceals the facts to induce the other party to convey a wrong meaning, it can be recognized as fraudulent act". There are different meanings, natures and characteristics of "fraud" in different domains. ① For example, in criminal offences, "fraud" is money cheating and cheating in love, while in the civil domain, "fraud" is goods and payment obtained by cheating.

In labor relations, "fraud" means a party in a labor relation provides false information to the other party which affects the other party to judge the quality and working ability of the laborer or the working environment and labor remunerations in the process of contract conclusion. Information exchange between both parties to a labor contract in the process of contract conclusion is the most important stage of the whole process of labor contract conclusion. In this process, if a party gives false information to the other party, and such information directly affects the basic information for labor contract conclusion, the act of the party providing false information is undoubtedly a fraudulent act of labor contract of the most typical and serious type.

Fraudulent acts in labor relations have self characteristics different from characteristics of common civil frauds, namely: (1) for employing units, academic qualifications and resumes are used to decide the basic quality and working ability of laborers, which are the most important basic information directly affecting whether a labor contract is concluded; (2) once laborers provide false basic information in relation to labor employment to employing units, a fraudulent act is established. Where a labor contract is concluded on the basis of such false basic information, the aim of the fraudulent act is

---

① To Hegel, "fraud" is an act in between "unintentional wrong" and "crime", which means that the doer commits a wrong act in the disguise of right. He believed that fraud means that the doer intentionally commits wrong in the disguise of right to reach his own aim. "In fraud universal right is abused, but the particular will is respected. The person on whom the fraud is committed, is imposed upon and made to believe that he gets his rights. The right, which is demanded, however, is merely subjective and unreal, and in that consists the fraud". "But to fraud penalties are due, since right is violated". (Georg Wilhelm Friedrich Hegel, *Elements of the Philosophy of Right*, translated into Chinese by Fan Yang, et al., the Commercial Press, 1982, pp. 94 – 95) Refer to Li Jianfei, Brief Analysis on the "Wrong Theory" of Hegel, *Foreign Legal Study*, Issue 3 of 1986.

achieved. ①

In this case, in the process of concluding the labor contract, Z willfully provides false academic qualifications to Company R, causing Company R to wrongly believe that Z has the corresponding basic quality and working ability, thereby concluding a high pay labor contract with Z. The act of providing false academic qualifications by Z constitutes a fraudulent act in law. Because of this fraudulent act of Z, Company R was induced to make a wrong decision to conclude a labor contract with Z. Company R, without knowledge of the false academic qualifications of the applicant, was misled in making judgment of the basic quality and working quality of the applicant, and the labor contract was wrongly concluded without knowledge of the true circumstances. Accordingly, the labor contract between Company R and Z was different from what was described by the second instance court as "voluntariness" of Company R. On the contrary, this is the outcome of the fraudulent act of Z, which is a strong evidence for the fraudulent act of Z. If the "voluntariness" in the second instance judgment is established, that means the act of the doer after being deceived can be assumed as "voluntary" act in law, fraudulent acts will then become legal, the person committing a fraudulent act will not be able to commit a crime as defined by legal provisions. It is obviously not the intent of law, nor the social impacts as expected by law.

The recognition of the court that "the academic qualification provided by Z is not true, but his act does not constitute fraud or threat in law", which comes from insufficient knowledge of the constitution, nature and characteristics of "fraudulent" acts in the labor employment domain, and also the erroneous

---

① In Germany, the provisions on invalid labor contracts are set out in the Civil Code, which also apply to the general principles of civil law. To protect the freedom of the party in the expression of meaning, the meaning conveyed out of fraud can be withdrawn. The withdrawal of meaning out of fraud must consist of the following elements: firstly, the fraudulent act must exist. Fraudulent act is an act to create, intensify or uphold erroneous knowledge of other party. Secondly, there is a co-relation between a fraudulent act and the expression of meaning. Thirdly, fraud is illegal. Fourthly, fraud is malicious. At interviews, the employer has the enquiry right. Upon enquiry, the candidate should make disclosure, it is reasonable that the employer is interested in the candidate if his reply is relevant to the work required. "If the applicant does not give a correct answer to reasonable questions, the employer has the right to dissolve the labor relation or dissolve the labor contract on the grounds of willful deception". Unusual dismissal mainly lies in acts and trust. "There must be serious errors in which the trust of the employer is destroyed to affect the usual existence of the labor relation". Clemens Appeal: Federal Germany Labor Contract Law—Legal Foundation, Issues and Experience, German Technical Cooperation and Ministry of Labor and Social Security of China, Joint Collection of Sino-German Labor and Social Law (1996 - 1999), pp. 61, 71.

application of prevailing legal provisions on the other hand. This error is presented by mixing up "fraud" and "threat", which are two different concepts in terms of statutory contents and legal liability. These two illegal acts and two separate legal liabilities are mixed into one. In view of the relevant provisions of the current labor laws in China, the act of Z is a typical fraudulent act in labor contract. Z should not only be liable to the legal consequence prescribed in law-automatic invalidity of the labor contract, but also compensate for the loss of the applicant according to Article 86 of the Labor Contract Law.

(Ⅳ) "Interviews" during Recruitment

The court held that "Company R interviewed Z and was entitled to verify the truthfulness of personal information of the applicant, but Company R did not exercise this right in a timely manner, accordingly it has to undertake the corresponding consequences".

Interviews at the time of establishing a labor relation can be broadly categorized as the rule of "face-to-face inspection of goods" in barter trade. The practice of undertaking the consequences of interview by the employing unit is equivalent to undertaking the liability of defects by the purchaser after the delivery of goods. Those who uphold this claim think that the job applicant is present in front of you and you are fine with the applicant, the employer or employing unit cannot query the real status of the job applicant, or it should undertake the liability for losing the lawsuit.

Face-to-face inspection of goods relies on the rule of "payment on delivery of goods" in barter trade. The payment of goods can prevent commercial dishonesty such as forgery, swindling, contractual fraud, etc. This rule cannot adapt to the modern society due to the cost of trade and difficulty in trade, which is also inappropriate for application to solve labor disputes because goods are different from humans. Goods are static but humans are dynamic, and the nature of goods can be seen but human ability is not. The use value of goods depends on the nature and the use value of humans depends on the ability.

Let's talk about goods first. Even in the trade of goods, there is a dilemma in face-to-face inspection of goods. I have experienced a real case in which face-to-face inspection of goods is made but the goods are not real. A non-domestic merchant leased a place in Beijing to operate a restaurant. The lease contract specified the floor area of the place rented. The tenant purchased a dining table according to the floor area stated in the contract, but the dining table cannot be moved into the place, because the actual floor area of the place leased is less than the floor area stated in the contract. The lessee applied for legal relief, and the judge held that: both parties have seen the place at the time of concluding the lease contract, even though the actual floor area of the place is less than the floor area stated in the contract, the lessee can only undertake the liability for losing the lawsuit. What I wish to challenge this judgment is: what is the basis for this judgment? The fact in "factual basis" is the true fact of the objective world, or the false fact wrongly recognized by people in the objective world? The justice upheld by law is true justice, or justice changing people by people? There is only one fact of the objective world, that is the actual floor area of the place. When the law upholds the false floor area in violation of contract, the false floor area is used to replace the real floor area, is it a reflection of justice in social life?[1]

Let us turn to humans. The major difference in the functions of humans and functions of goods is that measurement cannot be made from appearance. Accordingly, "education level" is valued by the employing unit, and "good match in social and economic status" becomes the only rule of spouse selection. If a person uses false certificates to deceive an employing or employing unit, which has no way to immediately distinguish whether the certificates are real, or look into the true self of the candidate. However, the Chinese stresses on "assessment of real ability", and the social world upholds "guarantee of truth". When a false certificate holder reveals his true self at work, thereby the employer or employing unit traces the source of certificate and confirms that the certificate is false, the employer cannot return or replace the employee, and no deduction of wages, change of job position or lay off is allowed. Otherwise, the false certificate holder will file a case at court, and the employer has to make compensation on reputation and various economic losses.

From modern people, I think of ancient people. I think of the adorable learnt man and feel pity for his life. If he could live up to the present era, even if the king intentionally criticized him, he could have stayed completely clam when his failure was marked in historical records. The reason is that the

---

① When a purchaser has acknowledged the defects of the subject matter and still makes the purchase, this is a willful decision subjectively, it is not necessary to offer protection in law. A scholar said: "In relation to known defects of the subject matter, two points should be noted, firstly, it must be specifically known without doubt. Secondly, it refers to knowledge at the time of contract conclusion, but not at a later time." Guo Mingrui, et al., *New Discussions on Specific Provisions of the Contract Law*, China University of Political Science and Law Press, 1997, p. 21.

adorable learnt man was interviewed by the father of the king and had been working for many years. ①

(Ⅴ) "Truth if not Questioned"

The court held that: "Under the condition that Company R cannot provide evidence to prove that academic qualifications and work experience are the decisive criteria for recruiting Z, the court confirmed that Company R had concluded a labor contract with Z on the basis of voluntariness, such contract does not belong to the invalid contract prescribed in the Labor Law and the Labor Contract Law". This can be said to be "truth if not questioned" in recruitment. It means that whether the labor relation formed through false certificates provided by a job applicant is valid, whether the employing unit can obtain the dismissal right and win the lawsuit does not lie in the false certificates, but whether the employing unit has requested the job applicant to provide proof of academic qualifications. If so, the false certificate holder will lose the case. The retrial ruling has stated this meaning more clearly: "although the academic qualifications provided by the applicant are not true, under the condition that the applicant for retrial cannot provide evidence to prove that academic qualifications and work experiences are the decisive criteria for recruiting the applicant, it shall be deemed that both parties have concluded a labor contract on the basis of voluntariness". After a second thought, I still cannot figure out the rationale for this view.

No request cannot be a reason for fraud. The reason is that when the employing unit does not request for proof of academic qualifications of the job applicant, the wrong doing of the false certificate holder seems to go against legislative intent, which cannot be proved in formal logic.

The focus of the question originally lies in whether the certificate is false. If so, the job applicant must undertake the legal liability for providing false certificates. This may either be a criminal or civil liability. In a labor dispute, the extinction of a labor relation arising from false certificates is the basic legal consequence, which is the bottom line of legal liability undertaken by a job applicant. His act is independent, self-initiated and irrelevant to others or his employing unit (the employing unit is a victim of his act). The employing unit did not request for proof of academic qualifications and certificates at recruitment, which logically creates a reason for impunity of academic qualifications

---

① Refer to Han Fei Zi: Inner Congeries of Sayings, the Upper Series.

and certificates of the job applicant during job application. During job application, the job applicant may not be required to explain his academic qualifications, and later provide the certificates as proof. It is impossible to justify the legality of the provision of false certificates by the job applicant, and it is even impossible that the illegal act of the job applicant is not legally liable. The labor relation established on the basis of illegal facts will become legally justified through the judicial system.

Secondly, active falsehood is worse than passive falsehood. A job applicant that provides false certificates at the request of an employing unit is passive falsehood, while a job applicant that provides false certificates without the request of an employing unit is active falsehood. The same behavior reflects different subjective attitudes, and the subjective attitude of the latter is worse than the former, which means the latter behavior is even worse, and should be negated legally. When a job applicant is requested to provide certificates, they provide false certificates even though they know they should not do so. To a certain extent, they have no way but to provide false certificates. In active falsehood, the job applicant is skillful in producing falsehood, getting a job without falsehood seems to violate his principle, which shows disrespect to his intelligence. If the law gives different treatment, does it mean that the law aids evil act?

A simple principle is that even though the employing unit does not make any request to the job applicant in the process of recruitment, the sole basis for the decision on employing the job applicant is the academic qualifications and work experience stated by the job applicant, and the judgment made by the employing unit on whether the academic qualifications and work experience are useful. In this regard, whether Company R provides evidence of requirements on academic qualifications for employment does not carry substantive legal significance and impacts on deciding this case, neither does it constitute the decisive condition for recruitment of Z. Following the logic of the second instance judgment, if the employing unit cannot provide evidence of requirements on academic qualifications for employment, the laborer can provide false academic qualifications and work experience at will, and enter into the labor contract "legally". Afterwards, the laborer will not be subject to legal liability but under legal protection. In addition, the legal consequences of providing false academic qualifications and work experience by the applicant will wholly be transferred to the employing unit in terms of legal liability and consequences. This "logic" does not make sense at all.

- 
- 
- 
- 
- Chapter Ⅵ

# Labor Conditions Law

Employers hiring laborers to work have to provide necessary labor conditions for laborers, not only out of the needs to protect the physical and mental health of laborers, but also the needs of social reproduction, or generally speaking, out of the needs of the progress of human civilization. With the development of the society, it is a global trend to gradually improve the labor conditions of laborers in the development of labor legislation.

This chapter focuses on labor remuneration, rest and vacation, elaborating the provisions of China's labor law on labor conditions.

## Section 1　Concepts and Legal Principles of Labor Remuneration

### Ⅰ. Basic Concept of Labor Remuneration

( Ⅰ ) The Basic Concept of Labor Remuneration

Labor remuneration, which we usually refer to as wages, can be interpreted in both broad and narrow sense. In a broad sense, wages refer to monetary income or valuables received by people for engaging in various types of labor services. It includes all incomes of civil servants and also the income of individual citizens from a variety of labor services including contracted processing, commission/consignment, transportation and invitation of contributions. In a narrow sense, wages ( also known as " salary", " earnings", " remuneration", " payment") specifically refer to various labor incomes obtained by laborers based on labor relations as regulated by the Labor Law, which includes hourly wages, piece-rate wages, bonuses, allowances and subsidies, wages for extended working period and wages paid under special circumstances, etc. The labor remuneration discussed hereunder refers to wages of the latter meaning. ①

Laborers with a proper job receive salaries from their working units every month. The difference is that wages vary in amount. Wages prescribed in the Labor Law carry normative connotation and denotation. Wages refer to all the remuneration obtained by laborers from the working units for the provision of labor services, including basic salaries in various forms, bonuses, allowances, subsidies, overtime wages and wages paid under special circumstances by employers, excluding insurance benefits paid to laborers and other non-labor income.

In the context of the labor law, wages include the statutory minimum wage and the wages negotiated and agreed upon by both parties in labor relations, which are referred to as "general wages". The Protection of Wages Convention enacted by ILO (International Labor Organization) in 1949 and the Proposals concerning the protection of general wages of laborers. The term "wages" referred in the Convention means remuneration or earnings, however designated or calculated, capable of being expressed in terms of money and fixed by mutual agreement or by national laws or regulations, which are payable in virtue of a written or unwritten contract of employment by an employer to an employed person for work done or to be done or for services rendered or to be rendered. Article 23 of the Universal Declaration of Human Rights prescribes that: "Everyone who works has the right to just and favorable remuneration ensuring for himself and his family an existence worthy of human dignity." The International Covenant on Economic, Social and Cultural Rights also calls for "remuneration which provides all workers, as a minimum, with: (1) fair wages and equal remuneration for work of equal value without distinction of any kind; (2) a decent living for themselves and their families". The European Social Charter provides that States Parties shall undertake that "all workers have the right to a fair remuneration sufficient for a decent standard of living for themselves and their families".

( Ⅱ ) Composition of Labor Remuneration

In China, labor remuneration for laborers mainly includes, in terms of composition, hourly wages and piece-rate wages; the supplementary forms of wages are mainly bonuses and allowances.

---

① In Article 11 of Japan's Labor Standard Law, wages are defined as: wages are a variety of expenditure paid by employers for remuneration of employees' work, whether they are called wages/ salaries, or allowances/bonuses, or any other names. The South Korean Supreme Court's precedent determines that wages are all the remunerations paid by designated users for labor use.

(1) Hourly wages. Hourly wages are defined as the labor remuneration paid to individuals based on standard hourly wages and working hours, including wages paid for work completed based on hourly working standards, basic salary plus duty wages or post wages paid to employees by units with the implementation of structural wage system, internship wages for newly workers and athletes' subsidies for physical training. In terms of the differences in time units adopted for the calculation of wages, hourly wages can be divided into monthly wage system, daily wage system and hourly wage system. The advantage of hourly wages lies in its simplicity and feasibility, i. e. hourly wages can be applicable to any businesses and types of jobs; the drawback lies in the use of working time as the basis for wage calculation, in which the remuneration cannot be adequately linked with the quantity and quality of labor services.

(2) Piece-rate wages. Piece-rate wages refer to the labor remuneration for completed work paid at piece rate, including wages paid to individuals in accordance with the quota or piece rate approved by the labor authorities or the competent authorities under the wage system of either excess progressive piece rate, direct infinite piece rate, quota piece rate, excess piece rate, or any other piece rates; wages paid to individuals by way of lump sum assignment; wages paid to individuals in the form of turnover commission or profit commission. They are wages based on the fruits of labor services within a certain period of time, calculated according to the indirect labor period; therefore, they are the transformation of hourly wages. The advantage of piece-rate wages lies in its ability to directly link the fruits of labor services with labor remuneration so as to better reflect the principle of distribution according to work. The drawback is that quality can be easily overlooked because of the pursuit of quantity, and sometimes safety in production can be jeopardized due to the same reason.

(3) Bonus. Bonus refers to the payment for additional labor remuneration paid to employees or the labor remuneration paid out of increased revenue and reduced expenditure. Bonus is additional labor remuneration and is a supplementary form of hourly wages. Bonus is paid according to the additional labor services provided by laborers, and is a reward for the outstanding performance of laborers. Bonus carries significant meaning in mobilizing workers' enthusiasm for production and better reflecting the principle of distribution according to work.

There are many different types of bonuses, mostly in the following forms: 1) Overfulfilling Award, calculated and paid according to the amount of additional labor services performed. 2) Quality Award, adopting the product quality pass

rate as the evaluation standard under the premise of the completion of production.
3）Conservation Award, calculated and paid according to the amount of
conservation of raw materials and fuel consumption under the premise of the
completion of production tasks. 4）Safety Production Award, awarded according
to the status of safety in production under the premise of the completion of
production tasks. The production award, conservation award, labor competition
award and the incentive payment and other bonuses of authorities, organs and
institutions all fall into this category.

（4）Allowances and subsidies. Allowances and subsidies refer to allowances
paid to workers for special or additional labor consumption or payments for any
other special reasons, or price subsidies paid to employees so as to ensure that
their wage levels are not affected by prices of goods. Various allowances can be
divided into the following categories: allowances for the compensation of the labor
consumption of workers under the special working conditions and any extra labor
consumption of workers, including mine and underground allowance, high
temperature allowance, field construction allowance, etc.; allowances for the
compensation of special labor consumption and additional living expenses of
workers, including forest benefits, mountain region allowances, island subsidies,
hardship allowances at meteorological observatories and stations, etc.; allowances
designed for special health care requirements, including health care benefits,
medical and health subsidies, etc.

（5）Overtime wages. Overtime wages refer to wages paid as required for
extra shifts and hours.

（6）Wages paid under special circumstances, including wages paid, in
accordance with the provisions of national laws, regulations and policies, based on
a certain ratio of hourly wages or piece-rate wages as well as any additional wages
and reservation wages due to illness, work-related injury, maternity leave, family
planning leave, wedding or funeral leave, casual leave, family leave, regular
leave, off-duty study, performance of national or social obligations and other
reasons.

（7）Wages paid for part-time employment. Employers shall pay part-time
workers the full amount of the wages in a timely manner. Hourly wages paid to
part-time workers shall not be less than the minimum hourly wage standards
enacted by local governments. Wages of part-time employment can be paid by
hour, day, week or month.

The following labor incomes of workers do not fall within the scope of labor
remuneration:

(1) Insurance and welfare costs. These refer to various labor insurance and welfare costs actually paid by working units to all the individual employees other than the total wages, including: funeral pension relief fund, hardship allowance, various non-wage subsidies (such as commuting expense subsidies, personal hygiene fees, child care subsidies, family planning subsidies, winter heating subsidies and sunstroke prevention fees) and the medical fees directly paid to individual workers of units with the implementation of public health system reform.

(2) Cost of labor protection. It refers to health food products, fees for antidotes, soft drinks and summer time cold drinks that workers get from the working units paid from labor protection expenses.

(3) Various types of labor remuneration not included in the total wages as required, including: Invention Award, National Spark Award, Natural Science Award, Scientific and Technological Advancement Award, Rationalization Proposal and Technical Innovation Award, and ranking awards, sports level awards and record-breaking awards paid to athletes, and the training achievement award of coaches, royalties, translation fees, lecture fees, project fees, income from a second job, part-time income, and for units organizing employees to engage in production, consulting services, scientific research, design and other activities in their spare time, cash and in-kind benefits paid to employees from the income received, and the commission paid to individual employees out of the income on rebates, rewards for go-between and handling fees collected from business dealings among units, etc.

(4) In-kind money. It refers to various in-kind payments not included in total wages and insurance benefits as required which individual workers get from both in and outside the units.

(5) Income from property, including the interest on deposits, debenture interest, stock dividends and share capital dividends which individual workers obtained from banks and enterprises.

(6) Transferred income, including the income employees obtained as a gift from people of strata other than that of the employees, meal sharing fees of relatives, estate income, and compensations obtained from accidents and donation income from non-profit organizations due to disasters, etc.

(7) Others. Refers to cash income workers receive other than the items mentioned above, including the risk compensation income for lessees of leasing business units, workers' subsidies for meals and dress allowance for overseas business trips and workers' net cash balances from travel grants and travelling

expenses and settling-in allowances in cases of job transfers.

## Ⅱ. Chinese Legal Principles of Labor Remuneration

Article 46 of Labor Law provides that: "Wages shall be distributed on the basis of work and under the principle of equal pay for equal work. Wage level shall be raised gradually on the basis of economic development. The State shall conduct macro-control of total wages." This is the basic principle of China's legal regulation of labor remuneration.

### (Ⅰ) The Principle of Distribution according to Work

Distribution according to work is defined as distribution of individual consumables according to the quantity and quality of labor services provided by laborers. Equal labor services shall be awarded equal pay. More pay for more work, less pay for less work. He who does not work shall not eat. Each laborer shall, according to the amount of labor provided by him, receive consumables of such amount equivalent to the amount of labor he provided.

The principle of distribution according to work is determined by public ownership of the means of production under socialism, and is the concrete realization of the laborers' ownership of the means of production under the system of public ownership. In a society of public ownership of the means of production, every laborer shall have equal rights and obligations of labor participation, and shall try their best to work for the society. The society shall, taking labor services as standard, upon the completion of various social deductions, distribute income according to the quantity and quality of labor provided by laborers. More pay for more work, less pay for less work.

Distribution according to work must fully reflect the differences between mental and physical labor, complicated and simple labor, skilled and unskilled labor, heavy and non-burdensome labor, and also reflect the principle of "reward the diligent and punish the lazy" and "reward the good and punish the bad", and in the meantime shall oppose both egalitarianism and the practice of unfair distribution and too much income disparity. It should be noted that, in a system of socialist market economy, distribution according to work is not and cannot be of the kind envisaged by the Marxist classical writers where the means of production belong to a society with no commodity and currency, and distribution is conducted directly within the scope of the whole society on the basis of labor. In a system of socialist market economy where the public ownership of the means of production plays the dominant role and co-exists with various forms of ownership, the market mechanism plays a fundamental role in the allocation of resources, which determines that the scope and form of realization of distribution according to work are bound to change to some extent. The dominant position of public ownership determines the dominant position of the principle of distribution according to work. The co-existence of diverse forms of ownership rules out the possibility of implementing a single principle of distribution according to work and justifies the existence of a variety of other forms of distribution. The basic role of the market mechanism determines that distribution according to work cannot be directly implemented within the scope of the whole society, but only within the enterprises. Distribution of wages shall follow the principle of distribution according to work, which also provides for the principle of the internal distribution of wages to be observed within the enterprises. This provision is the concrete manifestation of the dominant position of distribution according to work as well as the basic component of the distribution system where distribution according to work plays a dominant role and co-exists with a variety of distribution modes. It does not exclude the existence of interest, dividends, risk compensation, employment income and other forms of distribution as a supplement to distribution according to work. These forms of distribution shall, as long as they are legitimate, be allowed to exist and shall be protected.

( Ⅱ ) The Principle of Equal Remuneration for Equal Work

Equal pay for equal work means that employers shall pay equal amount of labor remuneration for labor of equal value of all employees. In the same deployment unit, laborers engaged in the same kind of work and with the same level of proficiency shall, regardless of gender, age, ethnicity and race, receive remuneration of the same value as long as they provide labor of the same value.

The ILO mentioned in its Constitution in 1919: "Men and women shall receive equal remuneration for work of equal value." The "recognition of the principle of equal remuneration for work of equal value" is also included in the preamble of the Constitution revised in 1949. The Convention concerning Equal Remuneration for Men and Women Workers for Work of Equal Value adopted in 1951 provides that labor of equal value of all labor forces, namely male labor force and female labor force, shall be awarded remuneration of the same value. This principle applies to all basic wages and other forms of income either in cash or in kind which are directly or indirectly paid by employers to laborers due to employment relations. "Equal remuneration for both genders for work of equal value" means remuneration rate is not differentiated by gender. The Convention also suggests that this principle may be applied by the following means: national laws or regulations, legally established or recognized machinery for wage determination, collective agreements or a combination of the aforementioned means. It also points out the measures to be taken by the government in exercising direct or indirect supervision, and the methods to promote the application of the principle of equal remuneration for equal work, such as job analysis, vocational guidance, employment counseling, placement work, welfare and social work, public awareness enhancement and research and survey, etc. The Chinese government has approved the Convention. In order to better implement this principle, equal remuneration for equal work has been included in the Labor Law to serve as a basic principle of wage distribution.

According to the principle of equal remuneration for equal work, employers shall not, in the process of wage payment, pay varying amounts of remuneration to workers engaged in the same kind of work and providing labor of the same value because of the differences in aspects including gender, race and age. The implementation of equal remuneration for equal work fully embodies the equality of Chinese citizens before the law, and is also the concrete manifestation of the implementation of the principle of distribution according to work. Only through the implementation of equal remuneration for equal work, Chinese citizens are guaranteed that they are entitled to genuine equality of right to labor remuneration. The provision of this principle is to protect the legitimate interests of all laborers and to prevent gender discrimination, ethnic discrimination, and other discriminatory practices. But it does not preclude that employers pay varying amounts of remuneration to employees engaged in the same kind of work yet with different skills and labor contributions. Nevertheless, it is worth noting that the principle of equal remuneration for equal work does not simply prohibits treatment of gender discrimination, discrimination in other aspects is also deemed a divergence from the principle.

---

### Typical Case Study: Different Pays for Equal Work Between Temporary and Regular Workers

In January 1998, Zhao Wu was hired as a temporary worker by Divine Land Freight Company for a period of one year. In December of the same year, the freight company decided to lay off all temporary workers and paid wages and economic compensation according to the original contracts. In March 2001, Zhao Wu filed an application for arbitration for not enjoying the treatment of equal pay for equal work as the regular workers of the plaintiff, the Divine Land Freight Company, during his stay in the company, and demanded for the award of the differences of wages and benefits while he was on duty. The Labor

Dispute Arbitration Commission ruled that the practice of Divine Land Freight Company was not in line with the law and that Divine Land shall pay Zhao Wu the differences of wages, bonuses and benefits at a total of 10,345 yuan. Divine Land Freight Company opposed the arbitral decision and instituted legal proceedings to the court. The Court, invoking Article 5 of the Interim Provisions of the State Council on the Administration of Temporary Workers of State Enterprises promulgated on October 5, 1989, which provides that "wages of temporary workers shall be stipulated in principle by people's governments of provinces, autonomous regions and municipalities directly under the Central Government with reference to wages of contract workers of the same jobs and same posts, with the specific criteria of which being determined through negotiations between the employing enterprise and the temporary workers, and being stipulated in the labor contract", citing the fact that Zhao Wu the defendant had known the differences between the wages offered and those of the regular workers before being employed as a temporary worker by the plaintiff Divine Land Freight Company, and had subsequently concluded with the plaintiff a labor contract stipulating a remuneration standard of minor difference with that of a regular worker, supported the claims of Divine Land Freight Company and ruled in favor of the plaintiff. The Court held: "This case shows that temporary and regular workers are equally protected by Chinese labor law, but interpretation of 'equal pay for equal work' shall not be simply construed as exactly the same pay, but rather remuneration of minor differences as compared with that of regular workers of the same jobs. The standard followed by the court when handling such labor contract disputes is also whether there are scenarios of 'too large' or 'too small' a gap. "[1]

Is there any difference between regular workers and temporary workers in terms of labor remuneration?

The inadequacy of this case lies in the differentiation between "regular workers" and "temporary workers" in terms of the identity of laborers, as they are all "laborers" under the Labor Law, and are equally protected and regulated by the labor law, and both are subject to the "equal pay for equal work" principle. The provision invoked by the Court was promulgated before the implementation of the Labor Law and was contradictory with the latter. On

---

[1] Compiled by the Legal System Publicity Department of Beijing Municipal Higher People's Court: Traps in Labor Contracts and Dispute Handling, p. 86, Beijing, China Democracy and Law Publishing House, 2003.

November 7, 1996, the General Office of the Ministry of Labor expressly pointed out in the Official Reply to the Request for Instructions on Issues Concerning Temporary Workers that: "As of the implementation date of the Labor Law, all employers shall fully implement the labor contract system with the employees, and all types of employees shall enjoy equal rights within the employing entity. Therefore, the name of a temporary worker in the past sense relative to the case of regular workers no longer exists. Employers hiring for temporary employment positions shall conclude labor contracts with workers and establish various social insurances for the latter, entitling them to the relevant welfare treatment, with differences permitted only in terms of the term of the labor contract. " Therefore, the so-called "temporary workers" only differ in terms of the term of the labor contract, but shall not be subject to discriminatory treatment because of their identities as long as labor rights are concerned.

## Section 2 Minimum Wage System

### Ⅰ. The Concept and Meaning of the Minimum Wage

The minimum wage refers to the minimum labor remuneration to be paid by the employer to the employee for the normal labor provided within the statutory working period. Among which, the statutory working period refers to the working hours prescribed by the State; the normal labor refers to the labor provided by laborers within the statutory working period in accordance with the relevant provisions of the labor contract. Laborers taking leave as required for reasons such as family visit, wedding, death of immediate family members, or participation in national or social activities according to law, shall also be deemed as having provided normal labor.

According to the relevant State regulations, the following items shall not constitute the minimum wage: (1) wages for extra shifts and hours; (2) allowances for middle shift, night shift, high temperature, low temperature, underground, toxic and hazardous and other special working environment and conditions; (3) labor insurance and welfare benefits stipulated by national laws, regulations and policies. Corporate training costs for workers, protective supplies given to employees according to the relevant State requirements and various corporate articles of use, family planning subsidies and special hardship subsidies received by workers, and housing subsidies granted to workers because of housing reform. The Circular of the Ministry of Labor on the Implementation of the Minimum Wage Guarantee System also stipulates that non-monetary income paid to employees by providing meal and housing allowances shall not be included in the minimum wage. The non-recurrent bonuses received by workers such as competition prizes, sports awards, awards for rationalization proposals must not be included as the minimum wage of the enterprise.

The implementation of a minimum wage guarantee system in China is in line with the need of economic development of the socialist market, and helps protect the basic livelihood of individual workers and their families, and promotes the improvement of the quality of workforce and fair competition among enterprises.

## II. The Scope of Application of the Minimum Wage System

The Provisions on Enterprise Minimum Wage formulated by the former Ministry of Labor in 1993 reflected the features of that particular period of time when China was in the early stages of economic system reform. However, after a lapse of 10 years, with the intensification of economic system reform and the gradual improvement of the socialist market economic system, some provisions of the Provisions cannot cater for the current external situation, hence it is necessary to revise and add new provisions. On December 30, 2003, the Ministry of Labor and Social Security promulgated the Provisions on Minimum Wage which came into force as of March 1, 2004. The Provisions on Enterprise Minimum Wage issued by the former Ministry of Labor on November 24, 1993 was repealed simultaneously. The Provisions on Minimum Wage have improved the current minimum wage system, in particular the establishment of hourly minimum wage standards, which contributed a lot to the development of flexible forms of employment.

The Provisions on Minimum Wage determine the scope of application of the minimum wage as enterprises, private non-enterprise units, and individual businesses with employees within the territory of the People's Republic of China and laborers with whom labor relations are established. State organs, institutions, social organizations and laborers with labor contract relations with the same will be governed with reference to these Provisions. The scope of application is broader than that of the relevant provisions previously formulated. The former Provisions on Enterprise Minimum Wage applied to enterprises of various economic types within the territory of the PRC and laborers receiving remuneration from the same. Individual economic organizations and laborers having established labor relations with the same, as well as state organs, institutions, social organizations and laborers with labor contract relations with the same will be governed with reference to the Provisions. In recent years, private non-enterprise units began to emerge as a new form of social organization, such as some private schools, hospitals, etc. It is necessary to include private non-enterprise units into the scope of application of the minimum wage so as to protect the legitimate rights and interests of workers of private non-enterprise units. In China, the enterprise minimum wage applies to enterprises of various economic types within the territory of the PRC and laborers receiving remuneration from the same. However, the applicability to township enterprises shall be decided by the respective people's governments of provinces, autonomous regions and municipalities directly under the Central Government. The provisions on minimum wage system do not apply to enterprises and workers in the scope below: (1) civil servants and staff of public interest groups; (2) leaseholders or contractors of leasing ventures or contracting businesses; (3) apprentices, work-study students during holidays, and the handicapped.

## Ⅲ. The Standards of Minimum Wages

The minimum wage standard refers to the minimum amount of wage in unit labor-time. Article 48 of Labor Law provides that the specific standards of minimum wages shall be formulated by people's governments of provinces, autonomous regions and municipalities directly under the Central Government and filed with the State Council for record, which indicates that China does not implement a unified national minimum wage, and that minimum wage standards will be determined by localities according to their respective situations.

As for the different practices of minimum wage standards, the Provisions on Minimum Wage define the minimum wage standard, namely the minimum labor remuneration to be paid by the employer to the employee for the normal labor provided within statutory working hours or working period stipulated in labor contracts concluded in accordance with the law. The Provisions also explicitly state the content of normal labor. "Normal labor" refers to the labor engaged by workers according to the stipulations of labor contracts concluded in accordance with the law in statutory working hours or working period agreed upon in labor contracts. Whereas maternity (child birth) leave and sterilization surgery leave are both rights to rest and vacation to which all workers are entitled by law, in order to more adequately protect workers' legitimate rights and interests during vacation breaks, maternity (child birth) leave and sterilization surgery leave are included in the scope of deemed provision of normal labor. Laborers are entitled to paid annual leave, family leave, funeral or wedding leave, maternity (child birth) leave, sterilization surgery leave, etc. Laborers on paid leave as mentioned above and laborers who participate in social activities in accordance with the law during statutory working hours shall be deemed to have provided normal labor.

Regarding the forms of minimum wage, the Provisions on Minimum Wage prescribe two minimum wage standard forms, namely monthly minimum wage standard and hourly minimum wage standard. Monthly minimum wage standard applies to workers on full-time employment, and hourly minimum wage standard applies to workers on part-time employment. This is to accommodate the needs of development of flexible forms of employment and encourage employment. The original monthly minimum wage standard is not suitable for workers on part-time employment, which is not conducive to the protection of their legitimate rights and interests. Beijing, Shanghai, Jiangsu and other provinces and municipalities have, according to the actual needs, made a breakthrough from the traditional full-time employment model, formulated and promulgated the local minimum wage standards to protect the legitimate rights and interests of hourly rate workers and other non-full-time workers, and promoted the development of flexible employ-ment forms. In formulating the Provisions, a total of 19 regions (including provincial municipalities) countrywide enacted minimum hourly wage standards, yet 8 of them determined the minimum hourly wage using a simple conversion of the monthly minimum wage, which cannot effectively protect the legitimate rights and interests of workers. In order to unify and standardize the development and implementation of the minimum hourly wage standards, addition of the relevant provisions on minimum hourly wage standards in the existing minimum wage provisions has become necessary.

The Provisions on Minimum Wage specifically state the factors to be considered when determining and adjusting the monthly minimum wage standards. In order to meet the needs of the establishment of social security system and intensifying the housing reform, the Provisions expressly included social insurance and housing fund paid by individual workers as factors to be considered in the determination of monthly minimum wage standards, which must, as required, refer to the minimum cost of living of the local working population and their dependents, the urban consumer price index, social insurance and housing fund paid by individual workers, the average wage of employees, the level of economic development and the employment status and other factors. The Provisions also state: the determination and adjustment of minimum hourly wage shall be based on the monthly minimum wage enacted with reference to the factors of basic old-age insurance and basic medical insurance to be paid by employers, and at the same time due attention must be paid to the differences in terms of job stability, working conditions and labor intensity, welfare and other aspects between full-time employees and part-time workers.

The Provisions on Minimum Wage provide the calculation method of minimum wage standards in the form of an annex. The minimum wage standards are determined by taking into consideration, in general, the living expenses of urban residents, social insurance and housing fund paid by individual workers, the average wage level of employees, the unemployment rate, the level of economic development and other factors, which can be expressed by the formula: $M = f(C, S, A, U, E, a)$: M for minimum wage standard; C for living expenses per capita of urban residents; S for social insurance and housing fund paid by individual workers; A for average wage of employees; U for unemployment rate; E for level of economic development; a for adjustment factors. The generic methods of determination of the minimum wage standard include the Method of Specific Gravity and the Engel's Ratio Method. The former method is based on urban household survey data and determines a certain proportion of households of the lowest income per capita as poor households, and gives the statistics of expenditure levels of living expenses per capita of poor households, multiplied by the coefficient of dependence on each employed person, coupled with an adjustment number. The latter is based on the annual standard food spectrum and standard food intake provided by the National Institute of Nutrition combined with the market prices of standard food, and works out the minimum food expenditure standard, divided by the Engel coefficient and comes up with the lowest cost of living standard, then multiplied by the coefficient of dependence on each employed person, plus an adjustment figure. The monthly minimum wage standard calculated this way will be subject to necessary adjustment with the consideration of social insurance and housing fund paid by individual workers, the average wage level of employees, the standards of social assistance and unemployment insurance benefits, the employment status and the level of economic development and other factors. The floating coefficient of the minimum hourly wage standard shall mainly focus on the differences in terms of job stability, working conditions and labor intensity, welfare and other aspects between full-time employees and part-time workers.

The Provisions on Minimum Wage revise the adjustment period of minimum wage standard. The Provisions on Enterprise Minimum Wage provided that "after the promulgation and implementation of the minimum wage standard, in case of change of any factors stipulated in Article 7 of these Provisions, or significant cumulative change of the price index of the cost of living of local workers, the minimum wage standard shall be adjusted in a timely manner, but not more than once a year." Nevertheless, the consolidated analysis of the situation of adjustment of the minimum wage standard countrywide in recent years found that in some areas the adjustment period of the minimum wage standard is too long and the level is on the lower side. In response to this situation, the requirement of adjustment of the minimum wage standard at least once in every two years was added to these Provisions for the protection of workers' basic livelihood.

## Section 3   Wage Payment Security

Article 50 of Labor Law provides that: "Wages shall be paid monthly to laborers in the form of currency. Wages of laborers shall not be deducted or accrued for no reason." Article 51 stipulates that: "Employers shall, in accordance with the law, pay laborers wages while they take statutory holidays, wedding or funeral leave, or participate in social activities in accordance with the law." The provisions mentioned above involve issues concerning the form of wage payment, the target of wage payment, the time of wage payment and the wage payment under special circumstances.

### Ⅰ. The Form of Wage Payment

Wages shall be paid in the form of currency rather than in kind.

Payment of wages in the form of currency is in line with the international practice. This is to limit and eventually eliminate payment in kind and to turn into currency and standardize personal income, which helps to enhance the transparency of distribution of income and strengthen the financial supervision over the employers' distribution of income, which at the same time is conducive to the establishment of personal income declaration system and strengthens the function of personal income tax in the adjustment of income distribution, and most important of all, safeguards laborers' incomes.

### Ⅱ. The Target of Wage Payment

Laborers themselves are the recipients of wages. The employers shall pay laborers wages at the workplace, which are directly received by the laborers themselves. In case the workers themselves cannot receive wages for some reason, wages can be collected by relatives authorized by the laborers. The purpose of this provision is to ensure that workers receive wages. According to the usual practice, employers will provide laborers a personal wage list with the amount of wages payable and items thereof, the amount wages deductible and items thereof, the actual amount of wages paid and so on. To facilitate inquiries, employers must record in writing the amount and time of the payment of wages, and the salaried person's name and signature.

### Ⅲ. The Time of Wage Payment

Wages should be paid monthly according to provisions. For employers implementing hourly wages, daily wages, or monthly wages or other time-based wage forms, or wages on the basis of piece-rate, employees must be paid wages monthly. For units adopting the annual salary system, wages should be paid in advance by a certain percentage each month.

### Ⅳ. Prohibition of Reduction of Wages

Employers must not reduce the wages of workers. Workers should receive full wages under the premise of provision of normal labor within the statutory working hours. This is also one of the legitimate rights and interests of workers protected by law. No units shall be allowed to reduce any wages; otherwise it would constitute an infringement of workers' legitimate rights and interests. Violations such as reduction or default of wages of workers often lead to serious consequences and must be given great attention, and the relevant perpetrators, in particular the person in charge or directly responsible of the working units shall be imposed legal sanction.

However, under the following circumstances, deducting part of the wages of workers does not constitute reduction of wages: (1) compensation as required for the damage to the property of the employer or other people due to accidents caused by the negligence of the workers themselves; (2) a certain amount of wages deducted according to the relevant management system of the units for the workers' absenteeism or over-due causal leave in violation of the labor discipline; (3) deductions of upbringing payment, alimony or compensation fees commissioned by the court; (4) debt to be reimbursed to employers by the workers; (5) social insurance premiums to be paid by the workers themselves as stipulated by law; (6) other fees to be withheld by the employer as required by law.

## V. Payment of Wages Under Special Circumstances

Article 51 of Labor Law stipulates that: "Employers shall, in accordance with the law, pay laborers wages while they take statutory holidays, wedding or funeral leave, or participate in social activities in accordance with the law. " Wages under special circumstances mainly include three aspects, namely wage payment for statutory holidays, wage payment for wedding or funeral leave and wages paid for participation in social activities in accordance with the law. In these three cases, the employer shall pay the worker wages in the same amount as of the payment for the performance of normal labor obligations.

### 1. Payment of Wages during Statutory Holidays

Statutory holidays refer to holidays stipulated by law. Workers' right to rest is a fundamental right protected by law. Statutory holiday is one of the leave systems. In accordance with provisions, the employing entity shall arrange vacation leave for laborers during the New Year Day, Spring Festival, International Labor Day, National Day and other statutory holidays stipulated by laws and regulations. Workers take leave in accordance with the above-mentioned provisions on statutory holidays, and the employer shall pay the employee wages in accordance with the law, otherwise it would constitute a reduction of wages of laborers.

### 2. Payment of Wages during Wedding or Funeral Leave

Wedding or funeral leave, a general term for wedding leave and funeral leave, refers to leave approved by the employing entity when the workers themselves get married or in case of the death of the immediate family members of the workers (including travelling time). Entitlement of wedding or funeral leave is the legitimate right of workers. 1 - 3 days of wedding or funeral leave will be granted by the unit. In some localities, in addition to the statutory 3-day leave prescribed by the state, additional paid leave of 10 days or so is granted to employees married at a mature age. The employer shall pay the employee wages during wedding or funeral leave (including travelling time).

### 3. Payment of Wages During Maternity Leave

According to the provisions of the Ministry of Personnel in 1993 on wages during maternity leave of women employees of authority organs and institutions, the wages of women employees of authority organs and institutions will be calculated and paid according to the total sum of the following items: (1) duty wages, rank wages, basic wages and seniority wages of the employee concerned for authority organs with the implementation of ranking wage system; (2) for skilled workers of authority organs, the position wages, skill level wages and bonuses calculated at the ratio stipulated by the State; (3) for ordinary workers of authority organs, the position wages, skill level wages and bonuses calculated at the ratio stipulated by the State; (4) for employees of institutions, the duty (technical grade) wages and allowances calculated at the ratio stipulated by the State (among which, for athletes, the basic allowance for physical training plus achievement allowances).

**4. Payment of Wages during the Participation in Social Activities in Accordance with the Law**

Participation in social activities in accordance with the law is one of the political rights of workers and is protected by law. Workers participating in social activities in the statutory working hours shall be deemed to have provided normal labor and shall be paid wages by the employer. The social activities mentioned herein mainly include: (1) exercising the lawful right to vote or stand for election; (2) representatives elected to attend congresses convened by government, political parties, trade unions and other legitimate social organizations; (3) serving as juror or witness at the people's court; (4) attending meetings or other activities organized and approved by the employing entity; (5) members of grass-roots trade union committee, appointed in accordance with the stipulation of the Trade Union Law who do not stay away from production and do not spend more than two working days of production time on union activities per month; (6) designated by corporate leaders to participate in meetings or mass working time; (7) other activities participated in accordance with the law.

**5. Payment of Wages During Family Leave**

In March 1981, the State Council stipulated in the Provisions on Family Leave Treatment of Employees that the travelling expenses of workers for visiting their spouses or of unmarried workers for visiting their parents shall be assumed by the employing entity; as for the travelling expenses of married workers for visiting their parents, expenses not exceeding 30% of the monthly standard wages of the workers concerned shall be assumed by the workers themselves, the portion in excess shall be assumed by the unit. Wages of workers during family leave shall be paid in accordance with the standard wages of the workers concerned.

**6. Wages Payment during the Downtime**

Article 12 of the Interim Provisions on Payment of Wages stipulates that where an organization is shut down or ceases its production due to reasons not attributable to its laborers and such period of shutdown or production cessation is within a wage payment cycle, the employer shall pay its laborers wages in accordance with the standards specified by the labor contracts. Where such period lasts for more than one wage payment cycle, the employer shall pay its laborers labor remuneration that is not lower than the local minimum wage standard if the laborers provide normal work; where the laborers fail to provide normal work, relevant matters shall be handled in accordance with relevant State provisions.

**7. Payment of Wages upon Bankruptcy of Enterprises in Accordance with the Law**

Article 14 of the Interim Provisions on Payment of Wages stipulates that, a laborer is entitled to obtaining his/her wages when his/her employer goes bankrupt in accordance with the law. Such employer shall, when conducting bankruptcy liquidation, pay its laborers overdue wages in accordance with the payment sequence as specified in the Enterprise Bankruptcy Law of the People's Republic of China.

**8. Issues Concerning Payment of Wages of Special Personnel**

(1) payment of wages to workers subject to penalties: 1) the wage remuneration for workers who still work at the original unit after administrative sanctions such as probation and demotion, or criminal sanctions, shall be primarily determined by the employing entity according to specific circumstances; 2) during the period of criminal sanctions of laborers such as sheltering for investigation, detention/custody, probation, serving a sentence out of prison or re-education through labor, their treatment shall be handled in accordance with the relevant national regulations; (2) wage treatment of apprentices, skilled workers and college graduates during the study period, training period, internship, probationary period and before substantive grading shall be determined independently by the employer; (3) wage treatment of newly employed demobilized soldiers shall be determined independently by the employer; wages and treatment of demobilized army cadres allocated to the enterprise shall be handled in accordance with the relevant national regulations.

## Section 4　The Right to Work and Right to Rest and the Significance

### I. The Right to Work and the Right to Rest Are Two Fundamental Rights of Workers

The right to work and the right to rest is constitutional fundamental rights of workers. Article 43 of Chinese Constitution states: "Working people in the People's Republic of China have the right to rest. The State expands facilities for the rest and recuperation of the working people and prescribes working hours and vacations for workers and staff. " According to this provision of the Constitution, the two rights are closely linked. Pursuant to this provision of the Constitution, the Labor Law prescribes specific provisions on workers' right to work and right to rest.

Workers' right to work and right to rest are reflected by working time and rest time. Working time refers to the time during which workers are supposed to engage in labor at the employing entity based on labor contract relations. Working time system is regulated by law. For example, the law provides for 8-hour working day system and 5-day working week system. Rest time refers to the time dominated by workers and staff outside working hours for recovery from physical and mental fatigue, arranging their lives, housekeeping, participating in social, recreational and sports activities and other aspects of life, including the intermittent time between working hours, the rest time between two working days, weekly rest days, statutory holidays and other breaks.

Working hours and rest periods consist of the entire time occupied by the workers within a day for production, activities and rest. Without limits established by law of the length of working time, the length of rest time will be shortened. Similarly, if no rest period is required by law, various forms of occupation of rest time for workers would emerge. In this sense, the provisions of the Labor Law on working hours, rest and vacation are protection of the working hours and rest periods of workers.

The right to work and the right to rest as the constitutional fundamental rights of workers have been specifically protected in the Labor Law, and carry important practical significance. The main purpose of the protection of the working hours, rest and leave of workers by the Labor Law is to protect the health of workers. After a day of intense labor, workers have physical and mental fatigue, and recuperate only through a good rest so that they have good health and abundant energy to carry out reproduction, participate in social activities and business learning, and take care of housekeeping and personal life as well as the education of children. A good rest is also conducive to ensuring that workers complete production and work tasks, improve work efficiency and labor productivity. The provision on working time ensures that workers work within the statutory time of a day; the provision on resting time not just compensates for the physical exertion caused by work of employees, more importantly, it is possible for workers to use leisure time to learn business and technology so as to improve the ability to work and the level of production technology. This is the only way for workers to make fuller use of working hours and ensure the completion of production and work tasks.

## II. Working Time and Working Days

### ( I ) Working Time

Working time is, as required by law, the time used by workers at the employing entity for the completion of their work. It is the time within which people engage in labor. It is the natural scale of labor and is the calculation unit for the measurement of each worker's labor contribution and the remuneration to be paid. Working time is the time within which employees engage in production and work for employers. Working time, generally calculated in the unit of hours, includes the number of hours worked daily and the weekly number of working days and hours. Working time is a limit stipulated by law which cannot be exceeded by employers when arranging the work of employees. According to labor contracts, workers must provide labor services to employing entities. The time spent by laborers in the work for employers is the working time. Wages and benefits are often affected by workers who do not spend enough time at work according to the labor contract. Workers who work additional shifts and hours receive overtime wages in accordance with provisions.

The main form of working time is working days. A working day refers to the length of working time of an employee as required by law in one day and night which is working time calculated based on the unit of a day. Working time includes daily working hours (i. e. the working time of a worker within one day and night) and weekly working hours (i. e. the working time of a worker within one week).

Determination of the working time is mainly based on the following aspects: (1) to ensure that every worker is able to provide the necessary labor for the needs of the society; (2) to guarantee workers time to rest. To ensure that workers have the time needed for the participation in social, political and cultural life and time required for learning and housekeeping; (3) to be in line with the level of national economic, technological and social development.

According to the Labor Law and relevant regulations, in China's current system of working hours, working days are divided into regular working days, irregular working days and piece-rate working days.

### ( II ) Regular Working Days

A regular working day is the fixed working hours required by law in every working day of a worker and is the main form of China's working time system. According to China's current working time system, a regular working day can be divided into a standard working day, a shortened working day and an extended working day. The Labor Law makes specific provisions on a regular working day. Working time refers to the time during which workers engage in production and work for employers. Working time is generally calculated in hours and includes the number of hours worked daily and the weekly number of working days and hours.

### ( Ⅰ ) Standard Working Days

A standard working day is the working day required by law to be commonly practiced in normal circumstances by State organs, social organizations, enterprises and institutions. Article 36 of the Labor Law provides that workers' daily working time shall not exceed 8 hours.

China's standard working day was previously implemented based on 8 hours per day, 48 hours per week and 6 days a week with one day of rest. This working day system was adopted following the provisions of the Common Program of the Chinese People's Political Consultative Conference. With the development of production and social advancement, shorter working time has become a worldwide trend. Convention No. 1 [1919] of ILO stipulated a standard working time as 8 hours per day and 48 hours per week which was subsequently reduced to 40 hours per week in Convention No. 47 [1935]. In recent years, a number of enterprises and workers have raised the requirements to shorten working hours, some enterprises also explored the practice of shorter hours, and achieved satisfactory results, hence, the conditions for a unified shorter working time in China were ripe. From March 1, 1994 onwards, pursuant to Article 3 of the Provisions of the State Council on Working Time of Employees, China began to implement the standard working time for workers as 8 hours per day, an average of 44 hours per week and an average of 5.5 working days per week. On March 25, 1995, the State Council promulgated the Provisions of the State Council on the Revision of the Provisions of the State Council on Working Time of Employees. Article 3 of the revised Provisions states that: "Workers and staff work 8 hours per day and 40 hours per week", i. e. from May 1, 1995 onwards, China's standard working time shall be a 5-day work week of 8 hours per day and 40 hours per week. Article 9 of the revised "Provisions" states that: "These Provisions shall come into force as of May 1, 1995. Enterprises and institutions having difficulties in implementing the Provisions since May 1, 1995 may be subject to an appropriate extension; however, institutions shall implement the Provisions no later than January 1,

1996, and the commencement for enterprises shall not be later than May 1, 1997".

( Ⅱ ) Shorter Working Days

A shorter working day refers to a working time of shorter length in each working day as compared with standard working days, which is, under normal circumstances, primarily applicable to workers engaged in toxic and hazardous trades and jobs, harsh conditions or highly stressful work, and workers engaged in particularly heavy physical labor.

The Labor Law does not make clear provisions on a shorter working day, yet in the Article 39 it states that: "where an enterprise cannot implement the provisions of Articles 36 and 38 of this Law due to its production characteristics, it may, upon approval by the labor administration department, arrange the laborers to work and rest in other ways", which offers a legal basis for the implementation of alternative work and rest ways according to the production features of enterprises. A shorter working day is one of these kinds of alternative ways.

For workers engaged in laboring under special conditions and workers of special conditions, the working time can, pursuant to the provisions of the State Council or the competent administrative departments of labor and personnel under the State Council, be further shortened to an appropriate extent. Where State organs and institutions need to shorten working hours, opinions shall be made by the provinces, autonomous regions and municipalities directly under the Central Government and the respective competent departments according to the subordinate relations, and shall submitted to the competent administrative departments of personnel of the State Council for approval. Where enterprises need to shorten working hours, proposals of enterprises directly under central management shall be subject to the examination of the competent departments and the subsequent approval of the competent administrative department of labor of the State Council. Proposals of local enterprises shall be subject to the examination of the local supervisory authorities and the subsequent approval of the local labor department.

According to China's special provisions on the working time of workers engaged in laboring under special conditions and workers of special conditions, circumstances in which shorter working days are applicable include the following:

(1) Night shift working time. Night shift working time generally refers to the time between 22: 00 of the day and 6: 00 of the next morning. Workers of enterprises, institutions, authority organs, organizations and other units who

engage in work of night shifts shall have their working time reduced by 1 hour as compared with the standard working day and shall be awarded as required of allowances for night shifts.

(2) Breastfeeding time. Breastfeeding time refers to the time occupied by female employees in infant nursing during working time who have babies of less than one year old. The Provisions of the State Council on the Labor Protection of Female Employees promulgated on July 21, 1988 provides in this regard: With respect to a female employee who has a baby under 12 months of age, the organization where she works shall grant her two breastfeeding (including bottle feeding) breaks within each labor shift with 30 minutes for each break. In the case of multiple births, an additional 30 minutes shall be granted for each breastfeeding break for each additional baby. The two feeding breaks for a female employee within each labor shift may be taken consecutively. The time for feeding breaks and spent on her way to and from the place of feeding inside the organization is deemed as labor hours.

(3) Special labor posts. Workers engaged in underground operations, mountain operations, seriously toxic and hazardous operations, or particularly onerous or overwrought manual labor jobs shall be entitled to a daily working time of less than 8 hours. For workers of generally toxic and hazardous operations, a "3 On and 1 Off System", namely three days of work with a one-day rest, can be adopted, as well as the practice of a 7-hour working day system, or the introduction of a "regular in-turn disengagement from exposure for one and a half months", which means that workers take turns annually disengaging from their operating posts for one and a half months, and go back to their original posts upon the expiry of the disengagement period. For workers of seriously toxic and hazardous operations, a combination of the "3 On and 1 Off System" and the "regularly in-turn disengagement from exposure" can be adopted, namely workers enjoying the system of three days of work with a one-day rest, plus an annual one-month disengagement from the original operation posts; or the adoption of a 6-hour working day system, or a regular in-turn disengagement from exposure for two and a half months. The forms of shorter working day adopted by other industries include the "4 Shifts of 6 Hours" working system implemented underground or at coal mines, the "5 Shifts in 3 Runs" pilot practiced by some individual chemical enterprises, as well as different forms of shorter working days implemented at industries such as construction, metallurgy, geological exploration, forest harvesting and loading and moving according to the situation of the industry.

## (Ⅲ) Extended Working Days

An extended working day refers to the working day system in which employees work longer hours in each working day as compared with the length of time of standard working days. It is mainly applicable to industries which, with production being limited by natural conditions or technical constraints, require concentrated efforts and are of seasonal characteristics, such as salt industry, sugar industry, vegetable gardens and farms. Working time can be either extended or shortened during busy or slack seasons of such industries. Workers working extended working days shall be entitled to compensatory time off or compensatory wages where compensatory time off is not applicable.

Currently, for some enterprises, China has implemented a comprehensive working day system. The adoption of a working system of consolidated calculation of industry working hours is based on the actual production situation of some enterprises, and allows the implementation of a working system with relatively concentrated time of work and rest, so as to ensure the normal production and workers' legal rights. Therefore, it is inappropriate to demand the compliance of enterprises with the provisions of a standard working time system in the process of examination and approval of the working system of consolidated calculation of working hours. However, enterprises shall be required to meet the following two points in the process of examination and approval of the working system of consolidated calculation of working hours: (1) consultations with trade unions and workers on the implementation of the working system of consolidated calculation of working hours as well as the working modes to be adopted in the implementation of the same; (2) for posts above Grade 3 (including Grade 3) of manual labor intensity, laborers shall not be subject to a daily continuous working time in excess of 11 hours and shall be entitled to at least a 1-day break every week.

For workers satisfying one of the following conditions, enterprises can implement the working system of consolidated calculation of working hours, i. e. to conduct consolidated calculation of working time based respectively on periods such as weeks, months, quarters and years, nevertheless the average daily working hours and average weekly working hours shall basically be the same as the legal standard working hours. (1) workers subject to continuous operation due to the special nature of jobs in industries such as transportation, railways, telecommunications, water carriage, aviation and fisheries; (2) some workers in industries subject to the limitation of seasons and natural conditions such as geology and resource exploration, construction, salt, sugar and tourism; (3)

workers of other industries suitable for the implementation of the working system of consolidated calculation of working hours.

## ( Ⅲ ) Irregular Working Days

Irregular working day refers to the working system of workers for whom, due to the unique nature of the duty requirements, it is difficult to implement a regular working day system. It applies to those jobs with scope of duty and working conditions not subject to the limitation of standard working time, such as field workers, special purpose vehicle drivers; some workers of enterprises such as railways, water carriage and post and telecommunications; people whose work cannot be calculated in hours (e. g. professional writers, field personnel, etc.); people of discretionary working time (e. g. forest patrol officers as well as some odd-job men, etc.); personnel of flexible working time due to the special nature of work (such as taxi drivers). Irregular working day also belongs to the category of alternative work and rest ways.

At present, there are no specific provisions in China on jobs applicable for the irregular working day system. The local people's government, industry departments and competent departments of enterprises can prescribe provision of their own regarding this issue. On January 1, 1995, the Ministry of Labor promulgated and implemented the Measures for the Examination and Approval of Enterprises Implementing Irregular Working Day System and the Working System of Consolidated Calculation of Working Hours which provide that: Enterprises can adopt irregular working day system for workers who meet one of the following conditions: (1) senior management personnel, field personnel, sales personnel, some operators on duty and other staff members of enterprises whose work cannot be evaluated with standard working time as the measurement unit; (2) long-distance transport workers of enterprises, taxi drivers and some loading and unloading personnel of railways, ports and warehouses as well as workers of flexible operations due to the special nature of work; (3) other workers applicable for the implementation of the irregular working day system due to special requirements associated with the characteristics of production, special needs in work or scopes of responsibilities.

However, whether the jobs of workers can be classified as occupations applicable to irregular working day system shall be subject to the examination and approval of State authorities. The Implementing Measures for the Provisions of the State Council on the Working Hours of Employees provide that: Workers not suitable for the implementation of regular working day system due to the limitation of the nature of work and responsibilities may be applicable to irregular working day system after opinions being proposed by the competent departments of industry or system under the State Council and the subsequent approval by the competent administrative departments for labor and human resources under the State Council. Article 7 of the Measures for the Examination and Approval of Enterprises' Implementation of Irregular Working Day System and the Working System of Consolidated Calculation of Working Hours provide that, enterprises directly under the central management shall be subject to the examination of the competent departments of the industry under the State Council and the approval of the administrative department for labor under the State Council prior to the implementation of the irregular working day system and the working system of consolidated calculation of working hours and other work and rest ways. The measures for the examination and approval of implementation of the irregular working day system and the working system of consolidated calculation of working hours and other work and rest ways by local enterprises shall be formulated by the administrative department of labor of the people's government of provinces, autonomous regions and municipalities directly under the State Council, and shall be filed with the labor administrative department under the State Council for record.

The provisions of the State Council on irregular working day system do not impose no limitations on working time but rather the implementation of a practice basically in accordance with standard working day. However, when working time within one day exceeds the standard working hours, the excess shall not be deemed as added shifts or hours and shall not be compensated with overtime wages but rather compensatory leave. For workers subject to the irregular working day system, labor quota or other assessment criteria shall reasonably be determined by the enterprise in accordance with the standard working time system, so that proper rest arrangements can be made for these workers, and the wages of whom shall be calculated and paid by the enterprise pursuant to the wage system and wage distribution methods in practice, according to the actual working hours and the status of the completion of the work quota. For workers meeting the conditions for paid annual leave, the enterprise shall arrange paid annual leave for them.

( Ⅳ ) Piece-rate Working Days

Piece-rate working day system refers to the working time system where the remuneration standard is based on the fixed labor quota completed by an employee. Piece-rate day is actually a special form of regular work purposes. Article 37 of the Labor Law provides for piece-rate working days as follows: "for piece rate workers, employers shall, in accordance with the system of working hours specified in Article 36 of this Law, reasonably determine their labor quotas and standards of remuneration on a piece-by-piece basis. " Under this provision, piece-rate working days shall come with reasonable labor quotas and piece-rate remuneration standards. The reasonable labor quota shall be based on the piece-rate amount which can be reasonably completed by an employee within the working time of a standard working day (8 hours per day) or a standard working week (no more than 40 hours per week). Any excess of this standard shall be deemed an extension of the working day and a violation of the employee's right to rest. In this sense, the reasonable determination of the piece-rate labor quota is the key to the implementation of piece-rate working days.

Piece-rate working time is actually the special transformation of the standard working time, and comes with greater flexibility. For laborers working on the basis of piece-rate, when the employer reasonably determines labor quotas and piece-rate remuneration standards, they can enjoy greater flexibility as compared with those working standard working days, that is, after they complete the quotas of the day or the month, they can rest or receive extra remuneration if they decide to work during the remaining time. In case of uncompleted quota of the day, extra hours besides the 8-hour working time can be spent for completion of quota.

Labor quota refers to the labor consumption standard predetermined for the production of a certain amount of qualified products or the completion of a certain amount of work under the condition of a certain production technology and production organization, or a predetermined standard number of qualified products completed in a unit time. Labor quota includes the time quota (time needed for the production of a unit of qualified products or the completion of a certain amount of work) and the yield quota (volume of qualified products to be produced within a unit time). The calculation of the labor quota level shall be based on the quota which can be achieved within the standard working time under the circumstance of normal production.

## Section 5  Rest and Vacation

### Ⅰ. Types of Rest and Vacation

Rest time/breaks refer to the time at an employee's disposal during which the employee does not have to be engaged in work or production in accordance with the provisions of the law, during the tenure of an employee of enterprises, institutions, government agencies and organizations and any other employing entities. It includes the time occupied by workers other than statutory working hours in order to eliminate fatigue, learn to conduct business, participate in social activities and do housework, etc. Rest time is the right of workers entitled under the law, and is closely linked to the working hours of workers. Without working hours, rest periods cannot exist; without time to rest, the working hours of workers cannot be better utilized.

Types of breaks change with the development of socio-economic situation and vary due to the differences of industry sectors. According to the Labor Law and other laws and regulations, China's current types and contents of rest periods are as follows:

### ( I ) Rest Time within One Working Day

Rest time within one working day refers to the rest periods and meal breaks of a worker in the process of production or working on one's daily post, which is also known as the interval time. Rest periods and meal breaks vary due to the differences of jobs and the nature of work, with normal breaks being one to two hours and at least not less than half an hour. The interval time usually starts four hours after the start of work, and is not counted as working time. For the type of work where production cannot be interrupted and therefore cannot afford a fixed interval time, workers shall be given proper meal breaks within the working time.

Some employing entities implement the work break exercise system, namely, during the 4-hour each working time in the morning and afternoon, a 20-minute rest period is arranged which usually starts after two hours of work. The time for work break exercises is different from the interval time and is counted as working time.

### ( II ) Rest Time between Two Working Days

Rest time between two working days refers to the rest time enjoyed by workers during the period between the end of the last working day and the beginning of the next working day, the length of which shall be decided based on a standard ensuring enough time for the workers' physical strength and working ability to get back to normal, usually 15 – 16 hours. Where a shift system is adopted, the shifts must be arranged on balance, usually come after a rest day. While arranging the shifts, no worker shall be put to work for two consecutive shifts, because such practice not only violates the worker's right to rest, but can also result in consequences of serious injuries to the worker.

( Ⅲ ) Rest Days

Rest days, also known as public holidays, are the rest time for workers after a full week of labor, namely 24 consecutive hours of uninterrupted rest at least once in a week. Article 38 of the Labor Law provides that: "Employers shall ensure that workers rest for at least one day in a week."

Previously, most workers were subject to a 6-day working week, namely 1 day of rest after 6 working days. The Provisions of the State Council on the Working Hours of Employees added 4 hours to the rest time of Chinese workers by changing the original 1 day of rest time every six working days to every 5.5 working days. The Provisions of the State Council on the Working Hours of Employees also stipulate that: "The State organs and institutions shall implement unified working hours and starting from the effective date of these Provisions, the first Saturday and Sunday shall be rest days, the second Sunday shall be a rest day, and such model shall be followed for the remaining Saturdays and Sundays." In this way, workers can enjoy a rest period lasting for two consecutive days every other week, and this model shall be followed without the limitation of any particular month or year. The Implementing Measures for the Provisions of the State Council on the Working Hours of Employees further provide for rest days that: any individual departments or units, which have difficulties in implementing the unified provisions mentioned above due to the need of work and need to keep shifts running to ensure the normal operation of the work, can make their own arrangements in accordance with their own circumstances and file with departments of human resources at all levels for record.

Under normal circumstances, Sundays and Saturdays (every other week) are public holidays. Workers who cannot rest on Sundays due to production or operational needs (such as telegraph, telephone, television, and other services which serve the needs of residents), or due to reasons concerning power supply or water supply as well as the needs to reduce traffic congestion and energy supply tensions, shall be arranged by the employer to rest on other days of the week. Where employees must take turns working due to special circumstances of the work, compensatory rest time of equal length shall be arranged. Workers of regular or irregular working time who are on duty on a rest day shall be awarded rest time of equal length as that of the on-duty time within a week. Therefore, the Ministry of Labor provides that "enterprises can, after consultation with trade unions and workers, arrange flexible weekly rest days according to the local circumstances of power supply, water supply and traffic conditions". The General Office of Shanghai Municipal People's Government also states in the circular on the implementation of the provisions of the State Council that: "enterprises shall make proper arrangements of weekly rest days in accordance with the requirements of integrated balance of the city's water, electricity and gas supply, and the competent departments shall strengthen coordination, organization and supervision".

For special industries implementing shorter working week, special provisions are prescribed on their rest days. Article 39 of the Labor Law provides that: "Where an enterprise cannot implement the provisions of Articles 36 and 38 of this Law due to its production characteristics, it may, upon approval by the labor administration department, arrange the laborers to work and rest in other ways. " For instance, in the "3 On and 1 Off System" implemented for workers of exposure to toxic and hazardous operations, and the "4 Shifts in 3 Runs" system generally practiced in the textile industry, each employee can rest for two days within 8 days.

(Ⅳ) Statutory Holidays (Rest on Holidays)

The time required by workers to eliminate fatigue, take care of personal life, engage in part-time study, cultural and recreational activities and social activities is called rest time. Vacations are part of the rest time. Besides rests on public holidays and the protective leave for female workers, employees can take vacations in the following forms:

**1. Rest on Holiday**

Article 40 of the Labor Law provides that: "Employers shall, in accordance with the law, arrange the laborers to take vacations during the following holidays and festivals: (1) New Year's Day; (2) Spring Festival; (3) International Labor Day; (4) National Day; and (5) Other holidays and festivals prescribed by laws and regulations. " On March 17, 2003, the Ministry of Labor and Social Security promulgated the Circular on Issues Concerning the Conversion of Annual Average Monthly Working Hours of Employees which provides, pursuant to the provisions of the Measures of the State Council for National Holiday Arrangements on Festivals and Memorial Days, that the length of holiday vacation for all citizens shall be changed from the original 7 days to 10 days, and pursuant to which the annual average monthly working days and working hours shall be adjusted to 20. 92 days and 167. 4 hours respectively and the daily and hourly wages of workers shall be calculated accordingly. On December 7, 2007, the State Council approved the Decision on the Revision of the Measures for National Holiday Arrangements on Festivals and Memorial Days which came into force as of January 1, 2008. The revised provision prescribes explicitly in Article 2 that "holiday festivals for all citizens" shall include: (1) New Year, a 1-day holiday (January 1); (2) Spring Festival, a 3-day holiday (Lunar New Year's Eve, Lunar New Year's Day and the day after); (3) Tomb Sweeping Day, a 1-day holiday (Lunar Tomb Sweeping Day); (4) Labor Day, a 1-day holiday (May 1); (5) Dragon Boat Festival, a 1-day holiday (May 5 of Chinese Lunar Calendar); (6) Mid-Autumn Festival, a 1-day holiday (August 15 of Chinese Lunar Calendar); (7) National Day, a 3-day holiday (October 1st, 2nd and 3rd).

### 2. Annual Leave

Annual leave refers to a continuous period of rest time in addition to public holidays during which employees enjoy reservation wages. China adopted paid annual leave system for some workers during the early years since the foundation of the PRC which was later suspended with the limitation of the national economic conditions. The Labor Law reinstates this system in Article 45 according to China's current situation and the situation of the pilot implementation in some units, namely: "The State shall practice a system of paid annual leave." It also provides for the conditions for workers to enjoy this system: "Laborers who have worked continuously for over one year may enjoy paid annual leave. The specific measures shall be formulated by the State Council."

The implementation of the paid annual leave system will allow workers to get better rest, which is not only conducive to the health of workers, but also beneficial for workers to engage in production and work with more abundant energy after a good rest. On June 15, 1991, the Central Committee of the Communist Party of China and the State Council promulgated the Circular on Issues Concerning Vacation of Employees, which provides that: (1) all localities and departments can arrange for employees to take annual leave under the premise of ensuring completion of work and production tasks without additional staffing and capacity; (2) when determining the number of vacation days of employees, factors such as the tasks and personnel qualifications and job posts shall be taken into consideration with differentiation manifested to some extent, and length of such vacation shall not exceed a maximum of 2 weeks. The vacation time shall be determined with attention to a balanced arrangement. Generally local vacation methods shall be given priorities, and no facility trips shall be permitted nor shall any money or goods be doled out to employees on the grounds of vacations either in cash or any other disguised forms; (3) vacation of workers of enterprises shall be determined according to their specific conditions and the actual situation, with reference to the spirit of the provisions mentioned above; (4) issues concerning the vacation of military cadres and workers shall be handled in accordance with the spirit of the Central Military Commission.

Length of service with annual leave entitlement shall include: (1) the actual working time; (2) the period of time not actually worked by workers during which the workers were reserved of jobs (positions) and all or part of the wages (including the forced absenteeism time resulted from incorrect termination of employment or the time of job transfer and return to work); (3) the period of time not actually worked by workers during which the workers were reserved of jobs (positions) and enjoyed state social insurance benefits, with the exception of the partially paid vacation time for workers to take care of their children till an age of a year and a half; (4) such other time as stipulated by law.

The order of vacation taking for workers shall be determined by administrative departments with the agreement of the corresponding trade union bodies. Annual vacation time can be set at any time of the year, but cannot disturb the proper work of enterprises, authority organs and public organizations. Annual leave shall be arranged once a year in accordance with the period prescribed, but shall be postponed or extended in the following circumstances: employees suffering from temporary loss of labor capacity; employees performing national or social mission; under other circumstances prescribed by law. In exceptional circumstances, for instance, when the employee's taking annual leave in the current year will bring impact to the normal operation of enterprises, authority organs and public organizations, the annual leave of the same employee can be postponed to the next working year with the consent of the employee concerned and after consultation with the relevant trade union body. In this case, within each working year, the employee shall be entitled to leave of at least 6 working days within 1 year since the date of the entitlement of the supposed annual leave, with the remaining unfinished days of which being incorporated into the next working year. Employees shall not be denied of annual leave for 2 consecutive years, nor shall employees of less than 18 years of age and employees entitled to extra leave due to work in hazardous working conditions be denied annual leave. Other than dismissal of workers having unused vacation time, monetary compensation in lieu of vacation shall be prohibited.

### 3. Family Leave

Family leave refers to vacation time awarded in the efforts to solve the issues of family visit for employees separated from their family members. The State Council prescribed in 1981 in the Provisions on the Family Leave Treatment of the Employees that, for regular employees of state organs, people's organizations, state-owned enterprises and institutions with a full year of work performance who do not live and cannot reunite with their spouses during public holidays, a family leave of 30 days shall be granted to either one of the couple once a year; for unmarried workers, a leave of 20 days shall be offered in principle once a year for the visit of their parents; and for married workers to visit their parents, a leave of 20 days once every four years shall be awarded.

## Section 6   Extension of Working Hours and Limitations

### Ⅰ. The Significance in the Prescription of the System of Extended Working Time

#### （Ⅰ） The Meaning of Extension of Working Time

Extension of working time refers to added shifts and hours. Added shifts are the time employees worked during statutory holidays or on rest days in accordance with the requirement of employing entities such as enterprises and institutions subject to certain approval formalities. Added hours are the extended hours employees worked other than the regular working days in accordance with the requirement of employing entities such as enterprises and institutions subject to certain approval formalities. Added shifts and hours will inevitably take up workers' rest time, therefore, shall be implemented strictly in accordance with the provisions of laws and regulations.

To effectively control added shifts and hours, China has promulgated several labor laws and regulations. The Labor Law also makes explicit provisions on the restrictive measures for added shifts and hours. Article 43 of the Labor Law provides that: "No employers shall extend the working time of employees in violation of the provisions of this Law. " The reason for the Labor Law to include this provision is that added shifts and hours would reduce workers' rest time and time for part-time study, housekeeping and participation in social activities, which is not conducive to the health of workers and the enhancement of the business and technology level; meanwhile, added shifts and hours would also inevitably affect workers' housekeeping and education for their children, which is not constructive to the strengthening of management, enhancement of work time efficiency and consolidation of labor discipline.

( Ⅱ ) Significance of the Limitation of Extension of Working Hours

**1. Helps to Improve the Organization of Labor, Improve Labor Productivity and Economic Returns of Enterprises, Institutions, Authority Organs and Other Units.**

With the social and economic development and the scientific and technological advancement, the general trend of working hour system is to gradually reduce working hours. This urges enterprises and institutions to adopt advanced technology and other measures to continuously improve labor productivity and economic efficiency, reduce product costs, and strictly implement various forms of post responsibility system and work contract, so as to complete production tasks in the statutory working time instead of through adding shifts and hours, extending working hours and occupying the rest time of workers.

To set legal limitations over added shifts and hours will force operators to continuously improve the organization of labor, adopt advanced technology, make innovation of equipment and process, improve the utilization of working time so as to increase labor productivity and economic efficiency, ensure the completion of production quotas and increase product yields.

**2. Alternates Work with Rest to Protect the Health of Workers**

The provisions of Chinese laws on working time and rest time are determined based on the social and economic development and productivity levels at various historical periods. To strictly limit added shifts and hours is determined by China's national system. The purpose of socialist production is to provide rich material conditions to improve people's lives and protect people's health, and adding shifts and hours is contrary to this purpose.

**3. Saves Expenditure on Overtime Wages**

According to the provisions of the Labor Law, where extension of working time does not come with compensatory time off, an overtime wage higher than the wages of normal working hours shall be paid to workers concerned. Too much overtime wages will affect the improvement of economic efficiency of enterprises, increase the production and operating costs, and reduce the profits and revenues of the state. To limit added shifts and hours in the legal form will do no harm to the State and enterprises.

## Ⅱ. The Content of the Extended Working Time System

Regarding the extension of working time, China has promulgated the corresponding laws and regulations one after another to expressly clarify issues concerned. The Labor Law made new provisions at the conclusion of the content of the original provisions. The main contents of the system of extended working hours are:

( Ⅰ ) The Statutory Conditions Allowing the Extension of Working Hours

Article 42 of the Labor Law provides that: "Under any of the following circumstances, the extension of working hours shall not be subject to the restriction of the provisions of Article 41 of this Law: (1) Laborers' lives, health and property safety have been threatened in case of natural disaster or accident or for any other reason, and emergency handling is needed; ( 2 ) Production equipment, transport lines and public facilities have broken down and affected production and public interests, and must be repaired promptly; and (3) Other circumstances prescribed by laws and administrative regulations. "

The Implementing Measures for the Provisions of the State Council on the Working Hours of the Employees also expressly provide that: "Under normal circumstances, the employing entity shall not arrange workers to work overtime, except in the following cases: (1) where work cannot be interrupted during statutory holidays and public holidays; ( 2 ) where equipment inspection and maintenance must be conducted at downtime during statutory holidays or public holidays; (3) where emergency repair must be performed upon temporary failure of production equipment, transportation lines, and public facilities, etc. ; ( 4 ) where the people's health and safety and national riches are seriously threatened due to the occurrence of severe natural disasters or other disasters, hence there is a necessity of emergency repair; (5) in order to complete production tasks of national defense emergency, or other emergency production tasks arranged by higher-ups besides the national plans, as well as urgent tasks of commercial, supply and marketing enterprises for the acquisition, transportation and processing of agricultural by-products in high seasons. "

According to the foregoing, it can be seen that, given any of the circumstances mentioned above, the employing entity can directly decide on the extension of working hours without consultations. This is because the situations described above are related to the public interest, and if not resolved in a timely manner will affect the production, living and even safety of life of the majority of the people. Therefore, it is of prominent necessity to solve these problems in a timely manner through the extension of working hours.

The Implementing Measures for the Provisions of the State Council on the Working Hours of the Employees also expressly provide for added shifts and hours for employees of authority organs and institutions that for State organs, institutions also made employees work overtime regulations: for employees of

State organs and institutions working added shifts and hours due to the need to complete urgent tasks, compensatory leave of equal time shall be arranged. This provision is a step forward from the provisions of compensatory time off for employees of enterprise working overtime, and protects the right to rest of employees of State organs and institutions.

( Ⅱ ) The Restrictions over the Extension of Working Time

As extended working time is directly related to workers' right to rest, the Labor Law prescribes restrictive provisions regarding the extension of working hours.

**1. Procedural Restrictions and Time Limits on the Extension of Working Hours**

Article 41 of the Labor Law provides that: "An Employer may, upon consultation with its labor union and laborers, extend working hours due to the need of production or business operations, provided that the extended time shall generally not exceed one hour per day; where working hours need to be extended for special reasons, the extended time shall not exceed three hours per day on the condition that laborers' health is guaranteed, but the total extended time per month shall not exceed 36 hours. "

Under this provision, it can be seen that extension of working hours cannot be a random decision and must undergo certain formalities and meet certain conditions, and the length of extended working time has to be restricted within the range prescribed by the State. Specifically, the conditions for extension of working hours are:

First of all, out of the needs of production and operation. The production and operational needs mainly refer to urgent production tasks, which, if not completed on schedule, will inevitably affect the economic efficiency of enterprises and the income of workers. In this case, extension of working hours must be allowed.

Secondly, the employing entity must consult trade unions and workers. Enterprises, prior to making the decision of extension of working hours, shall have to explain the grounds of the extension, the number of people concerned and the length of the extension and other factors to the trade union, and obtain its consent. The trade union may agree with the decision to extend working hours if it believes that the grounds of extension are justified. Otherwise, further consultations can be conducted. As extended working time is directly related to workers' time to rest and will take up the rest time of workers, consultations with trade unions and workers are essential. The purpose of formulating such provisions in the Labor Law is to make sure that the extension of working hours is a voluntary decision of laborers without compulsion. Enterprises can only extend working hours if agreed by laborers.

Last but not least, the length of extended working hours must also comply with the provisions of the Labor Law, i. e. not in excess of 1 hour per day; where working hours need to be extended for special reasons, the extended time shall not exceed 3 hours per day on the condition that laborers' health is guaranteed, but the total extended time per month shall not exceed 36 hours. Obviously, the extension of working time for more than 1 hour due to special reasons comes with a precondition that laborers' health shall be guaranteed, and the extension shall not exceed 3 hours per day and the total extension within a month shall not be more than 36 hours. Any violation of this provision shall be deemed violation of the law and shall be imposed legal liability depending on the seriousness of the circumstances.

**2. Restrictions via Wages Paid for Extended Working Hours**

Article 44 of the Labor Law provides that: "Under any of the following circumstances, employers shall, in accordance with the following standards, pay laborers remunerations higher than their wages for normal working hours: ( i ) Where an employer extends its laborers' working hours, it shall pay the laborers remunerations not less than 150 percent of their wages; ( ii ) Where an employer arranges its laborers to work on days off but cannot arrange compensatory time off, it shall pay the laborers remunerations not less than 200 percent of their wages; and ( iii ) Where an employer arranges its laborers to work on statutory holidays, it shall pay the laborers remunerations not less than 300 percent of their wages. "

According to the provisions mentioned above, remuneration for extended working hours is divided into three grades due to the differences in extension of working time, namely, 150% of the wages for extension of working hours on regular working days; 200% of the wages for work on rest days; 300% of the wages for extension of working hours on holidays and festivals. Hence, a clear legal standard is established for the payment of wages for extended working hours. The wages for extended working hours are significantly higher than those of normal working hours, which, hopefully, would force employers to minimize added shifts and hours so as to cut down the wages for extended working hours, and would thus serve the purposes of protection of laborers' health and workers' motivation.

Employers arranging workers to work overtime on a rest day must first arrange for compensatory time off, and where compensatory time off cannot be arranged, remuneration of at least 200% of the regular wages shall be paid.

Compensatory time off shall be equal to the length of overtime. Overtime arrangement on statutory holidays usually does not require compensatory time off arrangement, but remuneration of at least 300% of the regular wages shall be paid.

### 3. Workers' Attitudes towards Extension of Working Hours

Workers must show support to the arrangements of added shifts and hours which meet statutory requirements and procedures, and keep a positive attitude for production and work during extended hours, and strive to complete the tasks within extended working hours.

For extension of working hours that does not meet statutory conditions and procedures, workers have the right to report to trade unions and request the latter to settle the issue with the employer through consultation. Where the issue cannot be resolved through consultation, workers may also report to the competent departments of enterprises, through the supervision of which, to cease the illegal practice of extending working hours. Where labor disputes arise out of extension of working hours, workers may, pursuant to the labor dispute handling procedures, apply for mediation or arbitration or even institute legal proceedings in accordance with the law.

● Chapter Ⅶ

# Labor Protection Law

It is inherent in the protection of the legitimate rights and interests of laborers provided by the labor law to strengthen labor protection. With the gradual improvement of the market economy system of China and the increasingly diversified labor employment system and management methods, the labor protection work is facing many new problems and challenges.

This Chapter will introduce the legislations on work safety and health both at home and abroad and their main contents, and illustrate the scope of occupational diseases and legal liabilities. This Chapter will also put emphasis on discussing the special labor protection for female and juvenile workers.

## Section 1   Overview of Legislation on Work Safety and Health

Work safety and health refers to the legal protection provided to laborers in the course of labor in terms of safety and health, which includes work safety technology specifications, work health specifications and enterprises' management systems on work safety and health, etc. The work safety and health as mentioned in labor law is generated based on the labor relationship and is known as "labor protection" in the traditional legislation in China. Law in this respect is called occupational accident labor protection law or law on work environment rights.

The work environment issue involves all laborers, machines and equipments, raw materials and work flow. This issue is therefore applicable to all workplaces, including enterprises, family workshops, sites where the construction workers work, classrooms where the teachers teach, coal pits where the miners locate, football fields where professional footballers play and train, and race tracks where the professional cyclists compete. And the scope of work environment issue expands from machines, equipments and special dangers to sexual harassments in the workplace. The legislation in this field aims to ensure that the laborers work under safe environment, and to prevent laborers from physical and mental harm. In terms of codes and standards, the legislation specifically requires employers to continuously improve the work safety and health conditions for laborers in the wake with the technological development and social progress, so as to ensure that the laborers will obtain safe labor conditions and work environment.

## I. China's Legislation on Work Safety and Health

China's legislation on work safety and health began from China's revolutionary times. Due to lacking of the rudimentary protection for safety and health in the production, the casualty accidents occupational diseases of laborers in Old China were widely spread and uncurbed. Laborers in those days worked under bad labor conditions, with very humble and narrow factories and crowded machines. In some workshops, laborers even had to work, eat, sleep, urinate and defecate in the same place. According to the information on Shanghai in the national disasters statistics of 1935 retained by the Central Factory Inspection Office under the Ministry of Industry of the Kuomintang government, factories in Shanghai had 2,254 industrial disasters of all types, 325 workers died from work and another 2,496 got injured from work in that year (excluding the number of employee casualties in enterprises within the Concessions in Shanghai). In the Northeast under the ruling of Japanese puppet regime, the labor conditions of Anshan Iron and Steel Company were described as follows: "the dressing plant is as big as a large pigsty, and the bar mill is a kind of Palace of Hell. It's difficult for workers to work in there." At that time, 70% of the coal mines in China relied on natural ventilation, and the underground workers may only obtain 1 cubic meter air per person per minute, which was equal to 1/4 of the minimum requirement. The moving, loading and unloading of coal were all manual, and the load standards for the porters were 200 kilograms, and such porters may only be deemed as qualified if they can carry such load to fast walk 50 meters without leg shaking or panting. According to the incomplete statistics by the Kailuan Coal Mine, during the 35 years from 1913 to 1948, there were 4,973 workers died on their posts, averagely 138 workers died annually. In the Northeast under the ruling of the Japanese Militarism, there were five "mass graves" for discarding and burying dead workers just in Hegang Coal Mine[1].

---

[1] He Guang, *Labor Protection in Contemporary China*, Page 2 - 3, Beijing, Contemporary China Publishing House, 1992

From 1922 to 1948, there were resolutions on work safety and health made in the guiding lines and decisions adopted by all National Labor Conventions, and the Chinese Soviet regime had promulgated provisions on labor protection. The Labor Law of Chinese Soviet Republic promulgated in November, 1931 made provisions on the adding of new machines, work clothes and other protection items as well as the physical examination. During the anti-Japanese war period, the people's government of Shan-Gan-Ning Border Region formulated in 1942 the Regulations on Labor Protection of the Shan-Gan-Ning Border Region (Draft), which stipulated the work "safety and health" issue in a specific chapter. The government of Shanxi-Hebei-Shangdong-Henan Border Region amended the Tentative Regulations on Labor Protection of Shanxi-Hebei-Shangdong-Henan Border Region in 1943.

the Common Program, as adopted by the Chinese People's Political Consultative Conference at the eve of the founding of the People's Republic of China, specified that "private and public enterprises shall generally carry out the work hour system of 8 - 10 work hours", "the special interests of female workers shall be protected", "industry and mining inspection systems shall be carried out to improve the safety and health equipments in industrial and mining areas. " The first Constitution of China clearly specified that "the citizens' labor rights shall be guaranteed through gradually enlarging employment, strengthening labor protection and improving labor conditions and salary and benefits. ", "laborers shall be entitled to rest, and the State shall stipulate the system of work hours and vocation for workers and employees and gradually supplement the physical conditions for the rest and recuperation of laborers, so as to guarantee the enjoyment of this right by laborers", which laid legal basis for the legislation on work safety and health.

In September, 1951, the Ministry of Labor convened the first National Labor Protection Work Conference in Beijing. The State carried out a large-scale legislation on labor protection, and successively promulgated relevant regulations on safety technology education, preparing work safety technology measures plan, prevention of poisoning by asphalt and gasoline, prevention of explosions, prevention of silica danger, scope of occupational diseases and handling of occupational disease patients, labor conditions for loading, unloading and moving operations, boiler operation precautions, and temporary health standards for the design of industrial enterprises. Among them, most important of all are the Code for Factory Safety and Health, Safety Technology Specifications on Construction Installation Projects and Code for Reporting Casualty Accidents of Workers and

Employees promulgated by the State Council after deliberations under the host of Premier Zhou Enlai.

In 1982, the State Council issued the Interim Regulations on Safety Supervision of Boilers and Pressure Vessels, the Mine Safety Regulations and the Mine Safety Supervision Regulations, through which the labor safety supervision work was greatly strengthened and the system combining national supervision, industry management and public surveillance was thus gradually formed. In July, 1984, the State Council issued the Decision on Strengthening Dust and Poison Prevention, and put forward that the dust and toxicant treatments and safety measures in the infrastructure projects and factory technical transformation in all regions and departments must be designed, constructed, accepted and put into use at the same time with those of the main works. In December, 1987, the State Council issued the Pneumoconiosis Prevention Regulations, which stipulated that "where the dust concentration in workplaces exceeds the national health standards and is failed to be positively treated, which causes material adverse effect on the safety and health of employees, the employees may refuse operations." And regulations issued by relevant authorities in the same year expanded the scope of occupational diseases and stipulated the measures for treating occupational diseases patients. In addition, the Regulations on Labor Protection for Female Employees, a special regulation which systematically stipulated the labor protection legal system for female employees in China, was issued.

In 1991, The State Council issued the Code for Reporting Casualty Accidents of Employees in Enterprises, which replaced the Code for Reporting Casualty Accidents of Workers and Employees promulgated in 1956. The 28th session of the 7th National People's Congress held in November, 1992 adopted the Mine Safety Law, which was the first law on labor safety and health in China and had come into force on May 1, 1993. In January, 1993, the State Council approved and forwarded the Circular on Opinions Concerning Preventing the Disorder Mining and Suppression of Small Mines to Ensure the Work Safety in Mines issued by the Ministry of Labor together with other ministries and departments, and the Ministry of Labor also issued the Labor Supervision Regulations in August of the same year.

The Labor Law specially stipulates the provisions on "labor safety and health" in its Chapter 6, and makes provisions on the principles of labor safety and health by the means of basic labor law. In order to further carry out the provisions of the Labor Law, the Ministry of Labor has also issued a series of laws and regulations on labor safety and health to support the Labor Law, for example, the

Regulations on Labor Supervisor and the Regulations on Special Protection for Juvenile Employees.

China has also carried out and made great progress in standard legislations on labor safety and health, and the State has promulgated a series of national standards in respect of management standards, operation standards, work safety equipments, tool safety and health, production process safety and health, protective equipments, etc. For example, the national standards issued in China have reached over 150 standards, including the Helmet Standards, the Safety Color Standards, the Safety Sign Standards, the High-place Operation Standards, the Classification of Physical Labor Intensity, the High Temperature Operation Classification, the Classification of Productive Dust Hazard Degree, the Classification of Toxic Work, the Classification of Operations in Cold Water and the Classification of Low-temperature Operations. These standards lay the foundation for the legislation of the labor safety and health work in China and are important basis for carrying out labor safety and health supervision.

On June 29, 2002, the Production Safety Law was issued, which came into force on November 1, 2002. The Law stipulates the law principles on work safety, safety rules in production and operation, rights and obligations of the practitioners, supervision and management of work safety, the emergency rescue, investigation & handling and legal liabilities of work safety accidents.

The Occupational Diseases Prevention Law of the People's Republic of China has been adopted at the 24th session of the 9th National People's Congress on October 27, 2001. In order to prevent, control and eliminate the occupational hazards, prevent occupational diseases, protect the health of laborers and facilitate economic development, the Occupational Disease Prevention Law has introduced foreign legislation practices on the basis of summarizing the work experience in the prevention of occupational disease in China.

On December 31, 2011, the Occupational Disease Prevention Law has been re-promulgated after revision. The new Law has further specified and defined the supervision duties of relevant departments in the prevention of occupational diseases, strengthened the protection for patients of occupational diseases, made detailed provisions in respect of the diagnosis, authentication, arbitration and help, strengthened the efforts in the punishments against illegal acts and added the content of punishments or liabilities, and included the "dust of high hazard" into the legal provisions.

## Section 2　Content of Labor Safety and Health Law

### Ⅰ. Content of Labor Safety

( Ⅰ ) Safety of Building and Passageways

In China, the buildings in factory must be solid and safe and in compliance with the provisions on fire and explosion protection, and any found damage to or danger sign in the building shall be immediately fixed. The roads within factory must be flat and unblocked, and be equipped with sufficient night lighting equipments. The crossing points of roads and pathways must have conspicuous warning signs, signal installations or callers. The pits and trenches as required for the production shall be fenced or covered with plates. The piling of raw materials, finished products, semi-finished products and waste materials shall not impede the passage and convenience in loading and unloading. There should be protection net installed and obvious warning signs marked inside and outside the grid.

( Ⅱ ) Safety of Machines and Equipments

The safety installation of machines and equipments is an important content in the labor safety codes. In order to prevent and avoid any casualty accident to workers in the use of machines and equipments, the labor safety specifications in China require that machines and equipments shall have protection device, safety device, signal device, danger sign and identification mark.

( Ⅲ ) Safety of Electrical Equipments

Electrical equipments are equipments commonly used by many enterprises. In order to prevent any fire accident caused by electrical equipment or electricity shock accident to the workers in the production, the labor safety specifications in China have made corresponding provisions. For example, the Code for Safety and Health in Factories stipulates that, electrical equipments must have fuse cutout and automatic switch; protective grounding or neutralizing measures must be taken before the use of electrical tools and good insulation condition must be provided; the naked energized conductors shall be installed at places out of the general reach; otherwise, there shall be safety barriers set and conspicuous warning signs marked in the place. The voltage of red lights shall not exceed 36 V, and not exceed 12 V in case of metal containers or wet place.

For electric drills, electric picks and other hand-held motor-operated electric tools, protective grounding or neutralizing measures must be taken before their use. Workplaces with large amount of steams, air and dust must have closed electrical equipments. Workplaces with explosive gas or dust must have explosion-proof electrical equipments, and the switch of the electrical equipments must be managed by persons specially arranged for this purpose.

( IV ) Labor Protection Supplies

In order to prevent the occurrence of work-related accidents and protect the safety and health of workers in the production, China has made regulations on distributing labor protection supplies to persons engaging in relevant operations. Labor protection supplies use some shields to protect all or part of the body from the external toxic and harmful substances by the measures of obstruction, sealing, absorption, dispersion and suspension. Protection supplies are very important for the safety and health of laborers, the prevention of the occurrence of occupational diseases and chronic damage and the reduction or elimination of the occurrence of injury and death accidents. The types of labor protection supplies include: ( 1 ) dust-proof supplies, for example, respiratory dust-proof supplies, including respirator, dust-proof coat, shawl and cap; ( 2 ) anti-poison supplies, for example, anti-poison mask and anti-poison gloves; ( 3 ) noise-proof supplies, for example, earplug and ear-cap; ( 4 ) anti-power supplies, for example, insulating gloves and insulating boots and shoes; ( 5 ) high temperature and radiation prevention supplies, for example, safety goggles and heal insulation fire-resistant holes; ( 6 ) microwave and laser radiation prevention supplies, for example, anti-microwave glasses and laser radiation prevention glasses; ( 7 ) anti-radiation supplies, for example, calico and plastic protective overalls; ( 8 ) anti-acid and anti-alkali supplies, for example, rubber and plastic film; ( 9 ) oil-proof supplies, for example, rubber and latex; ( 10 ) water-proof supplies, for example, rubberized waterproof clothing and raincoat; ( 11 ) striking resistant supplies, for example, smash-proof shoes and bamboo leg-guard; ( 12 ) falling protection supplies, for example, safety belt and guard net; ( 13 ) mechanical trauma prevention supplies, for example, work clothes and elbow guards; ( 14 ) dirt resistant supplies, for example, overalls and gloves; and ( 15 ) cold proof supplies, for example, cold protective clothing and cold weather shoes.

## II. Content of Labor Health

( I ) Prevention of Dust Hazards

In order to eliminate the dust hazards in factories and mine enterprises and protect the safety and health of workers and employees, the labor health codes require that, for operation in dusty environment, efforts shall be made in realizing the mechanization and enclosure of production equipments and installing dust absorption, dust filtration and ventilation equipments, and in case of mines, wet drilling for rock and mechanical ventilation shall be used. Laborers will be vulnerable to all types of pneumoconiosis diseases caused by lung fibrosis if they inhale too much dust during work. Therefore, the State has made strict regulation on the dust concentration in workplaces, and the maximum acceptable concentration of dust or asbestos dust in the industrial workshops or workplaces with over 10% free silica per cubic meter is 2 milligrams. On December 3, 1987, the State Council issued the Regulations on the Prevention of Pneumoconiosis, which has made comprehensive provisions on the prevention of dust hazards. Such Regulations require that enterprises and public institutions with dust operations shall take comprehensive dust proof measures and new technologies, processes and equipments with no or low dust, making the dust concentration in the workplaces not in excess of the state health standards. The authentication and modeling system of the dust proof facilities shall be formulated by the labor authorities together with the health administration authorities. No enterprise or public institution shall cease the operation of or dismantle the dust proof facilities without the approval of the superior competent authorities, except under special circumstances. Any assignment of the work in dusty environment to the township or community enterprise or private business without anti-dust facilities by the ways of transfer, outsourcing and joint operation is strictly prohibited.

( Ⅱ ) Prevention of Hazards from Toxic and Harmful Substances

Long-term exposure to toxic and harmful substances will cause great physical health harm or even death caused by poisoning to the laborers. In order to prevent the damage from toxic and harmful substance and safeguard the health of workers in the labor, the labor health codes have made provisions on the prevention of hazards of toxic and harmful substances. The concentration of toxic and harmful substances in workplace shall not exceed the state standards. The toxic and dangerous substances shall be stored in specially designated place separately and under strict management. There shall be washing equipments in the workplaces where workers will be exposed to acid and alkali and other erosive substances and burning dangers. When processing the raw materials with danger of infectious diseases, stick protection measures must be taken. The handling of toxic wastes or wastes with infectious danger shall be conducted under the guidance of local health authority. The wastes and waste water shall be properly disposed to prevent their hazards to workers and residents in the neighborhood.

(Ⅲ) Prevention of the Stimulations by Noise and Hard Light

The noise and hard light produced in the working environment for such operations as connection, forging and pressing, gas welding, electric welding and smelting are harmful to the vision and hearing of workers. In order to prevent the harm or stimulation by the noise or hard light produced in industry enterprises, the labor safety codes require that the relevant working environment must have silencing equipments and meet the requirements specified by relevant regulations. Production with strong noise shall be conducted in the separate workshop equipped with silencing equipments as much as possible. Workers operated in the workplaces with noise, hard light, radiant heat, flying sparks, debris or fillings generated shall be separately provided with ear protectors, protective glasses and masks.

(Ⅳ) Ventilation and Lighting

Workplaces in which the workers carry out production activities shall be neat and clean, in good ventilation and have fresh air and reasonable lighting, so as to be conducive to the working of the workers and safeguarding the physical and mental health of the workers. Therefore, the Code for Factory Safety and Health stipulates that, for workplaces and passageways, there shall be sufficient light, and the luminosity of local lighting shall be in compliance with the operation requirements but not so glaring; ventilation equipments and heating equipments must be managed by full-time or part-time personnel; manual illumination equipments shall be kept clean and intact; and windows shall be wiped frequently, and start and close equipments shall be flexible, etc.

## Section 3  Reporting and Legal Liability of Occupational Diseases

### Ⅰ. Reporting System

In order to take control of the incidence of occupational diseases, formulate the prevention measures, protect the health of employees and enhance the labor productivity, the occupational diseases occurred in enterprises shall be reported by local health supervision authorities on a uniform basis.

The occupational diseases report in China can be dated back to the investigation, registration, statistics report of acute toxic accidents as provided in the Code for Reporting Casualty Accidents of Workers and Employees issued by the State Council in 1956. In the same year, the Ministry of Health and the Ministry of Labor jointly issued the Interim Measures for Reporting Occupational Poisoning and Occupational Diseases, whose nationwide and uniform enforcement in China was ceased in 1959 due to the practicability issues concerning diagnosis of occupational diseases.

In 1982, the Ministry of Health and the State Labor Bureau jointly issued the Circular on Resuming the Reporting System of Occupational Poisoning and Occupational Diseases. The Measures for Reporting Occupational Poisoning and Occupational Diseases was revised and renamed as Measures on the Report of Occupational Diseases in 1984. The circular on the "minutes concerning the work division in respect of labor health supervision between the health administration and labor administration" issued in 1986 specified that the health administration shall be responsible for the statistics and report work of labor health and occupational diseases.

1. The reporters shall be the enterprises with toxic and harmful substances generated, and all kinds of occupational diseases diagnosis institutions and medical health institutions at all levels.

2. Reporting Procedures: the statistics reporting shall be organized and carried out by health administrations at all levels and undertaken by the designated health supervision institutions at the same level. The health supervision institutions at all levels shall specially determine the person who is responsible for the collection, sorting, summary, analysis and reporting of materials. The health supervision statistics materials, both in the affiliated enterprises and public institutions under the ministries and commissions of the State Council and in the local enterprises and public institutions, shall be summarized and reported by the local health administration authorities and the health supervision institutions.

3. Contents of the Report: the seven reporting forms (cards) as approved by the State Statistics Bureau, including the Annual Report Form on Labor Health Situation of Factories and Mines with Harmful Work Condition, the Annual Supervision Form on Health of Workers Engaging in Harmful Work, the Annual Form on the Determination of Hazardous Factors in Production Environment, the Report Card for Pneumoconiosis, the Report Card for Occupational Poisoning and Occupational Diseases, the Report Card for Pesticide Poisoning and the Onsite Labor Health Investigation Form for Patients of Acute Occupational Poisoning.

An emergency reporting system is implemented for major occupational poisoning accident (i. e. any accident causing the death of one worker or the illness of three workers or more, or any accident in which at least one worker suffers occupational anthrax), and the reporting procedures for such accident shall be: any medical and health institution of preliminary clinic reception or other statutory reporter shall, within 12 hours upon being aware of the occurrence of the said accident, report the same to the local health supervision institution, and the health supervision institution first receiving the said report shall, upon the investigation and confirmation, immediately report the same to the health administration at the same level, report to the Ministry of Health by telephone within 24 hours, and submit a special report or the Onsite Labor Health Investigation Form for Acute Occupational Poisoning to the Ministry of Labor within 5 days upon the ending of handling work.

Pursuant to the Occupational Diseases Prevention Law, the employing unit in which the accident with acute occupational disease hazard has occurred or is likely to occur shall immediately take emergency rescue and control measures, and timely report the accident to the local health administration and relevant departments. The health administration shall, upon receipt of the said report, timely organize the investigation and handling together with other departments, and may take interim control measures whenever necessary.

## II. Legal Liability

Health administration department of the people's government at the county level or above shall, based on the responsibilities and duties they undertake, conduct supervision and inspection over the prevention, testing and assessment activities of the occupational diseases in accordance with the laws and regulations on the prevention of occupational diseases, state occupational health standards and health requirements.

### ( I ) Inspection and Control

When fulfilling their duties of supervision and inspection, the health administration departments may take the following measures: (1) to enter the unit under inspection and the place exposed to occupational disease hazards, to get to know the situation, conduct investigation and take evidence; (2) to consult or duplicate material related to violations of the laws and regulations on prevention and control of occupational diseases, and to collect sample; and (3) to order the unit or individual that violates the laws and regulations on prevention and control of occupational diseases to discontinue violation.

When an accident of occupational disease hazards occurs or there is evidence proving that the hazards may lead to occurrence of such an accident, the public health administration department may adopt the following measures to keep the situation under control: (1) to order suspension of the operation that may lead to an accident of occupational disease hazards; (2) to seal up for safekeeping the materials and equipment that has caused, or may lead to, the occurrence of an accident of occupational disease hazards; and (3) to get people to keep under control the place where the accident of occupational disease hazards has occurred. When the accident of occupational disease hazards or the hazardous situation has been kept under effective control, the public health administration department shall repeal the control measures without delay.

## ( Ⅱ ) Legal Liability

Where the construction unit commits one of the following acts, the public health administration department shall give it a disciplinary warning and order it to make rectification within a time limit; if it fails to do so at the expiration of the time limit, it shall be fined not less than RMB 100,000 yuan but not more than 500,000 yuan. If the circumstances are serious, it shall be ordered to discontinue the operation that produces occupational disease hazards, or the department may request the related people's government, within the limits of its powers specified by the State Council, to order the unit to discontinue construction or close down: (1) starting construction without making a preliminary assessment of the occupational disease hazards according to regulations or submitting a report on such assessment, or without obtaining approval of the report by the public health administration department after examination; (2) failing to have the facilities for prevention of occupational disease put into operation and use simultaneously with the main body of the construction project, as is required by regulations; (3) starting construction of a project which produces serious occupational disease hazards and the design of the facilities of which for prevention of such diseases does not meet the national norms and requirements; and (4) putting into use the facilities for prevention of occupational disease without assessing the effectiveness of their control of occupational disease hazards, as is required by regulations, or without inspection and acceptance by the public health administration department or without passing the inspection.

Where the employer commits one of the following acts, the public health administration department shall order it to make rectification within a time limit and give it a disciplinary warning, and may also impose on it a fine not less than 20,000 yuan but not more than 50,000 yuan: (1) failing to submit timely and truthful report to the public health administration department on the project that produces occupational disease hazards, as is required by regulations; (2) failing to assign special persons to carry out day-to-day monitoring of the factors of occupational disease hazards and failing to keep the monitoring system in normal working conditions; (3) when concluding or altering labor contracts, failing to inform the workers of the true situation of occupational disease hazards; and (4) failing to make arrangements for occupational health checkups, to keep files on occupational health monitoring and protection and to truthfully inform the workers of the results of the checkups.

Where the employer commits one of the following acts, the public health administration department shall give it a disciplinary warning and order it to make rectification within a time limit; if it fails to do so at the expiration of the time limit, it shall be fined not less than 50,000 yuan but not more than 200,000 yuan. If the circumstances are serious, the said department shall order it to discontinue operation that produces occupational disease hazards, or the department may request the related people's government, within the limit of its powers specified by the State Council, to order it to close down: (1) failing to keep the strength or concentrations of the factors of occupational disease hazards at the workplace from exceeding the national norms for occupational health; (2) failing to provide facilities for prevention of occupational diseases and to provide such articles for personal use, or failing to provide the said facilities and articles that meet the national norms and requirements for occupational health; (3) failing to maintain, overhaul and test the equipment for prevention of occupational diseases, the emergency rescue facilities and the articles to be used by individuals for prevention of such diseases, as is required by regulations, or failing to keep them in normal operation and use; (4) failing to monitor and assess the factors of occupational disease hazards at the workplace, as is required by regulations; (5) failing to discontinue work where the factors of occupational disease hazards exist, when such factors at the workplace still remain below the national norms and requirements for occupational health, even after treatment; (6) failing to make arrangements for patients of occupational diseases or suspected patients of such diseases to receive diagnosis and treatment, as is required by regulations; (7) failing to adopt emergency rescue and control measures immediately after the occurrence of an accident of acute occupational disease hazards or when such occurrence is likely, or failing to report such occurrence immediately, as is required by regulations; (8) failing to put up alarming indications with warning descriptions in Chinese at eye-catching spots of a post where serious occupational disease hazards are produced, as is required by regulations; and (9) refusing to accept supervision and inspection by public health administration departments.

Where the employer violates the relevant regulations, which has caused severe occupational hazard accident, i. e. having occupational diseases causing death or acute occupational poisoning of several people or more, or having other symptoms which shall be treated as occupational diseases damage accident as required by the State, such as occupational anthrax or radioactive isotope and ray accident (collectively "radiation accident"), or caused other severe consequence including but not limited to, forcing employees to continue to work after accident, damaging environment resources due to transfer of occupational diseases damage, impeding health administration authorities and occupational disease curing personnel to legally perform official business and disturbing social order by violence or forcing methods, if a crime is constituted, the person directly in charge and the other directly responsible persons shall be investigated for criminal liability.

If the manufacturers or operators of equipments or materials violate relevant regulations and cause occupational hazard, they shall be investigated for administrative and criminal liability. Pursuant to the Product Quality Law, industrial products relating to personal health, personal safety and property safety must be in compliance with the national standards and industry standards that protect the body health, personal and property safety; the requirements for protecting the body health, personal and property safety must be satisfied when there is no such national and industry standard. According to the Regulations on Radiation Protection from Radioactive Isotope and Ray Devices issued by the State Council, entities or individuals importing equipments containing instruments with radioactive isotopes must carry out registration and filing procedures at local health, public security and environmental protection authorities; and entities or individuals importing mine products and finished products with a radiation level beyond the radiation exemption level shall apply for radiation monitoring inspection with the local provincial health administration authorities where the port locates. In case of producing equipments, radiation devices or radioactive protection apparatus with radioactive isotopes, the radiation protection requirements must be complied with, and the unqualified products may not be delivered. In case of producing consumables and supplies with radioactive substance and electrical products producing X-ray, the radiation protection requirements must be complied with, and unqualified products may not be sold. The food, drugs, cosmetics, medical apparatus and other products used on human body, which have been irradiated by radioactive isotopes and ray devices, must meet the national health regulations and standards.

Where any health administration or its professional health supervision enforcement staff violates relevant regulations, which causes any occupational hazard accident and constitutes any crime, they shall be legally investigated for criminal liabilities; if no crime is constituted, the principal of unit, director directly responsible and other directly responsible persons shall be given such administrative punishments as demotion, dismissal or removal.

Where any member of occupational disease diagnosis committee accepts effects or other benefits from the party concerned, such member shall be given a warning and confiscated such effects, and may be given a fine not less than RMB 3,000 yuan and not more than RMB 50,000 yuan and cancelled off his/her qualifications for the membership of occupational disease diagnosis committee, and removed from the expert lists established by the health administrations of provinces, autonomous regions or municipalities directly under central government. The duties of occupational disease diagnosis committee include providing technical guidance to and examination over the occupational disease diagnosis, organizing the identification of the difficult and complicated cases submitted by the inferior occupational disease diagnosis committee, accepting the entrustment for identification and diagnosis of occupational diseases by the court, and undertaking other missions as entrusted by the health administration. The statutory requirements for occupational ethnics of the members of the occupational disease diagnosis committee are fundamentally for preserving the interests of the laborers.

## Section 4    Legislation and Significance of Special Protection for Female Employees

### I. Legislation of Special Protection for Female Employees

#### ( I ) Concept of Special Protection for Female Employees

"Female employees" refer to all women laborers in general, which include female mental laborers and female physical laborers. Special protection for female employees is an important integral part of the labor protection and the labor law of all countries in the world, and the personal characteristics of female employees have determined that female employees should be given special labor protection in law.

Female employees as mentioned in the Labor Law of China include all married and unmarried female employees engaging in mental or physical labor activities. Due to their own physical characteristics, female employees will generally face some special difficulties in labor and work. Meanwhile, they also undertake the responsibilities for giving birth to and nursing babies and infants. If no attention is paid to these characteristics of female employees in the labor, and no special protection is provided for these female employees, not only the personal safety and health of female employees will be affected, but also the safety and health of next generation will be affected.

Female will have to go through "four periods" in their lives, i. e. menstrual period, pregnancy period, perinatal period and breast-feeding period. During menstrual period, female will frequently feel tired and nervous and have big emotional fluctuations, and despite the fact that they can still participate in labor and production as usual, their physical and mental conditions will be affected considerately. Upon pregnancy, women will have a series of physical responses, for example, accelerated breathing, inconvenient mobility and the occurrence of physiological anemia, and in the later period of pregnancy, they often need to leave their positions, take a rest or do some extremely easy work. Women in breast-feeding period not only have to watch their babies, but also have to conduct their physical rehabilitation.

In terms of labor capacity, due to the features in respect of their body structure and physiological structure, women are not as good as men in terms of height and weight, and therefore have a poorer bearing capacity. Women's oxygen ability and ability in basic metabolism are weaker than those of men, but have a better patience and stamina than men. Women's physical power is relatively weak, and therefore less competent for physical work than men and having weaker adaptive capacity to environment than men, and work in toxic, tight and poor environment is extremely inappropriate for female. However, women have a good balance capacity and stamina, and can be quite qualified for the work requiring accurate hand's movement and high focusing attention, for example, electronics and textile jobs. Women have comparative advantage in observation ability, imagination, memory, ability of image thinking and language skill, and women have unique advantage in terms of labor activities concerning arts, education, social communication and service.

( Ⅱ ) Legislation on Special Protection for Female Employees

The Common Program of China of 1949 stipulated that the special interests of young and female workers shall be protected. In 1952, the Ministry of Textile and Industry and the National Committee of the Textile Workers' Trade Union of China jointly issued the Circular on Protecting Female Workers and Pregnant Women, which made specific provisions on the special protection for female textile workers. The Labor Insurance Regulations of the People's Republic of China amended and issued in 1953 stipulated that female employees shall be given a maternity leave of 56 days, during which their salary shall be paid as usual. In July, 1956, the Ministry of Labor issued and carried out trial implementation of the Regulations on Labor Conditions for Loading and Unloading and Transporting Operations (Draft), which provided that the bear load for a single female worker shall not exceed 25 kgs, and the total weight of load carried by two female workers shall not exceed 50 kgs. The Health Standards for Industry Enterprise Design issued in September, 1979, made specific provisions on the shower room, female worker health room, pregnancy worker rest room, breast-feeding and nursery room and other relating facilities of an industry enterprise. Since 1980, 14 entities including the State Labor Bureau, the All China Federation of Trade Unions, the All-China Women's Federation and the Ministry of Health have commenced to draft a special regulation on labor protection for female employees. The Regulations on Labor Protection for Female Employees issued by the State Council in 1988 made comprehensive provisions on special protection for female employees, and the Regulations on Prohibition of Use of Child Labor issued by the State Council in 1991 expressly prohibited all types of illegal use of child labor. In the Law of the People's Republic of China on the Protection of Minors adopted at the 21st session of the 7th Standing Committee of National People's Congress held in September, 1991 and the Law on Protection of the Rights and Interests of Women adopted at the 5th session of the 7th National People's Congress in April, 1992, provisions on special protection for female employees and juvenile employees have been made.

The Labor Law has summarized the effective experience in protecting female employees, absorbed the achievements made in legislation and practice in China, used the common practice in all countries of the world for reference and made provisions on the special protection for female employees in a separate chapter.

## Ⅱ. Significance of Special Protection for Female Employees

Special protection for female employees is an important integral part of the labor law and other labor protection regulations in China. Special protection should be provided for the labor of female employees, which is determined by the native features of female employees. The body structure and physiological characteristics of women are greatly different from those of men. Women have the physical stages including menstrual period, pregnancy period, perinatal period and breast-feeding period. If no special protection is provided for women under these circumstances who are in labor, not only the safety and health of the female employees will be affected, but also the quality of next generation will be affected.

Under the conditions of China's socialism system, it is of great political significance and economic significance to provide special protection for female employees and juvenile employees.

Firstly, the special protection for female employees embodies the superiority of socialism system. People are the masters of the country, and the special protection for female employees and juvenile employees reflects the will of the people, and is in the interests of people.

Secondly, the special protection for female employees is of great significance for promoting the productivity development of China. Women are great human resource. In China, women can participate in a lot of work and labor activities, covering all sectors. We must give special consideration to women and do a good job in the labor protection for female employees so as to enable them to maintain sufficient and enduring energy and to give full play of their role in all construction undertakings. This is an important measure to mobilize the initiative of female employees.

Thirdly, the special protection for female employees relates to the prosperity of the Chinese nation and the maintenance and improvement of the excellent physical fitness of the nation. Women shoulder the special responsibility for giving birth to next generation, so the special protection for female employees is not only the protection for female employees, but also the protection for the safety and health of next generation. For example, if female employees are engaged in extremely heavy physical labor and toxic and harmful operations, the development and growth of fetus and babies and infants will be affected, or even miscarriage, premature delivery and poisoning death and fetal malfunction of fetus will be caused. In order to ensure excellent physical fitness of next generation, it is necessary to safeguard the safety and health of female employees during labor in their pregnancy and breast-feeding period.

Fourthly, it is of greater practical significance to provide special protection for female employees under market economy conditions. Due to the fact that female employees have varies leaves during the "four periods", employers are reluctant to recruit female employees, and some employers even link the economic income of employees with the economic effects of the factory, under which the maternity leave of female employees will be calculated into absence time like personal leave and sick leave, and in this case, the salary income of female employees who have taken maternity leave would be reduced. In some other enterprises, employers will require that the work hours may be shortened on the precondition that the workload will not be lesser, which actually increases the labor intensity of the female employees who are in pregnancy or breast-feeding period. Thus, only improving the legal system for special protection for female employees can protect the intactness of special protection for female employees during reform and create more employment opportunities for female employees.

## Section 5　Content of Special Protection for Female Employees

According to the principle of protecting women by the constitution and in order to protect the special rights and interests of the female in the labor, China has issued different administrative instruments in different historical periods to guide the local governments to strengthen the labor protection for female employees. Local governments and relevant departments have also issued several regulations. Since 1986, China has successively issued the Interim Regulations on Health Care for Female Employees (Draft for Trial Implementation), the Regulations on Labor Protection for Female Employees and the Provisions on Scope of Forbidden Labor for Female Employees. In particular, the Regulations on Labor Protection for Female Employees issued by the State Council in July, 1988, is the first special regulation in China which has made systematical provisions on the legal system for labor protection for female employees. The said Regulations has made full provisions on female employees' recruitment, the forbidden labor activities, maternity leave and related benefits, and relevant protection facilities, providing a relatively defined legal basis for labor protection for female employees in China.

On April 18, 2012, the State Council adopted the Special Regulations on Labor Protection for Female Employees on its 200th executive meeting, which shall come into force on the date of its promulgation. The new Regulations has improved the Regulations on Labor Protection for Female Employees from three aspects: the first is adjusting the scope of labor forbidden to engage in by female employees, the second is regulating the maternity leave period and benefits, and the third is adjusting the supervision management system.

## Ⅰ. The Forbidden Labor Activities for Female Employees

Due to the different physiological functions and body structure between female and male, all poor labor conditions and all types of occupational hazards will produce adverse effects on the physical health of women. Article 59 of the Labor Law stipulates that work in underground mine is prohibited for female employees, as the work in underground mine has very hard labor conditions, poor operation environment, many hazardous factors and large labor intensity. Work in underground mine refers to all types of permanent work in underground mine, excluding temporary work such as the underground rescue and medical treatment as provided by the medical staff. At present, the work in underground mine is prohibited for women as stipulated by various countries in the world.

Article 59 of the Labor Law also stipulates that female employees are forbidden to engage in labor of Class 4 physical work intensity as provided for by the State, and no female employee may be arranged to engage in other forbidden activities. The work intensity index is measured by two factors, one is the average working time rate of the said work and the other is the average rate of energy metabolism. The greater the work intensity index, the larger the work intensity will be, and vice versa. The Classification of Physical Labor Intensity stipulates that, when the work intensity index $<15$, the work intensity is Class 1; when the work intensity index$>15$ and $<20$, the work intensity is Class 2; when the work intensity index$>20$ and $<25$, the work intensity is Class 3; and when the work intensity index$>25$, the work intensity is Class 4. The work as included in Class 4 work intensity is the work of 8 working hours per day with the average energy consumption value reaching 2700 Kcal per person and its working time rate reaching 77%, which equals to 370 minutes net working time.

The Regulations on Special Protection for Female Employees stipulates the scope of the forbidden labor activities for female employees as: (1) operations in underground mine; (2) operations of Class 4 physical labor intensity as provided in the standards for classification of physical labor intensity; (3) operations requiring at least six heavy loads per hour, each of which exceeds 20 kgs, or requiring intermittent heavy loads, each of which exceeds 25kgs.

## Ⅱ. Special Labor Protection for Female Employees During Pregnancy, Menstrual Period, Perinatal Period and Breast-Feeding Period

In addition to the production of social substances and materials, female employees also bear the main responsibility for the reproduction of human being. The menstrual period, pregnancy, maternity period and breast-feeding period are essential periods for the reproduction of human being, and female employees require special protection during these periods in which they have physiological functions changes.

### (Ⅰ) Pregnancy Protection

The scope of the forbidden labor activities for female employees who are in pregnancy includes operations in the workplaces relating to arsenic, benzene, mercury and cadmium and belonging to Class 3 and Class 4 as provided in the Classification of Toxic Operations. The employer may not arrange those female employees who are in pregnancy to engage in the work of Class 3 physical labor intensity as provided by the State or other labor activities as prohibited for pregnant women, and may not extend the work hours of female employees beyond the normal work days; and shall reduce the workload or arrange other work for those pregnant women who are incompetent to the original posts on the strength of certificate issued by the medical department.

Pursuant to the Regulations on Labor Protection for Female Employees, the forbidden labor activities for those female employees who are in pregnancy include: (1) the operations under the workplaces in which the concentration of lead and its compounds, mercury and its compounds, benzene, cadmium, beryllium, arsenic, cyanide, nitric oxide, carbon monoxide, carbon disulfide, chlorine, caprolactom, chloroprene, vinyl chloride, ethylene oxide, aniline, methanol or other toxic substances in the air exceeds the national health standards; (2) the operations relating to the production of anti-cancer drugs and diethylstilbestrol and the access to anesthetic gases; (3) operations relating to radioactive materials of unsealed sources, and emergency disposals for nuclear accidents and radiation accidents; (4) high-place operations as provided in the standards set forth in the classification of high-place operations; (5) cold water operations as provided in the standards set forth in the classification of cold water operations; (6) low temperature operations as provided in the standards set forth in the classification of low temperature operations; (7) operations of Class 3 and Class 4 as provided in the standards set forth in the classification of high temperature operations; (8) operations of Class 3 and Class 4 as provided in the standards set forth in the classification of noise operations; (9) operations of Class 3 and Class 4 physical labor intensity as provided in the standards set forth in the classification of physical labor intensity; and (10) operations in sealed room or high pressure room or diving operations, or operations with strong vibration, or operations in need of frequent bending, climbing and crouching.

### (Ⅱ) Menstrual Period Protection

During menstrual period, the body resistance of female employees will reduce, and their legs will feel weak and limp, and if they are required to engage in high-place operations, casualty accident is easy to happen to them. If they engage in low temperature cold water operations during this period, the moving of menstruation may be blocked and the stasis will accumulate in the pelvic cavity, which will cause dysmenorrheal and amenorrhea, and due to their reduced body resistance, they are more vulnerable to illness. And numerous haemorrhages may be suffered by them when they are exposed to toxic substances. Poor labor conditions will have a negative affect on the health of women during their menstrual period. Any lack of special protection in this respect will influence the health and fertility of female employees. Article 60 of the Labor Law stipulates that, "female employees may not be arranged to engage in labor activities of Class 3 physical labor intensity and high-place, low temperature or cold water operations."

The Special Regulations on Labor Protection for Female Employees set forth the scope of the forbidden labor activities for female employees during menstrual period as follows: (1) cold water operations of Class 2, 3 & 4 as provided in the standards set forth in the Classification of Cold Water Operations; (2) low temperature operations of Class 2, 3 & 4 as provided in the standards set forth in the Classification of Low Temperature Operations; (3) operations of Class 3 and 4 physical labor intensity as provided in the standards set forth in the Classification of Physical Labor Intensity; and (4) Class 3 and 4 high-place operations as provided in the standards set forth in the Classification of High-place Operations.

Pursuant to the Classification of High-place Operation, the so-called "working at heights", also known as high-place operation, refers to the operation at the place with the height of 2 meters or higher above the falling height datum with the risk of falling. And this type of operation is all addressed as high-place operation. Where the height of high-place operation is between 2 meters to 5 meters, it is called Class 1 high-place operation; where the height of high-place operation is between 5 meters to 15 meters, it is called Class 2 high-place operation; where the height of high-place operation is between 15 meters to 30 meters, it is called Class 3 high-place operation; and where the height of high-place operation is above 30 meters, it is called super high-place operation, it is forbidden for female employees who are in menstrual period to engage in operations of Class 2 or above in the national standards as provided in the Classification of High-place Operations.

The low temperature operations and operations in cold water will cause adverse effects on the physical health of female employees who are in menstrual period, therefore, low temperature operations and operations in cold water are forbidden for female employees who are in menstrual period. According to the Provisions on Forbidden Labor Activities for Female Employees issued by the Ministry of Labor in 1990, the forbidden labor activities for female employees include: (1) low temperature operations including operations within food freezer and cold water operations; (2) operations falling into the scope of Class 3 physical labor intensity as provided in standards under the Classification of Physical Labor Intensity; and (3) operations of or above Class 5 as provided in standards under the Classification of Physical Labor Intensity. Female employees in menstrual period may not be arranged to engage in labor of Class 3 physical labor intensity as provided by the State. Pursuant to the national standards as provided in the Classification of Physical Labor Intensity, labor of Class 3 physical labor intensity refers to the labor of 8 working hours per day with the average energy consumption value reaching 1746 Kcal per person and a working time rate of 73%, i. e. 350 minutes net working time, which is equivalent to the labor of heavy intensity.

( Ⅲ ) Perinatal Period Protection

Perinatal period protection refers to the protection provided for female employees during their perinatal period. Female employees may enjoy maternity leave period and maternity benefits within a given period during their perinatal period. Perinatal period protection includes natural delivery and miscarriage.

Article 62 of the Labor Law stipulates that "female employees may enjoy a maternity leave of no less than 90 days. " The Regulations on Labor Protection for Female Employees provides that the maternity leave for female employees shall be 90 days. The Special Regulations on Labor Protection for Female Employees have prolonged the maternity leave period to 14 weeks (i. e. 98 days) with reference to the provision in the relevant convention of International Labor Organization that "women must be entitled to a maternity leave of no less than 14 weeks". With regard to those female employees who have miscarriage, the Regulations on Labor Protection for Female Employees only stipulate "giving maternity leave of a certain period" in principle, and in practice, employers enforce this provision differently.

In order to protect the rights and interests of female employees who have miscarriage, the Special Regulations on Labor Protection for Female Employees have, with reference to the classification of maternity leave in case of miscarriage as provided in the Circular on Issues Concerning Maternity Benefits of Female Employees issued by the former Ministry of Labor, specified the maternity leave as follows: where a miscarriage occurs prior to the expiration of four months of pregnancy, a maternity leave of 15 days may be allowed; where a miscarriage occurs upon or after expiration of four months of pregnancy, a maternity leave of 42 days (6 weeks) may be allowed.

4. Breast-feeding Period Protection

Breast-feeding period, also known as "lactating period", refers to the period during which the female employee breast-feeds her infant. Article 63 of the Labor Law stipulates that "it is forbidden to arrange female workers who are breast-feeding their babies aged less than one year to engage in work with Class 3 labor intensity prescribed by the State or work prohibited during lactation. It is forbidden to arrange them to extend their working hours or work on the night shift", which has made a guideline provision on the protection for female employees during breast-feeding period.

The employer may not arrange the female employees who are breast-feeding their babies aged less than one year to engage in the labor requiring Class 3 physical labor intensity as provided by the State and other forbidden labor activities for female employees during breast-feeding period, and may not arrange them to work overtime and work on rest days. Such female employees may not be arranged to engage in night work. The forbidden labor activities for female employees during breast-feeding period include: (1) the operations under workplaces in which the concentration of lead and its compounds, mercury and its compounds, benzene, cadmium, beryllium, arsenic, cyanide, nitric oxide, carbon monoxide, carbon disulfide, chlorine, caprolactom, chloroprene, vinyl chloride, ethylene oxide, aniline, methanol and other toxic substances in the air exceeds the national health standards; (2) operations under workplaces in which the concentration of manganese, fluorine, bromine, methanol, organic phosphorus compounds and organic chloride exceeds the national health standards; and (3) operations falling into the scope of Class 3 physical labor intensity as provided in the standards under the Classification of Physical Labor Intensity.

Entities with large percentage of female employees shall gradually establish health room for female employees, pregnant women rest room, breast-feeding room, nursery, kindergarten and other facilities running by their own or with others in accordance with the relevant regulations of the State, and properly solve the difficulties of female employees in the respects of physical health, breast-feeding and feeding babies. In case of any female employee with infant aged less than one year, her entity shall enable her to breast-feed her baby (including artificial feeding) twice in a shift, with no less than 30 minutes for each feeding. In case of multiple births, an additional breast-feeding time of 30 minutes shall be allowed for each additional infant. The twice breast-feeding within one work shift as enjoyed by female employees may be used on a consolidated basis, and the breast-feeding time and the transportation time from and to the entity for the purpose of breast-feeding shall be calculated as work hours. The breast-feeding period for female employees will generally not be prolonged after their infants attaining the age of one. If the baby's body is very weak, the breast-feeding period may be prolonged on an appropriate basis with the certificate issued by the medical department. If the breast-feeding period is expired in summer, then such period may be prolonged one to two months. Enterprises and public institutions with required conditions may prolong the breast-feeding period for female employees in accordance with the actual situation.

## Ⅲ. "Sexual Harassment" of Workplace

### ( Ⅰ ) Sexual Harassment and Legislation

The term "sexual harassment" was first used in 1970s, and the de jure definition thereof came from a lawsuit brought by a female legal assistant of a law firm against her boss over his behavior and words made in the office in the late 1980s, on the ground that she thought her boss was "sexually harassing" her. The grand justices made a new precedence therefrom, and legally defined the term "sexual harassment" as that a party relies on its advantages in status, power and work to make sexual suggestion, sexual language teasing or sexual behavior to another party who is unwilling. Therefore, we could see that "sexual harassment" was connected to the "workplace" from the very beginning, and become a subject matter concerned in the field of labor law. ①

---

① Catharine A. Mackinnon, US jurist, pointed out in the Sexual Harassment of Occupational Female that sexual harassment in workplace shall not be comprehended as an individual event, nor caused by physical element, but shall be taken as causing by the combination of inequality of rights in sexual relations on the whole and the employment relationship (women are disadvantageous in the labor market); and we could find out from many cases that "sexual harassment is a sexual discrimination", and "sexual harassment in workplace is an employment discrimination". Study on the Jurisprudence and Judgment of Work Equality of Men and Women, Guo Linghui, Page 153, Taibei, Wunan Book Inc., 2000.

The " sexual harassments " defined by Equal Employment Opportunity Commission of the United States on November 10, 1980 include: (1) unwelcome sexual advances; (2) requests for sexual favors; and (3) other verbal or physical conduct of a sexual nature. These conducts will be considered as illegal if (1) the submission to such conduct is made either explicitly or implicitly as a term or condition for an individual's employment, or (2) the submission to or the rejection of such conduct by an individual is used as a basis for employment decisions affecting such individual, or (3) the purpose or effect of such conduct will unreasonably interfere with an individual's work performance or (4) the purpose or effect of such conduct will create an intimidating, hostile or offensive working environment.

The Declaration on the Elimination of Violence against Women as adopted by the United Nations in 1993 has included "sexual harassment in workplace, education institution and other places" into the scope of violence against women in Article 2. 1.

Discussions on sexual harassment so far are all around the relationship between male employees and female employees, and in most cases, the male are the harasser, while the female are the harassed party. Thus, "sexual harassment" mainly refers to that the person who has certain power, says words or puts forward requirements in connection with sex by taking advantage of his/her advantageous status, which cause hindrance to business. In the spring of 1999, the Ministry of Labor of Japan established the principles for prevention of sexual harassment in the workplace, and listed several matters to which the operators should pay attention in order to prevent sexual harassment. For example, forbidding words or behaviors, jokes or teasing, or pertinaciously asking for dinner or dating, in connection with or for the purpose of sex, or forcing others to listen to their own sexual experience, or disseminating materials or magazines with obscenity. Such words and conducts of sexual harassment will be investigated even if they happened outside the workplace, or during spare time. Sexual harassment is quite likely to happen in enterprises. The Ministry of Labor has conducted investigation over sexual harassment words and conducts in the workplace in 1989. According to this investigation, 8. 3% of the interviewed female employees answered that "there is" sexual harassment in the workplace, and 51. 4% of the interviewed female employees answered that " there is sometimes" sexual harassment in the workplace, by combining the above two, it is believed by approximate 60% of female employees that there is sexual harassment in the workplace. In those investigations on sexual harassment,

92. 2% of the interviewed persons believe that enterprises should take measures to prevent sexual harassment. ①

( Ⅱ ) Form and Case of "Sexual Harassment"

1. Sexual harassment for compensation, which means that the submission or objection to the implicit or explicit sexual requirement will result in an employment action against the victim, including promotion, demotion, loss of a position, or changes in work assignments. This type of sexual harassment usually happens between the supervisor who has management and supervision power and his/her subordinates, and the objection to such sexual requirement of their supervisor or boss, will result in the lose of job or promotion, or even demotion, decrease of salary or other difficulties in work or retaliation. This will create considerably large damage to the personal dignity and work rights and interests of such subordinates, and will directly affect the work performance of employees, for example, long-term tension or having powerlessness, self-accusation, insomnia, anger, tension, melancholy and other physical and mental symptoms in the confrontation, which will cause the involuntary resignation of the victim, and may lead to the mutual suspicion and hostility, low work efficiency and relatively high absence rate.

2. Hostile work environment. It is a kind of sexual harassment usually happening between colleagues, but it may also come from the customers or clients of the employer, for example, using words, behaviors or other measures in connection with sex to perplex employees or candidates in the workplace. Employer who has actually known about this situation but failed to take prevention and correction measures shall bear the corresponding legal liability.

( Ⅲ ) First Occupational Sexual Harassment Sentence Case in China

Case: on March 12, 2008, on the second day when Miss Chen, who has just graduated from a college in Chengdu, goes to work in a high-tech company, she was called to meet her supervisor, Mr. Liu, in his office, on the ground that he wanted to talk with her on her work. It was five o'clock in the afternoon, and the employees of the Company have started to get off work. Chen Dan walked into the office of Liu Lun without suspecting of any spite. However, after a few talks, she was astounded when Liu said he fell in love with her and hoped to be her boyfriend. Chen Dan refused immediately by saying "I already have a boyfriend. "

---

① (Japan) How to Deal with Sexual Harassment, the Sexual Harassment Issue Research Society, Page 3 & 14, Beijing, China CITIC Press, 2001.

This sentence exasperated Mr. Liu, who then turned off the light and held Miss Chen in arms forcibly with an attempt to kiss her. Miss Chen got her nuchal translucency hurt by the elbow of Mr. Liu, and struggled and finally ran out of the office. The head of another department who was working overtime saw this and called 110, and Mr. Liu was soon caught by the police. It has confused the policemen from Chengdu High-tech Development Zone at the very beginning that whether the conduct of Mr. Liu is just illegal, or has already constituted a crime? Policemen first believed that, the conduct of Liu Lun has actually caused certain damage to Chen Dan, however, the damage extent was not that serious, and he was only against the provisions of the Security Administration Punishment Law without constituting a crime. However, some policemen denied this view and believed that Liu Lun was suspected of constituting a crime. The people's procuratorate of High-tech Development Zone believed that Mr. Liu has used violence and caused the injury of nuchal translucency of Miss Chen, which was much more than the sexual harassment as understood by common people, therefore, he has constituted a crime and shall be investigated for criminal liability. The court admitted the latter view and Mr. Liu was sentenced to penal servitude of a period of five months.

Question: does the action of Mr. Liu constitute an occupational sexual harassment?

Comment: in the written judgment of this case rendered by the court, there is no sign of "sexual harassment". The relevant law cited by such judgment is Article 237 (1) of the Criminal Law of the People's Republic of China that, "whoever acts indecently against or insults a woman by violence coercion or any other forcible means shall be sentenced to fixed-term imprisonment of not more than five years or criminal detention." In China, there is no special regulation provided for the "sexual harassment", which is first referred to in the Law on Protection of Rights and Interests of Women and then in the Special Regulations on Labor Protection of Female Employees as a liability for employer, however, "sexual harassment" cannot become a basis for conviction and sentence.

The quo status of "sexual harassment", i. e. difficulty in determination on the nature and collection of evidence and lack of penalty standards, has led to the unfavorable results to victims of many sexual harassment cases due to insufficient evidence. "Sexual harassment" is usually committed in the secret places and mostly conducted by words, language, image, information and physical behavior, and it is not rare for female who have suffered sexual harassment to remain silent due to lack of evidence or compromise. The first domestic legislation on sexual harassment was the Law on Protection of Rights and Interests of Women as amended in 2005, however, there is no express definition in the said Law, because one of the important precondition of "sexual harassment" is the unwillingness of the harassed person, i. e. the sexual harassment is against the will of the other party, which is relatively difficult to be defined de jure. Therefore, legislation only makes an advocating provision, i. e. "sexual harassment is prohibited", without defining "sexual harassment". And occupational "sexual harassment" is difficult to be defined than the sexual harassment in public places. The occupational sexual harassment, in most of the case, is the harassment by the person having advantage to his subordinates, so the law requires that the employer shall bear the responsibility so as to urge the employer to take measures to prevent sexual harassment. Some suggest adding content on sexual harassment in the Labor Contract Law to stipulate the occupational "sexual harassment". [1]

## Section 6   Special Protection for Juvenile Employees

### Ⅰ. Concept and Significance of Labor Protection for Juvenile Employees

Special labor protection for juvenile employees refers to the special protection that is provided for juvenile employees during their labor process in consideration of their immature physical development. The physical development of juvenile employees has not been finalized and is on its way to become mature. Thus we shall pay attention to their physical characteristics when arranging the labor for juvenile employees. Heavy manual labor, poor work position, large labor intensity and inappropriate tools will affect the physical development of juvenile employees. In order to protect the normal physical development and safety and health of juvenile employees, they shall be given special protection in terms of work hours and workplaces in addition to the improvement of general labor conditions.

### Ⅱ. Main Content of Labor Protection for Juvenile Employees

( Ⅰ ) Minimum Employment Age

Pursuant to relevant recruitment systems applicable in China, juvenile

---

[1]   " 'First Sexual Harassment Sentence Case' Revealed Blind Zone, as the Judgment Mentioned no Sexual Harassment", www. 39. net, 2008 - 7 - 25.

employees refer to the juvenile workers aged from 16 to 18. This means the minimum employment age in China is 16. Special industry is required to obtain the approval from labor and human resource department when it is in need of recruiting persons under the age of 16 (for example, arts and sports and other sectors).

The minimum employment age is determined based on the consideration of the physical development conditions of teenagers and aims to guarantee a sufficient education time for them before their employment. Article 15 of the Labor Law stipulates that "Employers shall be forbidden to recruit minors that have not reached the age of 16. When recruiting minors that have not reached the age of 16, Employers engaged in literature and art, sports and special arts and crafts shall, in accordance with the relevant provisions of the State, go through the formalities for examination and approval and safeguard their right to receive compulsory education. " In order to safeguard the employment rights of minors, those minors reaching the age of 16 who are released from reeducation-through-labor or released from prison, who are exempted from criminal punishment or granted a probation by the people's court, or who is exempted from prosecution by the people's procuratorate shall not be discriminated against in terms of employment.

In order to guarantee the healthy growth of minors, the Japanese labor standard law has stipulated the minimum age of laborers, and taken the limitation on the employments of the minors under the age of 18 as a measure to protect the minors. It also makes provisions on the respect for the human rights and labor rights of minors and the special rules for the conclusions of labor contracts. The Japanese labor standard law stipulates that the employment of children who are under the age of 15, in the age of accepting compulsory education and have an immature body shall be prohibited. However, the said children may be employed if the work does no harm to the health and benefits of them, and the labor is not heavy, and such children are unwilling to continue their study, provided that the abovementioned matters must be proved by the principal of their schools, agreed by their parents and approved by the director of labor bureau. In case of movie, drama and other related undertakings, children under the age of 12 may be employed for that in their spare time, however, due to the fact that children are incapacitated to sign a contract, their performance contracts shall be the contracts entered into by and between their parents and the employers, under which their parents allow the employers to teach them how to perform and the employers pay remuneration to their parents. Minors are forbidden to engage in dangerous and harmful productions and work in underground by the laws. Due to the fact that minors are generally lack of social experience and accurate judgment, the Japanese labor standard law stipulates that only under the consent by their parents may minors personally sign labor contracts and collect wage for themselves. Besides, if the labor contract is detrimental to the interests of the minors and the parents fail to perform their custody duties and responsibilities, the labor contract may be terminated compulsorily.

( Ⅱ ) Work Hours of Juvenile Employees

In order to safeguard the normal physical development and physical health of minors, it is a common practice in China to shorten the work hours for juvenile employees and to forbid the night work and work overtime for juvenile employees. For some special industries which employ apprentices who are under the age of 16, the State has also specially stipulated the protection system for apprentices. For example, the Interim Regulations on Study, Labor and Rest Time for Students in School of Technology provides that the work hours for students who are under the age of 16 during their production internship shall be as follows: no more than 6 hours per day for the first school year, no more than 7 hours per day for the second school year and no more than 8 hours per day for the third school year. In the wake of the reduction of work hours in China, there will be new relevant provisions on the work hours for juvenile employees.

( Ⅲ ) The Prohibited Labor Activities for Juvenile Employees

Article 64 of the Labor Law stipulates that "juvenile employees may not be arranged to engage in underground mining, toxic and harmful and other activities falling into the scope of Class 4 physical labor intensity as provided by the State or other forbidden labor activities. " In order to thoroughly protect the physical health of juvenile employees, severe toxic and harmful types of work are prohibited for juvenile employees. The inspection and maintenance of dangerous mechanic parts are prohibited for Juvenile employees. The protection for juvenile employees shall be strictly implemented in accordance with this Article and the provisions of Regulations on Special Protection for Juvenile Employees; otherwise, in case of causing injury and death and great loss of state-owned assets, the responsible entity and directly responsible person will be investigated for liability; and in case of severe circumstance, which constitutes a crime, such entity and person shall be legally punished.

Other forbidden labor activities for juvenile employees include: (1) the logging, decking up and banishing operations in forestry industry; (2) operations in the high-place of 5 meters or higher above the falling height datum, with falling risks, i. e. Class 2 high-place operations; (3) operations in workplaces in which the radioactive substances exceeds the prescribed dose as set forth in the Radiation Protection Regulations; and (4) other operations that may be harmful to the development and growth of juvenile employees.

The employer may not arrange those juvenile employees who have a particular disease or some sort of physical problems (non-handicapped) to engage in the following labor activities: (1) high-place operations of Class 1 or above as provided in the national standards set forth in the Classification of High-place Operations; (2) low temperature operations of Class 2 or above as provided in the national standards set forth in the Classification of Low Temperature Operations; (3) high temperature operations of Class 2 or above as provided in the national standards set forth in the Classification of High Temperature Operations; (4) operations of Class 3 physical labor intensity or above as provided in the national standards set forth in the Classification of Physical Labor Intensity; and (5) operations which require the access to benzene, mercury, methanol, carbon disulfide and other substance which is likely to cause allergies.

(Ⅳ) Physical Examination System for Juvenile Employees

In order to protect the physical health of juvenile employees, a thorough physical examination shall be carried out for juvenile employees before their employment, and only those juvenile employees who are physical qualified for work and obtain the certificate of physical fitness may be officially recruited. Juvenile employees shall conduct physical examination on a regular basis after being recruited.

Regular physical examination for juvenile employees is a statutory obligation borne by the employer, and the employer may not cancel the same by any excuse. The Regulations on Special Protection for Juvenile Employees issued by the former Ministry of Labor in December, 1994 specially provide that (1) The employer shall arrange regular physical examination for those juvenile employees: who are going to start the work, who have worked over one year, who have reached the age of 18 or whose previous physical examination has been over half a year; (2) The physical examination over juvenile employees shall be implemented in accordance with the items listed in the Physical Examination Form for Juvenile Employees uniformly made by the former Ministry of Labor; (3) The employer shall arrange juvenile employees to engage in the labor activities suitable for them in accordance with their physical examination results; and a reduced workload or post shift shall be arranged for those juvenile employees who are incompetent for the original post as proved by the certificate of medical departments.

● Chapter Ⅷ

# Social Security Law

Social security is an important legal system in modern society. The essential issues of social security and social security legal system cover the concept and features of social security, and the subject matter, features and principles of social security law. An overview of the historical development of the social security system can help us understand the establishment and development of China's social security legal system and the on-going reform of the social security system in China.

## Section 1  Concept of Social Security Law

### Ⅰ. Concept of Social Security Law and its Subject Matter

( Ⅰ ) Concept of Social Security Law

Social security law is a general term of all legal norms adjusting social security relations. It includes social security law as a fundamental law, legal norms in other laws and regulations that are relevant to social security, and legally binding local regulations and rules concerning social security affairs.

In addition to regulating the project system, implementation scope and targets, source of funding, welfare standards, calculation formula, application procedures and approval procedures, the contents of social security law should also include the nature and functions of social security administration agencies, the structure and status of social security organizations, management of different social security targets, the relation between social security institutions and relevant departments, and the raising, application and payment of social security funds.

( Ⅱ ) Subject Matter of Social Security Law

The subject matter of social security law are various social and economic relations arising from social security activities conducted by the State, various types of units and all members of society. In other words, social security law regulates social security relations.

Social security relations can be classified into different categories from different perspectives. As to direct relationship, social security relations can be further divided into two sub-categories. With regard to contents, social security relations can be categorized as social insurance relations, social relief relations, social welfare relations and social special care relations; with regard to subjects, social security relations cover the relation between the State and members of society, the relation between social security institutions and the government, the relation between social security institutions and members of society, the relation among social security institutions, the relation between social security institutions and employers, and the relation between employers and laborers. As to indirect relations, in the management and operation of social security funds, social security relations cover the relation between social security institutions and various subjects on the investment market. All these relations require regulation and adjustment by social security law from different aspects.

Specifically, social security law regulates relations in the following eight aspects:

(1) Regulating the relation between the State and all members of society, i. e. the relation between the central government and local governments at all levels and all members of society. The responsibilities of governments in social security and the benefits enjoyed by members of society are required to be expressly stipulated in law.

(2) Regulating the relation between social security institutions and the government, i. e. the relation between social security institutions as organizations specifically managing and implementing social security projects and the government. The nature, tasks, status, rights and obligations of social security institutions are required to be defined by law.

(3) Regulating the relation between social security institutions and all members of society, i. e. the relation between managers of social security and participants and beneficiaries of social security. The responsibilities of social security institutions towards all members of society and the rights and obligations of all members of society participating in social security are required to be expressly stipulated in law.

(4) Regulating the relation between social security institutions and employers as well as rural collective organizations, i. e. the relation between managers of

social security and the participating duty-bearers of social security. The obligation of employers to pay social security fee and the responsibility of rural collective organizations to distribute social security payments and supplies are required to be expressly stipulated in law.

(5) Regulating the relation between employers and laborers, i. e. the responsibility of employers for laborers in social security and the social security rights and interests entitled by laborers. The employers' protection duties for laborers and the social security benefits enjoyed by laborers from employers are required to be expressly stipulated in law.

(6) Regulating the relation arising from the operation of social security system, i. e. the relation between social security institutions and other departments. The division of work, coordination and cooperation between social security administrations and other governmental departments, among social security administrations and among the internal agencies of social security administrations are required to be expressly stipulated in law.

(7) Regulating the supervisory relation arising from the operation of social security system, i. e. the relation formed in the process of supervision of social security operation through various supervisory methods. The establishment of appropriate supervisory organizations, the responsibilities and powers of and supervision procedures for all supervisory institutions are required to be expressly stipulated in law.

(8) Regulating the relation arising from the operation of social security funds, i. e. the relation occurred in the management and operation of social security funds. The rights and obligations of social security funds in operation in relation to State finance, investment market and related economic entities need to be expressly stipulated in law.

## Ⅱ. Features of Social Security Law

### ( Ⅰ ) Social Security Law is of Extensive Sociality

The extensive sociality is the overriding feature of social security law, which manifests the rights and obligations under social security law in relation to all members of society in a broad way. In terms of rights, the right-holders of social security are all members of society. The rights under social security system are jointly and equally enjoyed by all members of society. Furthermore, social security benefits will be improved and social security programs will be gradually expanded in the wake of the economic and social development of a country. Citizens from the cradle to the grave and particular laborers to any member of society of whatever status are all covered by social security. Internationally, some states have also concluded reciprocal agreements on social security treatment, in order to ensure that their own citizens residing aboard will equally enjoy social security rights and benefits in the residing state. In terms of obligations, social security obligations are borne by the entire society. By legislation, the State imposes mandatory requirements on the major systems of social security, demanding different entities in society to jointly assume social security obligations, jointly bear risks and jointly raise social security funds. In some particular security programs, the state may also raise funds from all members of society, international organizations and individuals for disaster relief, in case of any emergency or on basis of actual circumstances.

( Ⅱ ) Social Security Law is the Uniformity of Mandatory Norms and Non-mandatory Norms

In the major systems of social security, in relation to the programs concerning the fundamental protection of rights and interests of members of society, social security law stipulates mandatory norms, which expressly specifies the obligations the State (and local governments at all levels), society, enterprises, individuals and other related parties must carry out under social security, and the specific programs, implementation scope, fund raising, welfare standards and calculation formula of social security. The related parties must comply with the law, regardless of their preference. For instance, the insurance obligations under social insurance must be performed by the parties concerned with no choice. For some particular programs such as work-related injury insurance and maternity insurance, some parties only assume obligations without any right, while others only enjoy rights without any obligation. For these mandatory norms, the relevant entities and individuals must strictly observe the norms and make contribution to social insurance in full and on time, failure to do so will result in legal punishment. As to social security measures to be taken in temporary and contingent events, there are non-mandatory and voluntary measures in addition to the mandatory norms established under the fundamental systems of social security. For instance, donation for disaster relief and poverty relief is a non-compulsory and voluntary behavior of members of society.

( Ⅲ ) Social Security Law is the Uniformity of Humanitarianism and Mutuality

Humanitarianism, as the fruit of progression of human civilization, is the rationality and emotion of human beings in the wake of understanding of sociality. The important manifestation of humanitarianism in social life is the assistance and care for the weak by the strong. Through rational allocation of social security responsibilities and obligations among individuals in society, social security law has established a risk-sharing responsibility mechanism, in which social care and social support are provided by the rich, the healthy, the young and the strong to the poor, the sick and disabled, the old and the weak, reflecting the ethics and moral principles of respecting the old and taking good care of the young, assisting the weak and impoverished, fraternity and solidarity, and harmonious co-existence. Meanwhile, social security law also follows the principle of mutuality among members of society, exhibiting the social norm of "all for one and one for all". Take pension insurance as an example. The essence of pension insurance is the outcome of socialization of family model of providing for the aged, i. e. the model that parents are provided for by their son in a family has been extended to the model that the aged are provided for by the young in society as a whole. Since no one can stay young forever, the obligations of the young today are the rights enjoyed by them in the future when they are old. Likewise, for maternity insurance, maternity insurance premium is paid by society other than the persons who give birth, which is determined by the social nature of maternity itself. Even in unilateral behaviors such as "donation", the basis of social mutuality can be found. Provision of relief to people in disaster-stricken areas can maintain the stability of the whole society on the one hand, and help to reconstruct the disaster-stricken areas on the other hand, which in return enables people suffering disasters to provide relief to other victims in the same way in the future.

(Ⅳ) Social Security Law Can Achieve Social Equality

Social equality requires the society to treat each member of society in an equal manner and such equality ought to be manifested in the way of income distribution among members of society and their living conditions. Social security law defines the rights of members of society to equally participate in social security, providing that any member of society, regardless of their status, profession, wealth and so forth, is equally covered within the scope of social security, without existence of any privileged stratum or individual. Through social security, members of society are able to take part in social competition on the premises that their basic needs can be secured so that they will not lose an opportunity to equally compete in society due to strained circumstances caused by inadequate natural endowment or unsecured livelihood. Owing to disaster relief, unemployment insurance or unemployment relief, medical care security and the like, victims of disasters, the unemployed and the sick may quickly recover from disasters and difficulties and resume their usual lives, which to some extent enable social security law to serve the function of eliminating social inequality caused by unexpected disasters, failure in competition and illnesses or work-related injuries during the development of society. Implementation of social security law can to some extent minimize the unfairness of social distribution as well. Under the market economy, the discrepancy of social income distribution, which is caused by differences in education background, working skills and the number of family members among members of society, leads to polarization between the rich and the poor and even drives some members of society into poverty. Social security can to some extent narrow the gap of social distribution by redistribution of the income of members of society. The raising of social security funds requires that people with higher income will pay more, while people with lower income will pay less. As to social security benefits, well-off members or families of society with higher income have fewer opportunities to receive benefits, while poor families or the disadvantaged have more opportunities to enjoy more benefits. In this way, social security law, in fact and in general, leads to a result that the strong assume more obligations than rights they enjoyed while the weak enjoy more rights than obligations they assume, which objectively narrows the gap between the rich and the poor and achieves social equality.

## ( V ) Social Security Legal System Consists of Several Laws

It is impossible to use a single piece of law to regulate all affairs concerning social security since social security covers numerous issues, among which different issues require regulation by different legal methods. Conventionally, a country usually enacts various laws and regulations concerning social security which constitute the social security legal system in a coordinated way. Between social security law and other laws, between laws and regulations, and among different regulations, there is an objective division of labor to allow them to regulate the respective social security affairs within a certain scope as well as coordination issues. They cooperate with each other and jointly constitute a complete social security legal system.

For instance, in China, in addition to Article 44 of the Constitution of the People's Republic of China, which stipulates the retirement and pension security of members of society, and Article 45 of the Constitution which specifies the principles in accordance with which the State and the society shall provide members of society with material support and develop social insurance, social relief, medical care and health and social welfare, there are (1) special laws of social security adopted by the national legislation authority and other laws applicable to social security, such as the Law of the People's Republic of China on the Protection of Disabled Persons, the Law of the People's Republic of China on the Protection of Women's Rights and Interests, the Law of the People's Republic of China on the Protection of the Rights and Interests of the Elderly and other special laws, which are social security laws promulgated by national legislation authority and therefore form the basis of social security systems; (2) administrative regulations issued by the highest national administrative authority, such as the Labor Insurance Regulations of the People's Republic of China, the Regulation on Pensions and Preferential Treatments for Servicemen, the Regulations on the Work of Providing Five Guarantees and other regulations, issued by the State Council and specific implementing rules concerning social security law, which are the specific basis for implementing social security law; and (3) social security regulations promulgated in local areas by local legislation authorities, which are formulated under the instructions of national social security laws and regulations, based on the reality of local social security issues and aiming at regulating social security affairs for which local authorities are directly responsible. All these legal systems jointly constitute a multi-layer social security legal system within which there is relative independence as well as division of labor and coordination.

## Section 2   Development and Reform of Chinese Social Security Law

### I. Social Security Law from the Founding of PRC to the 3rd Plenary Session of the 11th Central Committee of the Communist Party of China

This period has witnessed the origination and development of the state security mode in line with the planned economy system, and its legislation. This process can be divided into three main stages: establishment stage, reform stage and stagnation stage.

( I ) Establishment Stage from the Early Years of the Founding of PRC to 1957

This stage mainly witnessed the establishment of a nationally uniform social security basic system and the promulgation of some fundamental laws.

In February 1951, the Government Administration Council published the Labor Insurance Regulations of the People's Republic of China. The Regulations secured the basic needs of employees who were temporarily or permanently deprived of labor capacity and made specific provisions on insurance against birth, old-age, illness, death, injury, disability and so forth. The Regulations also stipulated that insurance contribution shall be borne by enterprises and employees are not required to make any contribution, and the labor union shall be in charge of labor insurance affairs, and arrange various kinds of collective labor insurance services.

Since it was the economic recovery period, the State also promulgated decrees on relief to unemployed workers. In June 1950, the Government Administration Council published the Instructions on Providing Relief to Unemployed Workers, and the Ministry of Labor published the Interim Measures on Providing Relief to Unemployed Workers. In August 1952, the Government Administration Council issued the Decision on Issues Concerning Labor Employment. These decrees played an active role in solving the difficulty of unemployed workers and promoting the re-employment of unemployed workers.

In this period, the social insurance system for governmental agencies and public institutions were gradually established by specific regulations. In December 1950, the Ministry of Internal Affairs issued the Interim Regulations on Praise, Honor and Pensions for Revolutionary Comrades and five other regulations on preferential treatment for servicemen, i. e. the Interim Regulations on Preferential Treatment for Dependents of Revolutionary Martyrs and Soldiers, the Interim Regulations on Preferential Treatment and Pensions for Disabled Revolutionary Soldiers, the Interim Regulations on Praise, Honor and Pensions for Sacrifice and Death of Illness of Revolutionary Soldiers and the Interim Regulations on Pensions for Injury and Death of Militiamen and Migrant Workers. In June 1952, the Government Administration Council issued the Instructions on Implementing Free Medical Service and Care for State Functionaries of the People's Governments at All Levels Throughout the Country, Parties, Groups and Public Institutions and the Interim Measures on Treatment for State Functionaries of the People's Governments at All Levels During Illness in the same year. In addition, the Government Administration Council issued the Provisions on Maternity Leave of Female Staff in April 1954, the Interim Provisions on Treatment of Vacation of Office of Civil Servants in December 1955 and the Instructions on Several Issues of the Personal Life of Employees in 1957. These normative documents jointly constituted the basic system of social security of the new China.

( Ⅱ ) Reform Stage from 1958 to 1966

Since the beginning of the second Five-Year Plan in 1958, in order to get in line with the development trends on the basis of the completion of the first Five-Year Plan, necessary reform was made to the social insurance system not adapting to economic construction. In 1958, the State Council promulgated the Interim Provisions on the Retirement of Workers and Officials, the Interim Provisions on Wage Treatment of Ordinary Workers and Handymen in Enterprises, Public Institutions and State Agencies, the Interim Provisions on Training Period and Subsistence Allowance for Trainees of State-owned, Public-private Partnership, Cooperative and Private Enterprises and Public Institutions, and the Interim Provisions on Home Leave and Wage Treatment of Workers and Officials. In March of the same year, the State Council also published the Implementing Rules for the Interim Provisions on the Retirement of Workers and Officials (Draft).

These provisions were formulated on the basis of the overview of social security work of the past few years, which reflected an overall planning and all-round consideration and attention to both the internal relations in the working class and the relations between workers and farmers. They took note of (1) not only the immediate interests but also the long-term interests of employees; and (2) not only the interests of individuals but also the interests of the State. In terms of contents, legal norms at this stage have unified the retirement and resignation system of enterprises and governmental agencies, made appropriate reform on public healthcare service and labor insurance healthcare service, stipulated the social insurance treatment for downsized workers, specified the scope of occupational diseases and the treatment of patients suffering from occupational diseases, formulated the approval procedures for sick and maternity leave of staff, and adjusted the social insurance treatment for trainees.

In this stage, the State also promulgated considerable regulations and provisions on various aspects of social insurance, social welfare, social relief and special care, which pragmatically reformed the implementation scope, security level and qualification for benefits and other aspects of China's social security system.

( Ⅲ ) Stagnation Stage from 1966 to 1978

Social insurance system were severely damaged in the ten years of chaos: various regulatory agencies were revoked; labor unions responsible for staff social insurance service were forced to cease their activities; the Ministry of Labor, the Ministry of Civil Affairs, the Ministry of Health, the Ministry of Personnel and other related departments responsible for social security administration were paralyzed for a long time; social security affairs were left almost unattended; various social security laws and regulations and systems that were established since the founding of the new China were annulled de facto; social security work was not in order and the social pooling of retirement expenditure was cancelled. In 1969, the Ministry of Finance issued the Opinions on the Reform of Several Systems in the Financial Work of State-owned Enterprises, which stipulated that all state-owned enterprises must cease to withdraw labor insurance funds, salaries for retired staff and personnel on long-term sick leave and other labor insurance expenses, which must be disbursed from non-operating revenue. From then onwards, a situation where enterprise security system has gradually been formed and the situation where social insurance was planned and regulated as a whole and social mutuality disappeared. As a result, Chinese social security system was stagnated or even retrograded.

## Ⅱ. Social Security Law since the 3rd Plenary Session of the 11th Central Committee of the Communist Party of China

The 3rd Plenary Session of the 11th Central Committee of the Communist Party of China in 1978 established the opening-up and reform policy, which led to the radical change in China's political and economic trends. The 3rd Plenary Session of the 12th Central Committee of the Communist Party of China adopted the Decision of the Central Committee of the Communist Party of China on Reform of Economic System, which started the economic system reform by rejuvenating state-owned enterprises as the key and put on agenda the corresponding reform of the social security system.

During this period, the reform of China's social security system went through an exploration stage from the 3rd Plenary Session of the 11th Central Committee of CCP in 1978 to the 14th National Congress of the Communist Party of China in 1992, to the breakthrough stage in 1993 up to now. In the former stage, the reform of social security system, serving mainly as a supporting measure for the reform of state-owned enterprises, which explored the individual projects in relation to the reform of state-owned enterprises; the latter stage continued to support the reform of state-owned enterprises and in the meantime explicitly defined the social security system as an important element in the framework of Chinese socialist market economy. In addition to further exploration of the reform on individual social security projects, the general framework of the reform of China's social security system has been preliminarily shaped, entailing the establishment of a social security system commensurate with the socialist market economy.

The concept of social security was explicitly put forward for the first time in the Suggestions of the Central Committee of the Communist Party of China on Formulating the 7th Five-Year Plan of National Economy and Social Development in September 1985, integrating China's systems of social security, social welfare, social relief, social special care and so forth into a unified social security system. Legislation on social security in line with the reform of economic system was in full swing. The Interim Provisions on Unemployment Insurance of Staff of State-owned Enterprises promulgated in 1986 preliminarily established the unemployment insurance system in China. The Decision on Reform of Pension Insurance of Staff of Enterprises was published in 1991, which explicitly provided that pension insurance funds will carry out social pooling. The Standards for the Assessment of Work-related Injuries and Degree of Disability from Occupational Diseases were promulgated in 1992, which unified various standards on a national scale. The Circular on Public Healthcare Insurance was issued in 1989, to make a reform of public healthcare services. At the same time, the Law of the People's Republic of China on the Protection of Disabled Persons was adopted in 1990 and the Regulations on Pensions and Preferential Treatments for Servicemen were promulgated in 1988. These provisions have enriched and improved China's social security legal system.

The report of the 15th National Congress of the Communist Party of China put forward the key projects of the reform and establishment of social security system in four aspects, namely pension, healthcare, unemployment insurance and social relief, and established the objectives and tasks for the establishment of China's social security legal system in the next stage.

The reform and development of social security system have made prominent achievements during this stage. For instance, the coverage of social security has been extended, the pension, unemployment and other critical security projects have already been extended to non-publicly owned enterprises. By changing the pattern of "self-insurance" of enterprises, social insurance established a security framework of social mutuality. The source of social insurance funds has changed from the situation where the State undertook full responsibility to a situation of tripartite responsibilities, i. e. the State, the employer and the employee. Moreover, social pooling is adopted for principal projects, strengthening the regulation of social security funds, improving the social security financial system and avoiding misuse and embezzlement of social security funds. From 1978 to

1996, the total amount of national expenses on insurance and welfare increased 34 times to RMB 272. 53 billion, among which, that of state-owned entities was up 33 times and that of urban collective entities was up 35 times. National finance spent on special care, social welfare, disaster relief and so forth was up 600% from 1978 to 1996, reaching RMB 12. 803 billion.

On October 28, 2010, the Social Insurance Law was deliberated and adopted at the 17th Session of the 11th National People's Congress Standing Committee, and came into effect on July 1, 2011. The Social Insurance Law specifies the social insurance relations and the rights and obligations of employers and laborers, strengthens governmental responsibilities, explicitly defines the duties of social security administrative departments and social insurance agencies, stipulates legal liabilities of the parties concerned in social insurance and establishes the general framework, basic policies, basic principles and basic system for the establishment of Chinese social insurance system.

Pursuant to the Decision of the State Council on Amendment to the Work-related Injury Insurance Regulations published on December 20, 2010, the amended Work-related Injury Insurance Regulations would come into effect on January 1, 2011. The new Regulations are an important piece of supporting regulations for the Social Insurance Law. The new Regulations elaborate related provisions of the Social Insurance Law, increasing the feasibility of insurance against work-related injury. Its amendment and implementation are significant to the improvement of Chinese work-related injury insurance and better safeguarding the legal rights and interest of a large number of employees.

● Chapter IX

# Social Insurance Law

Social insurance is the main content of the social security system which takes all the social members as its objects, and is the legal system under which the State offers help and assistance to citizens when they get ill, injured, disabled, unemployed and old. The targets of Chinese social insurance are all laborers.

## Section 1    Concept of Social Insurance Law

### I. Definition and Features of Social Insurance

( I ) Definition of Social Insurance

Social insurance is the system established by the State through legislation which offers material assistance to the laborers when they are born, old, ill, dead, injured or disabled, or get unemployed and suffer other difficulties in life. The citizens have the basic right to be provided with material assistance when they are old, ill or incapacitated. Article 45 of the Constitution of the People's Republic of China stipulates that "Citizens of the People's Republic of China have the right to obtain material assistance from the State and society when they are old, ill or incapacitated. The State develops social insurance, social relief and medical and health services that are required for citizens to enjoy this right". This basic right of Chinese citizens conferred by Constitution, as for the laborers, is mainly achieved through social insurance. Article 70 of the Labor Law of China stipulates that "the State shall develop the cause of social insurance, establish a system of social insurance and set up social insurance funds to enable laborers to get help and compensations when they are old, suffer diseases, get injured in work, get unemployed and give birth to children. "

In terms of concept, the social insurance may be understood in broad and narrow senses. The social insurance in broad sense, which is targeted at all social members, refers to a general term of various systems that the State offers material assistance to them when they get ill, injured or disabled, unemployed and old. The social insurance in narrow sense means the only provision of economic securities for the employees of enterprises and staff and workers of public institutions and government staff and the dependants of the foregoing persons. In terms of content, the social insurance in board sense includes not only various social insurance programs, but also the subsidy program for the needy and other social assistance programs, and in terms of administration, the social insurance in board sense involves various administrative departments including civil affairs department, labor department, human resource department and other departments. The social insurance in narrow sense mainly includes maternity insurance, medical insurance, work-related injury insurance, unemployment insurance, and pension insurance.

As for definition of social insurance, though the understandings and expressions are quite different, however some common contents are contained. Firstly, it is a social security system regulated by statute; secondly, it requires the laborers and employers to participate in compulsorily; thirdly, it is a social responsibility for laborers undertaken by the State and also a basic right enjoyed by the laborers; fourthly, social insurance is an important component part of social security.

( Ⅱ ) Features of Social Insurance

**1. Sociality**

The sociality of social insurance mainly shows in three aspects:

(1) The sociality of insurance coverage. It means the scope of the targets enjoying insurance is extensive, including various laborers of different levels, industries, ownership forms and identities in society. The scope of social insurance targets is broad, which is one of the core features of social insurance. However, for a long time, some major social insurance systems that have been carried out in China were only targeted at State organs, public institutions and enterprises owned by the whole people. While in enterprises of town collective ownership, such systems were generally implemented on a reference basis. Laborers in other forms of economic organizations even have not been completely covered by the social insurance systems, and there was no unified benefits standard for them. This kind of social insurance systems completely deviated from the principles of unity and equality in current market economy. However, the Labor Law of China has changed this and extended the scope of social insurance to the laborers in all enterprises, public institutions, State organs, social

organizations and individual businesses within the territory of the People's Republic of China, which not only overcomes the previous defects of small coverage and differ standards, but also completely accords with the requirements of the socialist market economy system.

(2) The sociality of insurance purposes. The establishment and implementation of social insurance system not only reflects the political progress of the society, but also facilitates economic development of the society. Ensuring the laborers' basic living needs when they are old, suffer diseases, get injured in work, become unemployed, give birth to children or get disabled is of significance for the upholding of socialist humanitarianism, the stability and progress of society, protection of productivity, coordination of the social economy relationship and the sustained and steady development of economy.

(3) The sociality of insurance sponsorship and management. Social insurance is mainly a governmental insurance system. It is confirmed and regulated by the State through legislations and is organized and implemented by the government in terms of raising, distribution, adjustment and management of insurance funds.

## 2. Reciprocity

All the insurances have reciprocity, because they have to spread risks by means of centralizing and decentralizing funds, and extend the scope for spreading risk as far as possible. On the one hand, the reciprocity of social insurance manifests as insurance funds are raised by social pooling, centralized and used on the principle of adjustment, solving the particular basic life needs of laborers under different circumstances. Laborers can get help through helping each other when there are economic losses resulting from getting old, diseases, injured in work, unemployed, disabled, giving birth to children and so on. On the other hand, the situations of laborers can't be the same due to the affects of the factors that out of the controls of human beings, such as different lifetimes, being sick or healthy, severity of diseases, degree of diseases, injures and disabilities, being disabled or not. However the social insurance sticks to a single purpose, which is to ensure the basic living needs of the laborers. Therefore, social insurance in essence means the balance and adjustment in the funds pooled in many ways and the share of losses and burdens that incurred or borne by particular laborer under specific situation among the majority of laborers who have made contributions to the insurance premiums. This determines that laborers have to pay social insurance premiums according to a unified standard, but can not receive equal living subsidies from the society. This difference has fully reflected the feature of the reciprocity of the social insurance.

### 3. Compensatory Nature

The compensatory nature of social insurance mainly shows in three aspects:

(1) The value and wealth created by laborers, apart from the part that returned to the laborers as labor remunerations, are all brought into revenue of government as various deductions of the society. In the sources of social insurance funds, the part contributed by the State initially derives from the laborers' labor. The State returns this part to the laborers through social insurance, which, in essence, is a compensation for the past work of laborers.

(2) During the period when the laborers provide labor to the society and collect labor remuneration for that, they pay a certain percentage of their remuneration in accordance with the standards prescribed by the State as their contributions to labor insurance fund, and afterward receive subsidy in accordance with the standards prescribed by the State when they are old, sick, injured and unemployed, give birth or lose labor capacity, which is a specific reflection of the compensatory nature of social insurance.

(3) Under the circumstance of suffering work-related injury and disability or having occupational diseases, the social insurance benefits as enjoyed by the laborers directly reflect the compensatory nature of social insurance. Therefore, it is practical and scientific for Article 70 of the Labor Law to definite social insurance as the help and compensation obtained by laborers under particular conditions.

## II. The Concept of Social Insurance Law

Social insurance law is a legal norm that adjusts the legal relationship on social insurance. It makes provisions on the specific contents of social insurance, including its items system, scope and targets, source of funds, benefits standards and methods of distribution, and also specifies the nature and functions of social insurance institutions, sponsorship forms and status of social insurance, management and supervision of social insurance and other related matters.

The social relationships regulated by the social insurance law mainly include: the relationship between the social insurance administration and administrative counterpart, to which the social insurance law mainly specifies their respective rights and obligations; the relationship between social insurance agency and the employers and laborers, to which the social insurance law mainly standardizes the raising of social insurance funds and payment of social insurance benefits, guarantees the laborers to realize their social insurance rights and interests and regulates the employer's social insurance obligations to laborers; and the relationship between the social insurance supervision institution and social insurance management institution and handling agency and the employer and the laborers, to which the social insurance law regulates the establishment of supervision mechanism, and the duties and powers of different supervision institutions and their coordination.

There are mainly four subjects of the social insurance law: (1) the State or government. The State (via government) directly participates in the social insurance activities, and provides fiscal support for the operation and implementation of social insurance, and therefore becomes a unique subject in the social insurance legal system; (2) Social security management and implementation institutions. They directly assume the responsibilities of managing and implementing the social insurance, and are legally entitled to collect social insurance premiums from enterprises and individuals and obliged to specifically operate the social insurance projects and pay social insurance benefits to the laborers; (3) The employers. They assume the responsibility of contributing social insurance premiums to the social insurance institutions and are main resource of social insurance premiums, and are thus of special and important meaning to the normal operation and implementation of the social insurance legal system; (4) Laborers and their family. Laborers and their family are direct beneficiaries of social insurance, and the laborers need to assume the responsibility of contributing certain social insurance premiums, and are therefore important factors in the social insurance legal system.

## Section 2 Principles of Social Insurance Law

The principles of social insurance law are the basic spirits and guiding thoughts that followed by all social insurance laws and regulations. According to the features and functions of the social insurance law, the social insurance law mainly observes the following principles.

### Ⅰ. Principle of Unification of Rights and Obligations to Social Insurance

The operation and development of social insurance system largely depends on the establishment of the social insurance funds, while the establishment of the social insurance funds can not be achieved only depend on a particular institution or a little group of persons, it requires the joint efforts and sharing of responsibilities among the State, the employer and the laborer. The social insurance funds shall be socially pooled by the social insurance agencies which are entrusted by the State through compulsory measures in accordance with relevant state laws, and the funds so raised and contributed by the enterprises and laborers that enrolled in the social insurance shall be used for a centralized and unified purpose.

In this regard, employers and laborers who bear the social insurance responsibilities must first fulfil their obligations to pay the social insurance premiums, which is a premise for their rights to social insurance benefits. The risks incurred by laborers may only be solved and shared by centralizing the strength of the whole society to the maximum extent. During the planned economy period of China, the obligations of social insurance are mainly borne by the State and enterprises. One of the key reforms carried out currently is to gradually reduce the part of social insurance premiums borne by the State, to cause the part borne by the employers to become the main source of social insurance funds, and to increase the part borne by the laborers gradually.

## II. Principle of Unifying the Integration and Socialization of Social Insurance

Under market economy conditions, the marketization of labor force is an important aspect for achieving the optimum allocation of resources, and the integration of social insurance is a necessary maintenance mechanism for the marketization of labor force. In this regard, social insurance systems shall carry out the principle of integration, i. e. unifying the items of social insurance, unifying the standards of social insurance or basic social insurance, and unifying the management and implementation mechanism of social insurance; in this case, laborers will be always under the protection of the same social insurance system despite their mobility, which provides security conditions for the optimum allocation of labor force resources and the free flow of laborers. Meanwhile, social insurance as a re-allocation method for national income, aims at adjusting the income gap. Therefore, for the full functioning of the mutual assistance and reciprocity of social insurance, the difference in insurance benefits among laborers shall be less than the difference in first distribution, and the social insurance burden among employers shall be substantially balanced.

The realization of the socialization of social insurance is an important condition for the healthy development of social insurance. Social insurance in modern society is a common undertaking for all social members, and all members in the same country shall be encouraged to proactively participate in the social insurance affairs, including participating in the share of contribution and participating in the implementation of the supervision of social insurance systems, so as to lay more solid social and economic foundations for the social insurance undertaking. For example, in terms of selection of social insurance mode, other countries have some successful experience on socialization, such as the provident fund system in Singapore and the private-running endowment social insurance funds in Chile, both show that there are various forms of social insurance to be chosen. To achieve socialization of social insurance management, which is also an objective requirement of social insurance, we should gradually transform the scattered administration by various departments into an unified and socialized management, transform the routine work in relation to social insurance as assumed by the employer into a public service, and gradually perfect the unified public service organization.

### Ⅲ. Principle of Establishing a Multi-channel Social Insurance System

Prior to the promulgation of the Labor Law in China, only a single channel exists for social insurance. When the employees of the enterprise lose their labor capacity due to age or other reasons, they have to receive statutory social insurance benefits from the only available channel—enterprise. Besides such benefits, no other economic resource is available for them, which make their living is unsecured under many circumstances, for example, when the enterprise suffer loss or economic hardship, the living of laborers will become much more unsecured. Thus the Labor Law of China stipulates that "the State develops social insurance undertaking and establishes social insurance system."

This multi-channel social insurance system includes:

(1) Social insurance taking social insurance fund as the main channel. Article 72 of the Labor Law stipulates that "sources of social insurance funds shall be determined by insurance type, and social pooling shall be practiced gradually". This is the most fundamental channel for social insurance, which is usually contributed by the State, the employers and the laborers. Certainly, these three sources of funds are not all necessary, there are some exceptions, such as maternity insurance and work-related injury insurance, etc.

(2) Employer's supplementary insurance. Supplementary insurance refers to the social insurance measure established for the purpose of enhancing the insurance benefits or maintaining the insurance benefits unchanged under special

circumstances. It is established and paid by the employer. Currently, the supplementary insurance maintained by the employer carries out the principle of willingness, and the employer may determine to establish it or not based on its own situation. For this, Paragraph 1 of Article 75 of the Labor Law of China stipulates that the State encourages the employer to establish supplementary insurance for laborers in accordance with its own actual situation.

(3) Savings insurance. It refers to the measure taken by the laborers themselves for ensuring their living needs in case of any hardship by the mean of savings. Savings insurance is suitable for the traditional habits of Chinese laborers, and is of common significance for securing the economic needs of laborers when they suffer unexpected hardships. So Paragraph 2 of Article 75 of the Labor Law stipulates that "the State advocates laborers to conduct savings insurance. "

● Chapter X

# Endowment Insurance Law

Endowment insurance is a legal system ensuring that laborers who become incapacitated with age will receive the material assistance and that the basic late-life of laborers will be materially safeguarded, through legislation. Endowment insurance is the most social and extensive system in the social insurance systems.

**Section 1**   **Concept and Functions of the Endowment Insurance**

## Ⅰ. Concept and Legal Features of Endowment Insurance

Endowment insurance, also known as old-age social insurance, pension insurance or annuity insurance, refers to a social insurance system by which the State and society offer certain material assistance to the laborers who have reached the statutory age for the old and engaged in a particular work for legal length of service in order to maintain their lives in the old age. As long as the laborers have reached the legal age and engaged in a particular work for legal length of service, they may, after duly discharge of their labor obligation, enjoy old age pension benefits. Endowment insurance is an important integral part of the social insurance system and the outcome of market economy development that arises especially when the human society enters social large-scale production stage.

As an integral part of the social insurance, endowment insurance has following legal features:

(1) Having reached the statutory age for the old and engaged in any particular work for legal length of service is the legal eligibility condition as required by laws for the laborers to enjoy endowment insurance, which is the main feature that distinguishes endowment insurance from other types of social insurance. The targets of endowment insurance are the aged, which means the

person who enjoys old age pensions must reach the statutory age for the old. Therefore it is crucial to define the so-called "old-age". The definition of old age varies from country to country and depends on such factors as labor resource status, development of social economy and laborers' physical conditions. Reaching old age is just one of the eligibility conditions for old age pensions, and the other is having engaged in a particular work for legal length of service as required by laws; in this case, the length of service and physical conditions of the laborers and the labor conditions are stipulated as supplementary conditions.

(2) The duly discharge of a laborer's labor obligation is the factual premise to enjoy endowment insurance. Reaching the statutory age for the old and having engaged in a particular work for legal length of service will satisfy the statutory eligibility requirements for old age pensions, but the actual enjoyment of old age pensions also requires the satisfaction of factual premise, i.e. the laborer shall be duly released his/her labor obligations. In reality, some laborers who have reached the statutory age for the old and engaged in a particular work for legal length of service but have not terminated the labor relation with the employer, are still obligated to work and may not enjoy old age pensions.

(3) The legal provision of certain material assistance by the State and society to the laborers whose labor obligations have been discharged for the purpose of maintaining their lives in old age is the aim of endowment insurance. Given that the only purpose of endowment insurance is to provide particular material assistance to laborers whose labor obligations have been discharged in order to maintain their lives in old age, thus the endowment insurance benefits is distributed not by labor or on demand, but depending on the basic life requirements of laborers upon the discharge of labor obligations, contributions of the laborers and the social economy development status and other relevant factors.

(4) Endowment insurance is a type of social insurance with the most extensive coverage. As one of the types of social insurance, endowment insurance is featured with the most extensive coverage. Due to physiological reasons, becoming old is an inevitable problem faced by each laborer. Hence, the coverage scope of endowment insurance shall be all laborers.

## II. Functions of Endowment Insurance

Endowment insurance, as the major content of the social insurance system, plays an important role based on its inherent meanings and features.

(1) The primary function of endowment insurance is to guarantee the old-age life of the laborers, which means ensuring the provision of living security to the

laborers after the duly discharge of their labor obligations. So that the laborers may comfortably work during their employment, free of worries and struggles for the old-age life which will definitely affect their work enthusiasm.

(2) Endowment insurance plays a role in adjusting income distribution. Endowment insurance may redistribute the income, which leads to the achievement of reasonable income distribution between labor period and retirement period. The laborers have the obligation (right) to work and certainly own the right to enjoy endowment insurance after their retirement. It is the basic function of endowment insurance to ensure that the laborers who have created material wealth during labor period shall obtain the life compensations upon the discharge of their legal labor obligations in addition to the salary and other income they obtained during work.

(3) Endowment insurance has the function of motivating the laborers and improving labor productivity. Endowment insurance ensures the basic life of the laborers after the discharge of their legal labor obligations and relieves their worries and concerns, which is helpful for the motivation of work enthusiasm of laborers and according improvement of the labor productivity.

(4) Endowment insurance has the function of ensuring society stability. Each laborer cares about their old-age life security a lot, so that a reliable old-age life security available for each laborer will certainly facilitates the stability and the development and progress of the society.

## Section 2  Legislation and Reform of Endowment Insurance

### I. Legislation of Chinese Endowment Insurance

Since the establishment of the People's Republic of China, the endowment insurance legislation in China has experienced the following stages:

(1) The initial stage of endowment insurance was in 1950s. The Labor Insurance Regulations of the People's Republic of China promulgated in 1951 marks the basic formation of the endowment insurance legal system. The endowment insurance in this stage carried out a two-fold system: one is the endowment insurance system for the staff and laborers of enterprise owned by the whole people (the former name of state-owned enterprises before 1992) in urban

areas as stipulated in the Labor Insurance Regulations; the other is the endowment insurance system for the civil servants in the State organs as governed by several specific regulations. The main difference between these two systems lies in the insurance benefits.

(2) The adjustment and development stage of Chinese endowment insurance was between 1958 and 1966. The regulations on the retirement and resignation of laborers were revised and the legal system of Chinese endowment insurance was further perfected. In 1958, the State unified the endowment insurance system for enterprises and the endowment insurance system for State organs and public institutions on the basis of properly loosening the restrictions on the eligibility for endowment insurance benefits and improving the benefits standards, and separated the legislation on endowment insurance for enterprises' laborers from the Labor Insurance Regulations.

(3) The third stage was Great Cultural Revolution-era during which the Chinese endowment insurance system was badly damaged. Soon after the commencement of Great Cultural Revolution, the Ministry of Finance promulgated the Reform Opinions on Several Systems Concerning the Financial Work of State-owned Enterprises in February of 1969, which stipulated no more "labor insurance premium" shall be withdrawn from the state-owned enterprises and the retirement pension contributed by enterprises shall be listed as "non-operating disbursement of enterprises". In 1978, the State, for the sake of properly resettling those old cadres who have participated in the revolution for a long time but are no longer competent to their current jobs because of their old age and bad health, promulgated the Interim Measures of the State Council for Arrangement of the Old, Weak, Sick and Disabled Cadres and the Interim Measures of the State Council on the Retirement and Resignation of Laborers to respectively regulate the endowment insurance for cadres and laborers on basis of the regulations on cadres and laborers' endowment insurance in 1958. From that on, the nationwide enterprise retirement funds became a history and the endowment insurance became the "enterprise-contributed insurance" completely. In this stage, the endowment insurance system showed backsliding and breakdown, which lasted till the convention of the third Plenary Session of the 11th CPC Central Committee in 1978.

(4) Since 1980s, Chinese endowment insurance had entered into the reform period, and a new endowment insurance system had gradually formed. The major contents of this endowment insurance reform in this stage were: the gradual promotion of the social pooling of retirement pay, which first started from the

level of cities and counties, and then expanded to the level of provinces, autonomous regions and municipalities directly under central government; the establishment of endowment insurance program for contractual laborers; the reform on the computing and distribution of the basic pension; and pilot projects of the supplementary endowment insurance, which laid a foundation for establishing a multi-channel endowment insurance system.

Based on the reform experience as concluded from various regions, the State Council promulgated the Decisions on the Reform of Endowment Insurance System for Employees of Enterprises on June 26, 1991, which made guideline provisions on the principles of endowment insurance reform, endowment insurance system, fundraising channels and methods, benefits standards and management of insurance funds.

The reform of enterprise laborers' endowment insurance system, which had been carried out since 1980s, played an important role in maintaining the basic life of the enterprises' retired laborers, protecting the society stability and improving the economy development. But the reform was in a groping stage and cannot meet the requirements for establishing socialist market economy system, and the major problems such as narrow coverage, simple channel and difficulties in collecting insurance funds still remained.

(5) Deepening reform stage of endowment insurance. In order to guide the deepening reform of endowment insurance, the State Council promulgated the Circular on Deepening the Reform of the Endowment Insurance System for Employees of Enterprise on March 1, 1995, which further defined the directions, principles and major tasks of the reform on enterprise laborers' endowment insurance. At the same time, the establishment of pilot projects of endowment insurance in rural areas was on agenda. The State Council authorized the Ministry of Civil Affairs to carry out the pilot projects of society endowment insurance in 20 counties in rural areas all over China and promulgated the Basic Scheme of Rural Social Endowment Insurance at County Level (for Trial Implementation) in 1992; and the Ministry of Agriculture promulgated the Measures on Endowment Insurance for Laborers of Township Enterprises in December of 1992.

The Ministry of Labor and Social Security passed the Trial Measures for Enterprise Annuities on the 7th ministerial meeting on December 30, 2003, which came into force on May 1, 2004. It is stipulated that the enterprises meeting the required conditions may establish enterprise annuities. Enterprise annuities program applies to the laborer whose probation period has expired. The Ministry of Labor and Social Security, the Ministry of Finance and the China Disabled

Persons' Federation jointly promulgated the Circular on Issues Concerning the Provision of Appropriate Allowance for Urban Poor and Disabled Self-employed Businessmen's Participation in Basic Endowment Insurance on June 10, 2005, which stipulated that allowance measures shall be taken to help the disabled self-employed businessmen participating in insurance if they have particular difficulties in participating in the basic endowment insurance and are unable to pay the contributions.

The former Ministry of Labor and Social Security and the Ministry of Civil Affairs jointly promulgated the Circular on Issues Concerning the Participation in Endowment Insurance by Full-time Laborers of Social Organizations on March 18, 2008, which required that, all the social groups as legal registered at civil affairs department (including branches and representative offices of such social groups), foundations (including branches and representative offices of such foundations), private non-enterprise entities, overseas NGOs' representative offices in China and their full-time contractual laborers (excluding part-time laborers, outsourcing laborers, re-employed retirees and personnel under administrative staffing), shall participate in local enterprise laborers' basic endowment insurance pursuant to the territorial jurisdiction principle. Social organizations and their full-time staff shall pay the basic endowment insurance contributions as required, of which, the base of contributions for social organization shall be the total payroll of all full-time staff who participate in insurance. For the full-time staff of the social organizations who once worked in government organizations and public institutions, the length of service reaching the State's requirements shall be considered as the years of contributions towards basic endowment insurance; for the staff who have participated in insurance individually or in enterprises, their endowment insurance relationships may be transferred and continued according to the related rules.

On December 28, 2009, the General Office of the State Council forwarded the Interim Measures for Transferring Basic Endowment Insurance Relationships of the Urban Enterprise Laborers promulgated by the Ministry of Labor and Social Security and the Ministry of Finance. Such measures are of especially importance for improving the rational configuration and orderly flow of human resources, and guaranteeing the smooth transfer of the basic endowment insurance relationships when the participants transfer across provinces, autonomous regions and municipalities directly under the central government and are employed in urban areas.

According to the Social Insurance Law of China, the State shall establish a social insurance system including basic endowment insurance, basic medical insurance, work-related injury insurance, unemployment insurance and maternity insurance, in order to protect the rights of the public to receive material assistance from the State and the society when they are old, sick, work-related injured, unemployed, pregnant and so on. Such legislation has summarized the reform experience of Chinese endowment insurance, and made overall provisions on the coverage, basic mode, fund source, benefits, eligibility conditions and adjustment mechanism of the laborers' basic endowment insurance and established the sick and disabled allowance and survivor benefit system. The legislation has also specified the major principles of new rural social endowment insurance. In addition, relevant laws have also provided that, the State shall establish and perfect the social endowment insurance system for urban residents and authorize governments of provinces, autonomous regions and municipalities to combine the enforcement of urban residents' social endowment insurance with new rural social endowment insurance based on actual situations, for the purpose of building the legal foundation of overall urban-rural endowment insurance system.

Above all, the endowment insurance of China has gone through the stages of establishment, adjustment, breakdown, reform and further reform. The endowment insurance legal system needs to be further improved to guarantee and norm the health development of the endowment insurance project.

## Section 3   Raising of Pension Funds

### I. The Raising Model of China's Pension Funds

According to the conditions of social and economic development and population aging in China, it would be most scientific to adopt the model of partial funding for the raising of pension funds. Article 3 of the Decisions on the Reform of Endowment Insurance System for Employees of Enterprises promulgated by the State Council provides that, the basic endowment insurance funds shall be uniformly raised by the government based on the principle of deciding contributions according to expenditure, having slight balance and reserving partial accumulated funds, according to the actual needs of payable expenses and the affordability of enterprises and their employees. Establishing the partially-funded model for the raising of endowment insurance funds shall pay attention to the following things:

(1) Establishing a predictable stabilized mechanism based on the maintenance

of fiscal balance and actuarial equivalent to guarantee a relatively long period with a stable contribution rate of insurance funds.

(2) Establishing an information dynamic system closely related to the collection rate. To determine the collection rate, the influence caused by relevant factors such as salary increase, inflation index, interest rate, population change, average life expectancy and unemployment rate shall be taken into consideration.

(3) Strengthening the supervision over the use of partially-funded pension funds. Adopting legislative method to establish strong auditing, administrative and social supervision and practically guarantee the integrity of pension funds and the return of operative gains.

(4) The accumulation of pension funds shall seek return on investment. According to the State Council, in addition to the reserved fund with its amount equal to two months' payable expense, 80% of the accumulated funds shall be used to purchase the State-issued social insurance bond of a particular kind. This is a stable but conservative investment through which the aim of preserving and appreciating the value of endowment insurance funds is difficult to be achieved; the feasible measures shall be set out to enable the pension funds to participate in the investment in stock market, fund market, trust investment market and real estate market in a proper way.

(5) Under the model of partial funding for pension funds, the combination of social pooling and individual account has laid down the specific criterion with respect to contributions to pension funds respectively made by enterprises and individuals. The fiscal responsibility of government is realized on the premises that the basic endowment insurance contributions are paid before the taxation, the individual endowment insurance premium does not change and the individual income tax payable is undefined, and when there is a lack of payment ability in pension funds, the fiscal support from the government at the same level will be given so as to determine the final fiscal responsibility of the government at the same level.

## Ⅱ. The Contributions to Pension Funds

### (Ⅰ) Principles for the Contributing of Pension Funds

From the practices of countries carrying out the pension insurance in the world nowadays, most of the countries adopt the principle of common contribution to the funds by the State, employer and the laborer with the enterprises and individuals acting as the chief ones.

Under the traditional planned economic system, the Chinese endowment insurance premiums are totally contributed by the State and enterprise without contribution made by the laborer. Article 2 of the Decisions on the Reform of Endowment Insurance System for Employees of Enterprises promulgated in 1991 provides that the total contributions to endowment insurance by the State and enterprise shall be changed, the State, enterprise and individual shall make endowment insurance contributions together, and the employees shall also pay a certain amount of contributions. Thereafter, China has established the fundraising principle of common contributions to pension funds by the State, employer and laborer, and reasonably defined the contribution responsibilities of such three parties.

( II ) The Contributors of Pension Funds

The contribution to pension funds is also called as the fundraising channel or source for pension funds, and accordingly the contributors of pension funds refer to the persons who are responsible for the contributions to the endowment insurance. According to the principles for contributing pension funds, the contributors of pension funds shall include the State, employer and the laborer, and the employer and the laborer shall be the primary contributors.

**1. Contribution towards Endowment Insurance by the Employer**

At the present stage of China, the contribution towards endowment insurance by the employer is the main source of pension funds.

The contribution towards endowment insurance by the employer is generally collected before the taxation according to the total payroll of all employees of the employer and the contribution rate as prescribed by the local government, and the amount so collected may be directly transferred by the opening bank of the employer on a monthly basis. In the areas where the conditions are not mature, the endowment insurance contribution may be paid before the State's collection of enterprise income tax according to the prescribed wages and the actual dependency rate of local place. Paragraph 2 of Article 4 of the Decisions on the Reform of Endowment Insurance System for Employees of Enterprises promulgated by the State Council on June 26, 1991 expressly provides that the contributions towards basic endowment insurance by the enterprise shall be collected before taxation according to the total payroll of all employees of the enterprise and the contribution rate as prescribed by the local government, and may be directly transferred by the enterprise's opening bank on a monthly basis.

The contribution towards endowment insurance by the employer collected before taxation is actually a kind of subsidies given by the State for supporting endowment insurance in the form of tax concession, which means that, 30% of the endowment insurance premium, as estimated, is contributed by the State.

This has fully embodied the principle of common contributions made by the State, the employer and the laborer together.

As to the ratio of contribution, it shall be uniformly decided by the competent authority of social insurance after detailed calculation, and realized through the legislation procedure after reporting to the government. The ratio may remain unchanged for a quite long period, or may be adjusted once a year or every several years.

### 2. Contribution towards Endowment Insurance by the Laborer

The contribution towards endowment insurance by the laborer is also an important source and component part of the pension funds.

It's an obligation to make individual contribution towards endowment insurance for every laborer who enjoys the pension benefits. The Decisions on the Reform of Endowment Insurance System for Employees of Enterprises promulgated by the State Council on June 26, 1991 has expressly provided such an obligation. One of important contents of the reform on endowment insurance system is determining the contribution obligations of the laborers. This reform matches the international trend and China's actual conditions.

With respect to the proportion and method of contribution towards endowment insurance by the laborer, Paragraph 3 of Article 4 of the Decisions on the Reform of Endowment Insurance System for Employees of Enterprises promulgated by the State Council on June 26, 1991 made guideline provision that: the contribution towards basic endowment insurance by the employee shall be gradually carried out on the basis of wage adjustment, and individual contribution rate shall be no more than 3% of the individual standard wage at the beginning, and may be gradually increased with the economic development and individual wage adjustment. The contribution towards basic endowment insurance by the employee shall be deducted by the employer from employee's payroll.

The Decisions on the Reform of Endowment Insurance System for Employees of Enterprises promulgated by the State Council on March 11, 1995 and the two Implementing Methods for the Combination of Enterprise Employee Basic Endowment Insurance Social Pooling and Individual Account have specific provisions on individual contribution: the average monthly wage of the last year shall be the wage base for individual contribution towards endowment insurance. The average monthly wage shall be calculated according to the items prescribed by the State Statistics Bureau to be listed into the total wages, including wage, bonus, allowances, subsidies and other incomes. The retired employees do not need to pay the endowment insurance contributions. As to the proportion of individual contribution, the Implementing Method provides that the employee shall pay the contributions at the rate of no less than 3% of the wage base, and such rate will be usually increased by one percent every two years until the amount so contributed has reached 50% of the endowment insurance contributions of the individual account. The individual business, the private enterprise owner and other non-wage income earners shall, taking the local average monthly wage of the last year as the contribution base, make individual contributions at the rate of about 20%, of which, the 4% will go to the social pooling funds and the 16% will go to the individual account.

Article 10 of Chapter II (Basic Endowment Insurance) of Social Insurance Law provides that "workers shall participate in basic pension insurance and the basic pension insurance contributions shall be paid jointly by the employing entities and the workers. Sole proprietors who are not employed, non-full time practitioners and other workers in flexible employment who have not participated in the basic pension insurance in the employing entities may participate in the basic pension insurance and pay the basic pension insurance contributions on their own. Measures for the pension insurance of civil servants and staff governed by the civil servant laws shall be prescribed by the State Council. " On June 29, 2011, the Human Resource and Social Security Department promulgated the Several Provisions on Implementing Social Insurance Law of People's Republic of China, which expressly provides that "when an individual who participates in the employee basic endowment insurance has reached statutory age for retirement, but the accumulative period of his contributions is less than 15 years, then his contribution period may be extended to 15 years. If an individual participates in the endowment insurance before the implementation of Social Insurance Law, and his contribution period is still less than 15 years after adding the extended 5 years, he may pay the balance in a lump sum".

### 3. State Fiscal Subsidy

The State's subsidy from fiscal revenue is a reliable guarantee for the normal operation of the pension funds. Article 44 of the Constitution of the People's Republic of China passed by the fifth session of the fifth National People's Congress in December, 1982 expressly provides that the State shall carry out the retirement system for the employees of enterprises and institutional units and civil servants according to laws. The livelihood of the retirees is secured by the State and society. This is the legal basis for the State to be responsible for the endowment insurance, but in the endowment insurance, the government's fiscal subsidy only plays an auxiliary role.

The contributions to pension funds supported by China's finance include the following methods: (1) tax concession: collecting insurance contributions before taxation, no tax is levied on the appreciation of pension funds, and no regulation tax is levied on the exceeding amount when the pension exceeds a certain amount; (2) profit sacrifice: giving a relatively high rate to the pension funds deposited in the national financial institutions; (3) subsidy: financial allocation will be made when the pension funds cannot make ends meet.

## Section 4  Distribution of Pensions

### I. Conditions for the Distribution of Pensions

The conditions for the distribution of pension, also known as the eligibility requirements for pensions, include three main conditions of age, length of service and contributions years, and other conditions irrelevant to the employment or contribution, such as that the insured must be a permanent resident or national resident or domestic resident who has lived for a certain period of time and so on.

( I ) Age Requirement

The age of the senior is prescribed by a country according to the need of social and economic development, the average life expectancy of the population and the supply and demand conditions of labor. The prescription of the age of the senior normally takes the method of prescribing the beginning of the senior years.

The level of the age of the senior influences the raising and distribution of pension funds directly. Lowering the age of the senior will not only relatively increase pensions amount payable, but also significantly affects the supply of national human resources.

The existing laws of China provide that men reaching sixty and women reaching fifty will be deemed as the senior and are entitled to enjoy the pension benefits. Where the laws and regulations have special provisions on the age of the senior for the laborer, they shall be followed.

( II ) Requirement for Length of Service

The length of service is an important basis for distributing pensions. The length of service is the laboring years during which the salary income is the total or main source of income for the laborer. Different countries have different provisions on the length of service with the shortest as fifteen years and the longest as forty years, and some countries provide different length of service for retirement for men and women employees. In countries where the laborer individual contribution towards the endowment insurance is carried out, the length of service for retirement are the years for contributions, which is stipulated as three years in some countries, and generally between fifteen to twenty years in most countries.

China provides that employees may retire in advance if the continuous length of service reaches ten years, the civil servants can retire in advance if the continuous length of service reaches twenty years, and those who have a continuous length of service for thirty years may retire in advance without any limit on age; the retirement of employees who have totally lost their labor capacity due to industrial injury is not preconditioned on the continuous length of service. The pension benefits can only be enjoyed when the condition of length of service is satisfied.

( Ⅲ ) Years of Contribution

The years of contribution refer to the years in which the enterprise and the employee jointly pay the endowment insurance contributions. The provision on the years of contribution aims at: (1) avoiding the behaviors that some people for the purpose of obtaining pensions intentionally start to pay the insurance contributions only when they are close to the age for retirement; (2) avoiding the immigrations by some new migrants purely for obtaining retirement security; (3) embodying the fairness towards the participators in endowment insurance; (4) embodying the equal relationship between the laborer's rights and obligations.

There is a minimum contribution years prescribed in various countries generally, which is also known as the minimum qualifying years The minimum qualifying years is decided by the estimation with reference to the normal life expectancy and the possible length of service, combined with the financial expenditure status of pensions. In terms of the length of the minimum qualifying years, the International Labor Organization suggests it to be fifteen years, while some areas of China prescribe it as ten years. There are two methods used for the calculation of the minimum contribution years, including continuous calculation and accumulative calculation. Applying the accumulative calculation method to calculate the minimum qualifying years is more proper. If the continuous calculation method is applied to calculate the minimum qualifying years, the distinction between interruption of work and interruption of paid contributions shall be defined, but as to the interruption of work or paid contributions caused by involuntary reasons, the length of service shall be deemed as being consecutive.

## II. The Distribution Standard of Pensions

( I ) Distribution Items of Endowment Insurance Benefit

According to the existing provisions of China, the endowment insurance benefits for Chinese employees are that, from the second month after their retirement, the salary payable to them will be ceased and monthly pensions according to the prescribed standard will be distributed to them until their death. The medical care treatment and death treatment are the same as those during their employment. Other treatments such as the accommodation allowance and winter heating allowance will be executed according to the prescribed standard.

If a laborer is under resign circumstance, namely having totally lost labor capacity as certified by the hospital and left from the working position after being approved, but does not satisfy the conditions for retirement, he will get certain material helps with the treatment level lower than that of the retirement, the items of which include: (1) monthly pensions for living expense with its amount equal to certain proportion of the wages payable to him before his resign and no less than the lowest standard as prescribed by the State; (2) the medical care treatment and death treatment are the same with those of the employees on the job.

( II ) Distribution Standard of Pensions

### 1. Determination of Standard of Pensions

The pensions, also known as annuities, refer to a certain amount of living expenses received by the retirees according to law. It is the main part of the endowment insurance benefits.

The pensions are usually calculated based on the salary income when the laborers are on the job and supplemented by the length of service or years of contributions and retirement age. It is generally believed that the pension level shall under no circumstances be higher than in-service income, so the retirement pensions cannot be 100% of the pre-retirement wage, but a certain percent of that with such percent called as "pension/wage replacement rate". No. 128 Invalidity, Old-Age and Survivors' Benefits Convention 1967 of International Labor Organization provides that the normal pension benefits payable shall not be lower than 40% to 50% of the wage income when a retiree has a qualifying period in contribution or employment and a spouse who is eligible for pensions.

### 2. Determination of Chinese Pension Standard

The base of pensions for employees in China is established on the basis of hierarchical wage system and determined as the standard wage, which has not been changed since the determination in 1954. However, with the deepening of wage system reform, the wage structure has changed a lot, and the proportion of standard wage in the wage income of employees has expressly decreased from 85.7% in 1978 to around 55% in recent years, which gives great shock to the method of taking standard wage as the calculation and distribution base of pensions. If it is calculated according to the planned pension standard of 75% as prescribed by the State, the amount of pensions received after the employee's retirement in fact only equals to 40% of the wage income on the job, and it is hard to secure the normal life of the senior to depend on such low pensions.

Therefore, Paragraph 1 of Article 6 of the Decisions on the Reform of Endowment Insurance System for Employees of Enterprises promulgated by the State Council on June 26, 1991 provides that the calculation and distribution method of basic pensions after the retirement of employees shall remain unchanged presently, and the amount of pensions shall be gradually increased in combination with the wage system reform in the future and through increasing the proportion of standard wage in the total payroll. However, from the practices of reform, under the conditions of total payroll relating to the economic efficiency, the phenomenon that the low proportion of the standard salary in the total payroll is difficult to be adjusted. Therefore, we think that the standard of pensions shall be calculated by taking actual wage income of laborers drawn from employment as the base, other than taking the current standard wage as the base.

Article 15 of Social Insurance Law provides that "the basic pension is made up of the coordinated pension and the pension in the personal account. The basic pension is determined based on factors such as the individual's cumulative premium payment period, the wage from which premium payment is made, the average wage of the local workers, the amount in the personal account and the average life expectancy of the urban population."

## Ⅲ. Distribution Method of Pensions

### (Ⅰ) The Laws on the Distribution of Pensions

The Labor Law provides that the social insurance benefits enjoyed by the laborer shall be paid on time and in full amount. How to distribute the pensions is a matter quite important, and generally speaking, the distribution of pensions includes the distributions by the employer and by the social insurance institution. As to the distribution of pensions, the Decisions on the Reform of Endowment Insurance System for Employees of Enterprises promulgated by the State Council provides, "all regions and competent authorities shall actively create conditions to increase the socialized degree of endowment insurance management service and gradually change the distribution of pension by the enterprise to the socialized distribution. In the regions with relatively good technical conditions and solid foundations, the pensions may be directly distributed by the bank or post office; in the regions where the above conditions are not satisfied, the pensions may be distributed by the social insurance agency. The social insurance agency may also provide management service for the enterprises' retirees through setting up resident agencies in large enterprises and other methods. "

( Ⅱ ) Work to Socialize the Distribution of Pensions

The following work must be done to socialize the distribution of pensions:

(1) The Employee Endowment Insurance Handbook according to the social insurance number as issued by the State Bureau of Quality and Technical Supervision shall be established, with the contents of such handbook mainly including the records of contributions to basic endowment insurance, to enterprise supplementary endowment insurance and to personal savings of old-age insurance.

(2) The Enterprise's Employee Roster and Summary Sheet of the Enterprise's Employee Compositions, Personnel Changes and Contributions shall be established, and the enterprise shall name a specially-assigned person to record the contributions to basic endowment insurance respectively by the enterprise and employees in the "Roster" and "Summary Sheet".

(3) The endowment insurance management authority shall examine and record the contributions made by the enterprise and employees on a yearly basis and the data so recorded shall be used as the payment base of basic endowment premiums contributed by the enterprise and employees of next year, until the employee is retired.

(4) Computer management shall be gradually carried out. Because the benefits for the retirees are adjusted with the changes of pensions contributed every year and the workload is very huge, so it is necessary to establish and complete endowment insurance database for employees and gradually carry out computer management.

To improve social insurance handling service and maintain the rights and interests of the insured, Social Insurance Law has made express provisions on the following aspects: Firstly, the establishment of a social insurance handling service mechanism. The first is providing the establishing principles of social insurance handling agency. The legislation provides that there is social insurance handling agency set up in social pooling region. The social insurance agency, as required by work and after being approved by the local social insurance administrative authority and administrative authority for agency allocation, may set up the branches and service network stations in the social pooling area. The second is providing the fund security for the social insurance agency. The social insurance agency's personnel costs and basic operation fees, administration fees arising from the handling of social insurance are secured by the fiscal support from the government at same level according to relevant provisions of the State. The third is providing the following basic duties of the social insurance agency: social insurance registration and the verification and collection of social insurance premiums according to law; paying the social insurance benefits on time and in full amount; signing service agreements with the medical care agency and medicine business units as required by management service to regulate the medial care service; the prompt, complete and accurate records of the contributions to social insurance by individual and enterprise and social insurance benefits and other individual interests and the regular and free delivery of such records to the right person; the free provision of inquiry service for employers and individuals; and the provision of social insurance consultancy and other relevant service. Secondly, the guideline provisions on the construction of social insurance information system. The construction of social insurance information is the groundwork for social insurance administration and handling service, and the aim of a lifelong record, service and security is unable to be achieved without the support of a perfect information system. The relevant legal provisions are embodied in two respects: the one is the establishment of a nationally-unified social security number for each individual, which provides the legal basis for the making and issuance of the nationally-unified and multifunctional social security card; the other is the construction of national social insurance information system, which is under a nationally-unified planning and constructed by the people's governments at the county level and above together based on the principle of graded responsibility.

## Section 5   Supplementary Endowment Insurance

### I. Legislation on Supplementary Endowment Insurance

China makes provisions on the supplementary endowment insurance in the forms of basic laws and administrative regulations, and the specific provisions are:

(1) The Decisions on the Reform of Endowment Insurance System for Employees of Enterprises promulgated by the State Council on June 26, 1991

provides: the system combining basic endowment insurance with enterprise supplementary endowment insurance and employee individual endowment insurance of a saving nature shall be gradually established along with the development of economy. Since then, the enterprise supplementary endowment insurance system in China has emerged and been put into effect.

(2) Article 75 of Labor Law provides: The State shall encourage Employers to provide supplementary insurance for laborers in light of their actualities, which establishes the status of supplementary endowment insurance from the legislation.

(3) The Circular on Deepening the Reform of the Endowment Insurance System for Employees of Enterprise provides: while establishing the basic endowment insurance to secure the basic life of the retirees, the State also encourages enterprise supplementary endowment insurance and individual endowment insurance of a saving nature. After paying the basic endowment insurance contributions as required, the enterprise may, under the guidance of state policies and according to the economic benefits condition of the enterprise itself, establish supplementary endowment insurance for its employees. This further demonstrates the condition for establishing the supplementary endowment insurance, namely, the establishment of the supplementary endowment insurance is based on the economic benefits of the employers.

(4) The Suggestions on the Establishment of Enterprise Supplementary Endowment Insurance System of the Ministry of Labor have detailed provisions on the supplementary endowment insurance from the aspects of implementing bodies and conditions, source of fund, calculation and distribution method and investment and operation, etc.

## II. Features of Supplementary Endowment Insurance

The supplementary endowment insurance, as a new system, has the following features:

(1) Semi-compulsory legislation. On the one hand, the State encourages the employer who has economic capability to establish the supplementary endowment insurance according to their economic benefits in the form of legislation, which is compulsory; on the other hand, the employer may choose not to establish the supplementary endowment insurance when the conditions to carry out supplementary endowment insurance are not satisfied, which is quite flexible.

(2) The directness of distribution. The distribution of supplementary pensions among the employees may be directly carried out by the employers or entrusted to the handling agency, and there is no problem of social pooling and no

adjustment function.

(3) The singleness of fund source. The supplementary pensions are mainly contributed by the employers, or jointly contributed by the employers and laborers, but the individual contributions should not account for too much.

(4) The flexibility in implementation. The supplementary endowment insurance is set up and altered with the employer's economic development. And in terms of time, the employer may set up or cease it at any time and no consecutive period is required for it. The employer may determine the distribution level differing from person to person and from time to time at its solely discretionary. There is no uniform standard among the employers, and differences are allowed.

## Ⅲ. The Application of Supplementary Endowment Insurance

(1) The scope of application of supplementary endowment insurance: the scope of application of supplementary endowment insurance is the laborers of enterprises of all kinds in urban areas.

(2) The conditions of supplementary endowment insurance include: the employers have participated in the social pooling of basic endowment insurance and have pay endowment insurance contributions in full amount as scheduled; the employers have relatively stable production & operation conditions and good economic benefits; the employers have good basis for democratic management.

(3) Source of supplementary endowment insurance funds: the funds of enterprise supplementary endowment insurance are mainly burdened by the enterprise with the payment of such expense coming from the wage reserves of enterprise; the social insurance agency may also return the part exceeding 300% of average wage of all employees that contributed by the enterprise towards basic endowment insurance to the enterprise as supplementary endowment insurance funds; the part not exceeding a certain proportion of the total payroll of the enterprise can be written into the relevant costs of the enterprise after being approved by the local government. Under the circumstance that funds are jointly contributed by the enterprise and the individual, the individual contributions shall not exceed half of the total contributions, and the individual contributions shall be paid based on a prescribed proportion in individual wage income or a defined contribution amount.

(4) The calculation and distribution of supplementary endowment insurance funds: there is individual pension account usually established for the enterprise supplementary endowment insurance, and the supplementary endowment insurance benefits shall be calculated and distributed by the enterprise or entrusted agent according to the balance amount of individual pension account.

● Chapter XI

# Unemployment Insurance Law

The unemployment insurance constitutes an important part of the social security system. To establish a unified labor market under market economy entails the establishment of unemployment insurance scheme.

## Section 1 Overview of Unemployment Insurance and Its Significance

### I. Concept of Unemployment

Unemployment refers to a state that laborers with labor capacity and willingness to work fail to acquire labor opportunity or lose their job after being hired. The definition of unemployment varies from country to country. For example, U. S defines the unemployed as people above 16 who are without job or actively seeking one. The International Labor Organization specially makes a definition of unemployment as follows: the unemployment comprise all persons above a specified age who during the reference period were: (1) "without work", i. e. were not in paid employment or self-employment; (2) "currently available for work", i. e. were available for paid employment or self-employment; and (3) "seeking work", i. e. had taken specific steps in a specified reference period to seek paid employment or self-employment.

Chinese conception of the unemployment has the following characteristics:

(1) The unemployed only refers to urban laborers with a non-agricultural household registration (Hukou), excluding rural laborers. As a result, a huge number of migrant workers rushing into cities are excluded from the statistics. Persons without corresponding labor capacity cannot be deemed as the unemployed, such as the mental patients and totally disabled persons who cannot engage in any social labor. With regard to people who are currently without job

but not in need of one, they are not deemed as the unemployed. These people have given up their rights to work of their own free will. In this way, they withdraw from the labor team, not belonging to labor force. Therefore, there is no unemployment issue concerning them.

(2) The specified age limitation for the unemployed is in general 60 for males and 50 for females. Men reaching 60 and women reaching 50 in enterprises, and men reaching 60 and women reaching 55 in governmental institutions and public institutions can retire from work; for workers engaging in toxic and hazardous work and qualified workers suffering diseases or being disabled by work-related injuries, the default retirement age can be lowered.

(3) The calculation of the unemployment rate is not based on the international practice which is a monthly calculation; instead it is calculated at the number of the unemployed as of the last day of each calendar year.

The reasons for unemployment are various, which can be categorized based on international practice as follows: frictional unemployment, caused by time gap between the job-hunting laborer and the potential post, for example the transitioning period between jobs when a new laborer who is still looking for the first job or a worker who is transitioning from one job to another; seasonal unemployment, caused by changing demand for labor force with seasonal shifts, as the production conditions or products in some industry sectors are sensitive to climate change, social morals or purchasing customs; technological unemployment, caused by labor surplus of local society that is the result of updating machines and materials and adopting new productive technology and managerial methods; structural unemployment, caused by the adjustment of labor structure in response to new change of economic or industrial structure and production methods or scale; cyclical unemployment, caused by cyclical economic shrink in market economy countries.

## Ⅱ. Concept and Features of the Unemployment Insurance

The unemployment insurance refers to a social insurance system in which the State establishes the unemployment insurance funds to provide unemployment insurance benefits in a legal period for unemployed workers who are temporarily without income, in order to guarantee their basic living needs. The unemployment insurance constitutes an important part of the social security system. Its features are as follows:

First, the insured of unemployment insurance are the unemployed workers, i. e. unemployment insurance is provided only for people who have labor capacity and the willingness to work but are temporally out of job. In China, the targets of unemployment insurance are furthered limited to laborers who have had a job but have lost it out of their own will and have been through the unemployment registration, excluding those who have never been employed.

Since the unemployment insurance aims at guaranteeing the basic living needs of unemployed laborers who have had salary income during post-layoff period, its coverage includes most members of the labor force. Employers enrolled in the insurance are equally treated regardless of their sectors or industries or the nature of their ownership structure; their employees who are released or terminated their labor relationship and eligible for the benefits are all entitled to the unemployment benefits, regardless of their employment forms, household location (urban or rural).

Secondly, there is time limitation to the unemployment insurance benefits. Unlike pension insurance or work-related injury insurance, under which workers can enjoy the insurance benefits for a long term, the unemployment insurance can be received only within the legal period, beyond which even if the worker is still unemployed there will no longer be any benefit. For instance, in China the maximum period for a laborer to receive the unemployment benefits is 24 months.

Thirdly, the unemployment insurance premium is jointly contributed by enterprises and laborers. Among the various social insurance, for the work-related injury insurance and maternity insurance, only the enterprises are required to contribute while the laborers are not. The outdated Chinese unemployment insurance scheme provided that unemployment insurance contribution was only paid by enterprises, and laborers were eligible to receive unemployment benefits during the unemployment period. The establishment of the new unemployment insurance scheme has changed the old method that laborers were not required to pay contribution. Instead, it provides that laborers can enjoy unemployment insurance benefits only when they have paid the insurance contribution in a certain proportion based on their salary. According to the provisions, it is mandatory for employers and employees under the coverage of the unemployment insurance scheme to contribute to the unemployment insurance. Employers and employees who fail to pay the contribution are subject to legal liabilities.

The unemployment insurance funds are mainly collected from social pooling, and assumed by a tripartite of employer, individual and the State. Its payment ratio and payment methods are relatively stable. The collected unemployment insurance contributions are all included into the unemployment insurance funds regardless of their source channel or the nature of contribution units, and are used for mutual assistance and reciprocity in the pooling areas under unified arrangement.

## III. The Positive Role of Chinese Unemployment Insurance Scheme

A decade and more has been passed since the establishment of Chinese unemployment insurance scheme. The positive role it has played is revealed as follows:

(1) It has effectively guaranteed the basic living needs of the unemployed. The basic living needs of the employed have been secured, through the unemployment insurance scheme which grants unemployment insurance benefits to them in order to help them go through difficulties. With particular to recent years, the number of people who were benefited from the unemployment insurance funds is over 300 million. It has played a positive role in maintaining social stability.

(2) It has promoted the re-employment of the unemployed. According to applicable Chinese regulations, part of the benefits from the unemployment insurance funds are used for the unemployed to conduct self-relief production, job-transitioning training and employment hunting activities, which has helped more than half of the unemployed go back to the employment post and realize their re-employment.

(3) It has supported the enterprise reforms. The unemployment insurance scheme, which secures the basic living needs of the unemployed, has not only reduced the employment pressure assumed by the state-owned enterprises and the reform pressure, but also pushed the successful adoption and implementation of reform measures. A lot of local regions also apply the funds to support the liquidated, suspended, merged or transferring enterprises to make appropriate arrangement of redundant workers.

(4) It has promoted the corporate management of public institutions. Along with the furtherance of the reform, the reform on the employment mechanism in public institutions has further speeded. An optimal personnel structure with reducing staffs & improving efficiency based on the market principles will be a must for public institutions. Therefore, including the staffs of public institutions into the scope of unemployment insurance scheme is of great significance in carrying out the personnel management based on the market employment mechanism and promoting self-development for public institutions, especially for state-owned public institutions.

## Section 2　China's Unemployment Insurance Legislation

### Ⅰ. Unemployment Insurance Legislation at Early Days of New China

As early as the beginning of New China, in order to solve the unemployment issue left from the old China, China has begun its legislation on solving unemployment issue. In 1950, the Government Administration Council promulgated the Interim Measures for Relieving Unemployment Workers and the Instructions on Relieving Unemployed Teachers and Handling Students Dropout Problems. In order to relieve the unemployed workers, the government adopted the measures such as "welfare-to-work", self-reliance production projects and return to the native to produce, and for unemployed workers who have extreme difficulty in living, the government has carried out the measures of granting relief funds, and the Government Administration Council decided to appropriate 200 million kilos grains as the relief funds for unemployed workers under very tight fiscal budget, so as to guarantee the basic living of the unemployed workers. In the mid 1950s, along with the full recovery and development of China's economic construction, the unemployment rate was greatly reduced. In 1957, China's government announced that the unemployment has been eliminated, and the relevant measures on unemployment relief were then abolished.

### Ⅱ. Reform on Unemployment Insurance Legislation

The real establishment of unemployment insurance system in China was in the mid 1980s. With the comprehensively deepening reform of economy system, China has begun its labor system reform which mainly focused on the implementation of labor contract system. In July, 1986, the State Council promulgated the Interim Provisions on the Implementation of Unemployment Insurance for State-owned Enterprise Workers, which marked the real establishment of Chinese unemployment insurance. The Provisions only applied to state-owned enterprises with its scope covering staff and workers of the enterprises which have legally declared bankruptcy, staff and workers of the enterprises facing bankruptcy laid off during the statutory period of reorganization, staff and workers who have terminated or canceled their labor contracts and staff and workers fired by the enterprises. The unemployment insurance funds are contributed by enterprises with the amount equal to 1% of the payroll of all staff and workers. The distribution standard of unemployment relief funds shall be equal to 50% to 75% of individual standard wage.

In 1989, the Ministry of Labor promulgated the Measures on the Administration of Unemployment Insurance Funds for Employees of State-owned Enterprises to strengthen the overall planning and management of the unemployment insurance funds. In 1990, the Ministry of Labor promulgated the Circular on Solving the Living Problems for Part of the Unemployment Enterprise Workers with Unemployment Insurance Funds, which requires that living problems of the workers of the liquidated or suspended enterprises shall be well solved during the period of reorganization. In April, 1993, the State Council promulgated the Regulations on Unemployment Insurance for Staff and Workers of State-owned Enterprise, in which, in addition to the 4 circumstances as provided in 1986, the following items are covered by the scope of unemployment insurance coverage: staff and workers of the enterprises closed or dissolved in accordance with relevant regulations of the State; staff and workers laid off in periods during which the enterprises ceased production in order to be streamlined in accordance with relevant regulations of the State; staff and workers who have been removed or dismissed by the enterprises; and other staff and workers entitled to unemployment insurance in accordance with the laws and regulations or the regulations of the people's governments of the provinces, autonomous regions and municipalities directly under the Central Government. In terms of source of unemployment insurance funds, it provides that enterprises shall contribute unemployment insurance premiums on the basis of 0.6% of the payroll of all staff and workers. The distribution standard of unemployment relief funds shall be equal to 120% to 150% of the amount of social relief benefits regulated by the local civil affairs department, and the specific amount shall be determined by the people's government of the province, autonomous region or municipality directly under the Central Government.

In order to change the situation and establish more perfect unemployment insurance system, in January, 1999, the State Council promulgated the Regulations on Unemployment Insurance, replacing the Regulations of 1993, which also meant the initial establishment of unemployment insurance system adaptable to the market economy in China. The Regulations on Unemployment Insurance, which not only absorbed the practice experience of establishing and developing Chinese unemployment insurance system, but also learned beneficial practices from foreign countries, have made huge adjustments in many aspects, reflected the requirements of socialist market economy to unemployment insurance system, embodied the spirit that unemployment insurance system serves for the reform and social stabilization, and built the firm foundation for the formation of basically perfected unemployment insurance system with Chinese characteristics.

Social Insurance Law contains a special chapter of stipulation on the unemployment insurance, covering the contents of the unemployment insurance's coverage, system mode, source of funds, benefits and so on, which provides a legal safeguard for the further development of unemployment insurance.

## Section 3　Targets and Scope of Unemployment Insurance

### I. Targets of Unemployment Insurance

Unemployment insurance is established for the unemployed who suffer from unemployment risk or lose wage incomes temporarily, so the scope of its coverage in the initial stage was clearly and strictly defined. Generally, its targets are limited to the wage laborers that participate in formal economic activities, have a stable career but temporarily lose their jobs. In other words, the temporary workers with unstable and informal jobs, seasonal workers, domestic servants, agriculture workers, national public servant with quite stable jobs, individual workers with independent income and the graduates from secondary schools or above are all excluded from the insurance coverage.

With the development of the social economy, the explanation to the concept of unemployment has changed and the coverage of unemployment insurance has expanded correspondingly. The 75th Labor Congress held by International Labor Organization in 1988 defined the word "unemployed" as that, laborers who have the ability to engage in economic activities and look for jobs, are indeed looking for jobs but fail to get proper positions, and have no income and poor living conditions are all under unemployment and shall be covered by unemployment insurance. Nowadays, International Labor Organization and developed countries have made a new definition on unemployment that, any person who reaches certain age and has labor capacity, but has no job or his load capacity fails to reach certain standard, is engaging in searching for a job and has registered in a job introduction agency, is under unemployment and shall be the object of unemployment insurance. The unemployment insurance in United States started in 1935, the same year of the establishment of social security system. The Parliament authorized every state government to establish unemployment insurance system by legislation. The unemployment insurance scheme is administrated by the state government, while the federal government only enacts some measures to encourage the establishment of unemployment insurance scheme by each state government and to maintain the interstate consistency. This scheme covers 97% of the wage-earners. In 1933, there were about 1. 7 million people received weekly unemployment relief with the average of each person 172 US dollars a week.

There is no specific provision on the targets of unemployment insurance made in the Social Insurance Law of China. In practice, application scope of unemployment insurance as stipulated in the Regulations on Unemployment Insurance shall be followed.

## II. Eligibility for Enjoying Unemployment Insurance

The unemployed who are expecting to obtain the right to unemployment insurance shall satisfy certain eligibility requirements. So, in order to grant the unemployment insurance benefits to the unemployed within the stipulated scope, and prevent the unemployed form physiological dependence and the concept of reap without sowing, the eligibility requirements of unemployment insurance in each country are all stipulated quite strictly and specific. To sum up, they are mainly as follows:

(1) The unemployed shall meet the working-age requirement, that is to say only the laborers who are between the statutory minimum working-age and the retirement age may enjoy unemployment insurance. Unemployment insurance does not cover the person whose working-age is lower than the statutory minimum working-age or higher than the retirement age. In this respect, different countries have different requirements. In Britain and Australia, the eligible age for men is from 16 to 64, while the eligible age for women is from 16 to 59; and the World Bank uniformly stipulates that the eligible age for men and women is from 15 to 65. This is because only employees in working age can have the chance to become unemployed, and are entitled to enjoy the unemployment insurance benefits. Persons under the working age or retired workers in excess of the working age do not undertake the statutory social labor obligations, and countries in the world all expressly prohibit the use of child laborers so as to protect their health; persons in

excess of the working-age have already enjoyed the endowment insurance, so in this regard, these two types of persons are excluded from the labor force of the social production, and there is no unemployment issue concerning them, and they are certainly not the targets of the unemployment insurance.

(2) The employed must be under involuntary unemployment. The reasons for unemployment must not be out of willingness, but rather, all types of social or economic factors beyond their control. In this respect, countries in the world all have regulations on preventing the obtaining of unemployment insurance benefits due to intentional unemployment. Voluntary unemployed workers are not within the scope of payment of unemployment insurance benefits, because the liability for voluntary unemployment is on the part of the unemployed persons themselves, or out of the consideration for a better job position or a higher salary, or out of other personal considerations. This type of temporary unemployment due to voluntary separation from the original job position shall be attributed to the individual's decisions, and the enterprise and the State are of no obligation to provide unemployment insurance benefits for such persons. In contrast, the liability for involuntary unemployment does not lie in the unemployed, but some other reasons irrelevant to the unemployed and out of their controls, so under this kind of unemployment, unemployment insurance benefits should be provided.

(3) The unemployed must satisfy some conditions on qualified period. In order to carry out the principle of equality of rights and obligations of the social insurance, the unemployment insurance requires that the unemployed must reach certain length of service or pay unemployment insurance premium for a certain period and of a certain amount; and for the period of payment and length of service, most countries will subject to six months in the previous year before the unemployment. Some countries also provide that, the unemployed must live in relevant countries for a certain period before they are eligible for unemployment insurance benefits.

(4) The unemployed must have the labor capacity and willingness to work. What the unemployment insurance protects are the unemployed who have labor capacity and willingness to work. In order to inspect the willingness to work and labor capacity of the unemployed, all countries stipulate that the unemployed shall first apply for registration of employment tutoring with the employment service agency, and report regularly to the employment service agency during the period when they receive unemployment relief. This mainly includes: 1) the unemployed must register for work with the occupation introduction office or unemployment insurance management agency within the prescribed period; 2) During the

unemployment period, they must contact with the unemployment insurance agency regularly to report their personal information, which aims to timely update any change in the employment willingness of the unemployed and transmit employment information to the employment agency; 3) The unemployed show their willingness to accept occupational training and reasonable work arrangement. If the unemployed workers refuse to do so, they will be recognized as having no re-employment willingness and the distribution of insurance benefits to them will be ceased. The unemployed must be qualified for the said conditions to enjoy the unemployment insurance benefits.

## Section 4   Distribution of Unemployment Insurance Funds

### I . Expenditure Items of the Unemployment Insurance Funds

How to utilize the unemployment insurance funds is a matter related to the bearing capacity of the unemployment insurance funds, as well as the full functioning of the unemployment insurance. Many countries regulate the expenditure items of the unemployment insurance funds through legislations.

The main expenditure items of the unemployment insurance funds as stipulated in China are as follows: (1) Unemployment Insurance Benefits; (2) medical subvention during the period of receiving unemployment insurance benefits; (3) funeral allowance for the unemployed died during the period of receiving unemployment insurance benefits and the pension for the spouse and direct relatives supported by such dead person; (4) subsidy for accepting vocational training and vocational introduction during the period of receiving unemployment insurance benefits; (5) other expenses related to the unemployment insurance as regulated or approved by the State.

Unemployment Insurance Benefits is the basic living allowance paid to the unemployed who are qualified for certain requirements by the unemployment insurance agencies according to the laws, which is the main part of unemployment insurance benefits.

Medical subvention during the period of unemployment insurance means the subsidy which is payable to the unemployed for the medical expenses incurred during the period of receiving unemployment insurance benefits. The insurance system of China is immature at present, the free medical care system and the labor medical care system that have been carried out for a long time are all targeted at the laborers who are under employment, while the unemployed are not brought into the scope of medical insurance. In the regions where the reform on medical insurance system is implemented, there is individual account for medical insurance established for the laborers in recent years. When a laborer becomes unemployed, the medical expense can be withdrawn from the individual account established before his unemployment in accordance with the laws. However, because of the limited funds in the individual account and the weak affordability for medical care expenses by the employed, it is very hard to guarantee the basic medical needs of the unemployed during the unemployment. Under such circumstance, the necessary subsidy granted for the unemployed, which is sourced from unemployment insurance funds, can reduce the economic burden of the unemployed in some extent, and also be an important measure to ensure the basic life of the unemployed. The medical subvention generally adopts the mean of combining the fixed subsidies for outpatient service and subsidy in proportion for hospitalizations. Specific criteria and application procedures are determined on the basis of actual situations and vary from place to place.

The funeral allowance for the unemployed died during the period of unemployment insurance and the pension for the spouse and direct relatives supported by the dead person are the expenditure items targeted at the relatives of the dead unemployed. For a long time, the funeral expenses and subsidy of living expenses for the spouse and direct relatives supported by the dead employee in urban areas in China are borne by the employer by which the dead employee was employed. This is a kind of social security measure with Chinese characteristics. At present, in consideration of the purpose of relieving the burden of businesses and the economic burden of the relatives of the unemployed during the reform of the labor personnel system, the Chinese government regulates that, the funeral allowance for the unemployed died during the period of receiving unemployment insurance benefits and the pension for the spouse and direct relatives supported by the dead person can be withdrew from the expenditure of unemployment insurance funds.

The subsidy for the vocational training and vocational introduction during the unemployment insurance coverage period means the fund which is disbursed from the unemployment insurance fund to promote the re-employment of the unemployed. The purpose of providing this part of funds for the unemployed is to relieve the economic burden of the unemployed, help them get employment service timely, promote them to take active part in the vocational training, improve their labor skills and re-employment abilities and gain the re-employment opportunities.

## II. Payment Standard of the Unemployment Insurance Benefits

The key for the unemployment insurance to really achieve the purposes of helping the unemployed maintain their basic life and promoting their re-employment lies in the correct determination of payment standard of the unemployment insurance.

### ( I ) Determination of the Principles for Payment of Unemployment Insurance Benefits

At present, the following principles are generally followed by various countries:

### 1. Guaranteeing the Basic Life Need of the Unemployed and Their Dependents

Unemployment insurance benefits are the major income source of the unemployed. Therefore, the life standard of the unemployed and their relatives is determined by the payment levels of the unemployment insurance benefits. The unemployment insurance benefits play a security role to maintain the basic life needs of the unemployed. The minimum standard of living is the lowest limits of the unemployment insurance. Neither should the payment standard of unemployment insurance benefits be less than the earnings as required for guaranteeing the lowest living standard nor should it be equal to the same. This is just because that the unemployment insurance is aimed to ensure the unemployed enjoy the basic standard of living, rather than the minimum standard of living. So if we take the lowest living standard as the payment standard for unemployment insurance benefits, we may confuse the function of unemployment relief with the function unemployment insurance.

### 2. The Payment Standard Should Be Appropriately Lower than the Original Wage of the Unemployed

The reason is that the payment should be subject to contribution. The unemployed make no contribution to the enterprises, State and the society during their unemployment, so a payment less than the wage which is payable for their labor with a certain time limit attached hereto would be a matter of course. In case of the time limit for payment is exceeded, the payment will be made based on the standard of social relief, which would be helpful for prompting employment. But if the payment standard is the same as the original wage standard, not only the financial burden of the unemployment insurance will increase, but also the difference between employment and unemployment will be confused, resulting in negative effects on the re-employment of the unemployed.

### 3. Principle of Quality of Rights and Obligations of Unemployment Insurance

Upon unemployment, the laborers are entitled to obtain basic living guarantee, and before unemployment, the laborers are obliged to conduct social labor and pay the premiums. In this case, the payment of unemployment insurance benefits shall be connected with the length of service, period of payment and original salary income of the insured, which means the longer length of service, more contributions made to insurance premium and higher original wage the unemployed have before their unemployment, the more benefits they will gain when they become unemployed, and vice versa.

( II ) Content of Unemployment Insurance Payment Standards

### 1. Waiting Period

This refers to that the unemployed workers have to wait for a period of time before obtaining the unemployment insurance benefits. This provision is conducive to reducing the tedious work on small amount payment, and can control the payment amount. Most countries stipulate that the waiting period will be 3 - 7 days, and in some other countries, such as Belgium and Switzerland, the waiting period could be as long as 36 days. Meanwhile, most countries stipulate that there must be a waiting period before each claim for unemployment insurance benefits, but only once waiting period in a year. For example, if a worker becomes unemployed again in the same year, there is no waiting period before his second claim for unemployment insurance benefits.

### 2. Unemployment Insurance Benefits Ratio

This refers to the benefits ratio and benefits amount of the unemployment insurance. There are several common systems in this respect: (1) salary ratio system, which refers to a manner by which the unemployment insurance benefits shall be determined as per a percentage of the average wage in certain period before the unemployment of the insured. This manner is usually subject to the factors such as, the length of service, period of insurance, wage level and years of payment of premiums. The benefits ratio is usually 45%—75% of the wage and varies from country to country; (2) Uniform system, also known as fixed amount system, which refers to a manner by which a fixed and equal amount will be given for all persons who are eligible for unemployment insurance benefits, without regard to their wage incomes before their unemployment. Under this system, the benefit is usually calculated by day or in week; (3) Mixed system, which means the unemployment insurance benefits are calculated and distributed in combination of the ratio system and uniform system. Under this system, the unemployment insurance benefits are paid partially as per a percentage of the wage income before unemployment, and partially as per a fixed amount; (4) Payment in a lump sum. This means that a certain amount will be paid in a lump sum to eligible persons as unemployment insurance benefits or severance pay, with its specific amount depends on the their wage and length of service.

### 3. Benefits Period of Unemployment Insurance

The benefits period of unemployment insurance is the longest period during which the unemployed can receive their unemployment insurance benefits. Most countries stipulate it as a limited period between 8 to 36 weeks, which generally is 26 weeks. In 1952, the International Labor Conference stipulated the unemployment insurance benefits period as 26 weeks in 12 months, and later in 1988, changed it as 30 weeks in 24 months, and 52 weeks for particular circumstance. The stipulation on this period mainly aims to promote the re-employment.

In terms of the eligibility requirements for benefits, there are general provisions as follows: for the involuntary unemployment, the certain premiums contribution period or certain service years in the insured profession is required and the claimant shall have work ability and willingness to seek for another job. Besides, for those who voluntarily leave their jobs without proper reason, or are fired due to misconduct, or become unemployed for the involvement in suspension of production arising out of labor dispute, the disqualification for unemployment benefits or reduced benefits ratio or additional delay in benefits will be imposed on them.

The standard of unemployment insurance benefits is equal to a certain percentage of the average wage during the recent period prior to the unemployment. The replacement ratio of unemployment benefits in many countries is stipulated as between 40% and 75% of the average income. Some countries stipulate that if the unemployed have families, additional benefits for their spouse and children shall be distributed in addition to the basic benefits.

## Ⅲ. Eligibility Requirements for Unemployment Insurance Benefits

The standardization of the eligibility requirements and procedures for receiving unemployment insurance benefits is conducive to protecting the legitimate rights and interests of the unemployed and intensifying the functions of the unemployment insurance. Various countries have made legal stipulations on the eligibility requirements for unemployment insurance benefits. In China, there is a stipulation that the employees of urban collective-owned enterprises and public institutions enrolled in the unemployment insurance who want to receive unemployment insurance benefits after they become employed must meet the following conditions:

(1) Having participated in the unemployment insurance as required, with the period of contribution respectively made by the employer and individual no less than 1 year. This is the uppermost requirement. Participating in unemployment insurance as required refers to that the unemployed have worked in urban collectively-owned enterprises or public institutions for a period and are not new labor force; and they are not eligible for receiving unemployment insurance benefits after they become unemployed when their contribution period is less than 1 year.

(2) Involuntary suspension of employment. Generally speaking, the reasons for suspension of employment may be divided into two types: involuntary suspension of employment, which means the persons are unwilling to suspend employment, but are forced to suspend employment due to reasons out of their controls; and voluntary suspension of employment, which means the persons become unemployed due to voluntary leaving of post. It is a basic principle in unemployment insurance legislations followed by most countries in the world that only employees under involuntary unemployment are eligible for unemployment insurance benefits, which aims to prevent employees from obtaining unemployment insurance benefits by intentional losing their jobs. By referring to the international common practices, China also excludes those who are under voluntary unemployment from coverage of persons who are eligible for unemployment insurance benefits.

(3) Having completed the unemployment registration and be willing to be re-employed. Unemployment registration is a necessary procedure for receiving unemployment insurance benefits, with an aim to know the basic situation of the unemployed and confirm their eligibility. Unemployment registration is an important mark for the unemployed to enter into the claim procedure for unemployment insurance benefits. The unemployed who want to receive unemployment insurance benefits must be willing to be re-employed. This is to consider that one of important functions of unemployment insurance is to promote the re-employments of the unemployed. To achieve this purpose, on the one hand, we have to accelerate the economic development to create more jobs and develop and improve the employment service undertakings to provide services for the re-employments of the unemployed; on the other hand, the unemployed shall proactively take advantage of all types of employment opportunities and employment service facilities to continuously improve their own capacity, enhance

their ability to compete for the job and realize re-employment as soon as possible. In determining whether the unemployed is willing to be re-employed, the measurement shall be subject to whether the unemployed have registered for work with employment agencies and participated in the re-employment activities.

The provision of China's Social Insurance Law stipulates that an unemployed person meeting the following conditions may collect unemployment insurance compensation from the unemployment insurance funds: (1) the employing entity and the unemployed person has paid the unemployment insurance premiums for one year before the person becomes unemployed; (2) the unemployed person unintentionally terminates the employment; (3) the unemployed person has gone through the formalities for unemployment registration and is seeking employment. According to Article 4 of the Measures on Claim for and Distribution of Unemployment Insurance Benefits issued by the Ministry of Labor Security, involuntary suspension of employment refers to the following persons (1) whose labor contracts have expired; (2) whose labor contracts are terminated by the employer; (3) who are fired, dismissed and removed by the employer; (4) who terminate labor contract with the employer under Item 2 and 3 of Article 32 of the Labor Law; and (5) as otherwise provided by the laws and regulations.

China's legislations also stipulate that, during unemployment insurance benefits period, the unemployed may participate in the basic medical insurance for employees and enjoy the basic medical insurance benefits. The basic medical insurance premiums that shall be contributed by the unemployed shall be deducted from the unemployment insurance funds, and the unemployed individuals are not required to pay the basic medical insurance premiums. Where an unemployed worker dies during unemployment insurance benefits period, the funeral subsidy and pension for the family of the deceased shall be granted to his/her family in a lump sum with reference to the regulations on death of incumbent employees. All funds as required for that shall be disbursed from the unemployment insurance funds. Where the personal death simultaneously meets the requirements for receiving funeral subsidy from the basic endowment insurance, work-related injury insurance and unemployment insurance, the family of the deceased may only choose one of them.

Where the unemployed become re-employed or have other means and sources to support their livings during the unemployment insurance benefits period, then their unemployment insurance benefits in this case shall be ceased.

Article 51 of the Social Insurance Law stipulates that, if an unemployed person is involved in any of the following situations during the period in which unemployment insurance compensation is collected, he/she shall stop collecting the unemployment insurance compensation and stop enjoying other unemployment insurance benefits: (1) is re-employed; (2) applies to serve in the military; (3) migrates to a foreign country; (4) enjoys basic pension insurance benefit; (5) refuses to accept the appropriate job referred by or training provided by the department or institution designated by the local people's government without proper reason.

● Chapter Ⅻ

# Medical Insurance

Medical insurance aims at providing medical expenses, making up the lost income and assisting in the restoration of working ability for those laborers who are sick or become disabled due to the reasons not directly related to work. Medical insurance is significant to secure the health of the laborer and the living of the laborer and his family.

## Section 1 Concept and Significance of Medical Insurance

### Ⅰ. Concept of Medical Insurance

Medical insurance refers to a social insurance scheme under which laborers and their dependants can obtain material supports in respect of living and medical care when they suffer sickness or non-work-related injury. Such scheme involves the material support in respect of medical care, so it is referred to as medical insurance.

Features of medical insurance are as follows:

(1) Immediacy. Health walks hand in hand with diseases. Laborers may suffer sickness or non-work-related injury at anytime in their everyday life. Therefore, diseases are lifetime risks for an individual. Medical insurance is a kind of social insurance designed to against the risks of diseases. For an individual, medical insurance is the most frequently used social insurance and also a short-term compensatory measure.

(2) Universality. The universality of the disease-catching targets determines the universality of medical insurance. Unlike maternity insurance which is only targeted at female laborers, nor does it like pension insurance and unemployment insurance which are respectively targeted at the retirees and laborers who have temporarily lost their jobs, medical insurance is targeted at all laborers.

(3) Overlapping. The universality of medical insurance in turn leads medical insurance to form an interconnected and overlapping relationship with other social insurances. For instance, work-related injury insurance covers the treatment and recovery of work-related injury and prevention of occupational diseases; maternity insurance covers medical costs and services such as delivery operation expense, hospitalization expense and expense for medicine.

Medical insurance benefits and medical insurance are two associative concepts with some differences as well. Pure medical insurance benefits are the expenses directly used to cover medical care costs, while medical insurance includes relieves in terms of recuperation, wages and disease & injury, and medical care services for the insured during their medical treatments.

Since the 1950s, the Labor Insurance System established for urban employees in China has included the content of medical insurance, under which the targeted employees who suffer sickness or non-work-related injury will be given living relieves and sick pays. With regard to medical care service, there were labor medical treatment targeted at employees in enterprises and free medical services targeted at the staff of governmental agencies, public institutions and social organizations established in China. However, with the development of situation and the deepening of reform, the old system has exposed more and more problems: for instance, the drastic increase of medical care expenses, which was too costly to be borne by some entities; the inconvenient for employees to seek medical treatment and the difficulties in the reimbursement of medical care expenses; serious waste of medical treatment costs; the limited coverage of insurance, etc. Under such circumstances, the imperative reform on medical insurance system was urgently needed by most enterprises and the masses.

In the wake of the establishment of socialist market economy system and the further deepening of state-owned enterprises reform, the reform on China's medical insurance system is also in progress. Since 1994, the State Council has formulated the implementation scheme for the medical insurance system reform after obtaining success in pilot projects, and issued the Decision of the State Council on Establishing the Basic Medical Insurance System for Urban Employees in late 1998. The medical insurance reform aims to establish a medical insurance system tailored to meet the particular medical demands from persons of different levels or different crowds, which takes basic medical insurance as primary part, takes large amount of mutual medical expense, medical subsidies for public servants and supplementary medical insurance for enterprises and public institutions as secondary parts, and takes commercial insurance as supplemental part. It requires all employers and employees to participate in medical insurance on a compulsory basis. The core of medical insurance system reform lies in the principle that basic medical insurance premiums are jointly contributed by the employer and employee and under social pooling. The basic medical insurance funds are composed of two parts: social pooled funds and individual saving account.

The basic medical insurance system will secure the corresponding medical insurance benefits entitled by the participants of insurance according to the principle that obligations are equal to rights. Entities and persons who participate in the medical insurance should pay the medical insurance contributions in full and on time, which is the due obligation of every insurance participant. At the same time, whoever pays the medical insurance contributions in full and on time is entitled to enjoy the medical insurance benefits according to the provisions.

## II. Significance of Medical Insurance

Illness does not only directly harm people's physical health, but also affects people's ordinary life and work and leads to social restlessness. The implementation of medical insurance is of great significance for people to get rid of disease, restore health, prompt production and development, and secure social stability.

(1) Implementing medical insurance is helpful for regulating the income gap and achieving social equality. Medical insurance system is an important method for government to redistribute incomes among citizens. Medical insurance adjusts the income gap and demonstrates social equality by the collection of medical insurance premiums and the reimbursement of costs and expenses for medical treatments and services. The implementation of medical insurance is helpful for regulating social relationships and maintaining social safety.

(2) Medical insurance provides life support and medical treatment for ill employees, which not only contributes to the elimination of the social unstable factors caused by illness, but also serves as an important social mechanism of regulating social relations and social conflicts.

(3) Implementing medical insurance is helpful for the promotion of social civilization and progress. Medical insurance is an insurance mechanism featured with social mutuality through which the medical insurance fund is established for sharing the risks of incurring medical expenses among the participants of insurance. It not only demonstrates a new social relation that can be illustrated in a Chinese proverb "when one place is in difficulty, help comes from all sides", but also helps to promote social civilization and progress.

## Section 2　Contents of Chinese Medical Insurance

### Ⅰ. Coverage and Targets of Chinese Medical Insurance

Like other insurance items, the coverage and targets of Chinese medical insurance were first provided by the Labor Insurance Regulations of the People's Republic of China promulgated by the Government Administration Council in 1951.

On April 15, 1966, the Ministry of Labor and the All China Federation of Trade Unions issued the Circular on Several Issues concerning the Improvement of Labor Medical Insurance System for Employees of Enterprises, which stipulated new provisions on labor medical insurance.

Before 1953, the funds of labor medical insurance were all borne by enterprises. But after the change in 1953, the funds of labor medical insurance were contributed by enterprises at the rate of 5% to 7% of total payroll according to the nature of the business.

From 1980s, the reform of Chinese medical system began. The seminar group for national medical insurance system reform drafted the Ideas on the Reform of Medical Insurance System for Employees (Draft), pointing out that the direction of the reform of Chinese employees' medical system is: to gradually establish a multi-mode and multi-layer medical insurance system for employees that is suitable for Chinese national situations with a high degree of socialization and the insurance premiums reasonably contributed by the state, entities and individuals. The basic contents of the medical system reform are: the establishment of employees' medical insurance funds with its source pooled from the state, the employer and individual according to certain proportion of total payroll in principle; changing the subsidy method from underground subsidiary to open subsidiary. In 1988, the State Council made a decision concerning the reform of the basic medical insurance system for urban employees, including all urban employees into the coverage of medical insurance. The Social Insurance Law stipulates the fundamental medical insurance system of China and makes provisions as that, "all employees shall participate in the employee basic medical insurance with the insurance premiums jointly contributed by the employer and employee according to the relevant provisions of the state regulations. Individual businesses without employees, non-full time employees who have not taken part in the employee basic medical insurance at enterprise and other flexible employees may take part in the employee basic medical insurance, but the contribution to insurance premium is paid by individuals according to the relevant provisions of the state. The state shall establish and perfect the New Rural Cooperative Medical Scheme. The measures for administrating New Rural Cooperative Medical Scheme are stipulated by the State Council. "

As there are more and more international exchange and cooperation, China has also signed some agreements on mutual exemption of social insurance with interested countries. After the signing of mutual exemption agreement, the country in which a Chinese citizen works and participates in the social insurance will pay related social insurance benefits when any accident happens to such Chinese citizen.

## Ⅱ. Contributions to Chinese Medical Insurance Premiums

China's Urban Resident Basic Medical Insurance is sourced from two parts: individual contributions and government subsidies. The Guiding Opinions of the State Council on Carrying out Pilot Projects for Urban Resident Basic Medical Insurance provided that, the Urban Resident Basic Medical Insurance is mainly sourced from household contributions, and supplemented by appropriate subsidies from government. In 2007, the government granted an annual subsidy of no less than RMB 40 Yuan per person to insured residents in pilot cities. For the central and western areas, the central government granted a subsidy of RMB 20 per person; for the eastern area, appropriate subsidies were granted by reference to the subsidy measures of New Rural Cooperative Medical Insurance Scheme. In addition, the government granted extra subsidies for the household contributions of the poor residents receiving the minimum subsistence security. The specific measures of financial subsidy were drafted and determined after discussion by the Ministry of Finance, the Ministry of Labor Security and the Ministry of Civil Affairs. The subsidiary spending was included into the financial budget of governments at all levels.

In 2008, the Ministry of Human Resources, the Ministry of Social Security and the Ministry of Finance issued the Circular on Carrying out Pilot Projects for Urban Resident Basic Medical Insurance in Year 2008, which increased the subsidies for insured residents in pilot cities to RMB 80 Yuan per person with a subsidy of RMB 40 per person from central government for the central and western areas and a simultaneously increased subsidiary standard based on New Rural Cooperative Medical Scheme for eastern areas. In 2010, government subsidies at all levels for the Urban Resident Basic Medical Insurance increased to RMB 120 Yuan per person per year, and the standard of individual contributions also increased appropriately with its specific standard of contributions determined by provincial governments.

Moreover, the government provided an extra annual subsidy of RMB 10 Yuan per person for the household contributions of the residents receiving minimum subsistence security or students and children who are severely disabled, with a subsidy of RMB 5 Yuan per person from the central government for the central and western areas; the government provided an extra annual subsidy of no less than RMB 60 Yuan per person for household contributions of the residents receiving the minimum subsistence security, the severely disabled persons who have lost labor capacity and the seniors aged 60 years or more and minors of low-income families, with a subsidy of RMB 30 Yuan per person from the central government for the central and western areas. The specific measures of financial subsidy were drafted and determined after discussion by the Ministry of Finance, the Ministry of Labor Security and the Ministry of Civil Affairs. The subsidiary spending should be included into the financial budget of governments at all levels. The persons who are eligible for the subsidies for household contributions of the Urban Residents Medical Insurance include: the residents receiving the minimum subsistence security, the severely disabled persons who have lost labor capacity and the seniors aged 60 years or more and minors of low-income families.

## Ⅲ. Contents and Standards of Medical Insurance Benefits

The Decision of the State Council on Establishing Basic Medical Insurance System for Urban Employees provides that the basic medical insurance funds are composed of social pooled funds and individual accounts. The social pooled funds and individual accounts set their own scopes of payment with separate accounting. Individual accounts are mainly used to cover outpatient expenses for non-critical illnesses, while the pooled funds are mainly used to cover inpatient expenses for catastrophic diseases. Medical expenses below the deductible are paid from individual accounts or paid out of pocket by individuals. Medical expenses above the deductible and below the reimbursement cap are paid mainly from the pooled funds with a portion paid by individuals. The specific amount of the deductible and the reimbursement cap of social pooled funds and the specific proportion borne by individuals for the medical expenses above the deductible and below the reimbursement cap are determined by specific pooling regions in accordance with the principles of determining payments on the basis of incomes, maintaining the balance of incomes and payments.

(1) The deductible from the basic medical insurance pooled funds. The deductible from the pooled funds stipulated by the State Council is generally fixed as approximately 10% of the average annual wage of local employees.

(2) The reimbursement cap from the basic medical insurance pooled funds. In general, it is determined by the measurement of demographic features of large-sum medical expenses. In 2009, the State Council decided to increase the reimbursement cap to 6 times of the average wage of local employees.

(3) The proportion payable by individual for the medical expenses above the deductible and below the reimbursement cap. According to the regulations of the State Council, the medical expenses above the deductible and below the reimbursement cap are mainly paid from the pooled funds with certain proportion borne by individuals. Such proportion payable by individuals is fixed and determined by specific pooling regions in accordance with the principle of determining payments on the basis of incomes, maintaining the balance of incomes and payments. In practices, the proportion payable by individuals is in relation to the grade of the chosen hospital, i. e. the higher the grade of the chosen hospital is, the higher the proportion is.

The Decision of the State Council on Establishing Basic Medical Insurance System for Urban Employees also makes provisions on the medical insurance benefits of special groups:

The medical benefits for the retirees and Red Army veterans remain the same. Their medical expenses are be covered by the previous finance channels. If not possible, local people's government may provide support. The measures for the retirees and Red Army veterans Health administration are formulated by the people's government at provincial, municipal or autonomous regional level.

The medical benefits for revolutionary soldiers with disability level B or above remain the same. Their medical expenses are be covered by the previous finance channels, recorded and managed separately by social insurance agency. The insufficient part is covered with the financial support from local people's government.

For the retirees who participate in basic medical insurance, no individual contribution to basic medical insurance is required. Appropriate preferential treatments are given to the count-in amount of their individual accounts and their individually payable proportion.

National civil servants are entitled to medical subsidies on the basis of basic medical insurance.

### 2. Benefit Standard of the New Rural Cooperative Medical Scheme

The Circular of the General Office of the State Council on Forwarding the

Opinions on Establishing New Rural Cooperative Medical System provides that the New Rural Cooperative Medical Scheme (NRCMS) is mainly used to subsidize the large-sum medical expenses or inpatient expenses of the farmers enrolled in NRCMS. In the areas with good conditions, the method of combining the large-sum medical expense subsidy and small-sum medical expense subsidy is implemented, which can improve farmers' risk resistance capacity and benefit them at the same time. For those farmers who have been enrolled in the NRCMS but have not used the NRCMS funds within a whole year, a regular physical examination shall be conducted on them. Governments at provincial, autonomous regional and municipal levels shall formulate the lists of reimbursable basic medicine under NRCMS. Each county (city) shall, based on local reality and total pooled funds, in a scientific and reasonable way, determine the payment scope, payment standard and amount of the NRCMS funds, and the specific examination items and methods of the regular physical examination, so as to avoid the deficit spending or excessive surplus of NRCMS funds. Since the second half of 2009, the reimbursement cap (the maximum payment amount) of the NRCMS has exceeded 6 times of the net income of local farmers.

### 3. Benefit Standard of Urban Resident Basic Medical Insurance (UR-BMI)

The State Council does not expressly provide the deductible, payment ratio and the reimbursement cap of UR-BMI funds, but provides the principles of "determining payments on the basis of incomes and maintaining the balance of incomes and payments with appropriate surplus", and authorizes local government to formulate specific standards. From the perspective of practices, benefit standards provided by various local governments vary from each other, as the economic growth, medical consumption level and demographic structure are so different. Generally, the reimbursement cap for the medical expenses incurred by students and children is higher than that of adult residents; the proportion payable by individual is in proportion to the grade of hospital, i. e. the higher the grade of hospital is, the higher the proportion payable by individual is.

In June 2010, the Ministry of Human Resources and Social Security and the Ministry of Finance jointly issued the Circular on Carrying out Urban Resident Basic Medical Insurance in Year 2010, which requires that, the reimbursement cap of UR-BMI funds in 2010 shall be increased to 6 times of residents' disposal incomes; the proportion of payment for inpatient medical expenses from funds shall be gradually increased, with the proportion of reimbursement from the funds for medical expenses of the insured under the inpatient policy reaching 60% and that at the hospitals of second-grade or below reaching 70% in principle; it is defined that in 2010 the social pooling of urban residents' outpatient medical expenses shall be established within 60% of pooled areas.

### 4. Benefit Standard of Basic Medical Insurance for the Retirees

The retirees who want to enjoy basic medical insurance benefits in accordance with national provisions shall satisfy three eligibility conditions: having participated in the employee's basic medical insurance, having reached the legitimate retiring age and having reached the years of accumulative contributions as regulated by the State.

The retirees have made contributions to society in their previous working period and they are currently in an age that diseases are more likely to attack, so they are the vulnerable group in need of social care. In addition, the low incomes after the retirement and insufficient savings for medical expense make the burdens of medical expenses are too heavy to be borne by the retirees, in particular, by these employees who have retired before the establishment of the basic medical insurance. As a result, there are three kinds of preferential treatments for the retirees: first, the retirees are not required to pay individual contributions to the basic medical insurance; secondly, there are individual accounts of the basic medical insurance established for the retirees; thirdly, preferential treatment in respect of the proportion payable by individual for medical expenses is granted to the retirees and the standard of the deductible from the basic medical insurance funds is lower than that of acting employees. Some local governments also include outpatient medical expenses for certain chronic diseases by which the elderly are easily attacked into the payment scope of the pooled funds.

### 5. Exceptions to the Scope of Payment from the Basic Medical Insurance Funds

There are four categories medical expenses that are excluded from the payment scope of the basic medical insurance funds: firstly, the expenses shall be paid from the work-related injury insurance funds; secondly, the expenses shall be borne by the third party; thirdly, the expenses shall be borne by public sanitation; fourthly, the expenses incurred during the treatment aboard.

China's Social Insurance Law issued in 2011 specially provided Chinese Basic Medical Insurance System in the third chapter. As stipulated by such Law, employees shall participate in employee basic medical insurance with the insurance premiums jointly contributed by the employer and employee in accordance with the relevant provisions of the state. Individual businesses without employees, non-full time employees who have not taken part in the employee basic medical insurance at enterprise and other flexible employees may take part in employee basic medical insurance, but the contribution to insurance premiums is paid by individuals according to the relevant provisions of the state. The state shall establish and perfect the New Rural Cooperative Medical Scheme. The measures for administrating New Rural Cooperative Medical Scheme are stipulated by the State Council. The state shall establish and perfect the Urban Resident Basic Medical Insurance Scheme. The combination of individual contributions and governmental subsidies shall apply to Urban Resident Basic Medical Insurance. For the residents receiving the minimum subsistence security, the severely disabled persons who have lost labor capacity and the seniors aged 60 years or more and minors of low-income families, their individual contributions are subsidized by the government. Where an individual participating in the basic medical insurance for employees has paid premiums for a cumulative period reaching the number of years prescribed by the state when he/she reaches the statutory retirement age, he/she need not pay the basic medical insurance premiums any more after retirement, and shall enjoy the basic medical insurance benefits according to the relevant provisions of the state; or if the number of years prescribed by the state is not reached, he/she may pay premiums until the number of years prescribed by the state is reached.

● Chapter XⅢ

# Work-related Injury Insurance

The guarantee targets of the work-related injury insurance are the laborers who have suffered accident injuries and occupational diseases at their work, and the work-related injury insurance is of great significance to employees under modern production conditions.

## Section 1   Concept and Principles of Work-related Injury Insurance

### Ⅰ. Concept of Work-related Injury Insurance

Work-related injury insurance, also known as occupational accident insurance, refers to the social insurance system which affords material assistance and economic compensation to an employee or his/her dependants when any injury (occupational diseases), disability or death of such employee is caused by any accident occurred in the process of production and work or under any particular statutory circumstance or caused by any occupational detrimental factor.

Work-related injury insurance is one of the earliest social insurance projects in the world. Germany formulated its Accident Insurance Act for Workers in 1884, and at present, there are nearly 130 countries or regions that have established the work-related injury insurance system.

China's work-related injury and occupational disease system for employees of enterprises was established in 1950s. Article 12 of the Labor Insurance Regulations of the People's Republic of China promulgated and implemented by the Government Administration Council of the Central People's Government on February 25, 1951 has made provisions on the benefits of work-related injury insurance that: (1) where a worker or employee is injured in relation to work, then all medical treatment fees, medicine fee, food costs during the hospitalization period and travelling expenses for medical treatment so incurred by such worker or employee shall be borne by the administrator of enterprise or the employer. During such medical treatment period, the salary of the injured worker or employee shall be paid as usual; (2) Where a worker or employee becomes disabled due to work-related injury and becomes fully incapacitated and has to resign from office, if thereafter the diet and daily life of such worker or employee requires help or assistance from others, a sum equal to 75% of the salary of such worker or employee shall be paid to such worker or employee as work-related disability pension each month, till his or her death; (3) Where the worker or employee becomes disabled due to work-related injury and becomes fully incapacitated and has to resign from office, if thereafter the diet and daily life of such worker or employee does not require help or assistance from others, a sum equal to 60% of the salary of such worker or employee shall be paid to such worker or employee as work-related disability pension each month, till his or her death or the date when such worker or employee resumes labor capacity; (4) For those who are partially disabled but can still do some types of work, the enterprise shall arrange appropriate work for them, and pay monthly work-related disability subsidy equal to 10%—30% of the salary of them before disability based on the degree of their disability, till their death or resignation from office.

On February 28, 1957, the Regulations on Scope of Occupational Diseases and Handling Measures for Occupational Diseases Patients formulated by the Ministry of Health for the first time in China included the occupational diseases into the guarantee coverage of the work-related injury insurance and officially listed 14 occupational diseases which will do harm to the health of workers and employees or produce relatively severe influence on production or have relatively obvious occupational harmfulness into the scope of occupational diseases, including but not limited to occupational poisoning, pneumoconiosis and occupational dermatosis. Such Regulations also provided that, where a worker or employee who suffers occupational disease is determined as being disabled after termination of treatment or recreation or medical care, or is dead due to ineffective medical treatment, work-related benefits shall be granted to such worker or employee in accordance with the relevant provisions of the Labor Insurance Regulations of the People's Republic of China.

The Interim Measures of the State Council on Retirement Handling of Workers and Employees promulgated on February 9, 1958 and the Interim Measures of the State Council on Retirement and Resignation from Office of Workers promulgated on June 2, 1978 successively adjusted and enhanced the work-related injury insurance benefits for workers. Pursuant to the Regulations on Scope of Occupational Diseases and Handling Measures for Occupational Diseases Patients revised and re-promulgated by the Ministry of Health, the Ministry of Labor and Personnel, the Ministry of Finance and the All China Federation of Trade Unions on November 5, 1987, there are 9 categories of occupational diseases, including 99 types of occupational diseases in total.

The Labor Law of the People's Republic of China promulgated in 1994 stipulates that, laborers are entitled to enjoy social insurance and welfare benefits; laborers may legally enjoy social insurance benefits when they suffer work-related injury or disability or get occupational diseases. The Trial Measures on Work-related Injury Insurance for Employees of Enterprises promulgated by the original Ministry of Labor on August 12, 1996 took work-related injury insurance as an independent social insurance system for implementation. Article 6 of the Occupational Diseases Prevention Law of the People's Republic of China adopted at the 24th meeting of the Standing Committee of the 9th National People's Congress on October 27, 2001 and came into force on May 1, 2002 stipulates that, the employer must legally participate in the work-related injury social insurance. The Circular of the Ministry of Health and the Ministry of Labor and Social Security on printing and distributing the Category of Occupational Diseases on April 18, 2002 stipulates that there are 9 categories and 115 types of occupational diseases.

On April 27, 2003, the State Council promulgated the Regulations on Work-related Injury Insurance, according to which, work-related injury insurance is an important social insurance system that enables laborers and their dependents to realize their rights on work-related injury insurance through the establishment of work-related injury insurance funds which are sourced from social overall pooling and administered by the social insurance agencies. The Regulations on Work-related Injury Insurance plays an important role in facilitating the participation in work-related injury insurance by the employers, maintaining the legitimate rights and interests of the employees and diffusing the risks faced by employers, and also shows its shortages such as narrow coverage, low guarantee level and single guarantee functions. In order to overcome such shortages, the said Regulations had been revised in 2006 and sought for opinions on that from general public in July, 2009. On December 20, 2010, the State Council promulgated the Decision on Amending the Regulations on Work-related Injury Insurance, which has come into force on January 1, 2011.

## II. Significance of Work-related Injury Insurance

In the field of labor, the dangers caused by external direct damages, i. e. industrial accident and occupational detrimental factors are in objective existence and often result in work-related injury and occupational diseases, while, for those individual employees, the impacts and economic losses so caused by work-related injury and occupational diseases are normally unbearable. So, it is of great significance to establish work-related injury insurance system, set up work-related injury insurance fund, carry out social overall pooling of work-related injury insurance funds and provide material help, economic compensation and social management services to employees suffered work-related injury.

(1) Ensuring the right of employees suffered from industrial accidents or occupational diseases to obtain the medical treatment and cure, economic compensation and occupational rehabilitation; ensuring the rights of employees suffered from work-related injury and their dependents to obtain material help, respecting and affirming the value of the work of laborers and their spirit to make contributions to work, and eliminating the economic worries of the laborers and their families, which will be conducive to the social stability.

(2) Diffusing the work-related injury risks assumed by the employers. In the process of production and work, it is an objective possibility for industrial accident to cause risks to the employers. The occurrence of industrial accident will not only cause harm to the health or even life of the employee, but also cause relatively large economic losses to the employer. The implementation of work-related injury insurance and the provision of material help and economic compensation to employees through the socially-pooled work-related injury insurance funds are conducive for diffusing work-related injury risks assumed by the employers and guaranteeing the normal operation of their production after the occurrence of industrial accident.

(3) Facilitating the prevention of work-related injury. The course to carry out work-related injury insurance is the course to thoroughly implement the policy of "safety first and prevention primary". It will be conducive to facilitating the prevention of work-related injury and reducing the damage caused by work-related injury dangers by adopting the measures of carrying out differentiated charging rate and floating charging rate in payment of insurance contributions, and urging employers to strengthen the labor safety and health work, protect the health and safety of employees and proactively improve labor conditions.

## Ⅲ. Features and Principles of Work-related Injury Insurance

( Ⅰ ) Features of Work-related Insurance

(1) The applicant of work-related injury insurance is the employer and the insured is the employee who has established labor relationship with such an employer. In this regard, the general principle of labor relationship, i. e. the targets guaranteed by the work-related injury insurance are laborers that have established labor relationship with the employer, applies equally here. The one who suffers occupational injury must be a laborer who qualifies with the statutory conditions as required for laborer by the Labor Law. Meanwhile, in the particular work-related injury insurance relationship, it is a precondition that the laborer who enjoys the work-related injury insurance benefits shall be the one who suffers occupational injury.

(2) The "risk" insured by the work-related injury insurance shall be a kind of occupational danger, which refers to a kind of danger to the health and life of the employee caused by any work-related accident or occupational detrimental factor in the production and work. This kind of danger is in objective existence and caused by external direct harm, and its occurrence is of uncertainty.

(3) The method of work-related injury insurance is to offer material help and economic compensation to those employees who suffer work-related injury damages and their dependents.

(4) Work-related injury insurance is a type of compulsory insurance and a type of social insurance that must be implemented to the employees by the laws. Article 4 of the Trial Measures on Work-related Injury Insurance for Employees of Enterprises (hereinafter referred to as the "Trial Measures") promulgated by the Ministry of Labor in 1996 stipulates that "enterprises must, pursuant to the regulations of the State and local people's governments, participate in work-related injury insurance, pay contributions of work-related injury insurance in time and in full amount, and safeguard the work-related injury insurance benefits of the employees in accordance with the measures set forth herein and as provided by local people's government. "

(5) Work-related injury insurance carries out the principle of liability without fault, which means no matter whether the occurrence of the work-related accident is attributable to the employer or the employee, the employer shall bear the insurance liability.

There is an essential distinction between work-related injury insurance and commercial personal insurance, despite that they are both insurance systems established for the life and health of the insured.

Firstly, the applicants are different. The applicant of the personal insurance refers to the citizen, legal person or other organization that has concluded insurance contract with the insurer and performed the premiums payment obligation in accordance with the insurance contract; the applicant of the work-related injury insurance is the employer who has established labor relationship with the insured.

Secondly, the insured are different. The insured of the personal insurance is the person who is guaranteed by the insurance contract and enjoys the right to claim for insurance proceeds, and such person can be any citizen; and the insured of the work-related injury insurance is only limited to the employee who has established labor relationship with the applicant.

Thirdly, the insurers are different. The insurer of the personal insurance refers to the insurance company that has concluded insurance contract with the applicant and assumed the liability for indemnity or payment of insurance proceeds; the insurer of the work-related injury insurance refers to the labor administration department and the social insurance institution. An insurance company is an enterprise for profit, while labor administration department or social insurance institution is a specific administration department under the government, and a non-profit organization.

Fourthly, their insurance purposes are different. Personal insurance is a voluntary insurance, and the insurance relationship is established based on the voluntary conclusion of the insurance contract by and between the parties; while the work-related injury insurance is a compulsory insurance, and the insurance relationship must be established as provided by law.

Fifthly, the applicable laws are different. Personal insurance is a type of civil legal relationship, to which the civil laws and regulations are applicable; the work-related injury insurance is a type of labor legal relationship, to which the labor laws and regulations are applicable.

( II ) Principles of Work-related Injury Insurance

(1) Differential treatments and benefits will be given to work-related injury and disability and non-work-related injury and disability. Relatively high benefits should be given to the laborer who suffers work-related injury or disability as such laborer pays a price in the work. Such benefits will not only be care in life, but also a mental award and comfort to such laborer. The social insurance benefits of such laborer are of a nature of "compensation for loss", and of the meaning of "material award". As to non-work-related injury or disability, though the person also pays a price, however, it is not a price paid for the social labor, thus the insurance benefits shall be properly reduced. Same as the social insurance benefits

for illness, the social insurance benefits for non-work-related injury or disability shall fall into the scope of "material help".

(2) The direct and indirect economic losses caused by work-related injury or disability will both be compensated, however, there is a difference between them. The so-called direct economic loss refers to the economic loss incurred to and suffered by the laborer individually after the occurrence of injury or disability accident. The direct economic loss of the laborer is the salary income which is related to the direct economic income of such laborer and constitutes the main part of all of his or her gross income. Direct economic loss affects the lives of such laborer and his or her dependents as well as the reproduction of labor force, so full compensation must be made for all direct economic losses suffered by the laborer. Indirect economic loss refers to the loss of economic income other than the direct economic income of the employee, including part-time income, other armature labor income etc. This part of income is not applicable to everyone, and is a type of unfixed and irregular extra income. Social insurance mainly aims to guarantee the basic life of the laborer, thus this part of economic loss cannot be treated equally with the direct economic loss.

(3) The principle of combining with compensation, prediction and rehabilitation. Work-related injury insurance system also includes the prevention of accident and the assistance for the rehabilitation of the injured. The legislations all over the world require the employer to bear liability for the rehabilitation of the laborers. The employer shall make efforts to reduce the occurrence of accidents, improve labor conditions, strengthen the safety training on laborers, timely find out and then eliminate any accident potential. Once there is any accident in need of timely treatment, the employer shall take measures to facilitate the early recovery of employees, such as vacation and medical treatment. The employer shall also help injured and disabled laborers to resume their labor capacity and provide life and labor conditions for injured and disabled laborers. Occupational rehabilitation aims to help injured and disabled laborers to resume their labor capacities as soon as possible and enhance their capacities for independent living. For this reason, the employer shall proactively run occupational recovery undertakings. Regions with required conditions shall collect funds by means of reservation of work-related injury insurance funds and public sponsorship, to gradually run work-related injury and occupational recovery undertakings, or to train disabled persons by taking advantage of current conditions. For those laborers who suffer work-related injury or disability, but have certain labor capacity and need to resume or enhance their labor capacity through professional training, the labor administration

department and the employer are responsible for proactively organizing professional training with all costs so caused paid from the occupational recovery expense of the work-related injury insurance funds.

## Section 2    Scope of Work-related Injury Insurance

From the very beginning, work-related injury insurance was only carried out in high-risks industries, high-risk professions and relatively large enterprises and was targeted at those workers who engage in dangerous work and only depend on their salary income, in other words, mainly the manual workers. Later, the work-related injury insurance gradually expanded to other laborers. To date, some countries still exclude agricultural workers, baby sitters, family workers and independent laborers from the coverage of work-related injury insurance. However, from the overall development trend, the countries all over the world are gradually expanding the scope of work-related injury insurance.

The Labor Law of China adopts territory principle in terms of the applicable persons. Article 2 of the Labor Law stipulates that "This Law shall be applicable to all enterprises and individual economic organizations (hereinafter referred to as 'Employers') within the territory of the People's Republic of China and laborers who have established a labor relationship therewith. " The Regulations on Work-related Injury Insurance (2003) stipulate that "All types of enterprises and individual businesses which have employees (hereinafter referred to as the 'Employers') within the territory of the People's Republic of China shall participate in the work-related injury insurance in accordance with the Regulations. " According to the provisions of the aforesaid laws and regulations, the scope of applicable persons of work-related injury insurance in China is as follows:

(1) All types of enterprises within the territory of the People's Republic of China, including state-owned enterprises, collective enterprises, private enterprises, Sino-foreign joint ventures, Sino-foreign cooperative enterprises, wholly foreign owned enterprises and other types of enterprises, as well as the individual businesses which have employees.

(2) Employees having established labor relationship (including labor relationship de facto) with the aforesaid enterprises and economic organizations.

(3) State organs, public institutions, social organizations and their employees who have established labor relationship with them.

(4) Dependents of employees. Pursuant to the Regulations on Work-related

Injury Insurance and the Regulations on Scope of Dependents of Employees of Work-related Death promulgated by the Ministry of Labor and Social Security of the People' s Republic of China on September 18, 2003, dependents include:

1) Dependents supported by the employee who is died of work-related accident refer to the employee's spouses, children, parents, paternal grandparents, maternal grandparents, paternal grandchildren, maternal grandchildren or brothers and sisters. The so-called children include legitimate children and illegitimate children, adopted children and step children who supported or were supported by such decedent. Of which, legitimate children and illegitimate children include posthumous children; the so-called parents include natural parents, foster parents and step parents who supported or were supported by the decedent; the so-called brothers and sisters include blood brothers and sisters, brothers and sisters of half blood, adopted brothers and sisters as well as step brothers and sisters who supported or were supported by the decedent.

2) The aforesaid persons who mainly depend on the support of the decedent and have any of the following circumstance, may apply for dependent pension in accordance with law: being completely incapacitated; in case of the spouse of the dead employee, the husband is over 60 or the wife is over 55; in case of parents of the dead employee, the father is over 60 or the mother is over 55; where the children of the dead employee are dead or completely incapacitated, the grandchildren of the dead employee are under the age of 18; where the parents of the dead employee are dead or completely incapacitated, the brothers and sisters of the dead employee are under the age of 18.

The dependents' eligibilities for survivor's benefits due to the work-related death of the employee shall be verified and determined by the social insurance agency at the pooling region. The labor capacity appraisal committee at the place where the dead employee located before his death shall be responsible for the labor capacity appraisal of the dependents of such dead employee.

In addition, with regard to any foreigner who suffers industrial accident within the territory of PRC, Article 1 of the Equality of Treatment (Accident Compensation) Convention (1925) ratified by the Chinese government made provisions that, "Each Member of the International Labor Organisation which ratifies this Convention undertakes to grant to the nationals of any other Member which shall have ratified the Convention, who suffer personal injury due to industrial accidents happening in its territory, or to their dependants, the same treatment in respect of workmen's compensation as it grants to its own nationals." China will grant to nationals of other membership states which have ratified such

Convention, who suffer industrial accidents within the territory of PRC, the same treatment as it grants to its own nationals.

The prevailing Regulations on Work-related Injury Insurance have expanded the scope of application of work-related injury insurance by stipulating that, in addition to the enterprises and individual businesses which have employees as currently stipulated by the Regulations, public institutions, social groups and private non-enterprise entity, foundations, law firms, accounting firms and other organizations shall participate in the work-related injury insurance in accordance with the Regulations.

With regard to employees dispatched to work outside China, the Regulations on Work-related Injury Insurance stipulate that, where a Chinese employee is dispatched to work outside China and is required to participate in local work-related injury insurance in accordance with the destination countries or region, such employee shall participate in local work-related injury insurance and his/her work-related injury insurance relationship in China shall then be suspended; where the employee cannot participate in the local work-related injury insurance, his/her work-related injury insurance relationship in China shall not be suspended.

## Section 3  Identification of Work-related Injury and Prevention of Occupational Diseases

There are certain conditions and procedures in respect of identification of work-related injury, determination of occupational diseases and appraisal of labor capacity must be met.

### ( I ) Conditions for Identification of Work-related Injury

Industrial accidents must be related to the work, work hours and workplace. In the Workmen's Compensation (Agriculture) Convention (1921) adopted by the International Labor Conference, the industrial accident mentioned herein refers to "the accident directly or indirectly caused by work". Article 32 of the Social Security (Minimum Standards) Convention (1952) stipulates that "The contingencies covered shall include the following where due to accident or a prescribed disease resulting from employment: (a) a morbid condition; (b) incapacity for work resulting from such a condition and involving suspension of earnings, as defined by national laws or regulations; (c) total loss of earning capacity or partial loss thereof in excess of a prescribed degree, likely to be permanent, or corresponding loss of faculty; and (d) the loss of support suffered by the widow or child as the result of the death of the breadwinner; in the case of a widow, the right to benefit may be made conditional on her being presumed, in accordance with national laws or regulations, to be incapable of self-support. "

The scope of industrial accident has expanded from the industrial contingency at the very beginning to the contingency on the way to and from work. The 1964 Employment Injury Benefits Recommendation required to include the following accidents as industrial accidents: (1) accidents, regardless of their cause, sustained during working hours at or near the place of work or at any place where the worker would not have been except for his employment; (2) accidents sustained within reasonable periods before and after working hours in connection with transporting, cleaning, preparing, securing, conserving, storing and packing work tools or clothes; (3) accidents sustained while on the direct way between the place of work which include: 1) the employee's principal or secondary residence; or 2) the place where the employee usually takes his meals; or 3) the place where he usually receives his remuneration.

In China, pursuant to the scope of work-related injury and deemed work-related injury as provided in the Regulations on Work-related Injury Insurance, a staff member or worker shall be identified injured at work in any one of the following circumstances:

(1) Injured in an industrial accident at the workplace during the working time.

(2) Injured in an accident when making work-related preparations or conducting work-related winding-up work at the workplace around the working time.

(3) Injured by violence or other unexpected hazards in performing work-related responsibilities at the workplace during the working time.

(4) Afflicted with an occupational disease.

(5) Durante adsent for work, injured due to work or the whereabouts thereof is unknown due to an accident.

(6) Injured in a traffic accident in which the injured person himself does not assume main responsibility or in an urban rail transit, passenger ferry or train accident on the way to work from home or back home from work.

(7) Other circumstances that shall be identified injured at work as provided by laws and administrative regulations.

The revised prevailing Regulations on Work-related Injury Insurance adjusted and expanded the scope of identified work-related injury. It provides that any employee who has sustained injury due to traffic accident caused not primarily due to his own responsibility or mass transit, passenger ferry or train accidents shall be identified as having suffered from work-related injury.

Besides, a staff member or worker is deemed injured at work in any one of the following circumstances:

(1) Died on the spot or within 48 hours after unsuccessful emergency medical treatment of an acute disease breaking out during the working time and at the work post.

(2) Injured in protecting the interest of the State and the public, such as in dealing with an emergency or providing disaster relief.

(3) The staff member or worker is wounded or becomes disabled in war or on duty during the term of military service and is therefore given a certificate for injured or disabled serviceman, but the previous injury recrudesces after working for the employing entity.

A staff member or worker who comes under the circumstances prescribed in Item (1) or (2) of the preceding paragraph is entitled to work-related injury insurance benefits in accordance with the relevant provisions of these Regulations. A staff member or worker who comes under the circumstance prescribed in Item (3) of the preceding paragraph is entitled to work-related injury insurance benefits in accordance with the relevant provisions of these Regulations except the lump sum injury or disability allowance.

Article 37 of the Social Insurance Law stipulates that "a worker who passes away or gets injured at work due to any of the following situations is not identified as suffering from work-related injury: (1) committing a criminal offense intentionally; (2) getting drunk or taking drugs; (3) inflicting harm on himself or committing suicide; and (4) Other situations prescribed by the provisions of the laws and administrative regulations. "

In 1952, the International Labor Conference agreed to add three diseases into the scope of occupational diseases, namely, lead poisoning, mercury poisoning and anthrax infection. The Employment Injury Compensation Convention (1964) included 15 diseases into the scope of occupational diseases. The International Labor Conference published the new international category of occupational diseases in 1980, which includes 29 groups of occupational diseases.

In China, occupational diseases refer to the diseases caused by getting access to occupational detrimental factors by the laborers in the production, labor and other occupational activities. According to the Category of Occupational Diseases printed by the Ministry of Health and the Ministry of Labor and Social Security on April 18, 2002, the scope of occupational diseases stipulated in China includes 13 types of pneumoconiosis, 11 types of occupational radioactive diseases, 56 types of occupational poisoning, occupational diseases caused by physical factors, occupational diseases caused by biological factors, occupational dermatosis, occupational oculopathy, occupational otolaryngological and stomatological diseases, occupational cancers and other occupational diseases, i. e. 10 categories and 115 types of occupational diseases in total.

Pursuant to the provisions of the Appraisal of Degree of Disability of Employees Caused by Work-related Injury and Occupational Diseases, the occupational diseases must be determined by the diagnosis certificate issued by the medical and health institution which has the authority to diagnose occupational diseases as approved by the health administrative departments.

### (Ⅱ) Procedures for Identification of Work-related Injury

Identification of work-related injury is a confirmation made by the institution as stipulated by law on whether any given injury falls into the scope of work-related injury, which is also the basis for the determination of work-related injury insurance benefits.

The identification of work-related injury must be subject to statutory procedures. In China, pursuant to the provisions of Regulations on Work-related Injury Insurance, the identification of work-related injury must follow the following procedures:

**1. Report and Application**

(1) The employer who employs the employee shall, within 30 days upon the date of occurrence of accident or the date of being diagnosed or identified as occupational disease in accordance with the Law on Prevention of Occupational Diseases, file an application for identification of work-related injury with the labor and social security administrative department where the employer locates. In case of any special circumstance, the period for such application may be appropriately extended upon the consent of the labor and social security administrative department.

(2) Where the employer fails to file application for identification of work-related injury as required, the injured employee or his or her immediate family or the trade union may, within one year upon the date of occurrence of the industrial accident or the date of being diagnosed and identified as occupational disease, directly file application for identification of work-related injury with the labor and social security administrative department where the employer locates.

The following documents shall be submitted when filing application for identification of work-related injury: Application Form for Identification of Work-related Injury (which shall specify the time, place, reasons and injury degree of the accident), Certificate on Labor Relationship between Employee and Employer (including labor relationship de facto), medical certificate and certificate on diagnosis of occupational diseases.

### 2. Acceptance and Identification

After accepting the application for identification of work-related injury, the labor and social security administrative department shall investigate and verify the injury caused by the accident in accordance with the review needs; and shall carry out the appraisal on the diagnosis of occupational diseases and diagnosis dispute in accordance with relevant provisions of the Law on Prevention of Occupational Diseases.

The labor and social security administrative department shall, within 60 days upon the date of acceptance of application for identification of work-related injury, make a decision on identification of work-related injury, and notify the employee or his or her immediate family who applies for identification of work-related injury and the employer of such employee of such decision in writing.

### ( Ⅲ ) Appraisal of Labor Capacity

Appraisal of labor capacity, also known as appraisal of loss of labor capacity, refers to the rank appraisal made by the appraisal body on the labor function impairment and daily living impairment of the laborers who have suffered industrial accident or occupational diseases in accordance with the statutory appraisal standards.

Labor capacity appraisal is an important link in the work-related injury insurance management and a major basis for the determination of the work-related injury insurance benefits that shall be enjoyed by employees and the arrangement of employees suffering work-related injury.

The standards for labor capacity appraisal are usually and expressly provided by laws, for example, the social security act of the UK lists 55 types of disability on the basis of the degree of disability by percentage, and Japan divides the degree of loss of labor capacity caused by work-related injury into 14 levels. The appraisal standards for disability obligations in the US include classification of disability caused by diseases, injuries and cancers in 11 fields, including muscle, ossature, special organs, respiration, cardiovascular, digest, uropoiesis and reproduction, blood and lymph, skin, internal secretion and nerve. In 1976, the World Health Organization adopted the international classification method put forward by the expert group on the consequences of diseases, and categorized the degree and scope of injuries, impairment and disability into 1476 types.

In China, pursuant to the provisions of the Regulations on Work-related Injury Insurance, the appraisal standards on labor capacity shall be jointly formulated by the labor and social security administrative department and the health administrative department under the State Council. The labor capacity appraisal will generally be under the organization and implementation by special institution, and the specific appraisal work shall generally be entrusted to medical institutions with required conditions or the expert groups consisted of the doctors who have appraisal qualifications.

The newly revised Regulations on Work-related Injury Insurance have simplified the procedures for identification of work-related injury, and stipulated that for the application for identification of work-related injury with clear facts and defined rights and obligations, the decision on identification of work-related injury shall be made within 15 days. The Regulation has simultaneously cancelled the administrative pre-review procedure that is originally applicable to disputes concerning identification of work-related injury and shortened the procedures and time for handling of disputes, which are conducive to protecting the legitimate rights and interests of the employees suffering work-related injury. The new provision that the payment for the medical expenses for cure of work-related injury of the employees shall not be ceased during the period of administrative review and administrative litigation enables the employee who have suffered work-related injury to obtain timely medical treatment and prevents some employers from malicious lawsuit institutionally.

## (Ⅳ) New Provisions of the Law on Prevention of Occupational Diseases

The Decision of the Standing Committee of the National People's Congress on Amending the Law of the People's Republic of China on Prevention of Occupational Diseases has been adopted at 24th session of the standing committee of the eleventh National People's Congress on December 31, 2011 and promulgated and come into force on the same day.

The amendment to the Law on Prevention of Occupational Diseases this time has fundamental change in term of legislation concept, which transfers from the previous concept of "focus on cure" for occupational diseases to "focus on prevention" of occupational diseases. This directly leads to enhancement in legislation technology and reform on legal content, for example, provisions on prevention executors of relevant occupational diseases and liabilities of the employer have been changed, and such change enables the Law to provide more feasible protection for laborers.

1. Administrators for prevention are changed. The Law on Prevention of Occupational Diseases issued in 2001 listed health administration as the only administrator for the prevention of occupational diseases. However, there was too much work to be completed only by the health administration. The revised Law on Prevention of Occupational Diseases not only includes the security supervision department and labor security department into the scope of administrators, but also puts the work of security supervision department as the priority of the whole prevention of occupational diseases, of which, the early prevention of occupational diseases is the work focus of the security supervision department.

2. The liabilities of the employer are strengthened. The new Law stipulates that the principals of the employers shall be fully responsible for the prevention of occupational diseases in their workplace. If a laborer is diagnosed as having suffered occupational diseases and the employer fails to legally participate in the work-related injury insurance, the medical and living security of such laborer shall be borne by the employer. This has directly strengthened the liabilities of the employer, especially that of the principal of the employer. Regardless of the place in which the laborer gets the occupational disease, to the extent that the employer does not make work-related injury insurance contributions for such laborer when he is sick, such employer will have to bear the costs for medical treatment and living security of such laborer.

3. Burden of proof is inverted The new Law stipulates that a diagnosis of occupational disease shall be concluded when there is no evidence can deny the necessary connection between the hazard factors of occupational diseases and the clinical manifestation of the patient. The employer shall truthfully provide the employee's occupational history record and details of exposure to occupational hazards, results of inspection on hazard factors of occupational diseases in the workplace and other materials as required for the diagnosis and appraisal of the occupational diseases; the administrative department of work safety shall carry out supervision and inspection and oversee the provision of the aforesaid materials by the employer; the employee and relevant authorities shall also provide materials in relation to the diagnosis and appraisal of occupational diseases. The parties concerned are liable to provide evidences to support their claims made in the course of arbitration. Where the laborer is unable to provide the evidences which are controlled or administrated by the employer and in connection with arbitration, the arbitral tribunal shall require the employer to provide such evidences within the prescribed time limit; if the employer fails to do so, the employer shall bear the adverse consequence.

In the identification of occupational diseases, the determination of labor relationship is always the most difficult part. Fortunately, the new Law has established the principle of inverted burden of proof in the identification of occupational diseases for the first time, which is a big shift in the legislation concept. If the employer takes control of some evidences, e. g. attendance sheet, but intentionally conceals them, the competent authority may demand the employer to provide the same. In this case, if the employer still refuses to do so, it will then undertake the legal consequence of losing a lawsuit.

4. The occupational hazards are expressly stated. The new Law stipulates that the employer, whose production will result in occupational hazards to its employees, shall set up bulletin board at a conspicuous place and announce the rules and operational procedures on the prevention of occupational diseases, emergency rescue measures in occupational disease accidents and the results of inspection on hazard factors of occupational diseases in the workplace. Many occupational diseases are caused by the insufficient statement on occupational hazards. And this time, the express statement on the work of occupational hazards has been clearly stipulated in the new Law, which will be very helpful for the prevention of occupational diseases.

## Section 4   Liability Principles of Work-related Injury Insurance

### Ⅰ. Concept and Origin of Liability Principle of Work-related Injury Insurance

The liability principles of work-related injury insurance refer to the basic principles on ascertaining who is liable for the work-related injury insurance liabilities for employees after the occurrence of any work-related injury accident.

Given that it is generally accepted that the occupational danger exists objectively in production and work, the Industrial Accidents Insurance Act, a work-related injury insurance act promulgated in Germany on July 16, 1884, for the first time expressly specified that, when a worker is injured, disabled or dead due to industrial injury, regardless of the attribution of negligence or liability, the employer shall be obliged to compensate the income loss of the worker and the injured worker shall be entitled to economic compensation. Thereafter, this principle is also called as the principle of "occupational danger" or "no-fault compensation". By the beginning of the 20th century, nearly all industrialized countries have written this principle into their labor laws and regulations, and the principle of "occupational danger" or "no-fault compensation" has become a commonly applicable standard for ascertaining liability for work-related injury insurance in all countries in the world.

In the labor relationship, it is the employer's obligation to protect the safety and health of laborers during the course of labor, which is also the employer's liability to the country. If a laborer suffers any occupational injury, which means the employer violates its labor protection obligations, so the employer shall be liable for providing compensation for the injured laborers. This kind of liability is generated from the compulsory provisions of law instead of contractual agreement, so neither can it be excluded or reduced by contract, nor can it be changed on the ground of negligence of the laborer. Besides, owing to that modern industrial production is in a workplace of high hazardous environment, the occupational hazard factor is a source of great danger under the conditions of machines production and modernization production. In case of any damage accident occurs, such source of great danger shall bear the compensation liability, without regard to the negligence or fault of the indemnifying party.

Pursuant to the principle of "no-fault compensation" or "strict liability", the legislations on work-related injury insurance require that the employer shall give economic compensation to the laborers in case of any work-related injury accident, regardless of whether the employer or the laborer should be blamed for that. This is because an injury resulted in the work-related accident will not only cause extremely great pain and torture to the laborer, but also will affect or cut off the normal income of the laborer. Thus, for the sake of providing timely material assistance for those injured laborers, it is necessary to carry out the principle of "no-fault compensation", which is also the first principle of the work-related injury insurance law.

## II. Liability Principles of Work-related Injury Insurance in China

China's work-related injury insurance carries out the principle of liability without fault, that is, where any employee is injured, disabled or dead due to any accident during the course of production work or under statutory special circumstances, the employer shall bear the compensation liability and the employee shall legally enjoy work-related injury insurance benefits, regardless of the attribution of liability. The content of the principle of liability without fault for work-related injury insurance as implemented in China includes the following contents:

(1) The work-related injury insurance premium is fully contributed by the employer, in other words, the employee is not required to contribute any of it. In the work-related injury insurance, the insurance premium is contributed by the employer, and the employee is not required to make any contribution for that. This is an obvious distinction between work-related injury insurance and other social insurances such as endowment insurance, unemployment insurance. Given that work-related injury does harm to the laborer, causing the laborer to lose all or part of the labor capacity and such loss is resulted in the work for the employer, so thus the laborer should not be required to make any contribution to the work-related injury insurance premium. For the sake of safeguarding the basic living of the laborer who has suffered work-related injury and of his/her family, the laws require the employer to make full contributions to insurance premiums for the laborer so as to bear all compensation liability for the laborer. After making contributions to the insurance premium as required, the employer immediately transfer its liability to the work-related injury insurance for the employee to social insurance agency, and the relevant work-related injury risks assumed by such employer are also shifted from the employer itself to the society.

(2) Any injury or death of the employee during working hours in the workplace for work reasons (including the injury and death caused by any traffic accident occurred in any work travel), even if the employee himself or herself shall be blamed to some degree, shall be deemed as work-related injury and such employee shall be granted work-related injury insurance benefits.

(3) Any accident under special circumstances stipulated by laws, for example, any injury resulted in any road accident not for the employee's fault or main fault occurred on the marked route within reasonable periods before and after working hours in connection with transporting shall be deemed as work-related injury.

However, the principle of liability without fault is not applicable to any injury, disability or death of the employee caused by its crime or contravention of law, suicide or self-mutilation, fight, excessive drinking, intentional breaking traffic rules and other circumstances as provided by the laws and regulations, in which case, such injury, disability or death shall not be deemed as work-related injury.

The identification of work-related injury of the employee and the grant of work-related injury insurance benefits to the employee do not affect the other punishment given by enterprise to the employee for any operation against the rules in accordance with its bylaws.

## Section 5  Work-related Injury Insurance Benefits

Work-related injury insurance benefit is a matter related to the vital interests of the laborers, which is always valued by the laws of all countries and international treaties. For example, with regard to work-related injury medical treatment, the Social Security (Minimum Standards) Convention, 1952 put forward that, the work-related injury insurance shall not allow a worker with work-related injury to bear the expenses for any type of medical treatment they need and provided to him/her, and a medical care without time limit shall be offered to a worker with work-related injury. The medical treatment provided by the Convention includes the general practitioner and specialist in-patient and out-patient care, including domiciliary visiting; dental care; nursing care at home or in hospital and other medical institutions; maintenance in hospitals, convalescent homes, sanatoria or other medical institutions; dental, pharmaceutical and other medical or surgical supplies; and the care furnished by such other professional as may at any time be legally recognised as allied to the medical profession, under the supervision of a medical or dental practitioner. The Employment Injury Benefits Convention, 1964 expanded the scope of medical treatments by adding emergency treatment of persons sustaining a serious accident and follow-up treatment of those whose injury is slight and does not entail discontinuance of work.

In China, according to the Regulations on Work-related Injury Insurance, the work-related injury insurance benefits mainly include:

1. Work-related injury medical treatment benefits. Employees who suffer work-related injury or have occupational disease shall accept medical treatment and enjoy work-related injury medical treatment benefits. Work-related injury medical treatment benefits shall be paid out of the work-related injury insurance funds, which include (1) work-related injury medical treatment expenses. This includes all costs as required for treatment of work-related injury given to the injured employees, which are in compliance with the category of diagnosis and treatment items under work-related injury insurance and the hospitalization service standards for work-related injury insurance. (2) Rehabilitation treatment expenses. (3) Costs for installation and purchase of assistive devices. Injured employees may, for the needs of daily life or employment and upon confirmation by the labor

capacity appraisal committee, wear artificial limbs, orthosis, ocular prosthesis and artificial teeth and equip themselves with wheelchair and other assistive devices, and the necessary costs shall be paid from work-related injury insurance funds at the standards stipulated by the State.

2. Disability treatment. Employees of level 1 to 4 disability are the ones who lose their labor capacity totally, and for such employees, the Regulations on Work-related Injury Insurance adopt the method of combining long-term treatment with one-off treatment, stipulating that a one-off disability subsidy and monthly disability allowance shall be paid to them. The standards for one-off disability subsidy for employees of level 1 to 4 disability are respectively equal to 27 times, 25 times, 23 times and 21 times of their monthly salary. Employees of level 5 and level 6 disability are the ones who have lost most of their labor capacity, and the standards for one-off disability subsidy for those employees are respectively 18 times and 16 times of their monthly salary. Employees of level 7 to 10 disability are the ones who have lost part of their labor capacity, and the standards for one-off disability subsidy for those employees are respectively 13 times, 11 times, 9 times and 7 times of their monthly salary.

Employees with work-related injury who have been given disability level and confirmed by the labor capacity appraisal committee as having need for living care may be divided into three degrees, i. e. completely self-care disability, substantial self-care disability and partial self-care disability, and may enjoy a monthly living care fee respectively equal to 50%, 40% or 30% of the average monthly salary of employees of last year in the pooling region.

3. Work-related death treatment. In the case of a work-related death of an employee, the immediate family of such employee may receive funeral grants, survivors' benefits for dependents and one-off work-related death subsidy from the work-related injury insurance funds as follows. Of which: (1) the funeral grants shall be equal to 6 times of the monthly average salary of employees of last year in the pooling region; (2) Survivors' benefits for dependents (which refer to relatives who have no labor capacity with their main living incomes depend on the dead employee) shall be made at a certain percentage of the salary of such employee. The standards are: 40% per month for the spouse, and 30% per month for other relatives, with additional 10% on the basis of the afore-mentioned standards per person per month in the case of an elderly person living alone or an orphan. The sum of the survivors' benefits payable to all dependents so determined shall not be higher than the salary of such employee before his work-related death. The specific scope of dependents shall be stipulated by the administrative

department of social insurance under the State Council; (3) the standard for one-off work-related injury subsidy shall be 20 times of the urban residents' per capita disposable income in the previous year.

In addition, if, during work-related travel, an employee's whereabouts became unknown in an accident or in any emergency rescue and disaster relief, payment of his/her salary shall continue from the month in which the accident occurred for 3 months and be terminated from the fourth month, and thereafter the dependents of such employee shall be paid monthly survivors' benefits for dependents from work-related injury insurance funds. Where such dependents have difficulty in maintaining a living, 50% of the one-off work-related death subsidy may be paid in advance. Where the employee is declared dead by a people's court, the case shall be handled according to the provisions on work-related death.

Pursuant to the provisions of the Regulations on Work-related Injury Insurance, an employee with work-related injury shall cease to enjoy the work-related injury insurance benefits if: (1) he has lost eligibility to receive the benefits. Where the employee with work-related injury has any change during his enjoyment of the work-related injury insurance benefits and therefore has lost eligibility to enjoy work-related injury insurance benefits, for example, if his labor capacity is fully recovered and thus they no longer require the security provided by the work-related injury insurance system, the work-related injury insurance benefits shall be stopped; (2) he refuses to undergo an appraisal of labor capacity. The conclusion of labor capacity appraisal is a scientific basis for ascertaining compensation of different degrees, reasonable adjustment of work position or resumption of work. Where an employee with work-related injury, refuses to undergo an appraisal of labor capacity without any justifiable reason, on the one hand, the work-related injury insurance benefits would not be ascertained, and on the other hand, it also shows that such employee is unwilling to accept the help provided by the work-related injury insurance system, and therefore such employee shall no longer enjoy the work-related injury insurance benefits. (3) he refuses to receive medical treatment. After suffering work-related injury accident or having occupational diseases, the employee shall enjoy the right to work-related medical treatment benefits, and shall also undertake the obligation to proactively cooperate with the medical treatment. The refusal of receiving medical treatment without any justifiable reason is in contravention of the purpose of promoting the occupational recovery as provided by the Regulations on Work-related Injury Insurance on.

In China, pursuant to the Regulations on Work-related Injury Insurance, a staff member or worker injured at work shall cease to enjoy work-related injury insurance benefits in any of the following circumstances: (1) Being no longer qualified for the benefits; (2) Refusing to receive work capacity assessment; or (3) Refusing to receive medical treatment.

● Chapter ⅩⅣ

# Maternity Insurance Law

The current insured targets and coverage of maternity insurance were established in the process of development of and changes in maternity insurance legislation of China. Relevant legislations have been made on the payment and management of maternity insurance funds as well as the contents and standards of maternity insurance benefits.

## Section 1　Concept and Significance of Maternity Insurance

### Ⅰ. Concept of Maternity Insurance

Maternity insurance refers to a social insurance system by which a female employee may receive material benefits from society when she loses her labor capacity temporarily and has her normal source of income discontinued for pregnancy and childbirth. It is a social insurance established specially for protecting female employees and is intended to provide antenatal and postpartum economic compensation and medical security for the female employees giving birth.

(1) Maternity insurance is a social insurance established particularly for female employees. Maternity is a matter related to the whole family consisting of a man and a woman and the economic burden caused by maternity will be borne by the husband and wife jointly. However, maternity insurance is intended to provide direct material assistances and compensation for a female employee's pregnancy and delivery only.

(2) Maternity insurance is a material security for the whole course of a female employee's maternity. It covers not only the compensation for the medical expenses associated with the female employee's pregnancy and delivery, including medical examination fee, delivery fee, operation fee, hospitalization expenses,

medicine expenses, etc., but also the compensation for the wage income that fails to be earned by the female employee for the work leaves in the prescribed maternity period.

(3) Maternity insurance is a social insurance implemented for a female employee's lawful maternity. A lawful maternity must meet some conditions, such as reaching legal marriage ages, having gone through the marriage registration formalities in accordance with the marriage law and abiding by the maternity laws, regulations, and policies of the State. In China, an insured female employee shall be entitled to the maternity insurance benefits, no matter whether her gestation period is long or short, whether she has aborted or not, and whether she has a stillbirth or live birth.

## II. Maternity Insurance Legislation of China

The maternity insurance system of China was established in the beginning of 1950s. The Labor Insurance Regulations of the People's Republic of China has made specific provisions on the maternity insurance benefits and the basic contents and benefits of the maternity insurance are as follows: (1) A paid maternity leave of 56 days shall be offered to a female employee for her maternity; (2) A paid maternity leave of not more than 30 days shall be offered to a female employee in case of a miscarriage occurs during the first 7 months of the pregnancy; (3) An additional paid maternity leave of 14 days shall be offered to a female employee in case of a dystocia or twin birth; (4) A female employee's antenatal examination expenses and delivery expenses shall be borne by her employer; (5) A sick leave treatment shall be offered to a female employee who, as proved by hospital, is unable to go for work after the expiration of her maternity leave; (6) A maternity subsidy of RMB 4.00 shall be paid from the labor insurance funds to a pregnant female employee or a male employee's pregnant wife,

On April 26, 1955, the State Council promulgated the Circular on Maternity Leave of Female Employees, providing the maternity insurance of female employees of the Party and government organs as well as public institutions and expanding the scope of the targets under maternity benefits from enterprise female employees to all female employees of government organs and public institutions. The Safety and Sanitation Rules for Factory promulgated in 1956 and the Hygienic Standards for the Design of Industrial Enterprises promulgated in 1979 have made specific provisions on medical room for female employees, rest room for pregnant women and nursery. Provisions on Labor Protection of Female Employees were promulgated by the State Council in July, 1988 for the purposes of reducing and solving female employees' special difficulties caused by physiological function changes in the process of work and protecting their safety and wealth. On December 14, 1994, the Ministry of Labor promulgated the Measures for Trial Implementation of Maternity Insurance of Enterprise Employees, which made provisions on the maternity insurance system of China in accordance with the requirements of reform.

Maternity insurance is provided in Chapter VI of the Social Insurance Law, which provides the coverage, system model, source of funds, and qualifications for receiving insurance benefits of the maternity insurance. On April 18, 2012, the Special Provisions on Labor Protection of Female Employees were adopted at the 200th executive meeting of the State Council and came into force as of the date of its promulgation. There were more specific provisions in respect of the scope of application stipulated in such Provisions, which intensified and specified the employer's legal obligations and liabilities, and offered a more comprehensive, fair and improved labor protection to female employees. The work content that may be refused by a female employee was included in the Special Provisions and the Special Provisions is more practical. Relevant government departments' responsibilities for supervising, inspecting, and punishing the employer had been specified.

## Ⅲ. Targets and Coverage of China's Maternity Insurance

China's Maternity insurance was established by the Labor Insurance Regulations of the People's Republic of China that promulgated by the State Council in 1951. According to that, the maternity insurance shall mainly apply to: (1) Factories and mines under State operation, public-private operation, private operation, or cooperative operation that have more than 100 employees (excluding the employees of business management entities of and affiliates to an entity) and affiliates thereto; (2) Railway enterprises, shipping enterprises, and enterprises of post and telecommunications, as well as the affiliates thereto; (3) Capital construction entities that are engaged in industrial business, mining business and transportation business; and (4) National construction companies. In addition, the Regulations also provide that any worker or employee employed by the enterprise which is enrolled in labor insurance, including female workers and staff members who are under the wage system or supply system or are apprentice, casual laborers, or probation staffs, and male staff members' wives, shall be entitled to receive maternity insurance benefits of different degrees.

On April 26, 1955, the State Council promulgated the Circular on Maternity Leave of Female Employees, providing the maternity insurance for the female employees of government organs and of public institutions and expanding the targets and scope of maternity insurance from the female employees of enterprises to all female employees of government organs and of public institutions.

After the 1980s, China started to reform the maternity insurance system. Many local regulations provide that the enterprises owned by the whole people, collectively-owned enterprises at country level or above, central subordinated enterprises, and provincial subordinated enterprises shall participate in the social pooling of maternity insurance; some local areas have even brought Sino-foreign joint ventures, the town-established or subdistrict office-established enterprises that enrolled in the social polling plan of endowment insurance and private enterprises into the scope of maternity insurance; some areas have brought the public institutions adopted independent accounting or own revenue and expenditure system into the scope of maternity insurance with the permanent female employees and contract female laborers as the insured; some areas have brought the casual laborers enrolled in the endowment insurance into the scope of maternity insurance; and some areas have brought the rural wives of male employees from the enterprise enrolled in the social pooling plan of maternity insurance into the scope of maternity insurance.

On December 14, 1994, the Ministry of Labor promulgated the Measures for Trial Implementation of Maternity Insurance of Enterprise Employees by which various urban enterprises and employees were included in the scope of maternity insurance. Some areas have extended the targets of maternity insurance to the female employees of township enterprises and commune enterprises. In consideration of China's particular situation that there is over two thirds of total population lives in rural areas of China and 80% of nationwide women live in rural areas, villages and towns, so the development of rural maternity insurance has a significant influence on the development of national maternity insurance. Since the reforming and opening up, the noticeable changes in the rural areas of China and a historic progress in rural economy that caused by the emerging of township enterprises and development of commodity economy have laid material foundations and social conditions for rural maternity insurance. The scope of maternity insurance has been expanded gradually from female employees of childbearing ages to all childbearing-age women, from cities to countryside, and from economically developed areas to economically undeveloped areas, which is the development path of maternity insurance in China.

## IV. Differences between the Maternity Insurance Benefits and Medical Insurance Benefits

Maternity insurance and medical insurance provide living security and necessary medical services for the employees who lose their labor capacities temporarily. The person enrolled by maternity insurance benefits may be entitled to both maternity insurance benefits and medial insurance benefits simultaneously in special circumstances during the term of insurance. The following are main differences between maternity insurance benefits and medial insurance benefits:

(1) Maternity insurance benefits are generally for female employees and, in some areas, for male employees' spouses, while medical insurance benefits are for both female and male employees.

(2) Maternity insurance benefits are only received by those female employees of childbearing ages, and the female employees' age, marriage time, and birth order are also taken into consideration. According to the basic policy of family planning carried out in China, a female employee is entitled to maternity insurance benefits once in her whole life in general, with few exceptions for twice. Medical insurance benefit has no limitation for age and times, because any employee may suffer from an illness at different ages.

(3) The medical services for the person enrolled in maternity insurance are mainly health care and monitoring. Normal delivery needs no medical treatment, but needs only regular physical examination for the pregnant woman and delivery monitoring over the pregnant woman and fetus so as to ensure a smooth delivery. In the case of medical insurance, the insured who is sick may be adopted with the treatments of necessary medical examination, medicating, physiotherapy and surgical operation so that he/she can recover and return to work as early as possible.

(4) There are specific legal provisions on the period of maternity leave in China. For example, the normal maternity leave period is 90 days, of which, the antenatal leave period is officially stipulated as 15 days. No specific sick leave period is provided for the medical insurance, and generally the period ends with the recovering of the sick.

(5) The maternity insurance benefits are better than medical insurance benefits in general. In China, the medical insurance adopts the model of "Combining social pooling with personal account", by which an employee needs to pay insurance premium and open a personal account, while an employee enrolled in maternity insurance needs not pay the insurance premium. An employee may be provided with the childbirth allowance during the period of maternity leave, but no sickness allowance is provided for the medical insurance. ①

---

① China Labor Market Information Website Monitoring Center: "Relations and Differences between Maternity Insurance and Medical Insurance", June 1, 2004.

## Section 2  Maternity Insurance Funds

### I. Concept and Features of Maternity Insurance Funds

Maternity insurance funds are the funds established by the State uniformly in society for paying for maternity insurance expenses so that the funds for maternity insurance are guaranteed reliably.

Compared with other social insurance funds, maternity insurance funds have the following features:

(1) The fund has a single source. As a component part of social insurance, in terms of the fund source, maternity insurance also complies with the "law of large numbers" in social insurance, which is pooling social forces. Maternity insurance premiums are totally paid by the employer, and no individual contribution shall be made.

(2) Fund raising is foreseeable. Because of the targets of maternity insurance are women of childbearing ages and maternity insurance is closely connected with family planning, so maternity insurance expenses are foreseeable, the maternity insurance funds can be used as planned, and no fund reservation need to be made for emergency needs.

(3) Fund burden is equal. According to relevant provisions, all enterprises and employers participating in maternity insurance shall pay maternity insurance premiums in the same proportion of total wages, no matter whether they have female employees or not and how many female employees they have.

### II. Raising of Maternity Insurance Funds

In China, the raising of maternity insurance funds complies with the following principles and methods:

(1) Maternity insurance funds shall be raised in accordance with the principles of "Determining the collection on the basis of expenditure and making both ends meet". This is one of important features which make maternity insurance different from other social insurance in terms of the raising of funds. Firstly, maternity insurance is connected with family planning policy. Compared with other social insurance projects, maternity insurance funds can be foreseen more easily, are planned more widely and have less fluctuates, so no large reserves need to be provided for emergency needs. Secondly, it is good for lightening enterprises' burdens and establishing good social images. In terms of

purpose, maternity insurance funds are established for meeting the basic needs of the women who are pregnant or in labor. If the fund contribution amount is too large, the burden of the employer will be increased; while in terms of motivation, although maternity insurance is beneficial to society, the more the fund raised, the more negative effects will be caused to the society.

(2) The contribution to maternity insurance fund shall be determined by local people's government according to the number of infants within the ambit of family planning and other expenses such as childbirth allowances and medical expenses associated with the pregnancy or delivery. Its maximum rate shall not exceed 1% of total wages of the employee. The employer shall pay the maternity insurance contributions to local social security agency at the rate fixed by local government. The maternity insurance premium contributed by the enterprise shall be deemed as period expense and listed as the general and administrative expenses of such enterprise. Article 53 of the Social Insurance Law provides that "Employees shall participate in maternity insurance and the maternity insurance premiums shall be paid by the employing units in accordance with the provisions of the State. Employees need not pay the maternity insurance premiums." Those provisions reflect the support and care provided by the State and society for women during such a special period. In addition, the provisions have also balanced the burdens between enterprises, reduced enterprises' costs in employment of female employees, and helped women find jobs.

In practice, maternity insurance funds mainly have three raising ways: A. the employers make contributions for maternity insurance premiums at certain rate of an employee's total wages; B. the contribution for maternity insurance made by government organs and public institutions comes from the fiscal appropriation; and C. the employers make monthly contributions for maternity insurance premiums at fixed amount for each employee[1].

---

① When the Social Insurance Law (Draft) was exposed for pubic comments after it was reviewed the second time, some experts pointed out that, in theory an employee may only be exempted from his/her premium contribution to work-related injury insurance due to its special feature of being the converted form from employer liability insurance, which is also accepted by international practices. So they suggested deleting the provision that "Employees need not pay the maternity insurance premiums". But, the legislative authorities has not adopted such suggestion for they were convinced that such provision was in line with both the *Measures for Trial Implementation of Maternity Insurance for Enterprise Employees* promulgated by the Ministry of Labor and the current practices, and the implementation of such provision has not caused any problem in practice. Please refer to the *Interpretations of the Social Insurance Law of the People's Republic of China* published by the China Labor and Social Security Publishing House. Visiting http: //www. mohrss. gov. cn/page. do on January 14, 2013.

(3) Maternity insurance funds shall be organized on the principle of locality and raised through a social pooling system. The principle of locality refers to that the maternity insurance is carried out on a regional basis, which means every city or district (or county) is an independent raising unit for insurance funds, and all enterprises in the same administrative area, regardless of their forms of ownership or membership, shall uniformly participate in the maternity insurance organized by the administrative area and comply with local premium standards and relevant policies & regulations.

Social pooling of maternity insurance funds refers to that maternity insurance funds are raised and used uniformly by social insurance agencies within the scope provided for by the State for the aim of realizing mutual helps and sharing of risks and providing basic material assistances for the women giving birth. Social pooling of maternity insurance funds is the actual performance of the compensation responsibility for the women giving birth by society and has the following functions and significances:

(1) It is advantageous for promoting the fair market competitions of enterprises. Due to the imbalance distribution of female employees among enterprises caused by the division of labor in society and industrial characteristics, in some enterprises, female employees account for 60%–70% of total employees; while in some other enterprises, female employees account for less than 10% of total employees. Therefore, unbalance production expense burdens are so caused to different enterprises, hindering the fair market competitions and constricting the economic development of enterprises. The carrying out of social pooling of maternity insurance funds provides conditions for the fair competitions of enterprises.

(2) It is advantageous for ensuring the equal employment rights of women. Because of the intangible increase in the labor costs for the employment of female employees caused by the maternity expense, some enterprise are unwilling to employ female employees, which causes the difficulties in women employment. Even those employed women, in the occasion when the enterprise carries out new operation manner such as contractual operation, leasing, or optimization of labor organization, often fail to be given equal work arrangement as male employees for their work absence due to the childbirth. After the implementation of social pooling of maternity insurance funds, maternity expenses are paid uniformly by the social insurance agency, so that the worries about future of the enterprises that have many female employees are eliminated and female employees' equal employment is ensured.

(3) It is advantageous for protecting female employees' right to social

insurance benefits during the maternity period. In the past, it is the employer's liability to pay wages and related expenses for the maternity of female employers. So it's hard for the employers to afford the payment for maternity benefits to female employees when they have bad profits, accordingly the maternity insurance benefits for female employees are unable to be realized. After the social pooling of maternity insurance funds is implemented, maternity insurance funds are raised and used uniformly by the social insurance agency so that the funds' role of mutual aids is given fully play and female employees can receive their maternity insurance benefits.

In short, social pooling of maternity insurance funds is necessary for balancing enterprises' burdens, dispersing enterprises' risks, resolving the unbalance maternity expense burdens on enterprises, relieving the low employment of female employees and ensuring maternal and child health.

## Ⅲ. Payment and Management of Maternity Insurance Funds

In China, Maternity insurance funds are mainly used for the payment of the following two expenses: A. Childbirth allowance, also known as maternity wages in the past, is paid from the maternity insurance funds if employer has participated in social pooling of maternity insurance funds or paid from the employer's wage funds if the employer has not participated in social pooling of maternity insurance funds; and B. Medical expenses for maternity, including physical examination expenses, delivery fee, operation fee, hospitalization fee, charges for medicines and medical expense for the treatment of any disease caused by the childbirth.

There is a special agency provided for the management of maternity insurance funds by legislations in each country, In China, maternity insurance funds are collected, paid and managed by social insurance agency, the subsidiary of the administration of labor security department. Maternity insurance funds are deposited in the special account for maternity insurance funds opened at bank by a social insurance agency and are used for specified purpose only. The bank shall compute the interest of the maternity insurance funds at the interest rate of urban and rural individual saving deposits of the same period and all interests so incurred shall be included in the maternity insurance funds. No tax is imposed on maternity insurance funds. The budget and financial statement system is adopted for raising and using maternity insurance funds. The social insurance agency shall issue an annual report and be subject to the auditing and supervision of the department of finance at the same level.

## Section 3    Maternity Insurance Benefits

### I . Concept of Maternity Insurance Benefits

Maternity insurance benefits refer to all assistances and material compensations legally offered to a female employee during the period of maternity. The concept shall be understood from the following key points:

(1) Only the female employee herself is entitled to the maternity insurance benefits.

(2) A female employee may be entitled to the maternity insurance benefits only during her maternity period, and pregnancy, delivery, and breast-feeding are all included in the maternity period.

(3) Offering maternity insurance benefits to a female employee must comply with relevant laws, regulations and policies.

(4) Maternity insurance benefits include necessary health cares as required by the maternity and wage compensation for female employees. Maternity insurance benefit varies from country to country for many factors, and mainly depends on a country's economic development level, historical habits, and population policies.

### II . Contents and Standards of Maternity Insurance Benefits

The maternity insurance benefits in China mainly include maternity leave, childbirth allowance, medical services for maternity, special labor protection in maternity period and occupational security in maternity period.

#### ( I ) Maternity Leave

A female employee is entitled to a maternity leave of 98 days, including an antenatal leave of 15 days. In case of dystocia, an additional leave of 15 days shall be allowed; in case of multiple-childbirth, an additional leave of 15 days shall be given for each additional infant; in case of a miscarriage or abortion occurs prior to expiration of four months of pregnancy, a maternity leave of 15 days shall be allowed; in case of a miscarriage or abortion occurs upon or after expiration of four months of pregnancy, a maternity leave of 42 days shall be allowed.

The length of maternity leave varies from country to country, but it is 12 to 14 weeks in general. The Philippines provides the shortest maternity leave, which is 45 days, and Finland provides the longest maternity leave in the world, which is

258 days. The length of maternity leave extends with the birth of each additional infant in some countries which carry out the population policy of encouraging more births. For example in France, a female employee will be given a maternity leave of 16 weeks when she gives birth to the first or second child and will be given a maternity leave of 26 weeks when she gives birth to the third child, and an additional maternity leave of 2 to 12 weeks will be given in case of multiple childbirths.

### ( Ⅱ ) Childbirth Allowance

The childbirth allowance for a female employee during maternity leaves shall be calculated and paid on the basis of the average monthly wage of employees in the enterprise of the previous year. An employer who has not been enrolled in the social pooling of maternity insurance funds shall be liable for paying normal wages to female employees during their maternity leaves.

The Social Insurance Law of China provides medical benefit for maternity for an employee's unemployed spouse, i. e. the employee's unemployed spouse is entitled to medical benefit for maternity in accordance with relevant provisions of the State. The medical benefit for maternity mentioned herein mainly refers to the compensation for medical expenses associated with maternity and incurred by the unemployed-woman. .

### ( Ⅲ ) Medical Services for Maternity

The items of medical services for maternity include medical examination expense, delivery fee, operation fee, hospitalization fee, and other medical treatment expenses directly related to maternity. The expenses of female employees' medical examination, delivery, operations, hospitalization and medications shall be paid from maternity insurance funds. Expenses exceeding the standard charges as provided for medical services and medications ( including charges for medications at their own expenses and nourishing medications) shall be paid by the employees themselves. Medical expenses for diseases caused by childbirth after the female employees leave the hospital shall be covered by the maternity insurance fund; medical expenses for other diseases shall be paid in accordance with the provisions on medical treatment insurance benefits. In the event that the female employees require rest and medical treatment due to illness upon the expiration of their periods of maternity leave, they shall be entitled to relevant benefits in accordance with the provisions on sick-leave benefits and medical treatment insurance.

The Social Insurance Law of PRC provides the medical treatment expenses associated with family planning and expenses for other items as provided by the provisions of laws or regulations. The operation expenses associated with family planning refer to the medical expenses incurred for placing/removing the intrauterine device or conducting artificial abortion, induction of labor, sterilization or salpingostomy out of the need of realizing family planning. Expenses for other items as provided by the provisions of laws or regulations are provided for the consideration of potential expenses as may be incurred in the future. In addition, there is specific coverage of maternity insurance funds determined by local areas on the basis of actual situations of local economy, society, resources, environment and population development. For example, some provinces or cities provide a once-in-all nonrecurring nutrition subsidy for the female employee who is giving birth. Jiangsu Province provides that a general investigation of gynecological diseases shall be carried out gradually for the insured female employees.

### (Ⅳ) Special Labor Protection during Maternity Period

Special labor protection during maternity period refers to a special policy made for ensuring and protecting the basic income and personal safety of the female employees when they have special difficulties in work due to physiological changes occurred during their pregnancy, which includes income protection and heath protection. The major measure for income protection is keeping no decrease in basic wages for female employees during their pregnancy through State legislations. The major measures for health protection are: A. The employer shall not assign high-strength labor or the labor which is prohibited during pregnancy to those pregnant employees or extend labor time over the normal working days; B. for those pregnant female employees who are incompetent to the original labor, the employer shall reduce their workload or arrange a shift of work post; C. No overtime work or night shift work shall be arranged for those female employees who are pregnant for more than 7 months and some work time breaks shall be offered to them; and D. for those pregnant female employees, prenatal examination within normal working time shall be allowed and be included in the working time.

### (Ⅴ) Occupational Protection for Female Employees Giving Birth

In terms of occupational protection for female employees giving birth, a series of provisions were formulated in China to keep the female employees from unemployment for their pregnancy, delivery and breast-feeding. No employer shall terminate the labor relationship with the female employees who are in pregnancy, delivery or breast-feeding period. The labor relationship with female employees, regardless of the expiration of the labor contract period, shall be extended to the expiration of their breast-feeding period. In addition, the government also offers maternity assistances for those pregnant or lying-in women who have no income source through civil remedies. Maternal and infant health and safety insurance is established and transacted by family planning competent department and People's Insurance Company of China as a supplement to the maternity insurance.

## Ⅲ. Conditions for Maternity Insurance Benefit

The maternity insurance benefit in China is based on the establishing of labor relationship and also subject to the policy of family planning. The contributions to maternity insurance made by the employer and the time consistence of receiving the maternity allowances and maternity leaves are the two premises for female employees' receiving of the allowances.

● Chapter XV

# Other Legal Systems on Social Security

In this Chapter, other legal systems in respect of the social security of China will be introduced. Social welfare system is formulated for the purposes of improving the citizens' living quality and vulnerable groups' living conditions. Urban subsistence allowances system and its scope of relief, relief standard, relief manner, procedures and its fund source will be introduced in the section of social relief. The social special care system, its purpose and the specific contents including the granting of preferential treatment allowances, preferential treatments in social activities and economic subsidies will be also introduced in this Chapter.

## Section 1   Overview of Social Welfare System

Social welfare is a social security system aiming at improving the citizens' quality of life, in particular securing vulnerable groups' basic living and improving their living conditions. Social welfare system has a wide range of contents, covering public welfare for all members of society, occupational welfare only related to occupation, and the welfare for particular groups. Social welfare includes education welfare, housing welfare, personal livelihood welfare, maternal and child welfare, welfare for the aged, welfare for the disabled, welfare for employees and so on. In the patterns of manifestation, it may be certain assistances either in cash or in kind, or the free medical or educational services for poor groups and their offspring, or the provision of sanatorium or relaxation facilities for entitled groups.

### I. Concept of Social Welfare System

The concept of social welfare system can be defined in broad sense and narrow sense. In a broad sense, social welfare refers to the offering of comprehensive public services in respect of living, sanitation, environment, housing, education and employment by the State and society to all members as necessary for their whole lives. In a narrow sense, social welfare mainly refers to all kinds of policies and measures formulated and adopted by the State for resolving certain existing social problems, reducing social symptoms, and preventing social problems from occurring and getting worse so as to develop social insurance and social relief undertakings and meet the needs of social and economic development.

Social welfare, as a component part of social security, refers to the social security policies and facilities and related services adopted and provided by the State and society for the sake of securing and maintaining certain quality of life of members of society and meeting their basic material and spiritual needs. Social welfare is also a kind of public service that the State funds and sponsors various welfare undertakings and distributes various welfare subsidies. Social welfare includes the public welfare undertakings run by the State and targeted at all citizens, such as the utilities of education, science, culture, sports, sanitation, and environmental protection, particular welfare projects run by the State and targeted at certain groups such as various welfare enterprises established for the disabled, rest homes operated for the aged who are helpless, and orphan asylums, and various welfare subsidies granted by the State such as the non-staple food price subsidies granted to urban residents.

The Labor Law of China explicitly provides that "the State shall develop social welfare undertakings and build public welfare facilities to create conditions for laborers' rest, recuperation and rehabilitation. Employing units shall create conditions to improve collective welfare and laborers' benefits."

## II. Development of Social Welfare System of China

In the early days of new China, it was difficult to meet people's basic living sometimes because of the low industrial and agricultural productivity and low urban employees' low income. For the purpose of securing employees' living, the Trade Union Law of the People's Republic of China promulgated in June 1950 and the Labor Insurance Regulations of the People's Republic of China promulgated in February 1951 explicitly provided that the trade unions at all levels shall gradually improve employees' welfare and the government and enterprises shall provide necessary houses and facilities to the trade unions for carrying out collective welfare undertakings. Thereafter, the government formulated a series of social policies and adopted measures to develop social welfare undertakings, and the collective welfare facilities such as employee dining rooms, nurseries, and kindergartens have developed gradually from then.

During the period of Great Leap Forward, the scope of social welfare in China was constantly expanded and all welfare standards were over-enhanced, but such immoderate improvements were not suitable for China's actual situations and economic development level. During the period of Great Cultural Revolution, the State organs in charge of welfare were paralyzed, the employee welfare systems established previously by the trade unions at various levels were badly damaged, and the government reduced its social welfare projects day by day and only assumed the welfare for helpless urban elderly persons who had no family, orphans, and a few of disabled persons.

Since 1978, China has carried out a series of reforms on social welfare, such as amending and establishing several systems of welfare subsidies and changing the measures for the withdrawal and use of the employee welfare funds. Although the feature of "enterprises running social services" is still obvious in the welfare programs, most welfare programs are jointly contributed by the State, communities and individuals. Most of the welfare facilities such as nurseries, kindergartens, and clubs established by entities have been opened to public and the reform on housing welfare is also in process.

## III. Features of Social Welfare System

### ( I ) The Rights to and Duties for Social Welfare are not Equal

Social welfare, enjoyed by the whole society, is aimed at meeting people's welfare needs, providing basic living security to all social members, and promoting faster material progress and cultural and ideological progress as well as faster progress of whole society. It is the responsibilities of the State and society to develop social welfare undertakings, social welfare undertakings are mainly funded and financed by the State and society in a unidirectional manner, and members of society may enjoy social welfares without any pre-payment of expenses or any performance of other obligations, i. e. there is no corresponding and equal relationship of rights and obligations existed in social welfare system, which is also a significant feature for distinguishing social welfare from social insurance.

### ( II ) Targets of Social Welfare are Universal

In terms of the obtaining of security benefits, social welfare is provide by the State and society to all members of society in a unidirectional manner with the aim of "benefiting everybody", i. e. social welfare is shared by the whole society and is a kind of public benefit by which those who have special needs can be provided with material assistance and social services. There is no need to carry out an investigation on family economic conditions for the members who gain social welfares, which is the most remarkable feature for distinguishing social welfare from social relieves.

However, social welfare policies of each country (developing country in particular) have obvious policy orientation, so some welfare projects are particularly provided for special groups. For these special groups such as the disabled persons and elderly persons without family, social welfare measures are not increases in welfare, but some compensation to them for their welfare losses caused by certain social reasons. So, social welfare is also compensatory, but this does not conflict with its feature of "benefiting everyone". The compensation is helpful to realizing the true aim of "benefiting everyone" indeed. Besides, among these special groups who are entitled to be compensated, each person has equal opportunity to enjoy social welfare, so the social welfare is still universal.

### ( Ⅲ ) The Social Welfare Standards are Unified

Social welfare is aimed at social equity, and is different from "Distribution According to Work" in terms of distribution of resources. Besides, it is also different from social relieves in which the poorer the applicant is, the more relieves he/she can get, and different from social insurance in which the more obligations the insured has performed, the more social insurance benefits he/she can get. Social welfare standards are unified for all same targets, i. e. members from the same group share the same social welfare no matter whether they are rich or poor. It is obvious that the unified social welfare standard will generate different levels of satisfaction for different persons, but social welfare will no doubt have significant positive effects on the persons who are in urgent need of it.

However, the unified standard highlighted in social welfare does not mean equalitarianism. In fact, an imbalance in economical development among different areas shall be taken into consideration, particularly in China, a country with a vast territory and complex situations, in which the imbalance in economic and social development between areas and between urban and rural areas is more prominent.

### ( Ⅳ ) The Source of Funds for Social Welfare is Unidirectional

The funds for social welfare are not required to be contributed by individuals in advance, and they are borne by the State and society. Although the source of social welfare funds has been broadened constantly in recent years, it is still unidirectional, and this makes social welfare different from social insurance. At present, the welfare lottery industry has become an important pillar of social welfare in China. According to the data from the Ministry of Civil Affairs, during the period of the Ninth Five-Year Plan, the total sales volume of welfare lottery in China is RMB 35. 802 billion Yuan and the welfare funds so raised reach to RMB 10. 624 billion Yuan. During the period of the Tenth Five-Year Plan, China will try to issue welfare lotteries of RMB 100 billion to promote the development of social welfare undertakings.

( Ⅴ ) Social Welfare Standards are of Uncertainty

There is no rigid and compulsory indicator made for social welfare standards. Social welfare standards are adjusted according to social and economic development level and there is no certain and compulsory standard must be reached in social welfare, which is universal in all countries and departments. Generally speaking, the higher the social and economic development level is, the higher the social welfare standards are.

## Ⅳ. Significance of Social Welfare System

Social welfare is a form of income redistribution among citizens that the members of society may, in addition to their work incomes, be equally provided with all kinds of welfare facilities and services by the State. Therefore, social welfare is a State policy by which all members of society share the achievements of society.

(1) Social welfare is advantageous to the smooth reproduction of labor forces. As production is socialized and social productivity constantly develops, society will assume more and more responsibilities for laborers, some functions that belong to families before have became the responsibilities of society, and some necessary conditions for the reproduction of labor forces are also provided by society, such as child healthcare, education, occupation introduction and vocational training, and science and culture undertakings. The State provides the labors with facilities and services as necessary for their production by running social welfare undertakings, which is advantageous to the smooth reproduction of labor forces, the fostering of new and high-quality labor forces and the accommodation to modern production.

(2) Social welfare is advantageous to the improvement of people's material and cultural life and the achievement of stability and unity of society. The wealth created by laborers for society, except the part used by the State for maintaining necessary operation of the State, must be distributed among all members of society. By carrying out social welfare undertakings, the members of society benefit from the public welfare facilities and welfare subsidies offered by the State

together, people's material and cultural life improves constantly, and stability and unity of society are realized.

(3) Social welfare system may ensure minimum income of individuals and families, no matter whether they have labor capacity or not, whether they have property or not, and what the market value of their property is, especially those who have neither labor capacity nor property income. For example in capitalist countries, all kinds of transferred revenues sourced from social welfare policies, not only become an important integral part of workers' income in those countries, but also ensure the basic conditions of living, residence, medical care and education for workers, especially those low-income earners.

(4) Social welfare system can protect basic rights and health of women, minors, the aged and the disabled, as well as all citizens' rights to education.

## Section 2　Social Relief

Social relief is a traditional content in social security system and an effective way to provide subsistence allowances for the needy. Social relief system is significant for maintaining social stability. Social relief law refers to a legal system by which the State offers assistances to the poor who are unable to maintain minimum living standards for the reasons of themselves, nature, or society so as to secure their basic living. Social relief law consists of the law on social relieves, the law on disaster relieves, and the law on poverty relieves.

### Ⅰ. Subsistence Allowances System for Urban Residents

Subsistence allowances system for urban residents is a system by which the State grants subsistence allowances to urban residents on the basis of minimum subsistence standard, which is a new social relief system established for meeting socialist market economy system. From 1997 to March 2000, a total amount of RMB 4.98 billion funded by the finance departments at all levels had been put into this system, covering 3.01 million poor urban residents, of which, 2.36 million persons are enterprise employees, laid-off workers and retirees, accounting for 78% of the total number.

#### (Ⅰ) Relief Standards

Relief standard, known as "Minimum Subsistence Level", is a fundamental part of the system on subsistence allowances for urban residents. At present in

China, the minimum subsistence level is finally determined by local government on the basis of minimum expenditures of urban residents for maintaining basic living and price index by taking such factors as social average living standards and bearing capacity of government finance after estimate and demonstration are made. Furthermore, the minimum subsistence level shall be also adjusted along with the rise in price and other factors.

The urban minimum subsistence level is determined on the basis that urban residents reach the minimum subsistence. The so-called minimum subsistence includes two levels: 1. Absolute poverty, which means the enjoy of minimal conditions in respect of food, drink, clothes, and housing as necessary for maintaining survival; and 2. Relative poverty, which means the enjoy of minimum number of consumption goods and service that is suitable to local productive forces, it does not mean the shortage of food or clothes, but a sense of poverty compared with other residents. The urban minimum subsistence level shall center on "absolute poverty" first, and then give moderate consideration to "relative poverty".

The International Labor Organization holds that, in the industrialized country, the relief receipts that are unable to maintain the minimum subsistence refer to the families and individuals whose income is equal to 30% of average wage of manufacturing workers. The Committee of European Economic Cooperation holds that, an adult whose disposable income (after the income tax and insurance tax have been paid) is lower than 50% of the average level, shall be entitled to receive social relieves.

(Ⅱ) Targets of Relief

The system on subsistence allowances for urban residents is targeted at the urban residents who hold the permanent residence certificate, including the needy whose household income per capita is lower than the minimum subsistence level.

Those targets are the persons who have lost their working ability due to congenital or non-congenital factors; or who have work ability but are unemployed, or are unable to earn income, or are cut or reduced their incomes for the limitation of objective environment and are not covered by social insurance benefits; or who can not subsist without the offering of imperative aids after being hit by sudden natural or man-made disasters. Those factors have led to the results that they have no working ability or they have working ability but are temporarily in straitened circumstances. For the former, such as the poor who have no kin and can not support themselves and the disabled, long-term relieves shall be provided to support their living. While for the latter, persons who are encountered with sudden disasters or have living difficulties for the time being and can not support themselves, short-term relieves shall be provided to pull them through and help them return to normal life.

( Ⅲ ) Source of Funds

The funds for subsistence allowances: 1. are borne jointly by the finance department at municipal or district level and the government organs, enterprises, and public institutions. If a relief target has employing unit, the employing unit shall grant poverty allowance to him/her; if a relief target has no employing unit or the employing unit is unaffordable for aforesaid poverty allowance, he/she may be offered social relief by local finance department at municipal or district level; or 2. are solely borne by the finance department at municipal or district level.

To improve and develop the minimum subsistence allowance system, the government departments at all levels shall increase financial input and the Central Government shall set up special funds for urban subsistence allowances projects and regulate such funds in a unified manner. In addition, the sources of supporting funds shall be expanded, for example the initiating of such charity activities as donations and charity performances, the establishment of mutual assistance funds and anti-poverty funds by the folk force.

( Ⅳ ) Methods and Procedures of Relief

Cash relieves are adopted in general, including regular relieves and temporary relieves. In some areas, relieves are granted both in cash and in kind.

In terms of procedure, in order to gain social relief, the target of relief shall first apply to local neighborhood committee and complete the form of application for relief. Then the neighborhood committee will, upon preliminary examination, submit the application materials to the civil affairs section of the sub-district office for investigation and review. The civil affairs section of the sub-district office will, after investigation and review, put forward solving opinions and report the application to the civil affairs bureau at district level, and finally the civil affairs bureau will issue the relief certificate. The target of relief shall receive relieves on the strength of the relief certificate. Guangzhou City has expanded the coverage of needy families from the families that earn a monthly income per capita of less than RMB 300 to the families that earn a monthly income per capita of less RMB 390 and built their family files so as to provide a better basis for the researching, making, and implementing of poverty relief policies and measures by the municipal government and relevant departments.

Participation of urban basic organizations and basic mass autonomous organizations in social relief management is an effective method with Chinese characteristics. Those urban basic organizations are most closely and widely related to residents and the masses, they can, through the comprehensive adoptions of community rules, public opinions and democratic management force, manage the targets of relief, investigate the status of the targets' incomes and properties, grant special treatments for certain targets, directly provide necessities of life for some needy families, and arrange vocational training and create job opportunities for the unemployed. This will play an irreplaceable role in securing the accurate and effective implementation of the system on subsistence allowances for urban residents.

## Ⅱ. Social Relief in Rural Areas

Social relief in rural areas refer to a system by which the State and the collectives secure the basic living of the needy in rural areas by the means of offering material aids, supporting production, etc. Social relief in rural areas is mainly targeted to the aged, the disabled, and the minor who have no legal fosterer, no labor capacity, and no source of income as well as the persons who are poor for illness, disasters, or lack of labor capacity. By the end of 1999, the system on subsistence allowances for rural residents had been set up in 14 provinces, autonomous regions, and municipalities directly under the Central Government, and subsistence allowances of RMB 930 million had been offered to 3. 16 million rural residents[①].

( Ⅰ ) Government Relief and Collective Allowance

There is a larger poverty population in rural areas of China, and 85. 2% of the targets under relief are living in rural areas. It is difficult to secure the living of each rural target only by government relief. Therefore, social relieves in rural areas must adopt with the mean of combining government relief with collectives allowance, in which collective allowance is a principal part and government relief is a necessary supplement

( Ⅱ ) Government Relief and Social Mutual Assistance and Aid

Social mutual assistance and aid is also an important way to offer social relieves in rural areas. The people's government departments at all levels shall mobilize and organize the supports from cities to rural areas and from rich areas to

---

① Please refer to the report titled 6. 17 Million Chinese Urban and Rural Residents Received the Subsistence Allowances at http: //www. sina. com. cn, dated October 6, 2000, by Huasheng Daily.

poor areas, and encourage neighborhood mutual helps and aids so as to form a new mutual aid system at multiple levels and in multiple forms and participated in by the society, collectives and individuals. Social mutual assistance and aid can not only solve the living difficulties of targets of relief and relieve the pressure of the government and the collective, but also can increase the social participation and influence and foster good social morality fashions of mutual assistance, friendliness, supporting the weak and assisting the poor.

### ( Ⅲ ) Relief and Supporting Production

Supporting the self-reliance production of relief targets, as an extension of relieve programs, refers to a support manner by which the production funds are offered to the needy targets who have repaying capability for paid use and then the repaid funds can be re-used as the working funds for the poverty reduction. Such manner, combining free supporting with paid supporting, has changed the traditional singe mode of free supporting, and achieved remarkable results. Since 1982, certain funds have been appropriated from rural relief funds for supporting the self-reliance production of the needy targets in each year and each area.

### ( Ⅳ ) Relief and Work Relief

Work relief is one of the traditional relief manners in China and also an effective way for social relieves in rural areas. On one hand, the State will put a lot of funds in the construction of agriculture and forestry, water conservancy, and communications each year, particularly in some poverty-stricken areas and disaster areas where the infrastructure construction burdens are heavier and a good deal of labor forces are needed; while on the other hand, the poverty population in rural areas is larger than that in urban areas, but the relief fund is very limited, so it is impossible to secure the living of all rural targets. Therefore, the offering of the work relief to the needy who have working ability, to cause them solve their living difficulties by participating in national construction, is helpful to reducing the burden of social relieves in rural areas and giving a better play to the role of social relieves in rural areas.

### ( Ⅴ ) Rural Subsistence Allowances System

The targets of rural subsistence allowances system are the villagers whose household income per capita is lower than the rural minimum subsistence level. Rural subsistence allowances are granted both in cash and in kind. The minimum subsistence level is determined by the people's government at county or township level. Subsistence allowances are borne by the people's government at county level and the people's government at township level. To gain subsistence allowances, the person who is eligible for relief shall submit an application to the village committee, the village committee then will upon review submit the application materials to the civil affairs department of the people's government at township level for approval and to the civil affairs department of the people's government at county level for filing. The civil affairs department of the people's government at county level and the civil affairs department of the people's government at township level are responsible for the implementation and administration of local rural minimum subsistence level.

### ( Ⅵ ) Five-guarantee System

Five-guarantee system is a system to provide living helps and cares for those having no kin and can not support themselves and the disabled in rural areas.

The targets of five-guarantee system are the aged, the disabled, and the minor who meets the following conditions that: (1) He/she has no legal supporter or he/she has a legal supporter but the supporter has no supporting ability; (2) He/she has no working ability; and (3) He/she has no source of income. The aged, the disabled, or the minor are eligible for the five-guarantee system only when they meet all of the above three conditions.

The so-called Five-guarantee refers to five guarantees in five aspects: (1) supply of grain, edible oil and fuels; (2) supply of cloths, bedclothes, and pocket money; (3) supply of house meeting basic living conditions; (4) Timely treatment of diseases and cares for the person who can not take care of himself/herself; and (5) Proper arrangements for burial. In addition, a compulsory education shall be provided to the minor who are eligible for five-guarantee in accordance with the law. So, it is obvious that five-guarantee system is a system to give a comprehensive guarantee to those eligible persons in all respects.

## Ⅲ. Social Relief Targeted at Particular Groups

Social relief targeted at particular groups refers to the system by which the State grants living relieves or hardship subsidies to particular groups so as to secure their basic living. Those particular groups include the lepers who need medical treatment and relieves and the uprising members or surrenderors from Kuomintang troops, and some returned overseas Chinese who need resettlement and relieves. They are special because they are different from ordinary targets of relief. Therefore, the State grants special relieves for them and the social relief system targeted at particular groups is thus formulated.

Social relief law is composed of the law on social relieves, the law on disaster relieves, and the law on poverty relieves.

Social relieves include relieves for urban residents, for rural residents, and for particular social groups. The subsistence allowances system for urban residents is a system by which the State grants subsistence allowances on the basis of minimum subsistence level to urban poor residents, which is also a new social relief system established for meeting socialist market economy system. The subsistence allowances system for urban residents is targeted at the urban residents who hold the permanent urban residence certificate, including the person whose household income per capita is lower than the minimum subsistence level.

## Section 3　Social Preferential Treatment

Social preferential treatment is a system by which the State, society, and the masses offer aids and cares to the entitled groups such as family members of a revolutionary martyr or of a serviceman who has died on duty or of an illness, disabled revolutionary servicemen, servicemen in active service and their families, demobilized or retired servicemen returning home with illness, and the Red Army veterans, which is an important part of social special care system.

Social preferential treatment system includes the preferential treatment allowance system and economic subsidy system.

### Ⅰ. Preferential Treatment Allowance System

#### (Ⅰ) Granting of Preferential Treatment Allowances

The Chinese troops are mainly composed of young people from rural areas, so how to solve the living difficulties of the family members of rural revolutionary martyrs and rural servicemen due to the lack of labor force, has been an important part of preferential treatment work for a long period. As society and the economy change and develop, the manner of preferential treatment changes from cultivating land, then preferential working days, to preferential treatment allowances. Preferential treatment allowance is a main manner adopted in the current stage.

After the household contract responsibility system with remuneration linked to output was put into force in rural areas, the labor income is closed linked to the number of contributed laborers, so the reduction in the number of family laborers had direct influence on the family's economic income. In view of this particular situation, the Conscription Law promulgated in 1984 provided that, the people's government at township level shall granted the preferential treatment allowances in cash that pooled by all rural villagers by the means of balancing burden to rural compulsory servicemen's families. As to the families of compulsory servicemen living in city or town and having living difficulties, proper cash allowance may be granted by local people's government at the level of county, city, or municipal district. At present, generalized preferential treatment to the families of compulsory servicemen has been carried out in some provinces, municipalities, and autonomous regions.

Moreover, according to relevant provisions of the Regulations on Pensions and Preferential Treatments for Servicemen, in addition to the families of compulsory servicemen who are entitled to preferential treatments, the family members of revolutionary martyrs, disabled servicemen, old demobilized servicemen who are living in rural areas and have living difficulties, and retired servicemen returning home with illness, may also be entitled to preferential treatment allowances when their living level is lower than that of local masses after the receipt of government pensions benefits.

The preferential treatment allowances are sourced from: (1) financial allocation; (2) contributions by employing unit of a serviceman's family or a serviceman's former employing unit immediately before he/she enlists in the armed force; and (3) social pooling. The standard of preferential treatment allowances shall: (1) accord to local economic conditions and living level of the masses; (2) be equal to or slightly higher than the living level of local masses; and (3) be determined on the basis of the feasibility of raising preferential treatment allowances. At present, the scope, standard, and social pooling of preferential treatment allowances for the families of servicemen in active service are determined by the people's government of the province, autonomous region, or municipality directly under the Central Government on the basis of local actual situations.

Preferential treatment allowances are generally granted at the end of a year. The families of servicemen in active service may receive the preferential treatment allowances on the strength of the certificate of preferential treatment from the civil administration assistance division of the township government or the civil administration division of the subdistrict office. For the purpose of achieving better results, some areas have set up preferential treatment allowance foundations on a voluntary basis, by which the civil administration assistant reserves the preferential treatment allowances and then grants the preferential treatment allowances in a lump sum to a compulsory serviceman after he/she retires from active military service.

The period of preferential treatment allowances for the families of a compulsory serviceman shall be determined by the legal service life of such compulsory serviceman, in general three years for army solider and four years for the air force or navy solider. If a compulsory serviceman's service life is extended for military needs, then the military unit at or above the regimental level shall notify in time local government of extending the period of preferential treatments. Where local government does not receive that notice, the granting of preferential treatment allowances shall be discontinued upon the expiration of the compulsory serviceman's legal service life. The families of a compulsory serviceman shall not be entitled to preferential treatment allowances after such compulsory serviceman becomes a volunteer or is promoted as a cadre, because then such person will start to receive the troop wages. Moreover, the families of cadets directly enrolled from local area or of art soldiers and of other military professionals shall not be entitled to preferential treatment allowances.

The measures for raising preferential treatment allowances shall be made by the people's government of the province, autonomous region, or municipality directly under the Central Government according to local actual situations. At present in rural areas, the social pooling based on a township overall plan is mainly adopted in the raising of preferential treatment allowances and the civil affairs department and finance department of the township government are jointly in charge of the raising of preferential treatment allowances, moreover, a further expanded country-level overall plan is adopted on the aforesaid basis in some rural areas. The budget for preferential treatment allowances is made by the civil affairs department of the township government after estimating total amount of the allowances for the current year on the basis of the number of entitled households in the whole town and the per-capita income of the previous year, and then submitted to the township government. The finance department of the township government is in charge of raising preferential treatment allowances, and divides the budget amount proposed by the civil affairs department among all villages on the basis of the total agricultural population (or total number of farmland) of the whole town.

The system of allowances social pooling based on a township overall plan, which has been carried out for more than decade, has played an important role in securing the living of entitled groups such as the families of rural compulsory servicemen, but has also presented some problems in practice. For example, government input is insufficient and the standards of pensions and subsidies are low, so the entitled groups still have a low living level; it is difficult for some key entitled groups such as the family members of revolutionary martyrs, the disabled servicemen and the demobilized servicemen living in hometown to participate in competition in a market economy equally, because they are limited by their own conditions, in particular some of them are aged, so the relief only depended on preferential treatment allowances is insufficient to solve their actual difficulties in living, housing, or medical treatment; in terms of the sources of allowances, because the manner of social pooling based on a township-based overall plan is only restricted to be used in rural areas, thus the bearing of preferential treatment allowances is unbalanced, standards of preferential treatment allowances are not unified, total amount of preferential treatment allowances can not be increased greatly, and the standards of preferential treatment allowances can not be increased simultaneously as the economy develops and the living level of people increases. Therefore, in the process of establishing a mature preferential treatment system that is compatible with socialist market economy system, the pool level of preferential treatment allowances must be enhanced actively, the pool scope of allowances must be expanded, the scope of entitled targets must be expanded and the guarantee functions of preferential treatment allowances must be reformed.

( Ⅱ ) Preferential Treatments in Social Life

According to relevant provisions of the Constitution and the Regulations on Pensions and Preferential Treatments for Servicemen, the entitled groups may, in addition to the material preferential treatments provide by the public, be entitled to other cares and special treatments in other respects of social life.

( 1 ) Families of revolutionary martyrs. They are entitled to preferential treatment allowances in addition to the regular state pensions; if they are not entitled to free medical treatment and are unable to pay the medical expenses, appropriate medical cost relief may be offered by local department of health to them; if a martyr's son, daughter, brother, or sister is volunteered for the army and is qualified, one of them may be preferentially approved during the conscription period; when a martyr's son or daughter applies for the admission to technical secondary school or college entrance examination, the admission standards on literacy and physical conditions shall be softened moderately; after a martyr's son or daughter is enrolled in a public school (primary school, middle school, technical secondary school, vocational school, or junior college), he/she shall be exempted from tuition and fees and be entitled to student subsidies and student loans preferentially; and he/she shall be preferentially enrolled in a kindergarten or nursery.

( 2 ) Families of the servicemen who have died on duty or of an illness. They are entitled to preferential treatment allowances in addition to the regular state pensions; if they are not entitled to free medical treatment and are unable to pay the medical expenses, appropriate medical cost relief may be offered by local department of health to them; and if the serviceman's son, daughter, brother, or sister is volunteered for the army and is qualified, one of them may be preferentially approved during the conscription period.

(3) Disabled servicemen. They are entitled to preferential treatment allowances in addition to the regular and fixed-amount state pensions; when a disabled serviceman applies for the admission to technical secondary school or college, the admission standards on literacy and physical conditions shall be softened moderately; a disabled serviceman shall be entitled to preferential treatments on medical care, living welfare, artificial limbs fitting, and use of public vehicles. For example, a disabled serviceman entitled to disability health care subsidy shall be also entitled to medical treatment contributed by its employing unit; a disabled serviceman who suffers from the disability of Level 2B or more and is entitled to disability pension shall be also entitled to free medical treatment provided by the department of health; a disabled serviceman who suffers from Level 3 disability and is entitled to disability pension shall be entitled to local civil affairs department's reimbursement of necessary medical expenses on his/her recurring wound treatment, and a moderate subsidy may be granted by local civil affairs department for his/her illness if he/she is unable to pay the expenses incurred; if a disabled revolutionary serviceman who is entitled to disability pension for his/her disability caused on duty or in wartime suffers from a recurrence of wound and has his/her wound treated or his/her artificial limb(s) fixed non-locally as approved, the travel, board and lodging expenses and board expense during the hospitalization period thus incurred may be subsidized by the civil affairs department at country, city or municipal district level; if a disabled revolutionary servicemen who is entitled to disability pension suffers from a recurrence of wound and has his/her wound treated or his/her artificial limb(s) fixed non-locally as approved, the travel, board and lodging expenses shall be dealt with by his/her employing unit by referring to work-related injury policy; and when a disabled serviceman takes State-operated train, ship, long-distance bus, or domestic airliner, he/she is entitled on the strength of his/her Certificate of Disabled Revolutionary Serviceman to preferential purchase of tickets at a preferential price.

(4) Demobilized servicemen living in hometown and some retired servicemen returning home with illness. Demobilized servicemen living in hometown (including old retired Red Army soldiers, old West-Road Army soldiers, Red Army stragglers and demobilized soldiers living in hometown) and some retired servicemen returning

home with illness are entitled to the preferential treatment allowances from social pooling in addition to regular and fixed-amount subsidies. Old retired Red Army soldiers and old West-Road Army soldiers living in hometown are entitled to free medical treatments; old retired Red Army soldiers living in hometown are entitled to preferential treatments of commodity grains, and their spouses are entitled to regular and fixed-amount subsidies if their spouses have living difficulties after they die. Demobilized or retired servicemen returning home with illness are not entitled to free medical treatments, but if they are unable to pay for medical expenses incurred by illness, moderate medical cost relief may be offered by local department of health to them.

(5) Compulsory servicemen, military officers on active list, and volunteers, as well as their families. Compulsory servicemen enjoy the free delivery service for their ordinary letters from the troop; if a compulsory serviceman holds a permanent rural residence certificate before the enrollment, then the responsibility field and private plot previously distributed to him/her shall be reserved for him/her during his/her service life; if a compulsory serviceman is an employee of an enterprise or public institution before the enrollment, then the labor insurance benefits for his/her families shall not be discontinued; and if a compulsory serviceman lives in urban area, he/she shall be included when local department arranges house for his/her family. The pubic security organ in the place where the troop is stationed shall approve the settle-down of the families of the military officers on active list or of volunteers who follow the troop as approved; and if such families who follow the troop have regular jobs, local labor administration department and personnel department in the place where the troop is stationed shall offer appropriate jobs for them. The rural military officers who have served in the areas under harsh conditions such as frontier defence area and islands may have their registered rural permanent residence converted to registered urban permanent residence and may be offered appropriate jobs. Where the family member of a military officer on the active list or of a volunteer who does not follow the troop has housing difficulties, the employing unit shall offer working couple housing benefits to the family member; if such family member is unemployed, local housing administration department shall deal with the housing difficulties by overall arrangements. If the family member of a military officer on the active list is not entitled to free medical treatments and is unable to pay for medical expenses, moderate medical cost relief may be offered by local department of health to such person.

In addition, preferential treatments for entitled groups also include reasonable arrangement for the entitled groups' production, in particular appropriate care shall be provided to those who are old, weak, ill or disabled according to their physical conditions and living conditions. In terms of social aids, the targets of social special care may, under equal conditions, be given some priorities to social relieve, economic subsidies, loans, and social helps.

## II. Economic Subsidy

Economic subsidy for the entitled groups is another important way to ensure the living of entitled groups. Economic subsidy in China is granted regularly and at fixed amount, i. e. special funds appropriated by the State will be granted regularly (monthly) at a limited amount to an entitled group as living subsidy according to the qualifications and situations of the entitled group.

### ( I ) Entitled Groups to Economic Subsidies

(1) Retired old Red Army soldiers living in hometown. According to relevant provisions of the Joint Circular on Problems Concerning the Titles and Treatments of Retired Old Red Army Soldiers and Solving Opinions jointly promulgated by the General Political Department of PLA, the Ministry of Civil Affairs, the Ministry of Finance, the Ministry of Commerce, and the Ministry of Health on February 23, 1979, a person may be identified as a retired old Red Army soldier if he/she: ① Enlisted in the armed force and joined the Chinese Workers' and Peasants' Red Army (including the Anti-Japanese Amalgamated Army of the Northeast and guerrilla forces under the leadership of the Chinese Communist Party) before July 6, 1937; ② Has conclusive evidence which can prove his military service; and ③ Has not gone over to the enemy or turned traitor and has been keeping his/her good revolutionary tradition after retirement. A person who is eligible for all of the abovementioned conditions may be identified as retired old Red Army soldier living in hometown upon the completion of relevant formalities.

(2) Red Army stragglers. According to relevant provisions of the Circular on Properly Solving the Living Difficulties of the Red Army Stragglers promulgated by the Ministry of Civil Affairs and the Ministry of Finance on December 8, 1986, a person who officially joined the Chinese Workers' and Peasants' Red Army (including the Anti-Japanese Amalgamated Army of the Northeast) before July 6, 1937, straggled for illness or combat or left the troop as mobilized by the organization for dispersed concealment, and behaved well after leaving the troop may be identified as "Red Army straggler" after he/she is publicly recognized by local masses, reviewed by local township government, and approved by local people's government at county or city level. A Red Army soldier who straggled for

being captured or arrested, has not gone over to the enemy or turned traitor or was forced to hold an ordinary post contrary to his/her convictions after leaving the troop, and has not caused any damages to the revolution may also be treated as "Red Army straggler".

(3) Old West-Road Army soldiers living in hometown. According to relevant provisions of the Circular on Solving the Problems Concerning the Titles and Treatments of Old West-Road Army Soldiers Living in Hometown jointly promulgated by the Ministry of Civil Affairs, the Ministry of Finance, the Ministry of Health, and General Political Department of PLA on February 29, 1984, any West-Road Army straggler who is recognized by local government and is not subject to political or historical problems shall be identified as old West-Road Army soldier.

(4) Demobilized soldiers living in hometown and retired servicemen returning home with illness. According to relevant provisions of the Interpretations of Several Specific Issues Concerning the Implementation of the Regulations on Pensions and Preferential Treatments for Servicemen promulgated by the Ministry of Civil Affairs on April 17, 1989, a person who voluntarily joined the people's army under the leadership of the Chinese Communist Party before the compulsory service system was implemented in a trial manner on October 5, 1954 and holds the certificate of demobilized or retired soldier or was approved to be demobilized to his/her hometown shall be identified as demobilized soldier living in hometown. An unemployed demobilized soldier living in urban area shall be treated as demobilized soldier living in hometown. Retired serviceman returning home with illness refers to any person who joined the Chinese People's Liberation Army after November 1, 1954 when the compulsory service system was implemented in a trial manner and holds the certificate of demobilized or retired soldier and the certificate of returning home with illness issued by the troop.

( Ⅱ ) Standards of Economic Subsidies

Retired old Red Army soldiers living in hometown, old West-Road Army soldiers living in hometown, and Red Army stragglers are all entitled to the regular and fixed-amount economic subsidies.

In 1994, the Ministry of Civil Affairs and the Ministry of Finance issued the circular on adjusting the standards, providing the standards of economic subsidies as: RMB 851 for each retired old Red Army soldier living in hometown each month; RMB 135 for each old West-Road Army soldier living in hometown each month; RMB 55 for each Red Army straggler each month. Retired old Red Army soldiers living in hometown and old West-Road Army soldiers living in hometown are entitled to free medical treatments in addition to the regular and fixed-amount subsidies. If any of them is childless and can not take care of himself/herself, he/she may be supported by Homes for Disabled Veterans as agreed by himself/herself; if he/she is unwilling to be supported by Homes for Disabled Veterans, local township or village shall designate special personnel to take care of him/her and pay appropriate care service fees.

The grain ration, edible oil, and non-staple food of the retired old Red Army soldiers shall be supplied by the State with reference to the standards for local government functionaries.

The demobilized soldier living in hometown who is childless, old, weak, has lost labor capacity, and has living difficulties and the retired serviceman returning home with illness who is unable to participate in production frequently and has living difficulties shall be entitled to regular and fixed-amount subsidies. Some other retired servicemen returning home with illness are also entitled to such treatments.

● Chapter XVI

# Law on Labor Dispute Settlement

Labor disputes are the disputes arising from the labor rights and obligations between the parties to a labor relation. The existing mechanisms for settling labor disputes in China include mediation, arbitration, and litigation.

This Chapter will address the concept and type of labor disputes and the scope and characteristics of labor disputes settlement, and focus on the introduction to the mediation, arbitration, and litigation of labor disputes.

## Section 1   Overview of Labor Dispute Settlement

### I. Concept of Labor Disputes

Labor disputes are the disputes arising from labor issues between the parties to a labor relation. In this sense, all disputes arising from labor issues between a laborer and his/her employer, between two laborers, or between two employers can be called as labor disputes.

Seeing from the labor legislations of various countries around the world, labor disputes mentioned in the labor law generally refer to disputes arising from the exercise of labor rights or the performance of labor obligations between the parties to a labor relation. In narrow sense, labor disputes particularly refer to disputes arising from the application of laws & regulations, the conclusion, performance, modification or termination of the labor contract and other issues directly related to the labor relation between a laborer and his/her employer.

Since the Agrarian Revolution period, China has included the labor dispute settlement into the scope of legislation. After new China was founded, the All China Federation of Trade Unions formulated the Interim Measures for Resolving Employer-employee Relation in November 1949, providing that when the parties to Employer-employee relation in an enterprise fail to reach an agreement on the dispute between them, they shall request the representatives from the enterprise's labor union and trade association to settle the dispute through consultation; if such consultation fails, either party may bring the dispute to the arbitration committee for arbitration.

For the purpose of comprehensively establishing the legal system on labor dispute settlement in China, the Ministry of Labor, upon approval by the Government Administration Council, promulgated the Provisions on Procedures for Settling Labor Disputes in November 1950. The Provisions is applicable to the labor disputes occurred in all stated-operated, public, private, or joint state-private enterprises or enterprises operated by cooperatives. According to the Provisions, labor disputes cover: (1) Matters concerning employees' labor conditions (such as wages, working hours, and welfares); (2) Matters concerning employments, dismissals, rewards and punishments of employees; (3) Matters concerning labor insurances and labor protections; (4) Matters concerning labor disciplines and working rules of the enterprise; (5) Matters concerning collective contracts or labor contracts; and (6) Other matters involved in labor disputes. Procedures for settling labor disputes are as follows: (1) Consultations. In the event that any labor dispute occurs in any enterprise, the parties concerned shall settle the disputes through consultation first. Where such consultation succeeds and an agreement is reached between the parties, an application shall be submitted to local labor administration department for review and filing. The labor administration department, if holds that the agreement violates any labor policy or regulation, may require the parties to amend or annul the agreement. Where such consultation fails, the dispute shall be settled by the trade union at the next higher level and the competent department at the next higher level governing the enterprise concerned through consultations if such enterprise is a stated-operated, public or joint state-private enterprise or an enterprise operated by a cooperative, but if it is a private enterprise, the dispute shall be settled by the assistance of industrial labor union and trade association; (2) Mediation. If the dispute fails to be settled through the aforesaid consultation procedure, an application for mediation shall be submitted to local labor administration department; (3) Arbitration. If such mediation fails, the dispute shall be submitted to an arbitration committee for arbitration; and (4) Litigation. If either party to the labor disputes is dissatisfied with the arbitration award, it shall notify the labor administration department within five days upon the receipt of the arbitration award and file a lawsuit with the people's court for settling the disputes by litigation; otherwise the arbitration award shall have legal force.

On July 31, 1987, the State Council promulgated the Interim Provisions on

Settlement of Labor Disputes in State-operated Enterprises, which systematically provide the competent departments and the procedures for settling labor disputes in State-owned enterprises. The settlement of labor disputes in other enterprises or entities had also been provided in relevant legislations. Such as, the Provisions of the People's Republic of China on Labor Administration of Sino-foreign Equity Joint Ventures issued by the State Council on July 26, 1980, provides that, any labor dispute occurs in a Sino-foreign equity joint venture, if fails to be settled through consultation, may be settled by an application for arbitration submitted by either party to the labor administration department of the province, autonomous region, or municipality where it locates; If either party is dissatisfied with the arbitration award, that party may lodge a lawsuit at the people's court. The Interim Regulations of the People's Republic of China on Private Enterprises promulgated by the State Council on June 25, 1988 also provide that, labor disputes occur in private enterprises shall be settled in accordance with the Interim Provisions on Settlement of Labor Disputes in State-operated Enterprises.

From August 11, 1993, the Regulations of the People's Republic of China on Settlement of Labor Disputes in Enterprises started to prevail and the case number of the labor dispute accepted and filed by the labor dispute arbitration committees was up to 45,000 cases, of which 98% were settled by mediation or arbitration and only 2% were lodged to the people's courts for settlement. [1] As the labor system reform was deepened, some contents of the Interim Provisions no longer met actual needs and new contents needed to be supplemented. There were significant adjustments, amendments and supplements to the Interim Provisions with respect to the scope of labor arbitration and the organizational form of arbitration authority provided in the Regulations of the People's Republic of China on Settlement of Labor Disputes in Enterprises. in which, the objects for arbitration expanded from State-owned enterprises to all enterprises in China and the disputes concerning the resignation or demission or rising from wages, insurance, welfares, trainings and labor protections were also covered in the causes of arbitration. With respect to organizational form of arbitration authority, the Regulations provided that the arbitrator or arbitration tribunal system shall be adopted when a labor dispute arbitration committee settles labor disputes, and the arbitration tribunal shall handle cases legally to ensure a fair, accurate and efficient arbitration

---

[1]   *Interpretations of the Regulations of the People's Republic of China on Settlement of Labor Disputes in Enterprises*, P104, published by the China Peace Publishing House in 1994 in Beijing, by the writing group of the Interpretations of the Regulations of the People's Republic of China on Settlement of Labor Disputes.

procedure. .

## II. Type of Labor Disputes

In the world, labor disputes are classified into two types. One type is the dispute arising from application of labor laws or regulations or conditions specified by a labor contract. Legal issues are involved in this type of disputes, so this type of dispute is referred to as "Legal dispute" in some countries; employees' personal interests are generally involved in this type of dispute, so this dispute is also referred to as "Individual dispute" in some countries; and this type of dispute is over pre-existing rights, so this type of dispute is also referred to as "Right dispute" in some countries. The other type is the dispute arising from the making or modification of labor conditions. In general, majority of laborers are involved in this type of dispute, so this type of dispute is referred to as "Collective dispute" in some countries; this type of dispute is over the interests of a group, so this type of dispute is referred to as "Interest dispute" in some countries; and this type of dispute is intended to determine the labor conditions in the future, so it is also referred to as "Future dispute". The significance of classifying labor disputes is to set different dispute settling organizations and adopt different dispute settling procedures according to classification of labor disputes.

At present in China, labor disputes are classified into individual labor disputes and collective labor disputes. Individual labor disputes refer to the labor disputes in which the number of employees concerned does not reach the quorum of employees for collective labor disputes, no single and common disputed subject exists, and the petition is directly raised by the employee. Collective labor disputes refer to the labor disputes that involve at least three employees who have collective reasons for the disputes. Collective labor disputes refer to the labor disputes that involve at least three employees who have a common subject for the disputes.

In China, the differences between collective labor disputes and disputes over collective labor contract shall be noticed. According to Article 84 of the Labor Law of PRC, it is labor dispute mediation authority that is responsible for settling the disputes concerning the signing of collective labor contracts. When any dispute arises from signing of collective labor contract between the parties to the collective labor contract and fails to be settled by the parties through consultation, the labor dispute mediation authority under the labor administration department of the State shall assist the parties in the reaching of consensus, continuation of collective negotiations and signing of collective labor contract. Article 31 of the Provisions on Collective Contract provides that, the labor dispute mediation authority under the labor administration department of the people's government at county or higher level is the regular authority for accepting and mediating the disputes concerning the signing of collective labor contracts and its main duties and responsibilities are: (1) investigating the disputes; (2) making mediation solutions to the disputes; (3) mediating and settling the disputes; (4) drawing up of the Mediation and Settlement Agreement and monitoring the execution of settlement results; (5) summarizing, filing, and submitting the settlement results to the labor administration department at the next higher level; and (6) reporting and suggesting to government when necessary.

Disputes in regards to the performance of collective contracts shall be settled through any of the following procedures: (1) consultation by the parties concerned; (2) arbitration by the labor dispute arbitration committee. If the parties fail to settle the dispute through consultation, the dispute may be submitted to the labor dispute arbitration committee for arbitration; and (3) litigation at the people's court. If either party is dissatisfied with the arbitration award, such party may, within 15 days upon receipt of the arbitration award, bring a lawsuit to the people's court for settling the dispute through legal proceeding.

## Ⅲ. Scope of Labor Dispute Settlement

The scope of labor disputes differs from country to country. Article 2 of the Regulations of the People's Republic of China on Settlement of Labor Disputes in Enterprises carried out as of August 1, 1993 provide the following scope of labor disputes:

(1) Disputes arising from expulsion, discharge or dismissal of employees by enterprises, or resignation by employees or quitting their jobs of their own volition.

This provision was formulated on the principle of reciprocity between the parties to a labor relation. Both the disputes related to the expulsion, discharge or dismissal of employees made by the enterprise according to the employee's violations of disciplines or enterprise's operation status, and the disputes related to the resignation made by the employee according to the actual status of the enterprise and the individual, shall be accepted by the labor disputes settlement department.

(2) Disputes arising from implementation of relevant State regulations on wages, insurance, welfare, training and labor protection.

This provision was formulated according to the situations that there were a large number of regular employees who have not signed labor contracts with their employers in China then. Those regular employees' labor rights and obligations were mainly reflected in State laws & regulations and other normative documents in respect of wages, insurance, and welfare.

(3) Disputes arising from execution of labor contracts.

This provision is applicable to all kinds of employees who have signed a labor contract with their employers, such as the collectively contractual employees, contractual employees, temporary laborers, contractual migrant workers, etc. "Disputes arising from execution of labor contracts" specifically include the disputes arising from the implementation, modification, rescission or termination of labor contracts.

(4) Other labor disputes, as prescribed by the laws or other regulations, shall be handled according to these Regulations.

In consideration of the current immature labor legislations of China, it's not suitable to include some labor disputes (such as the disputes arising from admission or work allocation) into the coverage of settlement. However, as the legislation speeds up, these labor disputes will be specifically included in the application scope of the Provisions by relevant laws or regulations when necessary and the conditions for including them into the coverage of settlement by labor dispute settlement authority are satisfied.

Article 1 of the Interpretations of the Supreme People's Court on Certain Issues Concerning the Application of Law in Trying Cases Involving Labor Disputes adopted at the 1165th meeting of the Judicial Committee of the Supreme People's Court on March 22, 2001 provides that: Where one of the following disputes arises between a laborer and his/her employing unit and such dispute is a labor dispute as specified in Article 2 of the Labor Law and where a party concerned that is dissatisfied with the arbitration award made by the labor dispute arbitration committee files a lawsuit with a people's court, the people's court shall accept the case: (1) A dispute arising between a laborer and his/her employing unit in the process of performing a labor contract; (2) A dispute arising after the formation of a labor relation between a laborer and his/her employing unit although there is no written labor contract between them; or (3) A dispute arising between a retired laborer and his/her original employing unit that has not participated in the social pooling of social insurance from recovering his/her pension, medical expenses, work-related injury insurance benefits or any other social insurance compensation.

The Interpretations of the Supreme People's Court on Certain Issues Concerning the Application of Law in Trying Cases Involving Labor Disputes (II) issued on August

31, 2006 were directed against the situations that with respect to the illegal collection of labor contract deposits by some employers, the laborers dared not make complaints to a labor supervision department or bring an application for labor arbitration to the labor dispute arbitration department during the term of labor contract and hoped to recover the deposits by arbitration or litigation after the labor relation was severed; and that some employers punished the employees by detaining or discarding the employees' personnel files or refusing to transferring the social insurance relationship of the employee when the employees proposed to dissolve the labor contracts, which made the employments or re-employments of the employees are difficult. The Interpretations (Ⅱ) specifically provide that a people's court shall accept the disputes related to the employees' requests for returning the deposit, security, mortgage or pledge previously collected by the employer after the recession or termination of the labor contract between the employee and the employer. It also makes interpretations on the settlement of the disputes rising out of the procedures for transferring personal records and insurance relationship of the employees, and expands the jurisdiction coverage of labor case to the collateral obligations following the rescission or termination of the labor contract.

## Ⅳ. Characteristics of Labor Dispute Settlement

(Ⅰ) The Parties to A Labor Dispute, the Employer and the Employee, are Specific

"The employer and the employee" has a specific meaning, which refers to the employer and the employee between which a labor relation exists, i. e. the employer is an enterprise by which the employee is employed and the employee is a worker who works for the employer. The enterprise mentioned herein includes the enterprise with the legal person status and the enterprise without the legal person status. In the case of an enterprise with the legal person status, its legal representative shall act as the participant of the arbitration proceeding; in the case of an enterprise without the legal person status (such as a private enterprise, collective enterprise, individual business, or public institution), its principal shall act as the participant of the arbitration proceeding. "Employee" also has specific meaning, which refers to the laborer who has established a labor relation with an enterprise in accordance with nationwide and local laws and regulations, including the administrative staff, professional, worker, and foreign employee of the enterprise.

Article 2. 2 of the Labor Law of PRC provides that "State organs, institutional organizations, and social organizations and laborers who have established a labor contract relation therewith shall be subject to this Law. " Article 1 of the Interpretations of the Supreme People's Court on Certain Issues Concerning the Application of Law in Trying Cases Involving Labor Disputes provides that "The disputes arising between a laborer and his/her employing unit from performance of the labor contract are the labor disputes specified in Article 2 of the Labor Law. Where a party concerned that is dissatisfied with the arbitration award made by the labor dispute arbitration committee files a lawsuit with a people's court, the people's court shall accept the case. " It is worth noting that the natures of the different legal relationships established between a State organ and its employees, between an institutional organization and its employees or between a social organization and its employees shall be distinguished. Article 2 of the Interim Provisions on Settlement of Personnel Disputes issued by the Ministry of Personnel on August 8, 1997 provides that "The disputes arising from implementation of the employment contract or employment between a State organ or an institutional organization and its employee shall be settled by the Fair Personnel Arbitration Department or the Personnel Disputes Arbitration Committee". Therefore, if the employer is a State organ, institutional organization, or social organization that adopts civil servant system or similar system instead of labor contract system, it does not execute market-directed management and has its funds come from financial allocation in whole or in part, then the labor contract between it and its employee shall not be a labor contract and the dispute between them shall be deemed as a personal dispute, other than a labor dispute. Accordingly the authority to whom such dispute shall be acceptable shall be the personnel disputes arbitration committee, not the labor dispute settlement authority.

( Ⅱ ) The Scope of Labor Disputes is Defined and Limited by the Legislations of A Country

As mentioned above, labor disputes in China include the disputes arising from expulsion, discharge or dismissal of employees by enterprises, or resignation by employees or quitting their jobs of their own volition; the disputes arising from implementation of relevant State regulations on wages, insurance, welfare, training and labor protection; the disputes arising from execution of labor contracts, and other labor disputes that, as prescribed by the laws or other regulations, shall be settled according to these Regulations. In case of labor disputes between a laborer and its employer, complaints may be submitted to local labor dispute arbitration committee so long as the disputes are included in the abovementioned labor disputes.

The Ministry of Labor, upon approval by the Legislative Affairs Committee under the NPC Standing Committee, made a provision in the Circular on Several

Issues Concerning Labor Dispute Arbitration on September 1, 1995 as follows: in view of the lack of specific provisions on acceptable scope of labor dispute case in the Labor Law, the acceptable scope of labor dispute case shall be subject to these Regulations. Besides, according to Articles 2, 18, 24 to 32, 97 to 99, and 102, labor disputes shall also include: (1) Labor disputes arising between a State organ, an institutional organization, or a social organization and its employee who has signed a labor contract with it; and (2) Disputes arising from verification of invalid labor contract, execution of labor contract under specified conditions, turnover in staff, staff reduction of the employer, economic compensation and reimbursement. When handling the disputes between a State organ, institutional organization, or social organization and its workers or other persons who have established labor contracts with it, the labor dispute arbitration committee shall, in accordance with the specific characteristics of the disputes, apply the laws and regulations which are currently applicable to the State organ, institutional organization, or social organization.

Furthermore, with regards to the labor disputes arising from an employee's failure in the performance or incomplete performance of the contract on suspension from duty without pay, the employer may dissolve labor contracts, dismiss or discharge its employees according to the Regulations on Transforming the Operation Mechanism of an Enterprise Owned by the Whole People.

Furthermore, the Regulations on Transforming the Operation Mechanism of an Enterprise Owned by the Whole People provide that an enterprise may dissolve labor contracts, dismiss or discharge its employees according to laws, regulations and rules. Therefore, the labor dispute arbitration committee may settle the labor disputes arising from an employee's failure in the performance or incomplete performance of the contract on suspension from duty without pay in accordance with the rules and disciplines that are made by the enterprise and do not violate the national laws or regulations. The labor disputes arising from an employee's failure in the performance or part performance of the contract on suspension from duty without pay shall be accepted by the labor dispute arbitration committee. For example, the labor dispute between a farm or forest farm and its employee shall be accepted by the labor dispute arbitration committee if such farm or forest farm is an enterprise and the disputed content is included in the scope of labor dispute case acceptable to labor dispute arbitration committee. The contract, signed by and between an enterprise that carries out internal contracting responsibility system and its employee, is significantly different from labor contracts and is not deemed as labor contracts in general. However, if such contract includes the rights or obligations that shall be covered in the labor contract, such as wages and welfares, then such contract shall be identified as a labor contract. The dispute arising between the employee and the employer from the enforcement of provisions involving labor rights or obligations as provided in the contract belongs to labor disputes. According to relevant provisions of the Commercial Bank Law of PRC, a commercial bank is an enterprise with the legal person status, so the dispute between a commercial bank and its employee is a labor dispute and shall be accepted by the labor dispute arbitration committee. Article 243 of the Civil Procedural Law provides that "where a lawsuit is filed against a defendant that has no domicile within the territory of the People's Republic of China for contract disputes or disputes involving property rights, the case shall be under the jurisdiction of the people's court at the place where the contract is signed or performed if the contract is signed or performed within the territory of the People's Republic of China", so the dispute between a Chinese laborer and a foreign enterprise shall be accepted by the labor dispute arbitration committee. If there is a labor contract enacted by and between such laborer and such enterprise and performed within the territory of the People's Republic of China.

As provided by the Interpretations of the Supreme People's Court on Certain Issues Concerning the Application of Law in Trying Cases Involving Labor Disputes, the scope of labor dispute case acceptance covers: (1) Disputes arising between a laborer and the employing unit in the process of performance of the labor contract; (2) Disputes arising after the labor relation is formed although no written labor contract is signed by and between the laborer and the employing unit; and (3) Disputes arising between a retired laborer and the original employing unit from recovery of his/her pension, medical expenses, work-related injury benefits or other social insurance benefits. The Provisions on Several Issues Concerning Trial of Cases of Personnel Disputes in Public Institutions by the People's Court issued by the Supreme People's Court on August 27, 2003 provide that, for the purpose of properly hearing the personnel disputes cases between public institution and its employees, from September 5, 2003, the provisions of Labor Law shall be applied for the disputes arising from employees' registration, dismissal by the employing unit, or performance of employment contract between public institution and its employees. If the party concerned is dissatisfied with the personnel dispute arbitration award made by the personnel dispute arbitration agency established by the State in accordance with relevant provisions of the State, it may bring a lawsuit to the people's court within 15 days after receipt of the arbitration award and the people's court shall accept the case according to law. If the party neither files a lawsuit within the prescribed time nor performs the arbitration award, the people's court, upon the other party's petition for the enforcement of the arbitration award, shall conduct the enforcement procedure according to law. In fact, this judicial interpretation expands the scope of subjects to whom the Labor Law is applied. But whether the disputes about retired cadres' claims for changing their service time for revolutionary work are acceptable to the labor dispute arbitration agency or not? The answer is provided in the Official Reply to the Questions Whether a Labor Dispute Arbitration Agency Can Accept a Retired Cadre's Claims for Changing His/Her Length of Service for Revolutionary Work issued by the Ministry of Labor on July 25, 2002. Such Reply explicitly replies that, there are specific provisions in terms of the procedures for determining cadres' service years for revolutionary work before the foundation of PRC and their duties and powers stipulated in the Provisions on Determining the Length of Service for Revolutionary Work Prior to Founding of the People's Republic of China printed and issued by the Organization Department of the CPC Central Committee and the Ministry of Labor and Personnel Affairs in September, 1982. According to which, the disputes about the determination of service years for revolutionary work before the foundation of PRC are not accepted by labor dispute arbitration committee.

When recruiting rural migrant laborers, most of employers do not sign complete labor contracts with them because of their high motilities, low professional skills and weak legal consciousness. Therefore, disputes often arise between them during the term of the labor relation from performance or rescission of labor contracts or from actual labor relations. Many employers, when recruit rural migrant laborers, often ask them to pay deposits or detain their ID cards. So once disputes arise between them or the employers cease the employment of such migrant laborers, it will be very difficult for these migrant laborers to take back their deposits or ID cards from their employers. Generally, most of these migrant laborers engaged in are unskilled jobs with low payments which are often lower than local minimum wage standard. In addition, back pay, wage cuts and the lacks of overtime payment are happened to these migrant laborers frequently. Some employers often violate relevant provisions in recruiting rural laborers or refuse to pay social insurance premiums for laborers for the sake of avoiding social insurance obligations. The lacks of mature and complete labor security & protection measure, sufficient skill training and safety work education for these migrant laborers in some enterprise make the employment injury accidents without timely and legal resolution are easy to happen to those migrant laborers. All these problems are likely to cause labor disputes. Therefore, the Official Reply to Relevant Questions Concerning Application of the Labor Law to Rural Migrant Workers sent by the Ministry of Labor and Social Security to No. 1 Civil Tribunal of the Supreme People's Court on March 20, 2003 provides that the rural migrant workers (including the rural rotated workers) who have established labor relations with the employers shall be governed by the Labor Law. In case employment injury accident occurs, the Measures for Trial Implementation of the Work-related Injury Insurance for Enterprise Employees shall be applied.

The Circular on How to Settle the Labor Disputes Arising between an Employing Unit of a Troop or Armed Police and Its Employees without Military Status issued by the Ministry of Labor and the General Logistics Department provides that labor disputes arising between the employer (including the organ, public institution, or enterprise) of a troop or armed force and its employees without military status shall be accepted by the labor disputes arbitration committee at corresponding level in accordance with the provisions of the Labor Law and the Regulations on Settlement of Labor Disputes in Enterprises, and the superior authority of the employer shall provide assistance.

( Ⅲ ) Different Labor Disputes Shall be Settled through Different Procedures

General labor disputes have four kinds of settlement procedures including consultations, mediation, arbitration, and litigation. According to the provisions of Chinese law, if a labor dispute arises, the parties concerned shall settle the dispute through consultations; where the parties are unwilling to do so or the consultation fails, they may apply to the labor dispute mediation committee of the employer for mediation; where the mediation fails, they may apply to the labor dispute arbitration committee for arbitration. The parties may also directly apply to the labor dispute arbitration committee for arbitration. Where either party is dissatisfied with the arbitration award, such party may lodge a lawsuit at the people's court. If the laborer side involved in the dispute has a number of more than 3 persons and there is a single disputed-subject concerned, then a representative shall be elected by the laborer side to act as the participant of the mediation or arbitration proceedings.

In Germany, compulsory settlement for labor disputes is deemed as being illegal. The parties to a collective agreement will generally conclude a dispute resolution agreement first to ensure there is a dispute resolution procedure can be executed after the failure of negotiation and before the commencement of strike. In practice, the dispute resolution procedure will start upon the application filed by either party or both parties, and mediation agreement will automatically come into force and urge the parties concerned to reach a collective agreement once the negation fails. The mediation agency is consisted of the representatives respectively on behalf of the employers' association cornered and the trade union with their number equal to each other, and a neutral chairman shall be elected. The mediation proposal proposed by the mediation committee shall not be binding upon the parties, unless it is accepted by parties concerned in advance. But the mediation proposal shall have the same force as the collective agreement once it was accepted by the parties. If there is no mediation agreement reached or the mediation fails, either party may submit the dispute to the state committee. According to the Organization of Mediation and Arbitration in Conflicts between the Employer and the Employee, the dispute resolution procedure includes the following two steps: first, a mediator must be chosen by the labor department of the state upon the request of the parties concerned; then if the mediation fails, the parties may reach a consensus to submit the dispute to the state committee. The committee is an executive committee set up by the secretary of the labor department. The neutral chairman is selected, upon approval by both parties, by the secretary of the labor department from the list established by the Ministry of Labor, the organization of the employers, and the organization of the employees. The assistant is selected from the list established by the employers' association and the employees' association. The decisions made by the committee are binding upon the parties only when they are accepted by the parties concerned.

## Section 2   Mediation for Labor Dispute

### Ⅰ. Concept of Mediation for Labor Dispute

Mediation for Labor dispute refers to that the mediation committee of an enterprise, in accordance with labor law and regulations of the State, mediates a labor dispute arising between an enterprise and a laborer by the means of democratic consultations so as to cause the parties to reach an agreement and eliminate the dispute.

Mediation for Labor dispute is neither a judicial mediation made by the people's mediation committee, a mediation agency established by primary juridical organization, nor an administrative mediation made by the competent authority governing the enterprise, and it is also different from the labor dispute arbitration procedure and judicial mediation procedure. Mediation for Labor dispute is a mediation made by a primary-level organization inside of an enterprise and a basic form of labor dispute settlement in China.

Article 7 of the Regulations on Settlement of Labor Disputes in Enterprises provide that an enterprise may establish a labor dispute mediation committee, which shall be responsible for mediating labor disputes arising within the enterprise. The mediation committee shall be composed of the following persons: (1) representative(s) of employees; (2) representative(s) of the enterprise; (3) representative (s) of the enterprise trade union. The representative (s) of employees shall be recommended and selected by the congress of employees (or assembly of employees); the representative(s) of the enterprise shall be appointed by the enterprise director (or manager), and the representative (s) of the enterprise trade union shall be appointed by the enterprise trade union committee. The specific number of the component members of the mediation committee shall be proposed by the congress of employees and determined through consultation with the enterprise director (or manager). The number of enterprise representative(s) shall not exceed one third of total number of the component members of the mediation committee. The list of members of the mediation committee shall be submitted to local federation of trade unions and local arbitration committee for filing. The representative of the enterprise trade union shall act as the director of the arbitration committee. The regular office of the mediation committee shall be set in the enterprise trade union committee. The regular office shall be in charge of the daily work of the mediation committee, which mainly includes the acceptance of applications for mediation from the parties concerned in a labor dispute, the registrations of mediations, files managements, and statistics &. analysis. The mediation committee shall establish necessary working system and, as permitted by the actual conditions, be staffed with full-time staffs. In an enterprise without a trade union, the establishment and composition of the mediation committee shall be decided by the representative(s) of employees and representative(s) of the enterprise through consultation.

## Ⅱ. Principles of Mediation for Labor Dispute

### (Ⅰ) Principle of Free Will

Mediation shall be made by the labor dispute arbitration committee in accordance with laws and on the principle of free will of the parties. Where an agreement is reached by and between the parties upon mediation, a mediation agreement shall be made and be performed by the parties actively; where there is no agreement reached upon the mediation, either party concerned may apply to the labor dispute arbitration committee for arbitration within the specified period.

The principle of free will of the parties embodies in the following aspects: (1) the application for mediation to the mediation committee is chosen and determined by the parties themselves freely and neither party may be required to do so. The mediation by the mediation committee is not a necessary procedure for the labor dispute settlement in China. Therefore, the parties may determine whether applying to the mediation committee for mediation or not on their own free will. But the dispute shall be accepted by the arbitration committee if one party concerned applies to mediation committee for mediation, while the other party applies to the arbitration committee for arbitration; (2) the principle of voluntary consultation shall be followed throughout the whole course of mediation. As a mediation agency, the mediation committee has no power to make decisions, so the settlement of labor disputes depends on the free will of the parties. Whether to reach an agreement upon the mediation or not shall depend on the parties' free will and neither party shall be forced to do so. Neither the mediation agency shall forcibly or grudgingly cause the parties to reach a mediation agreement, nor shall it have power to act on the parties' behalf. Mediation is a process of voluntary consultations, the parties have equal legal status, and neither party shall force the other party to reach any agreement; and (3) the performance of the mediation agreement is on the parties' own free will. The mediation agreement reached through the assistance of the mediation committee is not compulsorily enforceable, so the performance of the mediation agreement is totally on the parties' free will.

( Ⅱ ) Principle of Persuasiveness

The principle of persuasiveness is determined by the nature of the labor dispute mediation committee. The mediation committee is neither an adjudicative organ nor an administrative organ of the State. Therefore, it has no jurisdiction, power to issue an administrative order, or arbitration power. When mediating a labor dispute, the mediation committee mainly persuades the parties to reach a mediation agreement through voluntary consultations in accordance with the laws of the State by democratic discussions and education. To adhere to this principle, the compulsive orders and behaviors shall be abandoned.

## Ⅲ. Acceptance of Mediated Cases and Mediation Procedures

The cases are acceptable to the mediation committee of an enterprise must be: (1) Labor disputes; (2) Labor disputes in the enterprise; (3) Labor disputes that are within the acceptable scope of case as provided by the laws of China; and (4) Labor disputes of which the mediation is chosen by the parties on their own free will.

Generally, the mediation of labor disputes by a mediation committee includes the following several stages: preparation stage, initial stage, execution stage and termination stage. After the occurrence of labor dispute, where the mediation procedure is chosen, the party concerned shall, within 30 days after the date on which it knows or should know its rights have been infringed, submit an application in oral or written form to the mediation committee, together with a Form of Application for Mediating Labor Dispute specifying the cause and course of the dispute and its specific claims. In the case of a labor dispute case involving three or more laborers who have the same reasons for the application, the laborers shall elect one of them as their representative to participate in the mediation proceeding. The mediation committee, after receiving the application for mediation from one party, shall seek opinions from the other party first. If the other party does not accept the mediation, the mediation committee shall make records and notify the applicant in writing within three days; if the other party accepts mediation, the mediation committee shall make a decision on acceptance or refusal within four days.

The mediation of a labor dispute by the labor dispute mediation committee of an enterprise shall be settled within 30 days. Where an agreement is reached by the parties through consultation within the period, the mediation committee shall make a mediation agreement and the parties shall perform the mediation agreement after it is served to the parties; where no agreement is reached within the period or either party or both parties violate ( s ) the agreement reached after the conclusion of the agreement, the mediation shall be deemed to have failed and either party may apply to the labor dispute arbitration committee for arbitration.

Article 17 of the Interpretations of the Supreme People's Court on Certain Issues Concerning the Application of Law in Trying Cases Involving Labor Disputes (Ⅱ) provides that a mediation agreement including contents of labor rights and obligations and reached in the presence of a labor dispute mediation committee shall have the same binding force as a labor contract and may be taken as a basis for a people's court to make a judgment or ruling. This provision is helpful for giving full play to the important role of labor dispute mediation committee in settling labor disputes, strengthening the carrying out of mediation work, improving the mediation efficiency, settling the contradictions of labor relation, and reducing the litigation pressure of the peoples' court. The second part of Article 17 of the Interpretation (Ⅱ) provides that where the parties concerned have reached a mediation agreement merely on labor remuneration in the presence of a labor dispute mediation committee, the employing unit refuses to perform the payment obligations determined in the mediation agreement and thus the laborer directly files a lawsuit with a people's court, the people's court may accept the case as an ordinary civil dispute. This means that, if either party concerned fails to perform the payment obligation under the mediation agreement after the conclusion of the agreement, a lawsuit brought by the other party to the people's court may be directly accepted by the people's court as an ordinary civil dispute. This provision is specially made for quickly settling disputes over labor remuneration. However, if the mediation agreement also includes other labor dispute contents such as confirmation that the labor contract between the parties has been terminated, then under this special circumstance, the labor dispute shall be settled according to the mechanism of "Arbitration first, litigation second". Therefore, it is clear that the nature of mediation agreement shall be determined by its contents covered. If the mediation agreement includes the contents of labor rights and obligations, then it shall be deemed as a quasi-labor contract, accordingly, the dispute concerned shall be settled through the procedures for settling labor disputes. If the mediation agreement merely includes the content of labor remuneration such as wages, then it shall be deemed as a quasi-civil contract, accordingly, the labor dispute concerned shall be settled as ordinary civil dispute without the adoption of arbitration precedence procedure for settling labor disputes.

## Ⅳ. Mediation and Conciliation for Labor Disputes

In abroad, mediation and conciliation are taken as synonyms in general and the difference between them is third party's interference degree. Mediation refers to that the mediator brings the parties to a dispute together, encourages them to make discussions on different opinions and assist and cause them to settle the dispute by themselves. Conciliation refers to that the mediator puts forward proposals for settling the problem to the parties on the basis of mediation. Mediation is a procedure through which the mediator or the mediation committee, as a third party, offers help to the employer and laborer concerned. When a labor dispute arises, the labor administration department of the State generally intervenes in the dispute by mediation or conciliation and the authorities responsible for investigating, mediating, or reconciling the dispute are a department subordinates to the Ministry of Labor or a semi-independent or independent organ separated from the Ministry of Labor, and some relatively independent arbitration agencies, quasi-judicial arbitration committees, and judicial labor courts. Most of those organizations independent to administrative body are often assisted by independent persons or the persons and consultants selected by the organizations of employers and workers.

The legal provisions on the mediation and conciliation for labor disputes in the Republic of Korea are specific. Mediation refers to that the mediation committee of the labor committee, upon the application for mediation by a party concerned, conducts the mediation and draws up the mediation agreement, and advises the laborer and the employer to perform their agreement. The advisement is non-mandatory and the mediation is based on the free will of the labor and the employer. Upon receipt of a party's application, the labor committee will start the mediation of a labor dispute in accordance with Article 53 of the Law on Trade Union and Labor Relation Adjustment. If the labor committee holds that the dispute is not a subject of mediation under the Law on Trade Union and Labor Relation Adjustment, the labor committee shall propose other solutions. In addition, according to 76. 12 of the Law on Trade Union and Labor Relation Adjustment, the mediation process will automatically start when the Minister of Labor decides to conduct an imperative mediation.

The mediation committee set up by the labor committee consists of three members, of whom one is the representative of the employing unit, one is the representative of the laborer, and the third one is neutral. The mediator who is a member of the labor committee shall be nominated by the chairman of the labor committee, the representative of the laborer shall be nominated from the members of the labor committee recommended by the employer, and the representative of the employer shall be nominated from the members of the labor committee recommended by the trade union. The labor committee, upon the requests or approvals of the parties to a labor dispute, may arrange a sole mediator dispatched by the mediation committee to conduct the mediation. The sole mediator shall be selected by both parties from current members of the labor committee or nominated by the chairman of the labor committee. The work of the mediation committee or the sole mediator is to understand the parties' opinions, confirm their claims, draw up the mediation agreement, and interpret the mediation agreement (or letter of undertaking). For the purpose of confirming the parties' claims, the mediation committee or the sole mediator shall regularly convene the meeting of the parties and confirm key points of their claims. The most important part in the mediation proceeding is the drawing up of mediation agreement, which is required to be acceptable to both parties. In this stage, additional reasons attached to the mediation case may be publicly announced by the mediation committee and if necessary with the assistance of the press and other broadcasting media. The reasons to do so are that the mediation agreement will have no binding force when it is not acceptable to either party and that public opinions are helpful for the settlement of the labor dispute. If the mediation process can not be continued due to the refusal of either party to the mediation, the mediation committee or the sole mediator may terminate the mediation and notify both parties. The mediation agreement shall be valid once it was accepted by the parties, regardless of divergence between the parties in understanding of specific meanings or performance measures of such mediation agreement.

Conciliation is used to settle the labor disputes in public welfare undertakings. According to Article 71 of the Law on Trade Union and Labor Relation Adjustment, conciliation shall apply to settle the labor disputes in the undertakings that are closely related to the daily life of the general public or have significant influence on national economy, such as regular-route passenger transportation undertakings, undertakings of supplying water, electricity, gas or petroleum, petroleum refining undertakings, and undertakings of public hygiene and medical services. The undertakings of banking, coinage, and broadcast communication are public undertakings and the suspension or termination of those undertakings will seriously affect the daily life of the general public or significantly obstruct the development of national economy, so the Minister of Labor may decide to carry out an imperative conciliation and both parties to the labor dispute concerned must discontinue their dispute unconditionally so as to avoid the long-term lasting of the dispute that has a significant influence on national economy and national life. An imperative conciliation may be adopted only when: (1) The dispute is over public welfare undertakings, or has a large scale or a special nature, or will harm national economy or cause risks to daily life of the nation; and (2) The Minister of Labor makes a decision on imperative adjustment after asking for the advices of the chairman of the Central Committee of Labor. That the Minster of Labor asks for the advices of the chairman of the Central Committee of Labor does not mean that the advices of the Central Committee of Labor have any legally binding force, but mean that the advices of the Central Committee of Labor that is responsible for the imperative conciliation will be fully respected and considered. After making the decision on imperative adjustment, the Minister of Labor shall promptly announce the decision and give the reasons and simultaneously notify the Central Committee of Labor and the parties concerned. The decision of imperative adjustment shall be announced by newspapers, radio, or other means that are promptly available to the general public. The Central Committee of Labor shall start the mediation after receiving the notice of the Minister of Labor. If the Central Committee of Labor believes that the mediation is impracticable, it shall within 15 days after receiving the notice of the imperative adjustment make a decision on whether it shall submit the dispute for arbitration. The arbitration shall start immediately after the Central Committee of Labor decides to submit the dispute for arbitration or both or either of the parties apply/applies for arbitration. After the decision on imperative conciliation is announced, the parties shall discontinue their dispute or cause any new similar dispute within 30 days after the announcement; otherwise any breach will be punished.

## Section 3  Arbitration for Labor Dispute

### I. Concept of Arbitration

Arbitration refers to a fair third party's judgment on the disputes between the parties. Arbitration for labor dispute refers to the activities that a labor dispute arbitration committee legally judges the dispute between an employer and a laborer on the basis of finding facts, making the right and the wrong clearly, and identifying liabilities. A labor dispute may be submitted for arbitration in the following three circumstances (1) an application for arbitration is directly submitted to the laborer dispute arbitration committee after the occurrence of labor dispute; (2) there is no mediation committee established by the employer after the occurrence of labor dispute; or (3) the mediation for the labor dispute by the mediation committee fails. In the case of any labor dispute meets any of the abovementioned circumstances and is covered by the scope of case acceptable to the arbitration committee as specified by law, either of the parties is entitled to submit an application for arbitration to the arbitration committee. Arbitration for labor disputes in China is mandatory, i. e. arbitration for labor dispute is a necessary procedure for settling labor disputes and a precondition for initiating a lawsuit at the people's court. Unless a lawsuit is brought to the people's court by a party who has objection to the award, the arbitration award for labor dispute shall be performed by the parties consciously and in time. If a party neither brings a lawsuit to the people' court nor performs the arbitration award, the other party is entitled to apply to the people's court for enforcement.

In accordance with Article 12 of the Regulations on Settlement of Labor Disputes in Enterprises, counties, cities and municipal districts shall establish labor dispute arbitration committees. Counties mentioned herein include autonomous counties in minority areas and cities mentioned herein include county-level cities and prefecture-level cities. In minority areas, autonomous prefectures and leagues enjoy the same status as people, government, so autonomous prefectures and leagues may be deemed as prefecture-level cities and shall establish arbitration committees. Whether a province, autonomous region, or a municipality directly under the Central Government establishes a labor dispute arbitration committee is at the province, autonomous region, or municipality's discretion based on their actual situations.

A labor dispute arbitration organization mainly includes the arbitration committee, the regular office of the arbitration committee, and the arbitration tribunal. An arbitration committee is a special organization established as authorized by the State to independently settle labor disputes legally, and has the duties to settle the labor dispute cases under its jurisdiction, employ full-time and part-time arbitrators, and administrate the arbitrators. An arbitration committee is composed of: (1) Representative(s) of the administrative authority governing enterprises; (2) Representative(s) of the trade unions; and (3) Representative(s) of comprehensive economic administration departments designated by the government. The director of an arbitration committee shall be a person in charge of the labor administration department. The labor dispute settlement organ of a labor administration department acts as the regular office of an arbitration committee and is responsible for handling daily affairs of the arbitration committee.

The composition of an arbitration committee complies with the tripartite principle, i. e. the arbitration committee is composed of the labor administration department on behalf of the government, trade union on behalf of the employees, and comprehensive economic administration department on behalf of enterprise operators with the common aim of settling labor disputes together. In the International

Labor Organization, the tripartite principle, also known as "Principle of Three Parties", refers to that the delegation of each member country consists of two representatives of the government, one representative of the laborers, and one representative of the employers, such three parties as the government, the laborers, and the employers may participate in the meetings of classes and join organizations, and the representatives of the laborers and of the employers may have free discussions and make independent speeches. The creation of such principle may date back to 1919 when the International Labor Organization was established. Part VIII of the Treaty of Versailles signed on June 28, 1919 provides the objectives and goals of the International Labor Organization, as well as the composition, organization, and working procedures of a member country's delegation. With respect to a member country's delegation attending the International Labor Conference, Part VIII provides that it consists of four representatives of each member country, of whom two are government representatives, one is an employer representative, and one is the employee representative. Each representative is entitled to vote against or for all matters transacted at the Conference on his/ her own behalf. Later, the tripartite principle has not only been adopted by all conferences and departments of the International Labor Organizations, but also been implemented at all stages of making the international labor standards. On August 13, 2002, the Ministry of Labor and Social Security, All China Federation of Trade Unions, China Enterprise Confederation, and China Enterprise Directors Association promulgated the Guiding Opinions on Setting up and Improving the Tripartite Coordination Mechanism in Labor Relations, pointing out that the tripartite coordination mechanism in labor relations is an important component part of the labor relation adjustment mechanism of China and an effective approach for coordinating the labor relations under the socialism market economy. By now, more than twenty provinces, autonomous regions, and municipalities directly under the Central Government have set up the tripartite coordination mechanism in labor relations. The provinces that have not set up the tripartite coordination mechanism in labor relations shall take practical measures on the basis of its local actual situations to set up provincial tripartite coordination mechanism in labor relations to be participated in by labor security administration departments, trade unions, and enterprise representatives. The areas that have set up the tripartite coordination mechanism in labor relations shall expand the mechanism to cities and counties (or districts) gradually to form a local multilevel tripartite coordination mechanism. The provincial tripartite coordination mechanism is responsible for investigating and researching the collective labor disputes and mass disturbances that have significant influence, putting forwarding opinions and suggestions on settlement or precaution, and guiding the set-up of the tripartite coordination mechanism at the prefectural level.

In general, a comprehensive economic administration department is the economic and trade commission or, in case of no economic and trade commission, the economic commission or commission for planned economy at the same level. On March 18, 1996, the Ministry of Labor, All China Federation of Trade Unions, and the State Economic and Trade Commission promulgated the Circular on Further Improving the Tripartite Mechanism for Labor Dispute Arbitration, requiring the compliance of the tripartite mechanism, those areas at county or higher level that have not established the arbitration committee shall establish the arbitration committee in accordance with the tripartite principle as soon as possible, those arbitration committees with a incomplete composition of three parties shall be re-composed as soon as possible in accordance with the law, and the arbitration committee that is composed of three parties but is not sufficiently staffed shall be sufficiently staffed with professionals as soon as possible. Working system must be established and improved to give full play to the third-party role of the arbitration committee and guarantee the arbitration committee's leadership of, supervision over, and management of the arbitration committees' office, arbitration tribunal, and arbitrators. In the arbitration proceeding of labor dispute cases, the arbitrator from any of the three parties shall be offered the opportunity to act as the presiding arbitrator, attend the arbitration tribunal, and hear cases as a sole arbitrator. In the hearing of major cases, the arbitrators of three parties shall attend. Each arbitrator shall stick to justice and shall not be biased towards either party. To further improve the tripartite principle for labor dispute arbitration, the working principle that the labor administration department, trade union, and comprehensive economic administration department shall coordinate with each other closely must be followed. The labor administration department at any level shall avoid the tendency of exclusive arbitration, actively strengthen coordination with the trade union and comprehensive economic administration department at the same level, and create advantages for the three parties to do a good job in labor dispute arbitration. All trade unions and comprehensive economic administration departments shall specially designate personnel to be responsible for labor dispute arbitration, and closely coordinate with the labor administration department. The three parties shall strengthen the awareness of cooperation, transpositional consideration, and integrity in the respects of arbitration agency set-up, system establishment, case hearing, arbitration fee and propaganda and consulting, give full play to the role of the tripartite principle, and do a good job jointly in labor dispute arbitration.

In addition to arbitral mediation, arbitration award is also a part of the labor dispute settlement procedure proceeded by an arbitration committee. Voting is generally required for the cases over which an arbitration award is made, so the number of arbitrators must be an odd number and the arbitration committee must adopt the majority rule. The arbitrator or arbitration tribunal system is adopted in the labor dispute settlement procedure proceeded by an arbitration committee. The so-called arbitrator or arbitration tribunal hearing system refers to that an arbitration committee selects one arbitrator or three arbitrators from the full-time or part-time arbitrators appointed or engaged under certain conditions to form an arbitration tribunal, and such arbitration tribunal will exercise the powers to process labor disputes on behalf of the arbitration committee. An arbitration committee may engage officials from labor administration department or any other department of the government, trade union staff, experts, scholars, and lawyers as full-time or part-time arbitrators. A part-time arbitrator has the same power as a full-time arbitrator in performing arbitration duties.

The regular office of an arbitration committee has the duties to: (1) Finish daily work for labor dispute cases; (2) Manage arbitrators and form an arbitration tribunal as authorized by the arbitration committee; (3) Manage the documents, files, and seals of the arbitration committee; (4) Provide the services of consultation concerning laws, regulations, or policies on labor dispute settlement; (5) Report work to and ask for instructions from the arbitration committee; and (6) Handle other matters as authorized or assigned by the arbitration committee.

## II. Arbitral Jurisdiction

Arbitral jurisdiction is a legal system determining the competence and jurisdiction of each arbitration agency and clearing the specific arbitration agency to whom the party shall submit an application for arbitration. It is actually an internal work division of each arbitration agency. Primary arbitral jurisdiction is territorial jurisdiction, supplemented by level jurisdiction.

### (I) Territorial Jurisdiction

Territorial jurisdiction refers to the distribution of jurisdiction over labor dispute cases among arbitration committees at the same level. In principle, jurisdiction among arbitration committees at the same level is distributed by the administrative area. Article 17 of the Regulations on Settlement of Labor Disputes in Enterprises provides that, the arbitration committees established in counties, cities and municipal districts shall be responsible for handling labor disputes arising in their respective administrative areas. The scope of jurisdiction of the arbitration committees in cities divided into districts and municipal districts in handling labor disputes shall be prescribed by the people's governments of the provinces and autonomous regions. Article 18 of the Regulations on Settlement of Labor Disputes in Enterprises provides that, if the enterprise and the employee involved in a dispute are not from the same area under the jurisdiction of the arbitration committee, the dispute shall be handled by the arbitration committee located in the place where the employee concerned has wage relations.

( II ) Level Jurisdiction

Level jurisdiction is to determine which arbitration committee shall accept and hear what kinds of labor dispute cases. Main standards and basis for determining level jurisdiction are the nature and degrees of materiality and complexity of the cases. In practices of arbitration for labor dispute, level jurisdiction is also determined by business type and administrative level. Seen from the current actual situations of China, there are two levels of level jurisdiction in general: (1) Jurisdiction of a municipality directly under the Central Government. An arbitration committee of a municipal district in a municipality directly under the Central Government is responsible for handling the labor dispute cases within that district and the arbitration committee of the municipality is responsible for handling the labor disputes within the municipality that have significant influences (such as a collective labor dispute), are complicated (for example, the application of regulations is ambiguous), or involve foreign-funded enterprises or large enterprises; and (2) Jurisdiction of a province or autonomous region. In general, an arbitration committee at provincial level does not directly accept a labor dispute case and is merely responsible for guiding the labor arbitration work of the whole province (or autonomous region). The arbitration committees of municipalities with independent planning status, provincial municipalities and districts only accept those labor disputes within their administrative area that have significant influence, or are complicated or involve foreign-funded enterprises and large enterprises.

Articles 17 and 18 of the Regulations of the People's Republic of China on Settlement of Labor Disputes in Enterprises as well as Article 8 of the Rules for Handling Cases by the Labor Dispute Arbitration Committees specify the jurisdiction over labor dispute cases. With respect to the provision that "if the enterprise and the employee involved in a dispute are not within a same area under the jurisdiction of the arbitration committee, the dispute shall be handled by the arbitration committee at the place where the wage relation of the employee exists", "the place where the wage relation of the employee exists" mentioned is explicitly defined and further interpreted as "the place where the enterprise that pays wages to the employee locates" by the Ministry of Labor in the Interpretations of Several Issues Concerning the Regulations of the People's Republic of China on Settlement of Labor Disputes in Enterprises. If an employing unit's registered address and its principal place of business are not under the jurisdiction of the same arbitration committee, the case concerned shall fall within the jurisdiction of the arbitration committee having jurisdiction over the employing unit's registered address.

## III. Arbitration Participants

Arbitration participants refer to those persons who protect their legal rights and interests by participating in the arbitration proceeding, including legal persons, other enterprises and entities legally established and natural persons. Therefore, the claimant, respondent, the third party, and the joint claimant are arbitration participants. Arbitration agents (including entrusted agents, statutory agents, and appointed agents) are to the persons who protect the lawful rights and interests of the party on the behalf of the party concerned, so they are arbitration participants. For an employee without or with limited capacity for civil conduct, or an employee who is dead, his/her statutory agent may participate in the arbitration on his or her behalf; if the employee has no statutory agent, the arbitration committee may appoint an agent on his/her behalf to participate in the arbitration. In a labor dispute case involving three or more employees who have the same reason for the case, they shall elect a representative to participate in the arbitration.

The party concerned in a labor dispute arbitration enjoys wide rights, which include the right to apply for arbitration, withdraw the arbitration application and change the application for arbitration; the right of defense; the right to accept or object to the arbitration claimant's claims; the right to lodge counterclaims; the right to entrust an agent; the right to apply for challenge; the right to attend the hearing; the right to make a compromise; the right to request or reject a mediation and reach a mediation agreement; the right to present evidences and request investigation, inquest, and verification; the right to request adjournment of the hearing; the right to sue at the people's court if dissatisfied with the unexecuted award; and the right to apply for enforcement of an executed award.

## IV. Prescription for Arbitration

Prescription is a system that a party to a labor dispute will lose the right to claim if it fails to exercise such right within a prescribed period.

A time limit for exercising the right to claim is specified by law. A party concerned shall, within 60 days after the date when it/he/she knows or should know its/his/her right has been infringed, file a written application for arbitration to the arbitration committee. If the period expires, it/he/she will lose the right to claim and the arbitration committee will not accept its/his/her application for arbitration. On August 16, 1994, the Ministry of Labor provided in the Official Reply to the Questions Concerning How to Understand Article 23 of the Regulations of the People's Republic of China on Settlement of Labor Disputes in Enterprises that "The date when it/he/she knows or should know its/his/her right has been infringed" refers to the date when the party concerned knows its right has been infringed as proved by an evidence or as presumed by the operation of law, which is the date when the labor dispute arises. The time limit of claim for labor dispute arbitration is calculated from "the date when it/he/she knows or should know its/his/her right has been infringed". Therefore, "The date when it/he/she knows or should know its/his/her right has been infringed" shall not be calculated from the date when the infringement ends. Article 85 of the Opinions on Several Issues Concerning Implementation of the Labor Law of the People's Republic of China promulgated by the Ministry of Labor on August 11, 1994 provides that "The date when the labor dispute arises" refers to the date when a party knows or should know its/his/her right has been infringed. With respect to the prescription of claim for labor dispute arbitration under special circumstances, Circular on Several Issues Concerning Labor Dispute Arbitration Work issued by the Ministry of Labor in 1995 pointed out that, Article 82 of the Labor Law has provided the prescription of claim for arbitration under normal circumstances and Article 23. 2 of the Regulations on Settlement of Labor Disputes in Enterprises that "If a party applies for arbitration beyond the prescription of arbitration as prescribed by the preceding clause due to force majeure or other proper reasons, the arbitration committee shall accept the application" is a special provision for special circumstances, which shall be implemented.

Article 3 of the Interpretations of the Supreme People's Court on Certain Issues Concerning the Application of Law in Trying Cases Involving Labor Disputes provides that, if a labor dispute arbitration committee makes a written ruling, decision, or notice of refusal in accordance with Article 85 of the Labor Law on the grounds that the prescription of 60 days has expired and the party is dissatisfied with such ruling, decision, or notice and file a lawsuit with the people's court according to law, then the people' court shall accept the case. The claim for action shall be refused by the people's court when the relevant application for arbitration was made after the expiration of the prescription for arbitration without force majeure or any other proper reason.

There are special provisions on the settlement procedure for disputes over employee's injuries and disabilities made in the legislations of China for the purpose of protecting the rights and interests of laborers who has been injured on duty. According to the Measures for Trial Implementation of the Work-related Injury Insurance for Enterprise Employees, an employee may submit an arbitration application or file a lawsuit for the certification of work-related injury only on the preconditions that a work-related injury certification and the evaluation of disability degree have been made by the labor and social security administration department. A labor dispute arbitration committee and people's court shall not make work-related injury certification or evaluation of disability degree by themselves. A dispute rising out of the declaration of work-related injury or the claims for work-related injury insurance benefits between an injured employee or his/her relative, and the employer shall be handled in accordance with the provisions on labor disputes. If the injured employee or his/her relative or the employer is dissatisfied with the work-related injury certification made by the labor and social security administration department and benefits paid by the work-related insurance agency, the administrative reconsideration or administrative litigation procedures shall be proceeded according to relevant laws and regulations. The employee who has objection to the evaluation conclusions of disability degree made by the labor evaluating committee, may apply for review to local labor evaluating committee; and may apply for re-evaluation with the labor evaluating committee at the next higher level if he/she is dissatisfied with the review conclusions. The final conclusions of re-evaluation shall be made by the labor evaluating department at provincial level. Where a dispute arises between an injured employee or his/her relative and the employer over the declaration of work-related injury or the claims for the work-related injury insurance benefits, the party to apply for arbitration shall file the application in writing with the labor dispute arbitration committee within 60 days after the date when the labor dispute arises. If either party to the labor dispute is dissatisfied with the arbitration award, the party may file a lawsuit with the people's court within 15 days after receiving the arbitration award. In the event that the employee who has been injured on duty files a lawsuit with the people's court claiming for compensation, the prescription shall be one year and calculated from the date when his/her disability degree is certified.

The Interpretations of the Supreme People's Court on Certain Issues Concerning the Application of Law in Trying Cases Involving Labor Disputes (Ⅱ) made more specific provisions on the computation of "The date when the labor dispute arises" as follows: Article 1. With regard to a dispute over wage payment arising during the existence of labor relations, where the employing unit is able to prove that the employing unit has notified the laborer in writing of its refusal to pay his/her wage, the delivery date of the written notice shall be the date when the labor dispute arises; where the employing unit is unable to provide such proof, the date when the laborer claims for his/her rights shall be the date when the labor dispute arises; with regard to a dispute arising from the dissolution or termination of labor relation, where the employing unit is unable to prove the date when the laborer receives the written notice on dissolving or terminating the labor relation, the date when the laborer claims for his/her rights shall be the date when the labor dispute arises; with regard to a dispute arising, after the dissolution or the termination of labor relation, from wage payment, economic compensation, welfare benefits and other reasons, where the laborer is able to prove that the employing unit makes commitment to pay him/her on a specific date after the dissolution or the termination of labor relation, the date when the employing unit makes such commitment shall be the date when the labor dispute arises. Where the laborer is unable to make such proof, the date when labor relation dissolves or terminates shall be the date when the labor dispute arises; Article 2. With regard to a dispute arising from delay in wage payment, where the labor relation still exists when the laborer files an application for arbitration and the employing unit asserts such wage not to be paid on the grounds of the laborer's application being filed beyond 60 days, the people's court shall not uphold such assertion, unless the employing unit is able to prove that the laborer has received the written notice of refusal to pay him/her wage; Article 12. Where a party concerned is able to prove that it is unable to file an arbitration application within the time limit for such application due to force majeure or any other objective reason, the people's court concerned shall hold that the time limit for arbitration application is suspended and the time limit for arbitration application shall be consecutively calculated as of the following day when the reason for the suspension is eliminated; Article 13. Where a party concerned is able to prove that it is under one of the following circumstances during the period of arbitration application, the people's court concerned shall hold that the time limit for arbitration application is suspended: (1) The party concerned claims for rights against the opposite party; (2) The party concerned files a request to the relevant departments for right relief; and (3) The opposite party agrees to perform obligations. With regard to a party concerned applying for a suspension of the time limit for arbitration application, the time limit for arbitration application shall be recalculated from the time when the opposite party clearly and definitely refuses to perform obligations, or from the time when the relevant authority makes a decision or clearly and definitely indicates a refusal to accept the case.

## V. Acceptance and Hearing of Arbitration Cases

To apply for arbitration with the arbitration committee, a party concerned shall submit the statement of claims and the counterparts of the statement of claims corresponding to the number of the respondents to the arbitration committee. The statement of claims shall specify the following matters: (1) The employee's name, occupation, address and work unit, the employing unit's name, address as well as the name and title of the employing unit's legal representative; (2) Claims and facts and reasons on which the claims are based; (3) Evidences as well as the name and address of each witness.

After receiving an application for arbitration, the staff of the office of the arbitration committee shall promptly complete the Form of Case Examination and Approval and submit it to the person in charge of the office for approval. The person in charge of the office shall, within seven days after the Form of Case Examination and Approval is completed, make a decision of acceptance or refusal. Where the arbitration committee accepts a labor dispute case, it shall, within seven days after making the abovementioned decision, deliver the Case Acceptance Notice to the plaintiff and the Notice of Responding to Action and the counterpart of the statement of claims to the respondent, and notifying respective rights and obligations of the parties in the arbitration in writing. Where the arbitration committee decides not to accept a labor dispute case, it shall make the Notice of Refusal, and deliver the Notice of Refusal to the claimant within seven days after making such decision.

The respondent shall, within 15 days after receiving the counterpart of the statement of claims, submit the statement of defence and relevant evidences. If the respondent fails to submit the statement of defence within the specified period or refuses to submit the statement of defence, the hearing of the case will not be affected. The respondent shall within the defense period raise an objection if it objects to the jurisdiction of arbitration. If the objection is raised after the specified period expires, the arbitration tribunal may reject the objection. The arbitration tribunal shall notify in writing the parties of the time and address of the hearing four days prior to the commencement of the hearing. The parties shall attend the hearing on time. Where any party, after receiving the written notice of the arbitration tribunal, fails to present in the hearing within 30 minutes after the commencement of scheduled shearing time without any justified reason or leaves the court in the course of hearing without approval, in the event that such party is the claimant, the case shall be deemed as being withdrawn; in the event that such party is the respondent, an arbitration award may be rendered against the respondent by default. The absence of the third party does not affect the case hearing.

A member of the arbitration committee or an arbitrator shall be challenged if: (1) He/she is a party to the labor dispute or a close relative of the party; (2) He/she has an interest in the labor dispute; or (3) He/she has any other relationship with a party to the labor dispute, which may affect the fairness of the arbitration. When handling a labor dispute, the arbitration tribunal shall mediate the case first to cause a voluntary agreement made by and between the two parties on the basis of clear facts. The content of the agreement shall not violate laws or regulations. The Arbitration procedure shall be suspended if: (1) A party to the labor dispute loses capacity for act and its/his/her legal representative or appointed agent has not been determined; (2) The laborer who is a party to the labor dispute is dead and it is necessary for his/her relative to participate in the arbitration; (3) A party to the labor dispute is unable to participate in the arbitration for irresistible reason; (4) This case is based on the verdict of another pending case; or (5) any other circumstance under which the arbitration shall be suspended.

Where an agreement is reached after the mediation, a mediation agreement based on the agreement reached shall be prepared by the arbitration tribunal and shall take effect as of the date when it is served upon the recipient; where no agreement is reached or a party to the labor dispute turns back before the service of the mediation agreement, the arbitration tribunal shall make an award in time. After making an award, the arbitration tribunal shall make a written award and serves it upon both parties. Where the claimant applies for withdrawing the claims before the award is made and the respondent does not raise a counterclaim, the arbitration tribunal may within seven days make a decision on the approval or refusal of withdrawal.

The hearing of a labor dispute by an arbitration tribunal shall be concluded in 60 days after the arbitration tribunal is formed. The hearing for those complicated cases may be extended a proper period with the approval of the arbitration committee, but such period extended shall in no case be longer than 30 days. The arbitration court shall strictly implement the provisions on time limit. Article 30 of the Rules for Handling Cases by the Labor Dispute Arbitration Committees provides the suspension of prescription for arbitration as follows: Asking for instructions and approvals, work-related injury certification, a party's failure to participate in arbitration for proper reason, or any other objective circumstance under which the arbitration is obstructed. The abovementioned circumstances shall be deemed as suspension of prescription for arbitration and reported to the arbitration committee for approval. Suspension of prescription for arbitration shall not be counted in the hearing period for arbitration case.

Labor dispute evidence, a kind of civil evidences, refers to the factual material that is presented or collected according to legal procedures, is verified as true by an arbitration agency or the people's court, and is used for certifying and supporting the claims of the parties to the labor dispute. When a claimant raises claims to the arbitration committee or the respondent raises counterclaims, the required and eligible evidences that support its claims shall be attached. It is the responsibility of the party who raises claims or refutes other party's claims to provide sufficient evidences that can prove the facts on which its claims or rebuttals are based. In case of no evidence or lack of sufficient evidences that can support the party's claims and facts, the adverse consequences so caused shall be assumed by the party that assumes the burden of proof. Originals shall be presented as documentary evidences or physical evidences. The duplicate, copy, or extract of a documentary evidence or the reproduction, photo, or video of a physical evidence may have the same probative force as the original only when it is checked as being consistent with the original, or confirmed by both parties, or certified as a true copy by a verification agency. Reproduction of such computer-stored materials as electronic data interchanges, E-mails, or electronic data that is fixed or shown by visible carriers may have the same probative force as the original only after being notarized or confirmed by both parties. If any evidence presented by a party to the arbitration committee was generated outside the territory of PRC, the evidence shall be notarized by the public notary office of the country in which it was generated and certified by the embassy and consulate of the People's Republic of China in that country or shall be handled according to the certifying procedures as specified by relevant treaty or convention between that country and the People's Republic of China. An evidenced presented by a party generated at the Hong Kong Special Administrative Region, the Macao Special Administrative Region, or Taiwan shall be handled in accordance with relevant agreements or provisions. The parties to participate in arbitration shall present evidences to the arbitration committee within the specified period. In general, the time limit for presenting evidences shall be determined by the arbitration tribunal on the basis of the case. If a party refuses to present evidences within the specified time limit without proper reason, the party shall be deemed as waiving the right to present evidences and shall assume the consequences of inability to present evidences. No cross-examination on the evidences presented by a party beyond the specified time limit shall be arranged by the arbitration tribunal in court hearing, except with the consent of the other party. If the respondent, without any justified reason, refuses to attend the court hearing after being legally notified or leaves the court in the course of court hearing and fails to present evidences, it shall be deemed as having waived the right to present evidences and the arbitration tribunal may make an award on the basis of existing evidences according to law. If the arbitration committee decides, upon the request of a party, or directly decides to carry out a appraisal, the appraisal expenses shall be pre-paid by the applicant or the party who is verified first, and then the arbitration committee will finally determine the liable party (parties) and amount on the basis of the parties' faults. With respect to the appraisal conclusions made by the appraisal institution or appraiser designated by the arbitration committee, no re-appraisal shall be required, unless there are conclusive evidences proving that the appraisal procedures are illegal, the appraisal conclusions are obviously erroneous, or there are other reasons that are able to affect the correctness of the appraisal conclusions.

The following facts need no evidences: (1) Well-known facts; (2) Natural law and theorem; (3) A fact that can be concluded from legal provisions, known facts, or daily life experience or rules; (4) Facts that have been confirmed by a valid award or judgment of the arbitration agency or the people's court; and (5) Facts that have been certified by a valid notarial document. After the labor dispute arises between a labor and an employer, the claimant shall submit the evidences proving the existence of the labor relation with the respondent, such as the labor contract and employee's card. In Beijing, if the claimant is a migrant worker working in Beijing, he/she shall present his/her ID card, temporary residential permit, and employment permit in addition to abovementioned evidences. If the claimant is an employee, he/she shall submit the certificate of the place of the respondent's industrial and commercial registration. If a labor dispute arises from the employer's decisions on discharge, dismissal, expelling, dissolution of the labor contract, reduction of labor remuneration, or computation of the employee's length of service, the employer shall assume the burden of proof.

In the hearing of labor dispute case, the arbitration tribunal shall adopt the majority rule. Dissenting opinions must be faithfully recorded in writing. After making an award, the arbitration tribunal shall make the written award and serve it upon both parties to the labor dispute. In the written award, the following shall be specified: (1) Name, gender, age, nationality, occupation, employer, and domicile, or the name, address, as well as the name and title of the legal representative (or person in charge) of the claimant and the respondent; (2) Reasons for the claims, and disputed facts and claims; (3) Facts recognized by the award, reasons, and the applied laws and regulations; (4) verdicts and burden of expenses; and (5) The time limit for filing a lawsuit with the people's court by the dissatisfying party. The written arbitral mediation (mediation agreement) may be made in the form of the written arbitration award. The written arbitration award (or written arbitral mediation or mediation agreement) shall be signed by the arbitrators and affixed with the official seal of the arbitration committee, and served upon both parties to the labor dispute. Where the award is made by the arbitration tribunal in court, the written arbitration award shall be delivered within seven days after the award is made; where the award is made on a scheduled date, the written arbitration award shall be delivered on the day on which the award is made.

In any of the following circumstances, the labor dispute arbitration committee may make upon preliminary trial a partial arbitration award requiring the employer to pay wages or medical expenses: (1) The employer has been in arrears of payment of wages, has deducted wages as penalties, or has suspended payment of wages without any justified reasons for more than three months, causing the employee's normal life is unable to be maintained; (2) The employee is injured on duty and the employer refuses to pay urgently needed medical expenses; or (3) The employee falls ill and the medical period has not expired, but the employer refuses to pay the urgently needed medical expenses. Where the employer is dissatisfied with the partial arbitration award made by the arbitration committee for abovementioned reasons, it may apply to the arbitration committee for reconsideration in accordance with Article 99 of the Civil Procedural Law once. The arbitration committee shall make a decision within seven days upon receipt of the application for reconsideration. Where the arbitration committee upholds the original partial award, the partial award shall have legal force. If the employer refuses to perform the partial award, the employee may apply to the people's court for enforcement.

Service of the arbitration documents is an important work of the labor dispute arbitration committee in the labor dispute arbitration proceedings. A receipt shall be required for every arbitration document that is served and it shall bear the date of receipt noted by the signature or seal of the person on whom the document was served. The date of receipt noted by the person on whom the document was served shall be considered as the date of service. The arbitration documents shall be sent or delivered directly to the person on whom they are to be served. Where such person is absent, the arbitration documents may be receipted by an adult member of his/her family living with him/ her; where the person on whom the documents are to be served has designated a person to receive such documents on his behalf and has informed the arbitration committee of it, the documents may be receipted by the person designated. Where the person on whom the documents are to be served is an enterprise or entity and no person has been designated by it for the receipt of the arbitration documents, the arbitration documents may be receipted by its principal. If the person on whom the arbitration documents are to be served refuses to accept the documents, the person serving the documents shall invite the representatives of relevant organization or other persons to appear on the scene, explain the situation to them, and record on the receipt the refusal and the date of it. After the person serving the documents and the witnesses have affixed their signatures or seals to the receipt, the documents shall be left at the place where the person on whom they are to be served lives and the service shall be deemed completed. Where direct service proves to be difficult, service of arbitration documents may be entrusted to the arbitration committee in the place where the party concerned locates, or done by mail. Where the documents are served by mail, the date stated on the receipt for postal delivery shall be deemed the date of service of the documents. If the whereabouts of the person on whom the documents are to be served is unknown, or if the arbitration documents can not be served by any other means specified by the Rules for Handling Cases by the Labor Dispute Arbitration Committees, the arbitration documents may be served by public announcement. 30 days after the public announcement is made, the documents shall be deemed to have been served. The reasons for service by public announcement and the process gone through shall be recorded in the case files.

## Ⅶ. Effect of Arbitration Award

Arbitration award is a decision that is made by the arbitration tribunal on a labor dispute for settling the dispute and is binding upon the parties to the labor dispute. If either party is dissatisfied with the arbitration award, it may within 15 days after receiving the arbitration award file a lawsuit with the people's court; where it fails to file a lawsuit with the people's court within the prescribed period, the arbitration award shall come into force. The parties shall perform the valid written arbitral mediation or written arbitration award during the specified period. If either party fails to perform the valid written arbitral mediation or written arbitration award during the specified period, the other party may apply to the people's court for enforcement.

Interpretations of the Supreme People's Court on Certain Issues Concerning the Application of Law in Trying Cases Involving Labor Disputes have some more specific provisions on the effect of arbitration award and they are as follows: Article 17. Where a party concerned is dissatisfied with part of the matters in an arbitration award made by a labor dispute arbitration committee, and thus the party concerned files a lawsuit with the people's court, the arbitration award on the labor dispute shall not have any legal effect; Article 18. Where, after a labor dispute arbitration committee has made an arbitration award on a labor dispute involving more than one laborers, some of the laborers are dissatisfied with the arbitration award and thus file lawsuits with the people's court, the arbitration award shall not have any legal effect on the laborers who file lawsuits; for the laborers who do not file lawsuit, the arbitration award shall have legal effect and the people's court shall accept the enforcement application filed by such laborers; Article 20. Where an employing unit has erred in its decision on dismissing, discharging, removing the laborer or in its termination of labor contract for any other reason, the people's court may make a ruling for cancellation thereof in accordance with the law. With regard to cases involving the recovery of labor remuneration, pension, medical expenses, work-related injury insurance benefits, economic compensation, training costs and other relevant expenses, where the amount is not paid properly, the people's court may make a change thereof; Article 21. When a party concerned applies to the people's court for enforcement of the written arbitration award and the mediation document of legal effects made by a labor dispute arbitration institution, and the respondent provides evidence to prove that the written award and the written arbitral mediation involves one of the following circumstances, which is verified to be true upon examination, the people's court may make a ruling of refusal to carry out the enforcement in accordance with the provisions of Article 217 of the Civil Procedural Law: (1) The arbitrated matters are not within the scope of labor dispute arbitration, or the labor dispute arbitration agency has no jurisdiction over the arbitration; (2) There is error in application of law; (3) Any arbitrator engages in the acts of practicing favoritism, committing irregularities, or perverting the law when arbitrating the case; or (4) The enforcement of the arbitration award on the labor dispute is determined by the people's court to violate social or public interests.

In the ruling of refusal to carry out the enforcement, the people's court shall state that either party concerned may within 30 days immediately following the date of receipt of the written arbitration award file a lawsuit with the people's court for the labor dispute matters.

## Section 4   Labor Dispute Litigation

### I. Concept of Jurisdiction over Labor Dispute Litigation

Labor dispute litigation refers to the activities that a party to a labor dispute is dissatisfied with the award made by the labor dispute arbitration committee, files a lawsuit with the people's court within the specified period and the people's court carries out court hearing of the labor dispute case after legally accepting the case. In addition, labor dispute litigation also includes the activity that a party to the labor dispute refuses to perform the valid written arbitration award or written arbitral mediation made by the arbitration committee and the other party applies to the people's court for enforcement.

The system of labor dispute litigation has fundamentally brought labor dispute settlement into legal system and ensures thorough settlements of labor disputes by the mandatory feature of the law. Moreover, this system has promoted the preliminary formation of the mechanism of judicial supervision on labor dispute arbitration committee, which is beneficial for improving the quality of arbitration. Besides, this system has protected the parties' litigation rights and provided the party that is dissatisfied with the arbitration award with the right to seek judicial relieves.

Labor dispute litigation is final procedures for settling labor disputes. The judicial proceedings as provided in the Civil Procedural Law of the People's Republic of China shall apply to the trial of a labor dispute by the people's court. According to relevant provisions of the Civil Procedural Law, a labor dispute case is generally under the jurisdiction of the people's court in the place where the labor dispute arbitration committee is located in consideration of the special features and requirements of labor dispute lawsuit, such as the participants of labor dispute lawsuit include legal person and natural person, and a labor dispute must be settled in time. Concretely speaking, the basic people's court in the place where the labor dispute arbitration committee is located generally has the jurisdiction as court of first instance over the labor dispute case that is simple and without significant influence. If a labor dispute case is complicated and has a significant influence, and it is difficult for basic people's court to hear it, the intermediate people's court has the jurisdiction as court of first instance over it.

The Interpretations of the Supreme People's Court on Certain Issues Concerning the Application of Law in Trying Cases Involving Labor Disputes provide that, where a party concerned is dissatisfied with a written ruling, decision or notice of non-acceptance that is made by a labor dispute arbitration committee on the grounds that the subject of the arbitration application is unqualified and thus the party concerned files a lawsuit with the people's court in accordance with the law, the people's court shall make a decision of refusal to accept the case or reject the lawsuit where the subject is truly unqualified upon examination and investigation. An additional claim made by the party after the acceptance of the labor dispute case by the people's court that is related and inseparable to the labor dispute case may be tried in combination; in case of such additional claim is an independent labor dispute, the party shall be informed of applying to the labor dispute arbitration committee for arbitration first. If the party concerned has objection to the matter arbitrated by the labor dispute arbitration committee and bring a lawsuit to the people's court, the people's court may make a ruling of refusal when such matter is not within the scope of case acceptance of the people's court.

A labor dispute case shall be under the jurisdiction of the basic people's court in the place where the employer locates or the labor contract is performed. Where the place where the labor contract is performed is not clear, the labor dispute case shall be under the jurisdiction of the basic people's court in the place where the employer locates. Where the parties bring the lawsuit on the same arbitration award to different people's courts that have jurisdiction over the case, the people's court that accepts the case later shall transfer the case to the people's court that accepts the case earlier. According to the latest provisions of the Interpretations of the Supreme People's Court on Certain Issues Concerning the Application of Law in Trying Cases Involving Labor Disputes (II), where both parties to a labor dispute are dissatisfied with the same arbitration award made by the labor dispute arbitration committee and respectively bring lawsuits to the same people's court, the people's court shall accept and try in combination, and either party shall be the plaintiff in its own claim and the defendant in the counterclaim raised by the other party against it.

Where an employing unit is merged with any other entity, the new entity shall be the party concerned to the labor dispute arising before the merger; where the employing unit is divided into several entities, the entity by which the laborer is actually employed shall be the party concerned to the labor dispute arising before the division; if it is not clear that which entity shall bear the labor rights and obligations with the employee after the division of the original employer, all the new entities emerging from the division shall be the party concerned to the labor dispute arising before the division; where an employing unit recruits a laborer who has not terminated the labor contract with his/her former employer, the current employing unit may be listed as a third party in the court hearing of the labor dispute case between the laborer and his/her former employer; the laborer may be listed as a third party in the hearing of infringement action raised by the his/her former employer only against his/her new employer; the laborer and his/her new employer shall be list as joint defendants in the hearing of the contributory infringement action raised by the former employer against the laborer and his/her employer. If the laborer has labor dispute with any party to or both parties to a contractual operation relation established by his/her employer and other entity with equal status during the terms of such contractual operation relation, and brings a lawsuit to the people's court according to law, both the parties to the contractual operation relation shall be list as the party to the dispute concerned.

Where a party concerned is dissatisfied with a written ruling, decision or notice of refusal that is made by a labor dispute arbitration committee on the grounds that the applied matter is not labor dispute and files a lawsuit with the people's court in accordance with the law, the people's court shall, in the light of the following situations, dispose of it accordingly: (1) If it is a labor dispute case, the people's court shall accept the case; or (2) If it is not a labor dispute case, but it is any other case over which the people' court has the jurisdiction, the people's court shall accept the case in accordance with the law.

Article 3 of the Interpretations of the Supreme People's Court on Certain Issues Concerning the Application of Law in Trying Cases Involving Labor Disputes (II) provides that, a rural migrant laborer may directly file a lawsuit with the people's court by taking the IOU issued by the employing unit as an evidence, and the people's court shall deem it as a dispute over arrears of labor remuneration and accept it as an ordinary civil dispute. This provision, to some extent, has protected laborers' litigious right to recover the wage receivable that he/she may lose after the expiration of the 60-day period for arbitration as provided by the Labor Law. In the hearing practice of wage arrear cases, we find that some employers often take advantage of this 60-day time limit for applying arbitration to achieve their aim of eliminating the creditor's right. So the Supreme People's Court make a further provision in the Opinions on Providing Judicial Safeguard by the People's Court for Constructing the New Socialist Countryside as follows: with regard to the dispute concerning the arrears of wages or labor remuneration payable to a rural migrant laborer and the labor dispute concerning property payment to a rural migrant laborer, the people's court shall timely make a ruling for advance execution when such disputes meet the legal conditions of advance execution. Such provision has more obvious effect of protecting the wages of rural migrant laborers.

## II. Labor Court and Labor Tribunal

In 1952, German labor court was separated from ordinary court and became an independent special court in German court system. Labor court has three levels: basic labor court, state labor court, and federal labor court, of which, basic labor court is the court of first instance, state labor court is the court of appeal, and federal labor court is the court of final appeal. In Germany, there are 123 basic labor courts and 840 professional judges with average three professional judges for each basic labor court. Germany has 16 states in total and has established 19 state labor courts, of which three state labor courts are in Nordrhein-Westfalen and two are in Bavaria. 200 professional judges are employed by these 19 state labor courts with average 10 professional judges for each state labor court. The federal labor court has set up 10 tribunals, of which each is staffed with three professional judges for case trial. Nearly 4000 employees will come before a judge in a basic labor court, and 16500 employees will come before a judge in a state labor court for the purpose of settling their labor disputes. [1]

According to the provisions of the Labor Court Law, a labor court shall be responsible for settling the following three kinds of labor disputes: (1) Disputes between a single employer and the employee under private law, including the disputes involving labor relations, disputes about the existence of labor relation,

---

[1] In 1995, the basic labor courts had tried 631,000 labor dispute cases in total and each judge had tried 752 labor dispute cases averagely. Of those cases, 42% were labor dispute cases involving protection against unfair dismissal. Taking those labor disputes for example, 23% were concluded within one month, 39% lasted for one to three months, 19.5% lasted for three to six months, and 17.5% lasted for six to 12 months or more. In 1995, the 19 state labor courts had tried 28,000 labor dispute cases in total and each judge had tried 139 labor dispute cases averagely. Data source: Cooperative Collected Works of Labor and Social Laws in China and Germany (1996 – 1999) published by German Technical Cooperation and the Ministry of Labor and Social Security of the People's Republic of China, P202.

disputes over termination of labor relations and relevant legal consequences, disputes arising form illegal acts related to labor relations, and disputes involving documents or files related to labor relations; (2) Disputes over collective contracts, including the disputes over the contents of collective contracts or the existence of collective contracts between both parties to a collective contract, and disputes arising between both parties to a collective contract and a third party from collective forbidden acts such as labor management struggles; and (3) Disputes arising from the Law on Articles of Association, mainly including the disputes arising between the employer and the enterprise commission form the execution or performance of enterprise agreements.

Labor courts in Germany adopt the system of three instances. A basic labor court is responsible for the first instance. A labor dispute which is covered by the scope of case acceptable to the labor court and complies with the provisions of the Labor Court Law on filing of a lawsuit shall be accepted by the basic labor court, regardless of its disputed subject's size and scale. The second instance is the instance of appeal. If any party concerned is dissatisfied with the judgment made by a basic labor court, it may lodge an appeal to a state labor court. If any property content is involved in the dispute, a party concerned may lodge an appeal to a state labor court only if the judgment made by the court of first instance states that an appeal is allowed or the value of the disputed subject is over 800 Deutsche Marks. If the case has a great significance in principle or meets other conditions specified by the Labor Court Law, the court of first instance shall allow a party concerned to lodge an appeal. The third instance is retrial and shall be carried out by the federal labor court. According to relevant legal provisions, the court of second instance must state in its judgment that whether retrial is allowed. If the dispute case has a great significance in principle, the court of second instance must allow a party concerned to apply for retrial. Even when the court of second instance has stated that the retrial is not allowed, the party concerned may appeal to the federal labor court for the decision on the inadmissibility of retrial made by the court of second instance. The federal labor court will not investigate facts, but just review the application of law. Therefore, the significance of retrial is to keep the uniformity of judgments and application of laws of the whole labor court system.

"Urteil" procedures and "Beschluss" procedures are two different judicial procedures adopted by a labor tribunal in trying different labor disputes. "Urteil" procedures are applicable to general labor disputes, such as the dispute arising between a single employee and the employer over the labor relation. "Beschluss" procedures are applicable to collective labor disputes, most of which are disputes concerning the Law on Articles of Association in practices, i. e. the disputes between an employer and workers council. In "Urteil" procedures, the disputed facts and claims shall be raised by the party concerned, and the court tries the dispute on the basis of the parties' statements; while in "Beschluss" procedures, the judicial proceedings are mainly determined by the court. In "Urteil" procedures, both parties concerned shall assume the burden of proof; while in "Beschluss" procedures, investigation for obtaining evidences is carried out by the judge. That is because that some of collective labor disputes involve the interests of all employees of an enterprise, the adoption of "Urteil" procedures will harm the interests of the majority, while the guidance and participating by the court in the whole juridical proceedings will settle the collective labor dispute easily and properly.

Judicial procedures of a labor court follow the following principles: (1) No trial without complaint. The court shall accept the case and carry out the trial only when a lawsuit was brought to the court by the party concerned who thinks that its rights have been infringed. (2) Mediation. Mediation procedure is a required procedure for settling labor disputes by a labor court. Many cases were concluded by mediation in the judicial practices. According to the statistics, 40% of labor dispute cases were concluded by mediation in some basic labor courts. (3) Full debate. A labor court is required to fully listen to the parties' statements and understand the facts before making a judgment. (4) Opened court session. Trail in court. In the trail with the presence of the parties, the judge may ask questions in court and parties shall answer the questions in court, which is helpful to the clarifying of the case details and the raising and change of the parties' claims.

● Chapter ⅩⅦ

# Legal Liabilities

Chapter XII of the Labor Law has provided the legal consequences for the violations of the labor law, and the legal liabilities for violations of labor or social security laws include administrative liabilities, civil liabilities, and criminal liabilities. The legal liabilities may be pursued only by labor administration department, public security department, judicial department and any other relevant department. Any other organization without legal authorization has no power to do so.

## Ⅰ. Concept of Legal Liabilities

Legal liabilities for violations of labor or social security laws refer to the legal consequences that shall be assumed by those persons who violate labor or social security laws or regulations. Those persons include the employer, laborer, labor administration department, or any other relevant department and their staff.

The relevant provisions on liabilities for labor law are mainly stipulated in labor and social security legislations. Liabilities for labor law are based on the existences of violations and lead to inevitable consequences of legal sanctions. Chapter XII of the Labor Law makes overall and systematical provisions on the legal consequences for violations of labor laws, for example, there are provisions on sanction measures such as warning, fine, and the payment for compensation.

Legal liabilities are intended to cause law violators to assume the legal consequences which are unfavorable to them through compulsory forces so as to reflect the protections of public interests, social security and individual interests by the State. Legal liabilities may be imposed by special State departments on those law violators within the scope of authorization as provided by law, and those special State departments are the authorities that are entitled to exercise the administrative power or judicial power of the State. No other social organization, institution or individual is entitled to exercise such power. For example, according to the labor law, liabilities for violations of labor law may be pursued only by labor administration department, public security department, judicial department and other relevant departments, and any other organization without legal authorization has no power to do so.

## II. Types of Legal Liabilities

Legal liabilities for violations of labor or social security laws are classified into administrative liability, civil liability, and criminal liability.

### ( I ) Administrative Liability

Administrative liability is an administrative sanction imposed by an administrative department on the person who violates labor or social security laws and fails to perform the duties provided by the labor law. Administrative liability may be classified into administrative punishment and administrative disciplinary sanction.

Administrative punishment for violations of labor or social security laws is an administrative sanction legally imposed on the employer or its principal, or laborer for violations of labor laws or regulations by the State administrative departments including labor security administration department and public security department. According to provisions of Labor Law, those persons against whom the administrative punishments are taken for violations of labor laws include the employing unit, its responsible person, and laborer.

### 1. Forms of Administrative Punishments

Administrative punishments provided by Chapter XII of the Labor Law mainly include warning, fine, suspension of license, administrative suspension of company activity, and administrative detention.

Warning refers to a punishment that labor security administration department warns those citizens, legal persons, or other organizations for their violations of labor or social security laws or regulations to cause them become aware of their violations and actively make rectification. Warning is not a simple punishment, but a punishment that is intended to rectify the violation and prevent repeated violation by affecting the violator's reputation. Warning is intended to prevent violators' continued or repeated violations by the means of reputation effects, other than the interferences in their personal freedom, property rights or capacities for action. Warning is the lightest punishment and mainly applies to those slight violations and the violations by which no actual damage has been caused. Warning is applicable to individuals, legal persons, and other organizations, and may be imposed independently or together with other punishment.

Fine refers to the punishment that labor security administration department legally forces the person (including legal person and other organization) who violates labor or social security laws or regulations to pay certain amount of money within a specified period. Fine is a kind of property punishment intended to prevent the violators' further violations by the means of causing economic loss to them.

In addition to warning and fine, there are other administrative punishments including forfeitures of illegal earnings or illegal belongs, administrative suspension of company activity, suspension or revocation of business license stipulated in local laws and regulations. For example, Article 29 of the Labor Supervision Regulations of Shanxi Province provides that, whoever establishes an employment agency or vocational training agency without approval or issues a training certificate or job qualification certificate in violation of relevant provisions shall be confiscated its illegal gains by the labor administration department.

**2. Contents of Administrative Punishments**

According to relevant provisions of the labor law, an administrative punishment shall be imposed:

(1) Where an employer violates the legal provisions on working hours, rest or vocation. Article 90 of the Labor Law provides that where an employer extends laborers' working hours in violation of this Law, the labor administration department shall give it a warning and order it to make rectification, and may levy a fine. While Measures on Administrative Punishments for Violation of the Labor Law of the People's Republic of China make a further and more specific provision on this legal liability as defined by the Labor Law, that is, where an employer, without consultations with the trade union or laborers, forces laborers to extend their working hours, it may be warned, or ordered to make rectification, and may be levied a fine of not more than RMB 100 for each extended working hour for each laborer; where an employer extends laborers' working hours by over three hours per day or 36 hours per month, it may be warned or be ordered to make rectification, and may be levied a fine of not more than RMB 100 for each extended working hour for each laborer.

(2) Where an employer violates the provisions of the Labor Law in respect of the protection of female employees or underage workers. Article 94 of the Labor Law provides that where an employer violates the provisions hereof by recruiting a juvenile who is younger than 16, the labor administration department may order it to make rectification and levy a fine upon it; where the circumstances are serious, the department of industrial and commercial administration may suspend its business license. Article 95 of the Labor Law provides that where an employer infringes upon the lawful rights and interests of a female employee or an underage worker in violation of the provisions of this Law on the protection of female employees or underage workers, the labor administration department shall order

the employer to make rectification and levy a fine upon it; where the employer has caused damages to a female employee or an underage worker, it shall bear the liability for compensation.

(3) Where an employer infringes laborers' personal rights. Article 96 of the Labor Law provides that where an employer forces a laborer to work by violence, threat or illegal restriction of personal freedom or humiliates, imposes physical punishment on, beats, illegally searches or detains a laborer, the public security organ shall detain the responsible persons for less than 15 days, levy a fine or give a warning if a crime is not constituted.

(4) Where an employer unreasonably obstructs the labor administration department, relevant department or their staffs from exercising the power of supervision and inspection or takes revenge against informants. According to Article 101 of Labor Law, labor administration department or relevant department may levy a fine on the aforesaid employer and its responsible person.

(5) Where an employer detains laborers' ID card or other certificates and harms the lawful rights and interests of laborers. Article 84 of the Labor Contract Law provides that, where an employer detains a laborer's ID card or other certificates, the labor administration department may order it to return the same to the laborer within a specified period and punish it in accordance with the provisions of relevant laws; where an employer collects money or things of value from a laborer in the name of guaranty or in other names, the labor administration department may order it to return the same to the laborer within a specified period and levy on it a fine of not less than RMB 500 but not more than RMB 2,000 for each person from whom it has collected money or things of value; where damages are caused to the laborer, it shall be liable for compensation; where an employer detains a laborer's personal file or other articles when the laborer has his/her labor contract revoked or terminated in accordance with law, it shall be penalized in accordance with relevant provisions.

According to the laws and regulations on social insurance, administrative punishments shall be imposed according to the following provisions:

(1) Where any entity that is obligated to make contributions to social insurance premiums, in violation of relevant provisions, fails to go through the formalities of social insurance registration, alteration registration or cancellation registration, or fails to declare the amount of its payable contributions to social insurance premiums, a fine of more than RMB 1,000 and not more than RMB 5,000 may be levied on its principal and other directly responsible persons in case the circumstance is serious; and under the particularly serious circumstance, a

fine of more than RMB 5,000 and not more than RMB 10,000 may be levied on its principal and other directly responsible persons.

(2) Where any entity that is obligated to make contributions to social insurance premiums, in violation of relevant laws, regulations or rules in respect of finance, accounting and statistics, forges, fabricates, alters or intentionally destroys relevant accounting books or materials or fails to establish accounting books, which causes the base of social insurance premiums can not be determined, administrative punishments may be imposed on it in accordance with relevant laws and regulations; and a fine of more than RMB 5,000 and not more than RMB 20,000 may be levied on its principal and other directly responsible persons in the event that it fails to pay its contributions hereof upon a call made by labor security administration department according to relevant laws.

(3) Where any entity or individual misappropriates social insurance funds for other purpose, its illegal gains, if any, shall be confiscated.

### 3. Administrative Disciplinary Sanctions

An administrative disciplinary sanction refers to the sanction imposed by the labor security administration department or other relevant department on its officials for their violations occurred in the performance of work duty. Administrative disciplinary sanctions include warning, circulating a notice of criticism, recording of a demerit, recording of a serious demerit, demotion, downgrading, reduction of salaries, in probation, and dismissal. Those sanctions are listed with an increase in the severity of punishment and one of them shall be imposed on the violator on the basis of the seriousness of its violation. Article 103 of Labor Law provides that, where a staff of the labor administration department or any other department concerned abuses his/her power, neglects his/her duties or plays favoritism or commits irregularities, which constitutes a crime, his/her criminal liability shall be prosecuted in accordance with law; where no crimes are constituted, administrative disciplinary sanctions shall be imposed.

According to the laws and regulations on social insurance, administrative disciplinary sanctions shall be imposed according to the following provisions:

(1) Where any entity which is obligated to make social insurance contributions, in violation of relevant laws, regulations or rules in respect of finance, accounting and statistics, forges, fabricates, alters or intentionally destroys relevant accounting books or materials or fails to establish accounting books, which cause the base of social insurance premiums can not be determined, administrative disciplinary sanctions shall be imposed on it in accordance with relevant laws and regulations.

(2) Where any staff of labor security administration department, social

insurance agency or tax authority abuses his/her power, neglects his/her duties or plays favoritism or commits irregularities, which causes loss of social insurance premiums, but does not constitute a crime, an administrative disciplinary sanction shall be imposed on him/her.

(3) Where any entity or individual diverts social insurance funds for other purpose, which does not constitute a crime, administrative disciplinary sanctions shall be imposed on the principal and other directly responsible persons.

### 4. Administrative Treatment

Administrative treatment for violations of labor or social security laws refers to specific administrative acts that labor security administration departments find and affirm the violations of the administrative counterparts which refuse to perform their legal obligations as provided by labor or social security laws, in violation of relevant labor or social security laws, through labor security supervision and administration activities, and make the written decisions on administrative treatment against these violations of labor or social security laws so as to administratively order those administrative counterparts to perform their legal obligations as provided by labor or social security laws,

Administrative treatment for violations of labor or social security laws shall be premised on the facts that the administrative counterpart violates labor or social security laws and refuses to perform its legal obligations as provided labor or social security laws. The purpose of such administrative treatment is to ensure the performance of labor and social security obligations by the administrative counterpart, which is also the legal duty of the labor security administration department. When the administrative counterpart refuses to perform the decision on administrative treatment for violations of labor or social security laws, the labor security administration department shall apply to the people's court for enforcement in accordance with the Administrative Procedural Law.

The contents of Administrative treatment for violations of labor and social security legislations are mainly based on Article 85 of the Labor Law, which provides that "labor administration departments of the people's governments at or above the county level shall, in accordance with law, supervise and inspect employers' compliance with labor laws and regulations, be entitled to deter the acts of violating labor laws or regulations and order employers involved to make rectifications. " Thus the contents of administrative treatment for violations of labor or social security laws generally include administrative order to the employer requiring the payment of wages, economic compensation, or damages to the laborer, administrative order to the employer requiring the, signing of labor contracts by the employer with the laborer, and administrative order to the employer requiring the removal of child laborers.

### ( Ⅱ ) Civil Liabilities

Civil liabilities refer to the liabilities that shall be borne by the subject of a civil legal relation for violating its civil obligations. Civil liabilities are intended not only to punish illegal acts but also to compensate the victims' losses. Therefore, civil liabilities are mainly property liabilities with the main form as compensation for losses.

Civil liabilities for violations of labor law refer to the civil liabilities that shall be borne by a party to a labor relation which violates the labor law or the agreement between the parties to the labor relation. According to Chapter XII of the Labor Law, civil liabilities for violations of labor law may be classified into two types of liabilities, one is the civil liabilities for the breach of labor contract, and the other is the civil liabilities for the infringement of civil rights of the laborer or the employer, which is abbreviated as civil liabilities for tort.

The main manner of bearing civil liabilities for violations of labor law is compensation for losses. Other forms of bearing civil liabilities, such as elimination of adverse effects and apology provided by the civil law are not covered by the labor law as the manner of bearing liabilities for the lack of the direct relationship with the civil offences as provided in labor laws. Moreover, Article 99 of the Labor Law provides that, where an employer recruits laborers whose labor contracts have not been terminated thus causing economic losses to their former employers, the employer shall, in accordance with law, bear joint and several liabilities for compensation.

#### 1. Civil Liabilities for Breach of Labor Contract

Civil liabilities for breaches of labor contract refer to the legal consequences that shall be borne by a party or both parties to a labor contract for breach of the obligations under the labor contract. According to the labor law of China, civil liabilities for breach of labor contract include:

(1) Civil liabilities for illegal terminations of labor contract by employers. Article 98 of the Labor Law provides that where an employer, in violation of the conditions specified in this Law, terminates labor contracts or deliberately delays the conclusion of labor contracts, the labor administration department shall order the employer to make rectifications; where damages have been caused to laborers, the employer shall bear the liability for compensation.

(2) Civil liabilities for illegal terminations of labor contract by laborers in violation of labor laws. Article 90 of the Labor Contract Law provides that, where

a laborer terminates the labor contract in violation of the provisions of this Law or breaches the confidentiality obligation or competition restriction stipulated in the labor contract, thus causing losses to the employer, he/she shall be liable for compensation.

(3) Civil liabilities for conclusions of invalid labor contract for employers' faults. Article 97 of the Labor Law provides that, where an invalid contract is concluded due to the employing unit's faults, thus causing damages to the laborer, the employer shall bear the liability for compensation. The conclusion of invalid labor contract for employer's faults refers to that an invalid contract between the employer and the laborer is concluded by the employer internationally or for negligence, under which the employer shall liable for compensation should any damage was caused to the laborer. According to the Measures of Compensation for Violating the Provisions of the Labor Law on Labor Contracts, where an invalid labor contract or a partly invalid labor contract is concluded due to the employer's faults, the employer shall make the payment of the deserved wages payable to the laborer plus the compensation with its amount equal to 25% of the deserved wages to the laborer if any wage loss was caused to the laborer.

## 2. Civil Liabilities for Tort

Civil liabilities for tort, as mentioned in labor laws, refer to the civil legal liabilities that shall be borne by the employer for infringements of lawful rights and interest of the laborer or any other employer protected by labor laws, mainly including the following two types of liabilities:

(1) Civil liabilities assumed by the employer for infringements of the laborer's legal rights and interests. This type of civil liabilities includes: 1) Civil liabilities that shall be borne by the employer for infringements of the laborer's lawful rights and interests; and 2) The civil liabilities that shall be assumed by the employer for the damage caused to the laborer in work.

In accordance with the Labor Law, the employer shall bear related civil liabilities for infringements of the laborer's lawful rights and interests under any of the following circumstances: 1) The labor rules made by the employer are contrary to laws or regulations and cause damages to the laborer; 2) The employer, in violation of the labor law, deducts or owes the wages of laborers without proper reasons, or refuses to pay wages and remunerations to laborers for extended working hours, or pays wages that are less than the local minimum wage standard to the laborer, or refuses to make economic compensation payments to the laborer after the termination of the labor contract between them; and 3) The employer, in violation of the provisions of the labor law on special protection of female employees or underage workers, infringes their legal rights or interests and causes damage to them.

(2) Civil liabilities assumed by the employer for the infringement of other employer's rights resulted in the new conclusion of labor contract. Article 99 of the Labor Law provides that, where an employer recruits a laborer who has not yet dissolved a labor contract, which causes economic losses to his/her former employer, the employer shall, in accordance with law, bear joint and several liabilities for compensation.

### (Ⅲ) Criminal Liabilities

Criminal liabilities refer to the legal consequences that shall be borne by the persons who have criminal capacity for their acts which are prohibited by criminal law and constitute crimes.

### 1. Criminal Liabilities for Violations of Labor Laws

Criminal liabilities for violations of labor laws are reflected as the criminal sanctions imposed by the judicial organ on persons whose acts violate labor law and criminal law, cause serious results and constitute crimes. According to Chapter XII of the Labor Law, the criminal liabilities shall apply to the following acts which are so serious as to constitute crimes:

(1) Where an employer forces a laborer to work by the means of violence, threat or illegal restriction of personal freedom, or humiliates, gives corporal punishment to, beats, illegally searches or detains a laborer, and the circumstances are so serious as to constitute a crime, the liable person shall be prosecuted for criminal liability.

For example, Article 88 of the Labor Contract Law provides that, where an employer commits one of the following acts, it shall be subject to an administrative sanction in accordance with law; if a criminal is constituted, it shall be prosecuted for criminal liability according to law; if harm is done to a laborer, the employer shall be liable for compensation: (1) Forcing a laborer to work by violence, threat or illegal restriction of personal freedom; (2) Giving instructions in violation of rules or regulations or giving peremptory orders to a laborer to perform hazardous operations, which endanger the laborer's personal safety; (3) Humiliating, imposing physical punishment on, beating, illegally searching or detaining a laborer; or (4) Providing a laborer with hazardous working conditions or a severely polluted environment, thus causing serious harm to the physical or mental health of the laborer.

(2) Where an employer commits an illegal act, which causes a casualty accident and leads to serious loss of life and property of laborers, it may be deemed as having committed a crime of major labor security accent, and its liable

persons shall be prosecuted for their criminal liabilities in accordance with Article 135 of the Criminal Law. Article 135 of the Criminal Law provides that, where the facilities for labor safety of a factory, mine, tree farm, construction enterprise or any other enterprise or institution do not meet the State requirements and no measures are taken to remove the hidden danger of accident after the warning given by the departments concerned or employees of the unit, so that an accident involving heavy casualties occurs or other serious consequences ensue, the person who is directly responsible for the accident shall be sentenced to fixed-term imprisonment of not more than three years or criminal detention; if the circumstances are especially flagrant, he/she shall be sentenced to fixed-term imprisonment of not less than three years but not more than seven years.

(3) Where an employer unreasonably obstructs the labor administration department, other relevant department, or the staff thereof from exercising the power of supervision and inspection or takes revenge against informants, and the circumstances are so serious as to constitutes a crime, the liable persons shall be prosecuted for criminal liabilities in accordance with law.

(4) Where the staff of labor administration department or of other relevant department abuses his/her power, neglects his/her duties or plays favoritism or commits irregularities, which constitutes a crime, he/she shall be prosecuted for criminal liability in accordance with law. Article 95 of the Labor Contract Law provides that where a labor administration department or another competent department or its staff neglects its/his/her duties and fails in violation of law to perform the statutory duties, or exercises its/his/her functions or powers, thus causing losses to a laborer or an employer, it/he/she shall be liable for compensation; the person directly in charge and the other directly responsible persons shall be given administrative discipline sanctions according to law; if a crime is constituted, it/he/she shall be prosecuted for criminal liability in accordance with law.

(5) Where a State functionary or a staff of a social insurance fund agency embezzles or misappropriates social insurance funds, which constitutes a crime, he/she shall be prosecuted for criminal liability in accordance with law.

### 2. Criminal Liabilities for Violations of Social Insurance Laws

Criminal liabilities for violations of social insurance laws are reflected as the criminal sanctions imposed by the judicial organ on persons whose acts violate the social insurance laws and constitute crimes.

According to the provisions of the Interim Regulations on Collection and Payment of Social Insurance Premiums, criminal sanctions shall apply to the following two types of acts that: (1) An entity that is obligated to make contributions to social insurance premiums, in violation of relevant laws, regulations or rules in respect of finance, accounting and statistics, forges, fabricates, alters or intentionally destroys relevant accounting books or materials or fails to establish accounting books, which violates the criminal law; and (2) A staff of labor security administration department, social insurance agency or tax authority abuses his/her power, neglects his/her duties or plays favoritism or commits irregularities, which causes loss of social insurance premiums and violates the criminal law.

图书在版编目（CIP）数据

中国劳动法与社会保障法＝Labor Law and Social Security Law of China：英文/
黎建飞著 . —北京：中国人民大学出版社，2014.6
ISBN 978-7-300-19680-0

Ⅰ. ①中… Ⅱ. ①黎… Ⅲ. ①劳动法-研究-中国-英文 ②社会保障-行政法-
研究-中国-英文 Ⅳ. ①D922.504②D922.182.34

中国版本图书馆 CIP 数据核字（2014）第 139851 号

中国法丛书（英文版）

**Labor Law and Social Security Law of China**
中国劳动法与社会保障法

黎建飞　著

Zhongguo Laodongfa yu Shehui Baozhangfa

| | | |
|---|---|---|
| **出版发行** | 中国人民大学出版社 | |
| **社　　址** | 北京中关村大街 31 号 | **邮政编码**　100080 |
| **电　　话** | 010 - 62511242（总编室） | 010 - 62511770（质管部） |
| | 010 - 82501766（邮购部） | 010 - 62514148（门市部） |
| | 010 - 62515195（发行公司） | 010 - 62515275（盗版举报） |
| **网　　址** | http://www.crup.com.cn | |
| | http://www.ttrnet.com（人大教研网） | |
| **经　　销** | 新华书店 | |
| **印　　刷** | 北京联兴盛业印刷股份有限公司 | |
| **规　　格** | 170 mm×240 mm　16 开本 | **版　　次**　2014 年 6 月第 1 版 |
| **印　　张** | 26.5 插页 2 | **印　　次**　2014 年 6 月第 1 次印刷 |
| **字　　数** | 525 000 | **定　　价**　78.00 元 |